CRITICAL ISSUES
IN BUSINESS CONDUCT

CRITICAL ISSUES IN BUSINESS CONDUCT

Legal, Ethical, and Social Challenges for the 1990s

Walter W. Manley II
with William A. Shrode

*Forewords by Robert H. Stovall
and Governor LeRoy Collins*

QUORUM BOOKS
New York • Westport, Connecticut • London

Library of Congress Cataloging-in-Publication Data

Manley, Walter W.
  Critical issues in business conduct : legal, ethical, and social
challenges for the 1990s / Walter W. Manley II and William A. Shrode
; foreword by Robert Stovall ; foreword by LeRoy Collins.
    p. cm.
  ISBN 0-89930-570-9 (lib. bdg. : alk. paper)
  1. Business ethics. 2. Industry—Social aspects. I. Shrode,
William A. II. Title.
  HF5387.M335 1990
  658.4'06—dc20   90-30009

British Library Cataloguing in Publication Data is available.

Library of Congress Catalog Card Number: 90-30009
ISBN: 0-89930-570-9

First published in 1990

Quorum Books, 88 Post Road West, Westport, CT 06881
An imprint of Greenwood Publishing Group, Inc.

Printed in the United States of America

The paper used in this book complies with the
Permanent Paper Standard issued by the National
Information Standards Organization (Z39.48-1984).

10 9 8 7 6 5 4 3 2 1

To my parents, Walter and Marjorie Manley, and my daughter, Marjorie.

To the Shrode family.

Contents

viii   Contents

Foreword

Assuming one can agree on what proper values and ethics are, can they be taught, and when and how? Ignatius Loyola said that if he had a child's attention for six years, is that person his forever? In the popular vernacular, many think that if ethics are not formulated at mother's knee, or in church, synagogue, mosque or school, they never will be.

In reality, the practice of ethics is a continuing process that incorporates a number of different disciplines. Most importantly, ethical behavior is based on the ideal of taking full responsibility for thinking through daily managerial problems and making everyday decisions with a view toward fair play.

Managers tend to be doers, competitors, goal-oriented, practical, good with facts and numbers, suspicious of sentiment and very busy. Attention spans may be short. They do not routinely pick up paperbacks by Loyola, Aquinas, Jeremy Bentham or Thomas More for in-flight reading. They define their jobs with precision and stick to chains of command, responsibility, and communication. They believe in loyalty up and down the organizational chart and sometimes subordinate their own personal values to the corporate-team culture. Many are greatly influenced by military codes of conduct practiced during their years of uniformed service.

These are good qualities and they may provide an essential foundation on which to build ethical behavior. But managers also need new tools that can encourage them to take in a broader view of the world, a longer sense of time and a better appreciation and understanding of their own experiences. Such ethical insights should be regarded as part of each responsible manager's everyday activity, and not at-home or weekend behavior.

Walter W. Manley II provides an extensive exploration into the critical legal, social and business conduct issues any manager must address now and into the coming twenty-first century. All the most relevant subjects come under scrutiny: the rights and responsibilities of the corporate family's members in the 1990s from all angles. William A. Shrode adds an important chapter concerning the effective and proper use of management information systems. The work extensively and unsparingly identifies, explains and offers executives, directors, managers, and proprietors useful guidance concerning those issues which dominate managerial energies now and into the foreseeable future.

Responsible decisions come after the right people have provided the needed input and participated in those decisions. Responsible decisions require that people and groups that may be affected have been correctly identified, and the consequences of the contemplated actions have been anticipated. It is especially important that ethical decision makers see the negative consequences—the harm, the dislocations—of their decisions. However, when people are very busy, that can be difficult. To become responsible managers, people need practice, special structures and experience-proven short cuts. There is simply no other way to insure fair play. This book can help managers do these things.

This well-documented and extensive compendium of case studies and interpretations correctly focuses on some of the biggest issues of modern corporate life—environmental considerations, employee chemical dependency, personal on-the-job harassment, discrimination, defining proprietary information, and safety, to list but a few. In sum, this very impressive work will take its place among other must-have references. Managers will give this book preferred space in their executive bookcases, close at hand, for day-to-day dipping.

Robert H. Stovall, CFA
President, Stovall/Twenty-First Advisers, Inc.

Foreword

I recall from my schooling, decades ago, the five steps a salesperson takes in advancing to and consummating a sale. First he must get the prospect's *attention*. Second, *interest* by the prospect in acquisition must then be developed. Third the interest of the prospect must then ripen into a strong *desire* to purchase, followed by a *demand* to do so. Then comes the final step, the execution of the *contract* itself. I believe these remain today as sound essentials of salesmanship, but this book is far more esoteric and comprehensive.

Walter W. Manley II, and William A. Shrode's book <u>Critical Issues in Business Conduct: Legal, Ethical, and Social Challenges for the 1990s</u> deals with fundamentals, yet it is a desktop reference for today's executives, directors, managers, business owners and students of management. As brilliant business leaders and teachers themselves, the authors identify and explain business issues which will dominate the 1990s. It is a compendium of invaluable information and advice previously unavailable in the business world. The authors provide their readers with sage counsel through their agile and cogent expression.

Professor Manley has had a lifelong concern about ethics and social responsibility. He holds advanced degrees in law and business from Duke and Harvard, teaches two courses at the Masters of Business Administration level at Florida State University, Tallahassee, Florida—"Ethical Aspects of Business Policy" and "Entrepreneurial Management"—and is recognized as one of the most outstanding teachers in the entire university. He has achieved outstanding success as a Florida businessman and lawyer.

Professor Shrode has held positions as Chairman of Management and Associate Dean for Graduate Studies and Research in the College of Business at Florida State University. He is past Chairman of the relatively new Department of Information and Management Sciences and has coauthored many books and articles. He is teaching basic and advanced courses in management information and decision support systems, and conducting research aimed at developing methodology for measuring information value in organizational information systems. He has worked in manufacturing and in research and development for several large corporations in the petro-chemical, food and machinery, and aerospace industries.

Private and public institutions play a significantly greater role in our society than every before; they are becoming the loci of power, authority, and responsibility. Consequently, this book discusses thoroughly how America's most successful firms are dealing with critical ethical and business conduct issues and adding value to their firms.

This book discusses the important legal, ethical and social issues of our time. These topical issues affecting business firms include those arising from the relationship between business organizations and their external constituencies—consumers, competitors, community groups, government agencies, the general public, and host countries—and between business organizations and their equally important internal constituencies—managers, employees, directors, and shareholders.

Two-hundred and seventy-six of America's most successful and well-managed firms actively participated in Professor Manley's two-year research project in which he conducted oral and written interviews with top executives of the participating firms. The reader will find the discussions of the critical issues challenging, dynamic, and contrasting with their diversity, length, and complexity.

LeRoy Collins
Governor of Florida, 1955-1961

Acknowledgements

For over two years I have conducted research in the area of business firms' response to issues in business conduct and their creation and use of codes of conduct. Much of the material in this book has come from the 276 participating firms, among the best managed in this country, including publications and codes, together with 1,000 pages of interviews and correspondence with 400 executives, including 85 CEOs and chairmen; 71 Executive and Senior Vice Presidents; 77 General Counsel; 105 Vice Presidents; and 65 Treasurers, Chief Auditors, and Directors of Human Resources, Employee Relations or Corporate Responsibility. I thank these gentlemen and ladies for their interviews and letters. I have examined over 10,000 pages of codes of business conduct and policy statements and appreciate the permission granted to publish in this book the most useful excerpts of such codes.

I owe many thanks to Kathy McCord, a dear friend and talented journalist, for her support during the writing of this book. Further, I wish to thank Professor William Shrode, Robert Stovall, Nicole Hiers, Kelly Shrode, Kathleen Rice, Paula Bryant, Kay Haberman, Ronald and Richard Garl, Rebecca Einolf, Geir Kjellevold, Patrick Schneider, and Terry Harris for their advice, typing, editing, proofreading, and editorial assistance. I particularly wish to thank Nick Sweers, a learned and accomplished journalist; Joe Riffe, my research assistant for part of 1989; and Barbara Baker and Lois Stille, my wonderful, cheerful typists, for their dedication. Larry Hopcraft, President of Parker-Hannifin's Automotive and Refrigeration Division, offered cogent advice and demonstrated in his encouragement the qualities which have allowed him to be so successful at such a young age.

Cambridge University, Oxford University, and Ridley Hall College have been kind to me and visiting membership on their faculties served as catalysts for writing the two books, including this one, which I completed in 1990. I particularly wish to thank Cambridge University Professors David Thompson, Stephen Watson, Anthony Giddens, J. N. Butterfield, and Lecturer Amy Cosh; Ridley Hall College Principal Hugo de Waal and Dr. Richard Higginson; and R. J. Smith, Chairman of the Oxford Faculty of Law, for their many kindnesses.

Further, I acknowledge the substantial knowledge, insight and encouragement I have received over the last several decades from certain teachers and friends. Harvard Professors

Rosenblum (now Dean of Virginia's Colgate Darden School), Stevenson, Thurston, Korten, Kassarjian, and Trevelyan were excellent teachers and motivators, as were Duke Professors Latty, O'Neal, and Pye. Professors Earl Sasser of Harvard and Robinson Everett and Kazimierz Gryzbowski of Duke were not only good friends but probably the best teachers I have ever had.   Professor Ken Goodpaster of Harvard has done much to advance the practical application of business ethics.   Duke Law Deans Paul Carrington and Pamela Gann and Fuqua School Dean Tom Keller have demonstrated a pursuit of excellence and have, through their ethical leadership, improved the already outstanding Duke School of Law and the Duke Fuqua School.

Former Florida Governor LeRoy Collins, the greatest living Southerner, Solicitor General Ken Starr, Judge Clifton Kelly, former Congressman and Florida Insurance Commissioner Bill Gunter, Hal Norvell, Bill Parks, and Babson Professor Farshad Rafii, Jim Meadows, former Florida Bar President Bob Ervin, Toni Burton, David C. Strong, and Wayne Todd by their personal examples, have greatly inspired me.

I owe particular thanks to my colleagues who have offered support and encouragement as well: Florida State University Professors Ross Heck, Charlie Conn, Mark Martinko, David Kuhn, Glenn Boggs, Bill Gallups, Tom Clark, Dean Ray Solomon, and Grantham Couch, among them.

Other persons who have taught me valuable lessons which have formed the basis of my frame of reference include: my daughter Marjorie, whose wisdom and infinite love belie her young age; my brilliant, talented loving parents, Walter and Marjorie, who encouraged me and demonstrated great patience with my many shortcomings; the dynamic businessmen George Barley and Jim Hewitt, who along with Bill duPont brought the Orlando Magic to Florida; Joe Moretz; Jackie Sharkey; Florida Judges Rick Bronson, Oliver Green, William Love, Jesse Willson, John Dewell, John Antoon, Jack Watson, Tom Langston, Dennis Maloney, Carolyn Fulmer, Randy Bentley, Bob Young, Susan Roberts, Randy McDonald, Ed Threadgill and Bill Norris; Florida Supreme Court Justice Ray Ehrlich; former Florida Attorney General Bob Shevin; Dale Williamson; outstanding college and preparatory instructors, headmasters, and administrators Bob Akerman, Walter Murphy, Harold Albert, Kelton Tidwell, Mario Rivela, Jack Heffner, John Morgan, Henry Whiteside, Elizabeth Spense, Genevieve Mitchell, Mrs. Lawrence and Lane Abernathy; Lucy Strong; Dr. Dan Bagley, whose book showed the way; Pulitzer Prize winner Vermont Royster; fellow trustees Jac Chambliss, Webb Follin, Woody Sims; Cliff and Lee Hinkle; Dennis Bradshaw; Commissioner Marlene Duffy Young; Diane Manley; Hope Strong, Jr.; S. E. Oot; Earl and Maurita Oot; Daisy Parks; classmate and lawyer extraordinaire David Hardee; lawyers Peter Munson, Larry Jackson, Ron Clark, Russell Crofton, Charles Sammons, Bill Mitchell, Tom Floyd, John Shannon, Joellen Farnham, Guerry Dobbins, Ray McDaniel, Gerald Medeiros, Bryan Thomas, Bob Stokes, Jim Kelly, Rick Nail, Jim Tompkins, Bob Sammons, Scott Bunn, Larry Jackson, Kingswood Sprott, Rodd Buell, Joe Morrison, Zollie Maynard, and Steve Salley; Oliver Horne; Joe Tedder; Gary Runnels; Iloe McKenzie; Keith Carpenter; Cal and Pam Peters; Charles Lydecker; Polly Hopcraft; Al Gadoury; Scott Smith; Richard Greaser; restaurateur and friend Mary Bacon; Ann Todd; Gary

Ralston; Charlene Padgett; Alice Starr; Hans Stumm; Mary
Keeler; DeeDee Floyd; Fred Moore; Richard Moore; Bill Spring-
field; Richard Ruis; my aunts, Margaret Cowell and Marie
Christie; my aunt and uncle, Ben and Kitty Watkins; my
grandparents, Ben and Clyde Watkins and Mr. and Mrs. William
Manley; John and Lynn Rau; Tim Cronin, Ezra Nilson; Dr.
Charles Inman; John Carver, a fine Marine and caring foreman;
Bob and Toby Wagner, and their wives Ruth and Margie, respec-
tively; my devoted, insightful secretaries Kate Shaw and Zulma
Pagan; Sam Burton; Norm Best; Fathers Lahey and White; Ann
Dobbs; Carol Albritton; Lester Abberger; Bill Dahl; Pfil Hunt;
Dr. Bob Schuchts; Barclay Wilson; David Porter; Tom Cooper,
Steve Owen; Diana Frazier; Nick Sudzina; Marjorie Owens; and
Congressman Bill Nelson.

I owe a special thanks to editors of the seven publishing
firms which extended contracts for my two books I wrote in
1989-90.   Specifically, I thank Tom Power of Prentice-Hall,
Liliane Miller and Lauren Nagy of Greenwood Press, John
Mahaney of Wiley, Ann West of Sage, and Karen Hansen and Bob
Bovenschulte of Lexington for their support and encouragement.

Finally, I owe my deepest thanks to my students.   They
have taught me much and have enlivened and enlightened my
life.

Walter W. Manley II

Introduction

OVERVIEW

This book is the most comprehensive publication available that thoroughly examines the critical management issues business firms will face in the 1990s. These wide-ranging issues, which the authors have complemented with current developments and notable Supreme Court decisions of the late 1980s, will affect firms' responses in significant areas such as punitive damages, affirmative action, age and sex discrimination, the environment, drug testing, AIDS, marketing, reverse discrimination, and a myriad of employer and employee rights and responsibilities.

One of two books published in 1990 as a result of Walter W. Manley's intensive two-year study on corporate business conduct, this publication is designed to advance the reader's comprehension of the critical issues of this new decade and how he or she can address them effectively and efficiently from a legal, ethical, and social vantage point. Consequently, this book affirms that confronting these issues intelligently, professionally, and proactively will assure success to a firm striving for enhanced efficiency, greater profitability, and improved employee morale. The other book derived from this study by Manley, <u>Complete Portfolio of Model Business Codes</u>, intends to further encourage the reader's understanding of values and critical business issues in the context of promulgating a firm's successful code of conduct.

Manley, who received valuable assistance in preparing the book from William A. Shrode, who wrote the chapter on management information systems, conducted an intense and focused study on 276 of America's most successful and best-managed firms. As a result of this study on business conduct, the author accumulated 1,000 pages of interviews and extensive in-depth correspondence with top executives. Additionally, he reviewed more than 10,000 pages from firms' codes of business conduct (from which he selected 440 self-contained, topic-related excerpts in the other book) and about 40,000 pages of source materials. The course of this research involved consultations with approximately 400 business leaders, including 85 chief-executive officers and chairmen of the board, 77 corporate legal counsel, 71 senior vice presidents and executive vice presidents, 105 vice presidents, and 65 others holding the positions of director of corporate responsibility, director of human resources, director of employee relations, treasurer, or chief auditor.

This book is based on factual evidence and on the experience and beliefs of the top executives who participated in the study. Clearly, this profound publication is a reflection of the critical issues for the 1990s as opined by these business leaders. Further, the book exhibits the balanced perspective of Manley, who has been a successful attorney, an outstanding university professor, a creative consultant, and an innovative owner of or partner in diverse business firms. Shrode, also a university professor, has worked in manufacturing and in research and development for several large corporations.

While the book seeks to share its findings with the esteemed executives who contributed to this exhaustive examination of corporate America, it also is intended and highly recommended for any person who owns, is a partner of, or manages a firm and who wishes to successfully address the critical business-conduct issues of the 1990s. Moreover, the book is a valuable reference and instructive tool for the lawyers who serve as counsel to business firms; members of boards of directors of firms; faculties, scholars and students in the disciplines of business, philosophy, social sciences, and law; and members of the general public who have demonstrated a keen interest in business-conduct issues.

WHY BUSINESS CONDUCT ISSUES ARE IMPORTANT

In the final months of the last decade, a brief report from the Harvard Business School painted the 1980s as disastrous for "sluggish, complacent companies." Conversely, the "leaner, more agile firms" found the last ten years to be difficult but gratifying. For managers of the most successful firms in the nation, the concept of time was a critical weapon in the competitive arsenal.

In the energetic business community of the 1990s, productive time management is even more crucial and profitable while wasted time is counterproductive and costly. By understanding and confronting business-conduct issues of this decade in an efficient manner, America's tough, lean, and fast firms will head toward the twenty-first century along a successful—and profitable—path.

Surveys indicate that the best single response to business-conduct issues (whether they rest in the realm of law, values, social responsiveness, or simply proper conduct) is the promulgation and enforcement of comprehensive codes. The 1987 Touche Ross survey of business executives and board members reveals that ninety-four percent of respondents believe the American business community is significantly troubled by improper conduct.

The emphasis in designing this book, of course, is to ensure that businessmen will embrace its wisdom while pursuing a timely explanation of those business-conduct issues that firms of all sizes (including 3.68 million U.S. corporations) must address to remain competitive. For example, there were 1989 developments in at least a dozen states—including California, New York, and Illinois—to protect nonunion workers and those without individual contracts from termination without "good cause." These extensions of employment rights are immolating the termination-at-will doctrine. Furthermore, in another important 1989 occurrence, OSHA's $1.5-million fine against Lockheed was the first settlement of a major case involving federal rules that require an employer to inform workers if they have been exposed to hazardous chemicals. Moreover, according to a Spring 1989 study, only one-quarter of the nation's companies—large and small—have formal AIDS policies, even though nearly sixty percent have had cases of AIDS among employees or dependents covered by their health plans. Employers risk discrimination suits from employees with AIDS as well as legal action from employees who demand a safe workplace.

The subject matter of this book reflects what the most current national surveys and polls indicate are the critical concerns of managers and executives of American business firms. For instance, nearly all firms are concerned with drug and alcohol abuse, advertising and marketing, financial accounting and reporting, safe workplaces, protecting the firm's proprietary and confidential information, consumer protection, product and services quality, negotiations, employer and employee rights and responsibilities, sexual and other harassment, affirmative action and discrimination, the environment, and balancing management responsibilities among various constituencies. In addition, many firms also address issues regarding international business, AIDS, social responsiveness, fair competition, and laws regulating insider trading, mergers, and acquisitions.

How to Use This Book. The authors of this publication methodically address the critical business-conduct issues—and their legal, social, and ethical challenges in the 1990s—in 14 detailed chapters. The reader has two paths to choose in employing this book. One direction to take, of course, is to completely digest all of the issues by reading the entire book. Another course of action is for a reader with a specific concern or curiosity to seek the chapter that best answers his or her questions. This reader can return to other topics in the book at a more convenient time. In this regard, the book is both an instructive and reference tool for those wishing to better understand these critical business-conduct issues.

In Chapter 1, "A Manager's Overview," the reader will acquire a better understanding of values and ethics, balancing management responsibilities among various constituents, social responsibility and responsiveness, and protecting the environment. The reader, for example, who wants to know more about acid rain or which avenues to take to confront difficult decisions in management, should review this chapter.

Chapter 2 highlights employers' and employees' rights and tackles relevant issues such as employment at-will, whistle blowing, employment privacy, and polygraph testing. Chapters 3 through 6 address, in order, drugs, alcoholism, AIDS, and genetics in the workplace; preventing sexual and nonsexual harassment; equal employment opportunity, nondiscrimination, affirmative action, preferential treatment, reverse discrimination, and comparable worth; and workplace safety, consumer protection, and product safety.

Next, the reader is encouraged to examine the issue of protecting a firm's proprietary and confidential information in Chapter 7.   In the following three chapters, numbers 8 through 10, the reviewer will absorb marketing and advertising issues for the 1990s, financial accounting and reporting, and management information systems, respectively.

In Chapters 11 through 13, one of the authors shares the study's findings on such issues ranging, in order, from business dealings and relationships to insider trading and securities laws to fundamental honesty and antitrust laws. Chapter 14 concludes the book with a thorough discussion and insight on international business relationships and practices.

CONCLUSION

Clearly, the subject matter of this book, which combines extensive business-conduct research and the exclusive input from top leaders of the 276 most successful and best-managed firms, provides a uniquely valuable and timely reference tool for managers at all levels and at any size firm.   It is a book for and about the 1990s; a significant product of a study born in 1988 with an intellectual concern for the critical business issues facing the twentieth-century's final decade.   Hopefully, it will secure a prominent spot on the reader's desktop or bookshelf as he prepares for the challenges of the future.

CRITICAL ISSUES
IN BUSINESS CONDUCT

1
A Manager's Overview

VALUES, MORALITY, AND ETHICS

Values, morality, and ethics are used in a variety of loosely connected contexts. Business ethics is philosophical thinking about issues of morality in business, including moral problems and judgments. Business ethics necessarily addresses ethical issues that arise in a competitive, economic environment, and these issues are similar to those raised by any human activity. There is a great public interest in business ethics primarily as a result of fundamental changes in societal attitudes about the proper conduct of business organizations.

Many factors have contributed to the increased public concern regarding business values and ethics, including: the growing inability of the market mechanism to govern many business decisions and activities because firms have become so large and powerful; a growth in government constraints and involvement in business firms' activities; concern about certain issues such as environmental protection, which are not normally regulated by the market; and the emergence of "quality of life" issues, which are of high priority among society's social values.[1] Moreover, firms have become larger and more bureaucratic, often inspiring less concern about proper conduct. In addition, industrial restructuring can lower the standards of employee behavior by its inexorable pressure to tighten budgets and increase profits. "Conscience is a fragile thing," notes Abraham Zaleznik, a psychoanalyst and Harvard Business School professor. "It needs support from institutions, and that support is weakening."[2]

Values are specific desires for objects or beliefs perceived as important, whereas ethics is a more general term that refers to conceptions of human welfare and the promulgation of principles to enhance human welfare. Morality, further, usually refers to traditional beliefs of proper and improper conduct, that have an historical context of years or centuries.[3] Business ethics is a sub area of ethics in general.

Ethics or moral philosophy is the attempt to understand the nature of human values, of how people ought to live, and of what constitutes right conduct.[4] Ethics is a branch of philosophy whose object is an inquiry into what is good for people and what is bad for people. Ethics involves moral thought and reflection, as well as moral judgments. "People make moral judgments and face moral problems constantly . . .

[people] give moral reasons for certain beliefs and decisions . . . [and] evidence by this fact fairly deep concerns about the course of human affairs," notes ethicist and Harvard Business School professor Ken Goodpaster.[5]   People assess others' actions in moral terms, such as "good," "bad," "right," and "wrong," with a moral frame of reference in mind.[6]   In addition, ethics is the study of what rules ought to govern human behavior that is done knowingly and, usually, willingly.[7]   "In essence, ethics is concerned with clarifying what constitutes human welfare and the kind of conduct necessary to promote it."[8]

The study of ethics is properly categorized into three approaches: descriptive, analytical, and prescriptive (normative). The descriptive approach comprises scientific studies or factual descriptions that describe or explain the similar or different moral behavior and beliefs of different persons or societies. The descriptive approach is interested in the phenomenon of morality in a nonphilosophic context, and seeks a deliberate neutrality concerning the validity, superiority, inferiority, or justifiability of the values, norms, and moral beliefs that are factually reported or explained.   In the descriptive approach, there is no advocacy of one set of values or beliefs. Related to the descriptive approach is the clinical interest in the phenomenon of morality.   This clinical approach, which includes the fields of clinical psychology and moral education, relates to behavioral and cognitive development or inculcation of morality and means to nurture that development.[9]

The philosopher's interest in morality and moral issues and judgments is neither descriptive nor clinical. Rather, philosophical thinking about morality comprises contemplation about the shape and the substance of moral judgments. Analytical ethics (metaethics) and prescriptive (normative) ethics relate to the shape and substance, respectively, of moral judgments. Analytical ethics, also called conceptual ethics or metaethics, has as its function the systematic examination of the foundations of ethical systems and the functions of ethics in society.   The analytical approach "involves clarifying and evaluating presuppositions and investigating questions of meaning and justification . . . [and it] attempts to transcend existing ethical theories and principles, which may lead to conflicting courses of action, and judge them in light of ultimate values of human well-being and welfare to resolve such conflicts."[10]

The aim of metaethics is not to discover what is good or what is right, but rather what is meant when a person says of something that it is, for example, "good" or "right." Metaethics is concerned with analyzing concepts such as "good" and "right," as opposed to employing such concepts to discuss human conduct. Thus the metaethicist poses questions such as "How do we know that one action is better than another?" and "Can we ever really know such a thing?"[11]

Issues of concern in metaethics include: whether the principles sought in ethics are ever more than personal predilection and, in fact, genuine knowledge; whether "proof" in ethics is similar in form to "proof" in other disciplines, like science; and whether the "moral frame of reference" is rationally compelling for normal individuals or is merely a matter of "irrational commitment"; and, if the "moral frame of reference" is in fact rationally compelling, whether other frames of reference, such as self-interest or business profit, relate in a complementary or antagonistic manner to it.[12] Hence, the primary concern in analytical ethics is "the overall location of moral judgment in the inventory of human thought and action, and not with the development of moral principles or judgments themselves."[13]

Two lines of thought in analytical ethics are cognitivism and noncognitivism. Cognitivists assert that moral judgments are directly true or false, such as postulates or laws in mathematics and science, and, consequently, they believe genuine knowledge is present in ethics. On the contrary, noncognitivists posit that moral judgments are not factual, as the laws of mathematics and science, but are, rather, mere expressions of attitude, feeling, or emotion.[14]

Prescriptive ethics, together with analytical ethics, constitute the philosophical interest in the phenomena of morality. Prescriptive (normative) ethics, the second major domain of reflection in ethics, is concerned with "the formulation and defense of basic moral norms governing moral life."[15] Prescriptive ethics is concerned with the question, "What kinds of action are good or right?"[16] Prescriptivists present a particular group of principles and standards that would be best for people to use as guides in all aspects of their lives. Consequently, prescriptive ethics is not morally neutral.[17]

Prescriptive ethicists are concerned with addressing questions such as the following: (1) What are valid or defensible principles of good or bad character, or of right and wrong conduct? (2) How do these general principles relate to each other and are there patterns of reasoning about ethical matters? (3) Are there other issues regarding values, which are not absolutely moral in themselves, which pertain directly to moral principles and judgments?[18] Whereas prescriptive ethicists seek to build theory by discovering, developing, and justifying basic moral values and principles, they also apply those principles of conduct and character when relevant to specific moral problems. Prescriptive ethicists, moreover, reflect on defensible prescriptive generalizations, as opposed to descriptive generalizations about defensible or indefensible prescriptive beliefs.[19]

Within the realm of prescriptive ethics are deontic and aretaic judgments. Deontic judgments of moral assessment are those that concern conduct actions, choices, or judgments. This rubric, comprised of theories of moral obligation, focuses on general principles of duties, right and wrong, and "oughts" and "should nots" regarding conduct. Examples of deontic theories are ethical egoism, utilitarianism, and contractarianism. On the other hand, judgments that have as their primary concern traits of character and motivation, not conduct or action, are promulgated under aretaic theories, which are theories of moral value. Issues arising in aretaic theories address the question "What type of person should I strive to be?" and relate to the necessity and sufficiency of such virtues as courage, prudence, and kindness.[20]

The topics of ethics are relevant to business administration for a variety of reasons.[21] Decisions in the business context involve assessments of conduct and character. Second, practical disciplines such as business administration share the lingua franca of normative language like "right," "wrong," "should," "good," and "bad." Moreover, business administration, as ethics, at times relates not only to judgments regarding actions, but also the motives and character traits that influence those actions. Economics and ethics, as fields of study, are interrelated as they both encourage substantive analyses of concepts such as "utility," "benefits," "welfare," "greatest good," and "costs." Further, when executives and managers seek to clarify certain issues of cultural diversity and relationships between morality and self-interest, they can benefit from an understanding of analytic (metaethics) ethics, which approach investigates questions of meaning and justification. In addition, the effective management of an organization includes assessing behavior and, particularly, the effects of behavior on the lives of persons other than the person making the decision. Last, business administration and ethics, both fields of practical and intellectual inquiry, seek a practical rationality or wisdom that can be nurtured.

In short, business ethics is a topic worthy of the executive's or manager's special consideration because "the daily conduct of business raises personal ethical issues similar to those raised by any other human activity."[22] Furthermore, business firms must deal on a daily basis with a myriad of subjects of ethical significance: employer and employee rights and duties; marketing ethics; corporate social responsiveness; and improper conduct in the firm. Finally, business ethics raises questions regarding ethical theory, for instance: Should ethical inquires arising in business be resolved by reference to general ethical principle, or does the business context preclude or constrain their resolution by such reference?[23]

BALANCING MANAGEMENT RESPONSIBILITIES

Business executives and managers must address certain problems and dilemmas that pose conflicts among various constituents. The most difficult pose distinct conflicts among managerial responsibilities that defy a "business as usual" resolution.[24] Often, a manager's economic responsibilities—to shareholders, suppliers, and lenders—conflict with duties owed to society, or with that manager's own values or moral beliefs. Certainly, carefully evaluating the impacts of decisions and balancing the various constituent interests, whether in the context of near-term or long-term effects, is an integral part of the firm's management process.

This process of balancing constituent interests is important, for managers who ignore consideration of these constituencies may ultimately inflict significant harm on their firms and themselves, to say nothing of the consequent deleterious effects on society or consumers. Resolving differences among constituents requires compromises. It is essential that the manager review all sides' viewpoints; however, there is no assurance that all constituents will be satisfied because of the mutually exclusive nature of the competing demands. It is the manager's duty to balance these various responsibilities to constituents in an ethical manner while attempting to provide a reasonable profit to the shareholders, except in the most extreme circumstances.

In most cases, a manager can make a proper business conduct decision by relying on general principles of fairness, promise-keeping, loyalty, obeying the law, and avoiding harm. In the more difficult decisions, however, such principles may conflict or may be inappropriate in resolving the issue at hand.   Answering three questions[25] will assist managers in resolving these various issues: (1) What are the responsibil- ities at issue in each situation? (2) What standards should guide the conflict's resolution? (3) Whose judgment should prevail in the situation—the manager's, colleagues', the firm's, or that of society? A manager's careful analysis will usually pinpoint the key responsibilities. Moreover, employ- ing the various avenues discussed later in this chapter provide standards for decisions.

Last, in answering the third question, the manager must examine his or her own assumptions about leadership. A "personal" leader will be inclined to believe that his or her values should control, "institutional" leadership relies on common values infused in the firm usually manifested by the manner past decisions have been promulgated, and a "political" leader usually exhibits more flexibility than presumption in seeking compromises.   Some firms have also responded to the need for making proper decisions and establishing values by creating policy instruments in codes of conduct, which provide guidelines in areas such as corporate disclosure, compensa- tion, fair pay and employment opportunity, privacy, freedom of expression, the environment, workplace safety, ethics in advertising, product quality, and corporate social responsi- bility.

External constituencies, such as government bodies, interest groups, labor unions, and the media, seek to influ- ence a firm's strategic goals or major operating policies.[26] These constituencies pose pronounced dilemmas for managers and executives unlike those presented by internal constituencies like shareholders and employees, whose major concerns general- ly do not threaten the firm's performance.   Executives and managers must assess various issues arising from external groups in a specific and objective manner, because such issues are often emotionally charged and managers are often unfamiliar with the gravament of such issues.   First, the manager must appraise the substance of the firm's current or proposed policies or goals, which external groups seek to affect, to determine their importance in terms of profits, growth, and organizational integrity.   Further, such policies and goals, beyond economic considerations, must be politically sensible and reflect a pragmatic assessment of the basic interests and power of the external groups.[27]

Moreover, managers must question the time-honored but antiquated presumption that setting the firm's goals and policies, as long as they consider capital and product markets, is their province alone.   Instead, the power to establish a firm's goals and policies may be shared to some degree with external, as well as internal, constituencies. The resulting goals often reflect a compromise between managers and external parties.   In this process of rational

assessment, the firm's managers should effectively respond to
three questions.   First, how can the exertions of external
groups impact the firm's strategy and competitive position?
Laws, regulations, and other government intervention and
pressure will variously effect different companies, because
each firm has a distinct mix of products, pricing, technology,
manufacturing, financing, and personnel policies.[28]

Competitive analysis may indicate that a particular
external demand will assist the firm in the long term.   For
example, if proposed regulations require a manufacturer to
modify an old process, a firm with exceptional technical
ability might alter the process faster and less expensively
than its competitors.   When confronted with severe external
pressure, a firm may offer accommodations that modify or
sacrifice economic objectives.   Nonetheless, a firm, after
determining which of its goals and policies is negotiable and
which is not, can pursue the course of concerted resistance to
outside demands.[29]

> Managers gain insight into the changes and the
> probability of having to alter policy and goals in
> response to outside constituencies, by asking the
> question: What are the agendas and strengths of
> those groups? Answering this second query requires
> a political analysis at two levels: determining
> the group's goals and strength as a political
> player, and examining the "broader implications of
> the various political strategies a firm could adapt
> in a particular situation."[30]

Even the activities of ostensibly weak or small external
groups, as the original environmental and consumer protection
movements, can herald fundamental social or political changes.
Moreover, the firm's political strategy in response to
external pressure regarding a particular issue will establish
precedents, form coalitions, publicize images, and counter or
mobilize opposition.   Myopic strategies, though perhaps
successful in the short term, can prove disastrous in the
longer term.

Furthermore, managers must address a third consequential
question: Do the external constituencies have advanced
concerns that the firm has a responsibility to accommodate?
Rather than reflexively reject such concerns about the firm's
economic or social responsibility as threats to management's
prerogatives, managers must determine the firm's accountability.[31]

After the managers respond to the foregoing three
questions, they should determine the correct composition and
communication style of decisions concerning goals and external
constituencies.   A pronounced top-down influence in these
regards rests on factors such as: responsibility for final
decisions inevitably lie in senior management, headquarters
specialists usually are more experienced in dealing with
external groups, and senior managers are in the best position
to weigh the alternative courses and balance entire firm and
divisional concerns.[32]   Yet, lower level managers probably
better comprehend the business issues at stake, are ultimately
accountable for the performance of their units, often have

prior experience dealing with external groups, and can focus the attention of media and other external groups on an isolated business unit, as opposed to the firm's policies and reputation.[33]

In addition, management's response, whether formulated at the top or at a lower level, can be precise or vague or a hybrid of the two. Clear decisions, precisely communicated to external parties, force difficult decisions, provide benchmarks to assess future performance, and evidence that the firm has seriously considered an issue. On the other hand, flexible goals and more vague communication permit managers to respond to developments as they arise and not commit the firm to a course of action that may prove regrettable.[34]

Many critics of ethical thinking in business base their disapproval on an avowed lack of self-interest, personally or of the firm. They posit that it is the firm's responsibility not to act with any ethical consideration, but only to assess and pursue economic growth and profits. Of course, they miss the point entirely, as other chapters in this book display, that concern for ethics and proper conduct benefit the firm's economic performance, and that rational self-interest is consistent with ethical thinking.[35] In the first pattern, referred to as "ethics as a means to self-interest," a manager maintains that one's core value is to further one's own interest in a rational way, and that one primary avenue is to be respectful of others. Respect, like honesty, may be "the best policy," and the "better his reputation for integrity, honesty, and decency the better his chances . . . of [success] will be in the long run."[36] Pursuant to this mindset, which is applicable to organizations as well as individuals, ethical behavior is instrumental to success. A prudent manager with this mindset will select a course of action after assessing the costs against the anticipated benefits. Still, this joining of ethics to self-interest does not necessarily respect ethics as an independent value—only as a means to achieve that self-interest. This "ethics as a means to self-interest" thinking exists when a person manages ethics or respect-oriented values with rational self-interest as the all-embracing object.[37]

A second broad pattern of thinking, "ethics as an external constraint," incorporates ethical considerations as a constraint on the choice of ends. One such representative mindset recognizes market forces as substitutes for ethical action; the other views legal and political intervention and constraints as acting for ethical values. The "invisible hand" proponents assert that ethics may be important to business administration, but that managing with an eye toward ethics is redundant—because ethics is built into the free market system. Adam Smith, eighteenth-century author of The Wealth of Nations, coined the term "invisible hand," and one interpretation of the doctrine holds that individuals and business firms cannot be "do-gooders" because no one has access to complete knowledge about the universe. Instead, profit maximization frees managers from making controversial value judgments. "In a free society," trenchantly notes Nobel Laureate economist Milton Friedman, "there is one and only one social responsibility of business—to use its resources and engage in activities designed to increase its profits so long as it stays within the rules of the game, which is to say, engages in open and free competition without deception or fraud."[38]   In this pattern, ethics is not merely a means of achieving one's self-interest; social and legal constraints provide moral authority beyond that of market forces alone.

By contrast, the "visible hand" pattern relies on noneconomic forces beyond the firm to provide direction.   In this way, just as a firm might conscientiously strive to adhere to the Environmental Protection Agency rules and procedures concerning pollution, the firm's managers place responsibility for promulgating moral judgement outside the managers' or the firm's economic realms.   Managers in this pattern acknowledge authority, but not their own or the firm's accountability concerning ethical values in managing the firm.[39]   If the action is not constrained by law or public policy, then, according to "visible hand" proponents, that action passes ethical muster.

The last pattern of thinking that reconciles ethical thinking and self-interest can be termed "ethics as an end." According to this manner of thinking, managing only with ethical constraints imposed by the marketplace (invisible hand) and by government, labor, and the media (visible hand) is inadequate.   Rather, managers and firms are accountable to blend ethical considerations in managerial actions.   Rational self-interest and concern for ethics are synonymous.   In this way, managers and firms reach beyond the minimal conduct imposed by self-interest alone, the marketplace, or external forces like government and the media.   The minimalist position is that businesses provide desired goods and services, compete fairly, and cause no apparent harm.   By following the "ethics as an end" mindset, managers do not abandon self-interest, but rather posit that ethical action is as fundamental as enlightened self-interest.[40]

At this point it is instructive to discuss certain philosophical frameworks that allow the manager to consider, if not actually integrate, ethics in practical decisions.   For instance, in the Harvard Business Review article "Why 'Good' Managers Make Bad Ethical Choices," the author identifies certain rationalizations that often lead to misconduct.   These rationalizations include: (1) a belief that the activity is in the firm's or individual's best interests and, hence, that the firm implicitly expects the individual to undertake the activity, (2) a belief that the activity will not be discovered or publicized, and (3) a belief that the firm will condone any act that assists the firm and, in the process, protect the perpetrator.   As the author asserts, "[t]he difference between becoming a success and becoming a statistic lies in knowledge—including self-knowledge—not daring . . . managers are not paid to take risks; they are paid to know which risks are worth taking."   In order to avoid such potentially deleterious rationalizations and resulting management failures, executives and managers benefit by employing certain guidelines, based on theories that moral philosophers have proposed in promulgating proper decisions regarding business conduct.

Managers can effectively use a number of general approaches to difficult business, moral, or ethical problems in order to reach proper decisions.   Each of these approaches suggests a critical question that the manager can use as a test of the correctness of proposed action.[41]

1.   What are the consequences of the manager's action for all affected parties?

Consequentialism or utilitarianism, one of the most influential normative ethical views, holds that the consequence of actions affect their moral value. Whether an act is morally right or wrong depends entirely on the consequences of the action or practice. It is the good or evil that the act produces, not the act itself, that determines the act as right or wrong. Actions are right if they produce happiness or prevent suffering, and wrong if they prevent happiness or produce suffering.[42] Ethical egoism and ethical altruism, both of which are teleological or consequentialist theories, assume that an act should be judged solely on how good or bad the consequences are for the actor or for others, respectively.

Utilitarianism combines both ethical egoism and ethical altruism, as reflected in the nineteenth-century British philosopher Jeremy Bentham's formula of "everybody to count for one, nobody for more than one." Utilitarians differ as to the nature of the "good" or ultimate utility by which the effects of the alternative actions are to be evaluated. There is wide variation as to the appropriate standard: happiness, peoples' welfare, friendship, knowledge, courage, or the promotion of nearly any value.

According to act utilitarians, an action is right if it produces consequences that are better than those of the available alternatives. Utilitarians accept the fact that a "good" may produce some consequential harm and that some people may be injured. In approaching problem solving, especially ones involving multiple constituencies, managers can achieve congruence between decisions and the moral point of view. Consequently, in every situation, the manager can consider a utilitarian analysis to determine the right action or practice. Along this line or analysis, the moral principles of conduct inculcated in a person are mostly irrelevant to act utilitarians. In addition, concepts of duty and rights are subordinate to the consequence of the action. Moreover, the morality of the actor is distinct and independent from the morality of the action. It is the consequence of the action, not the motives of the actor, that determines whether the actor is right.

A manager, contemplating a specific action or practice, who wishes to make a utilitarian decision must: (1) determine what alternative actions to the proposed course are available, (2) calculate the costs and benefits that a given action will produce for every affected person, and (3) select the alternative that produces the greatest sum of utility or the least amount of disutility.[43] In the context of management, "utilitarian reasoning frequently manifests itself as a commitment to the social virtues of the market system, both inside the organization and outside . . . [for] greatest good comes from competitive decision-making . . . and market forces can be relied upon to minimize social harm."[44]

Utilitarianism was the dominant normative ethical theory of the industrial nineteenth-century. Difficulties in applying this analytical process arise in the disregard of the minority, of measuring and comparing "goods" and "bads," the failure to account how equitably the utility is distributed, and the impossibility of determining the consequences of alternative actions.[45] An advantage is that the utilitarian approach provides a touchstone for ethical thinking in a structure that resembles a scientific, empirical method.[46]

2.   What are the consequences of the manager's adherence to the general rule which forms the basis for the proposed action?

Rule utilitarianism, as distinguished from act utilitarianism, which examines each individual action, asserts that utility can be determined regarding classes of actions. In this form of consequentialism, of which the nineteenth-century British philosophers John Stuart Mill and Henry Sidgwick[47] are the most well identified exponents, general rules or principles applied to classes of actions are paramount to highly specific rules. Consequently, rule utilitarians believe that general moral rules provide sound guidance in ordinary cases. Therefore, if the general rule or principle, such as promise-keeping or honesty, is justified on utilitarian grounds, then a person merely adheres to that rule or principle. Whereas an act utilitarian may inquire "Which actions will produce the greatest happiness?" a rule utilitarian would ask "What are the moral rules or principles, observance of which would produce the greatest happiness?"[48]

Rule utilitarians evaluate the moral value of individual actions in various ways. Some judge a particular action as right provided it conforms to a justifiable general rule, regardless of the consequences of that action. On the other hand, other rule utilitarians value the moral worth of a particular action on the basis of the consequences of that action; general principles are merely guides as to what is generally correct. When novel situations occur that are beyond the purview of established utilitarian rules or principles, the rule utilitarian either creates a new general rule or applies act utilitarian analysis to proposed actions responding to the new situation. Rule utilitarianism has particular relevance when cooperation of several persons is required to accomplish a desired result.[49] In cases, such as moving a stalled vehicle from a hilly road, if every person applied act utilitarianism to decide his or her individual course of action, the desired result of moving the vehicle from danger probably would be avoided. In such situations, following a general rule, such as every passenger's pushing the vehicle in the example, is the most feasible way of "achieving the coordination necessary for the desired result."[50]

3.   Can the manager prescribe universal acceptance of the principle upon which he proposes to act?

The deontological approach to ethical decision making affirms that factors other than outcomes determine whether actions and practices are right or wrong. Consequently, deontologists examine the intrinsic value of actions; the actor's motives, whether based on duty or self-interest, are the elements in determining the value of the action. To deontologists, fulfilling a person's duty "is a matter of satisfying the legitimate claims or needs of others as determined by applicable moral principles . . . [and the various] sources of duty can be a divine command, reason, intuition, or a social control arrived at by the members of a society."[51] For example, in the context of business administration, maintaining contractual promises to employees and repaying lenders are the proper actions to take because of duties owned, not because of the good or bad results of such actions.

The theories of the eighteenth-century German philosopher Immanuel Kant illustrate the deontological approach. Kant is the first philosopher to place the concept of "duty" at the center of ethical theory. He proposes that moral goodness comprises the performance of a generalized duty for its own sake, not in order to further human happiness or fulfillment.[52] In a single sentence, Kant proposed a principle to govern moral action: "I am never to act otherwise than so that I could also will that my maxim should become a universal law."[53] Kant asserted that practical reason, as opposed to intuition, conscience, or realization of utility, is the basis of morality.[54]

Kant excluded the elements that John Stuart Mill placed at the center of his moral theory of utilitarianism: the assessment of actions in terms of their consequences and ends, their endowment of human happiness, and their prevention of human suffering.[55] A person's demand to act morally is present in the form of a categorical imperative, that which all rational beings must do because reason commands it. In Kant's view, categorical imperatives are not hypothetical, but, rather, they instruct persons how to act in all circumstances and allow no exceptions.[56] Moreover, Kant distinguished between prudence and morality, as he posited that actions performed from a sense of moral duty, not those based on considerations of prudence, possess moral value.[57]

Kant's theories, often called "ethical formalism" because the form of the action determines its moral correctness, hold that general moral law, not the content of the action, provides the form an action must possess to be moral.[58] For an action or principle to be moral, it must satisfy three demands: (1) it must be possible for it to be made universal, (2) it must respect rational human beings as ends in themselves, and (3) it must respect people's capacity to choose for themselves.[59] Universalizability is that element of moral judgments that requires all logical people to judge the same circumstances alike, and to treat others as we wish to be treated. Consequently, if an action is moral for a particular person, it must be moral for everyone. For instance, an executive's attempt to break a valid contract with an employee cannot be universally applied, and, consequently, it has no moral value.

Further, the action in order to be moral must treat persons with dignity and respect. Therefore, there is a clear distinction between Kant's theory and utilitarianism, which allows certain rights to be violated in pursuit of the general good. Last, according to Kant, the action is morally right if it allows people to treat each other equally. As a consequence, the moral action or principle does not allow deception or coercion, which are immoral because they interfere with a person's right to autonomy.[60]

R.M. Hare[61] has constructed a two-tier theory of moral thinking that lucidly defines the universal aspect of moral judgments, and the relationship between universalizability and moral principles.[62] Moral thinking of the first tier, the intuitive level, exists by reference to basic moral principles that people develop through their upbringing.   Although necessary for all moral thinking, such principles are also insufficient in resolving conflicts of tier-one principles. For example, a manager who must choose between fairness, on one hand, and keeping a promise in a particular employee promotion situation, on the other, has reached the limits of intuitive thinking to select the morally right course. Instead, to resolve the conflict dilemma, that manager must proceed to the second-tier of moral thinking—the critical level—and, in so doing, must employ creativity, imagination, intelligence, and knowledge.   At Hare's critical level of moral thinking, moreover, universalizability of moral judgments is essential. Universalizability demands that if a person makes a moral judgment about a given case, he or she must make the same judgment about any other real or hypothetical situation that is precisely similar to the first case.[63]

In applying the principle of universalizability in a business situation, the manager must imagine him- or herself in the position of every stakeholder affected by the manager's judgment and with every stakeholder's concomitant needs, desires, and preferences. By constructing the situations of every stakeholder and analyzing the consequences for each of them regarding alternative judgments, the manager can determine which judgment is universally prescribable and, hence, morally correct.[64]

Criticisms of deontological theory include the following. First, it is insufficiently precise especially in allowing the discernment of whether people are treated as means or ends, whether people are autonomous, or whether that autonomy is respected.   Second, deontologists may, in fact, appeal covertly to the consequences of an action to demonstrate its rightness, although it may be impossible to separate the consequences of an action from the action itself. Last, how should a person or manager proceed when morally correct duties, rights, or principles conflict? Nonetheless, deontology has value in allowing managers to consider their duties and to examine motives in decision- making.[65] For example, the manager may conclude that truth- telling, promise-keeping, and avoiding any harming of innocent persons are morally correct. Consequently, if the manager intends to introduce a new product that promises great benefit to many but that may harm

some innocent parties, the manager should order further
testing or modification.

4. Does the managerial action conform to principles that would be selected behind a "veil of ignorance"?

Egalitarians ground their vision of justice on the proposition
that all human beings are equal in a fundamental way and,
therefore, each person has an equal claim to society's goods
and services.[66] One of this philosophy's central ideas is that
moral common sense should be governed, not by the maximization
of utility, but by fairness in that all individuals receive
equal respect as participants in any social arrangement.[67]
John Rawls, in his book A Theory of Justice,[68] clearly and
profoundly developed an egalitarian theory as a reaction to
the indifferent distribution of utility in utilitarianism.
Rawls objects to the emasculation of basic human liberties and
rights, which, in his view, deserve protection as a matter of
social justice.[69] Utilitarianism, according to Rawls, permits
infringement of some people's liberties and rights when such
infringement can produce a greater utility for other persons.[70]
Rawls presumes that inequalities among persons that reflect
physical, intellectual, or experiential differences are
undeserved.   Whereas equality is fair, inequality is undeserved.
     In this view, impartiality is a critical concept and is
closely related to universalizability.   The basic idea in
Rawls' theory is that persons can identify proper principles
of justice by "imagining a convention of rational persons of
equal liberty and status . . . [who] select the principles of
justice which will govern their society."[71]   The "original
position" is that situation in which the parties exist when
they begin the choosing of governing principles.
     A hypothetical social contract, further, assures each
person behind a "veil of ignorance" will agree to refrain from
tailoring the principles in a manner biased toward his or her
own fortuitous talents and characteristics.[72]   This veil of
ignorance, designed to exclude types of knowledge that create
schisms among people, empowers persons to freely and im-
partially select valid principles of justice.   As no one knows
his or her status in society, or fortune in the distribution
of natural abilities, strength, or intelligence, so no one is
consciously advantaged or disadvantaged in the selection of
principles.[73] According to Rawls, such a bundle of conditions,
in which the initial situation is symmetrical and all persons
fair and impartial, causes people to unanimously agree on two
fundamental principles of justice: (1) each person shall
possess an equal right to the most extensive basic liberty
compatible with a similar liberty for others, and (2) economic
and social inequalities shall be arranged to both be reasonably expected to be to everyone's advantage and, also,
attached to offices and positions available to all persons.[74]
     Persons in the original position do know general facts
concerning human society, including the bases of social
organization, laws of human psychology, and political and
economic principles.   The conclusion of this process of
selection behind a veil of ignorance is a social system in

which all primary social goods, including liberty, the foundation of self-respect, and opportunity to secure income and wealth, would be distributed equally unless unequal distribution would be to the advantage of those least favored persons.[75] Yet, many have criticized Rawls' theory because, first, it is not clear what principles people would chose behind the veil of ignorance, and, second, it would deny justice to those who, by being more diligent, creative, or innovative, deserve greater benefits.[76]

Another type of egalitarian theory of justice, proposed by William Frankena, asserts that the basic standard of distributive justice is equality of treatment.[77] In Frankena's theory, equality of opportunity, including special attention to persons with certain types of handicaps, is a primary foundation of distributive justice.   Nonetheless, whereas equality of results is not a requisite of equal treatments, justice does mean "equal help or helping according to need" or asking for sacrifice "in accordance with ability."[78]

In the context of business administration, managers may encounter egalitarian reasoning in a number of issues.   Such areas as concerns about employee rights, fair treatment of minorities, and consumer rights are manifestations of egalitarian thinking.

5.   **Regardless of the inequitable distribution of benefits, goods or utility, does the manager's action or course assure that rewards flow to persons according to their production for the benefit of the enterprise?**

Libertarian theories of justice propound that liberty rights must be recognized in economic practice and that people, free to select the nature of their contributions to the economic system, have a fundamental right to own and dispense their own labor as they choose.   Libertarianism advocates individual freedom to the extent that a person's actions do not infringe on the rights of another person.   This theory of justice emphasizes freedom of will and personal accountability. People, then, can act for their own purposes, even if such basic liberty creates an inequitable distribution of the benefits or burdens in society.[79] All society benefits from inequality—every individual's creative endeavors nurture the maximum development of everyone's unique talents and abilities.

Robert Nozick, developer of an entitlement theory of justice, holds that interference in people's voluntary transfer of resources or the taking of resources from someone whose own economic contributions gave rise to the acquisition of the resources violate people's basic rights and entitlements.[80] Consequently, if a manager derives his thinking from this view, he must act to reward the most productive members of his economic micro-system, even if inequalities of distribution result.   To deprive the best workers of the maximum fruits of their labor in order to compensate less productive workers violates the liberties of the former.   Further, because everyone should reap all of the consequences for his expression, laziness should be penalized.

Criticisms of this libertarian view characterize it as enshrining freedom from coercion by directly sacrificing all other rights and values. Further, the freedom of one person necessarily places constraints on others. In addition, the libertarian theory of justice can generate unfair treatment of the disadvantaged, because a person's portion of goods or benefits springs wholly from what that person produces or receives from others who voluntarily give him or her goods or benefits.[81]

6.   In what manner would a person of character conduct him- herself if in the manager's position?

Aristotle, the pupil of Plato and tutor of Alexander of Macedon, applied his techniques of observation and judicious analysis to logic and ethics. In the <u>Nicomachean Ethics</u>, Aristotle wrote regarding his investigations of the vagaries of human conduct. To Aristotle, "human good turns out to be activity of soul in accordance with virtue . . ."[82] and virtues are of two categories: the intellectual (prudence, and knowing how to acquire knowledge) and the moral (truthfulness, temperance, courage, and friendliness). In his analysis of the moral virtues, Aristotle "relies on the common conscience and refers constantly to the moral judgments men make in the ordinary course of life."[83]

By emphasizing virtues as desirable character traits or dispositions, Aristotle stressed the importance of how a person acts, as well as what that person does. A person's virtuous action flows from his or her right motive, in the right way, at the right moment. By habitually acting as someone who possesses those desirable character traits, an individual can cultivate desirable virtues.[84] This reasoning, applied in the contest of business administration, presupposes the manager's developed conception of the virtues. Without such conception, the manager may not comprehend what character traits are indeed virtuous or identify what person possesses those virtues. Nonetheless, in times of difficulty for many managers with an appreciation of admirable character traits, reflection on what action persons with such virtues would pursue provides a helpful reference.

SOCIAL RESPONSIBILITY AND RESPONSIVENESS

Business firms and their environment interact mutually and business firms also react upon their environment. Business activities do not merely provide economic effects, but also determine the conditions of community living and shape the intellectual and moral tones of the age.[85] Moreover, before discussing the concepts of social responsibility and social responsiveness, it is instructive to review the social contract that business firms maintain with society. Firms derive their existence, rights, and protection from a frame- work of government in which citizens determine the ends of governmental activities. Whereas, historically, private property has enjoyed a preferential status, in this century the government has taken steps to regulate private property, purportedly to direct its conduct toward the protection and benefit of society. Society, through the government, can revoke or amend any institution's charter if it fails to

fulfill society's expectations. As long as business firms are
not public property, corporate responsibility rests with those
who are legally and morally responsible and accountable for
the firm—directors, managers, and owners (if privately held).

Business Social Responsibility

After business ethics, business "social responsibility" is the
second important concept regarding attempts to evaluate the
social performance of business firms and to provide managers
with guideposts.   The essence of the social responsibility
concept is that business firms have societal obligations that
transcend the economic functions of producing and distributing
goods and services for profit.[86] Although the modern interest
in the doctrine dates to the 1950s, the roots of business
social responsibility lie in the late nineteenth century with
the view that "private business is a public trust."[87]
       Moreover, the growth of the notion of management as a
profession in the 1920s stimulated society's expectation that
corporate responsibilities extended beyond profit maximization.   A consensus developed in the mid-1960s through the
mid-1970s within academic and business circles that businesses
and their managers must be socially responsible.[88]   Included
in this consensus was the recognition that the major issues of
business social responsibility emanate from the "ongoing
business functions of the firm and not from company 'do
goodism'—that 'responsibilities' inhere in day-to-day
organizational operations . . . the question became how best
to insure that the . . . [firm] and its leadership would
operate in a 'socially responsible' manner."[89]
       There are a number of distinctions[90] between the modern
concepts of business ethics and business social responsibility: the former emphasizes ethical reflection by the
manager, whereas the latter focuses on organizational action.
The social responsibility doctrine stresses resolution of
specific   issues   and   identifiable   stakeholders,   whereas
business ethics posits a moral reflection as a generalized
activity involving all managerial actions.   Last, the language
of business ethics employs terms of moral philosophy in
analyzing business administration (right, wrong, utility,
rights, duties, justice); on the other hand, business social
responsibility analysis uses a lexicon of social science
(power and legitimacy).
       Social responsibility regarding business firms has many
definitions including: following "lines of action which are
desirable in terms of the objectives and values of our
society,"[91] the "ethical principles that ought to govern the
relationships between the corporation and society,"[92] and the
idea that the firm has "certain responsibilities to society
which extend beyond these [economic and legal] obligations."[93]
Generally the concept of business social responsibility means
that a firm has a broader constituency than its shareholders
or owners alone and that it has responsibilities to society
beyond the production of wanted goods and services at a
profit.
       Arguments in favor[94] of social responsibility assert that
business firms should accommodate the new expectations society

has regarding business. Further, business benefits itself by
helping to solve social problems because such amelioration
improves the environmental conditions favorable for long-term
survival, prosperity, and profitability.   In addition,
business gains a more desirable public image by acting
socially responsible. Also, socially responsible businesses
may avoid more stringent government regulation. Moreover,
since the business sector has great social power in its
influence on consumers, employees, society, and the environment, it also has a responsibility for the effects on them as
well.   Business has enormous resources useful in solving
social problems and, further, can turn social problems into
profitable opportunities. Finally, there exists the moral
argument that business has an obligation to help solve social
problems, such as pollution, unsafe workplaces, and discrimination in hiring and promotion, because it helped to
create or perpetuate them.

     Others, who oppose the concept of business social
responsibility either in whole or part, raise serious objections.[95] First, one commentator notes that social responsibility "has been used in so many different contexts that it has
lost all meaning . . . [and] has come to mean all things to
all people," thereby confusing business people and policy-
makers alike.[96] Further, since the market system does not work
to allocate resources for the provision of public goods and
services, the manager receives little information to aid his
or her decisions in solving social problems. Moreover, as
Milton Friedman has noted, business people affectively impose
taxes on the public by using consumers', employees', and
shareholders' money for a public purpose. No public process
selects these managers whose unaccountable actions in this
regard can be arbitrary. In addition, the sole responsibility
of a business firm is to its shareholders or owners, and
managers have no legal or moral right to pursue any course
other than profit maximization.

     Over three decades ago, Professor Theodore Levitt in a
Harvard Business Review article[97] pointed out the danger of
allowing business to assume social well-being activities
traditionally in the domain of other institutions, because
such a concentration of power in one institution would lead to
a collapse of pluralism. Also, business managers do not have
experience in dealing with social as opposed to private goals,
and individuals alone, not business organizations, have moral
responsibilities. Finally, business decision- making should
be economic not political; decisions that reflect the political power of interest groups subvert the principle of a free
enterprise system and would add cost to those products that
expense would inhibit American competitiveness.

     Given the above discussion, it is obvious that some of
the conflicts between proponents and critics of the social
responsibility of business firms may never be settled. One
clear need is to improve the level of debate, especially in
areas where managers are faced with decisions that, although
morally doubtful, are unambiguously profitable. Some matters
appear to defy solution: the concept of social responsibility
provides no clear guidelines for managerial behavior, the
concept does not fully consider the competitive environment in
which firms function, and the concept implies a moral obliga-

tion. Given the lack of precision in the concept's meaning, managers who strive to be socially responsible must follow either their own values or vague definitions of the concept.

Moreover, firms are severely limited in their ability to respond to social problems, because a firm that unilaterally engages in social action increases its production costs and product prices, thereby placing itself at a relative competitive disadvantage. Only the government can force such collective redirection by rewriting the rules under which all firms operate. Proponents of social responsibility have produced no generally accepted moral principle that imposes an obligation for firms to commit their resources to social betterment.[98] Instead, one proponent has suggested:

> What is required, then, in addition, is some change in consciousness—and conscience. Corporate social responsibility in this sense, if it is to be more than slogan, presupposes changes too far reaching and subtle to be achieved by playing around with the formal organizational charts. Focusing inside the firm, there have to be reforms in the corporate culture, in the attitudinal assumptions not merely of the executives, but of the entire work group, where so much of the trouble, the faulty brakes and so on, brews. Outside the firm, in the world at large, support has to develop for revised definitions of virtue and redirected vectors of loyalty. Changes of that sort cannot be imposed—not successfully, at any rate. They have to evolve, with some push from the people who care.[99]

Business Social Responsiveness

In response to the seeming intractability of the conflicts of social responsibility, a reorientation regarding the response of business firms to the social environment evolved into the morally neutral concept of "social responsiveness."[100] This novel concept refers to the capacity of firms to respond to social pressures. The concept of corporate social responsiveness reflects a marked shift in emphasis, on one hand, from philosophical definitions and specific social performance issues to, on the other, strategic management of values in business decision-making. Social responsiveness as a concept is related to searching within the firm for organizational elements (procedures and mechanisms) that enable the firm to respond to societal pressures.[101] This notion of responsiveness emphasizes proactive, not reactive, action embodied in organizational policies that enhance rational, empirical decision-making.[102] Business social responsiveness has complemented the explicitly normative orientation of business ethics and the "issue-outcome" stress of business social responsibility. Development of the social audit and codes of conduct are examples of the pragmatic orientation of social responsiveness.[103]

In one conceptual model of social responsiveness,[104] the three stages of a firm's response appear as awareness, commitment, and implementation. The awareness phase comprises key firm executives' recognizing a social problem as important, going "on record," and devising company policies to address the problem. The beginning of the second phase, commitment, is marked by the appointment of a staff specialist, who reports to the CEO or a senior executive and who coordinates the firm's activities regarding the problem and records feedback. Often, the staff specialist eventually is overwhelmed by the decentralized character of decision-making within the organization, as that specialist fails to educe a company response congruent with the company policy. The third phase, a response to the failure of phase two to accomplish the company's social policy, is characterized by the CEO's attempt to achieve the social policy by making it an institutional goal for all managers. Toward this end, the CEO may modify the firm's procedures concerning establishing objectives, reward systems, and performance measurement.

This model of social responsiveness has served as the catalyst for the development of other models. Another commentator emphasizes corporate behavior as social obligation, social responsibility, and social responsiveness:

> In the first state, social obligation, the corporation seeks legitimacy by meeting legal and economic criteria only . . . [as the] corporation believes it is account-able only to its stockholders and strongly resists any regulation of its activities. In the second state, social responsibility, the corporation searches for legitimacy by recognizing the limited relevance of meeting only legal and economic criteria and accepts a broader set of criteria for measuring corporate perfor-mance that includes a social dimension. Management considers groups other than stockholders that might be affected by its actions and is willing to work . . . for good environmental legislation. In the third state, social responsiveness, the corporation accepts its role as defined by the social system and recognizes that this role is subject to change over time . . . it is willing to account for its actions to other groups . . . and assists legislative bodies in developing better legisla-tion. Thus business becomes an active supporter as well as promoter of environmental and social concerns.[105]

There are many advantages[106] of the social responsiveness doctrine. First, this philosophy does not necessarily develop a moral perspective to validate its holdings. Rather, the issues in this pragmatic and action-grounded approach relate to the firm's ability to respond to certain social issues. The social responsiveness doctrine, it follows, has a man-agerial orientation. Moreover, this approach allows a rigorous analytical research in examining specific techniques, such as environmental scanning. Still, in spite of these advantages, the concept of social responsiveness does not clarify how the firm's resources should be employed to solve social problems. Moreover, the concept does not markedly consider the institutional and competitive context of the firm. Finally, the concept of social responsiveness does not construct an overriding moral reason for business to become engaged in addressing social problems or provide moral principles for business to follow in offering social responses.

The business sector is one of the few major loci of power and authority in our society. Since it is futile to believe that lawmakers can anticipate all socially deleterious behavior and would probably be more harmful if they could, all loci of power benefit society by encouraging people to act in socially appropriate ways. Responsible behavior through self-control is often preferable to doing nothing, an inaction that is a catalyst to additional regulation to enforce all desiderata by law with the concomitant diminishing of personal freedom.[107] Consequently, a discussion of what a business firm's social responsibility or responsiveness comprises is relevant and valid.

Protecting the Environment

One area in which the public's expectation of business social responsibility or responsiveness is substantial is that of protecting the physical environment. In 1962 Rachel Carson in Silent Spring warned of a "chain of evil," the growing contamination of earth, air, rivers, and seas by manufactured pollutants. The decade of the 1960s offered tinder for the environmental movement: the pesticide DDT's danger, whiskey-brown smog in major cities, rivers slimy with algae and toxic compounds, Lake Erie as the "North American Dead Sea," the spontaneous combustion of the oily Cuyahoga River, PCB poisoning of Japanese on Kyushu, the Torrey Canyon and Santa Barbara oil spills, and the Rhine River pesticide spill, which killed 40 million fish.

It will be many years before scientists determine the full extent of the damage wrought in the *Exxon Valdez* oil spill in Alaska in 1989. Ironically, even if the *Exxon Valdez* oil had safely reached its ultimate destination—power plants and auto engines—the millions of gallons of oil lost in the wreck would have released into the atmosphere approximately sixty million pounds of carbon in the form of carbon dioxide, a direct contributor to the greenhouse effect and air pollution. At the beginning of 1990, many old problems are unabated, whereas new concerns, such as acid rain, depletion of the ozone layer, and the greenhouse effect, occupy the headlines.

As a result of the environmental disasters of the 1960s, a few modest, state-enforced legislative initiatives (the 1963 Clean Air Act, the 1965 Motor Vehicle Air Pollution Control Act, and the 1967 Air Quality Act) gave way to the National Environmental Policy Act (NEPA) of 1969.[108] The NEPA established an advisory Council on Environmental Quality, and in a little-noticed section, mandated comprehensive environmental impact statements for nearly all large government-sponsored construction projects. No single body of law had such an immediate and powerful effect on all facets of American life.

In December of 1970 President Richard Nixon issued an executive order creating the Environmental Protection Agency; Congress enacted the 1970 amendments to the old Clean Air Act and the 1972 Federal Water Pollution Control Act. By 1973 business firms, government, and consumers were annually spending $13 billion (approximately 1% of the Gross National Product) on pollution-abatement measures, a figure that would since average 1.5-2% of the GNP, although key industries, often ailing, bore the brunt of the expenses.

The Council on Environmental Quality (CEQ) has responsibility for administering the environmental impact statement process by issuing regulations regarding their preparation, but it has no administrative authority for pollution control. The CEQ evaluates all federal programs to monitor their congruence with the national policy regarding the environment, advises and assists the president, and promulgates national environmental policies. The other federal agency involved in protecting and enhancing the physical environment is the Environmental Protection Agency (EPA), which has responsibility for controlling pollution in seven areas[109]: air, water, solid and hazardous waste, toxic substances, pesticides, radiation, and noise. EPA duties in these domains include: (1) establishing and enforcing standards, (2) monitoring pollution, (3) researching environmental problems, and (4) assisting state and local governments in their pollution-control efforts.[110]

Air Pollution. Normally, the total amount of pollution in the atmosphere over the United States comprises hundreds of millions of tons and the annual amount of pollutants discharged in the air amounts to over a ton for every inhabitant of the nation. The EPA regulates the artificial sources of pollution and has identified seven pollutants as pervasive and in need of immediate reduction: in 1971, sulfur oxides, carbon monoxide, ozone, nitrogenoxides, particulates, and hydrocarbons, and, in 1978, lead.

The EPA's primary legal bases to control air pollution are the Clean Air Act of 1963 and its extraordinarily rigorous amendments of 1970 and 1977. As a consequence, the EPA is empowered to manage the ambient air quality; control emissions from stationary sources (factories, for instance) and mobile sources (primarily vehicles); restrict industrial growth in areas where minimum national air quality standards have not been attained; and limit industrial growth in areas where the air quality surpasses the minimum national standards.[111]

To regulate ambient air quality, the EPA sets primary standards regarding the seven aforementioned pollutants to prevent people from becoming ill, without regard to expense or the adequacy of technology to allow the standards to be met. Whereas primary standards safeguard human health, secondary standards established by the EPA purportedly promote the public welfare and prevent damage to plant life, animals, and property. By 1975, although the states had reponsibility to promulgate plans to reach the target standards for air quality control regions within their areas, only 69 of the 247 regions were actually in compliance.

Investments of $58.3 billion by American industries and $12.8 billion by the federal government in smokestack scrubbers and other emission control devices from 1972 through 1987 have significantly reduced most air pollutants. By 1988, 1,600 (of 3,151) counties complied with air quality standards.[112] The 1977 amendments to the Clean Air Act added more muscle to the EPA to prevent significant deterioration of the air in regions that have satisfied the standards.   In nonattainment areas, moreover, the EPA has instituted an offset policy, which allows new industrial development and pollution in concert with offsetting reductions from existing pollutant sources.

Furthermore, the EPA controls stationary sources of air pollution, in addition to the ambient air quality discussed above. The EPA, although determining that all air pollutants are dangerous to a degree, has established strict limits on the discharge of particularly dangerous substances such as beryllium, mercury, arsenic, benzene, asbestos, and vinyl chlorides. Pursuant to the "bubble concept" introduced by the EPA in 1982, firms that limit or reduce their pollution within an area covered by an imaginary bubble can trade or sell credits to other firms that wish to expand but are violating clean air standards.[113] In 1986 the EPA expanded this concept to areas that had not satisfied federal air pollution standards. Under the "bubble" transactions, Scott Paper's mill in Chester, PA, and 3M's tape and packaging plant in Bristol, PA, saved $220,000 and $1.2 million, respectively, in annual operating costs, whereas 3M also saved $3 million in capital expenditures.

Last, the EPA establishes standards for automobile, truck, and aircraft pollutant emissions pursuant to its authority to regulate mobile sources. The Clean Air Act's motor vehicle standards focus on the reduction or elimination of nitrogen oxide, carbon monoxide, lead, hydrocarbons, and particulate matter.[114]

The Greenhouse Effect, Ozone Layer Thinning, and Acid Rain. The emission of pollutants into the atmosphere directly effects three major environmental problems that have a potentially devastating effect on the Earth's environment: the misnomered greenhouse effect, the thinning of the planet's ozone shield, and acid rain. The greenhouse effect, misnamed because greenhouses don't work in such a way, is a natural phenomenon. The earth's atmosphere, which consists primarily of nitrogen and oxygen, is virtually transparent to sunlight. Some of the outbound infrared radiation, which the planet emits after absorbing sunlight, is trapped by gases in the lower atmosphere before it can escape into space.   These "greenhouse gases," primarily carbon dioxide (CO^2) and water vapor, then heat the earth's atmosphere.[115] Most scientists[116] believe that the greenhouse effect will indeed considerably warm the earth during the next century: for example, by 3-9°F. above 1989 levels.

Scientists project that the global warming will reach a few degrees Fahrenheit above preindustrial levels by 2010, a temperature higher that any global mean in 100,000 years.[117] Whereas the planet's atmosphere contains 25% more carbon dioxide than at the birth of the (1850) Industrial Revolution based on the analysis of carbon from tree rings,[118] the level is increasing by .4% per year. Ten to 20% of the world's manufactured emissions of carbon dioxide are attributable to extensive logging and to land clearing—for plant matter, like the oceans, absorbs emitted carbon dioxide. Every year, approximately 27.2 million acres of tropical forest are permanently lost and 14.8 million acres of new desert are formed.

The greatest single source of CO^2, however, is the combustion of fossil fuels (coal, natural gas, and petroleum) in factories, homes, and vehicle engines. One- half of the CO^2 produced by humans remains in the atmosphere. Moreover, other greenhouse gases such as methane (CH_4) and nitrous oxide (N^2O) have increased more rapidly than CO^2. Factory smokestacks, vehicle exhausts, and the decomposition of chemical fertilizers emit N^2O into the atmosphere, whereas cattle are the chief producers of methane. Apparently, increasing quantities of these "greenhouse gases" produced by modern humans have destroyed the atmosphere's delicate equilibrium. Even to slow the warming to more recent historical rates of .2 of a degree Fahrenheit per decade would require reducing fossil fuel emissions by 60%; yet, economists forecast a doubling of the levels of such emissions over the next four decades. Serious conservation efforts would yield greater results than the substitution of alternative energy sources: the United States, for example, employs twice as much energy to achieve the same standard of living as Europe and Japan.[119]

The warming of the earth, notes Dr. James Hansen, director of NASA's Goddard Institute for Space Studies, will cause a rise in sea levels, wetter and drier regions, and longer summers and rising temperatures. Computer calculations and comparisons of past cold and warm years demonstrate an increase of $2°F$ will warm the high latitudes most and the regions close to the equator the least. Moreover, temperature changes imply alterations of rainfall and wind[120] with the result that U.S. corn and wheat belts would be parched. For example, by 2050 the oceans (heat causes water to expand) could be several feet higher (compared to the four to six inches increase between 1880 and 1985), thereby inundating coastal areas where tens of millions of people live, and making aquifers in Florida and Long Island and rivers providing Southern California drinking water useless.

A related unseen phenomenon, the depletion of the paper-thin ozone layer in the atmosphere, is caused by the decomposition of chloroflourocarbons, which liberate chlorine molecules, thereby destroying ozone. The phenomena of warming and ozone depletion will occur in the same atmosphere and "their effects not only will be intertwined, but also will perturb one another."[121] Chlorofluorocarbons, manufactured chemicals, have been banned as propellants in aerosol cans. Nonetheless, the chemicals are still used in a variety of ways: as industrial solvents, as propellants in producing styrofoam, and as refrigerants—all comprising a $750 million industry in the United States alone.

Chloroflourocarbons and methane act like high-altitude Pac-Men destroying the ozone, warned University of California chemists Sherwood Rowland and Mario Molina in 1974. Yet, the same year, the DuPont company dismissed the finding as "speculative" and asserted that any restriction of the use of chemicals in aerosols "would cause tremendous economic dislocations." Unfortunately, chloroflourocarbons remain in the atmosphere for approximately 100 years.[122] Then, in 1985 a team led by Joseph Farman of the British Antarctic Survey reported a 50% loss in the ozone layer of Antarctica—a hole as large as the continental United States.[123] Later measurements revealed an ozone reduction extending to the southern tips of South America, Australia, and New Zealand.[124]

Ozone loss increases the relative amount of a form of ultraviolet light, UV-B. Even a paltry 1% drop in ozone will increase skin cancer cases by 3% to 6% and damage the human immune system, relates immunologist Margaret Kripke of the University of Texas. Moreover, UV-B causes tissue and cell damage in many plant species; a 15% loss of stratospheric ozone would cause crop losses of $2.6 billion per year. Finally, UV-B causes mutations in microscopic organisms necessary for marine life. Meanwhile, in 1987 studies indicated that the planet's ozone shield has eroded by 1.7% to 3% since 1970—considerably more rapidly than earlier predictions.[125]

A third problem directly related to the release by human activities of chemical compounds into the atmosphere is acid rain or deposition, which contains small but significant amounts of sulfuric acid (H^2SO^4) and nitric acid (HNO^3). Oxidation in the atmosphere converts the gaseous forms of sulfur and nitrogen into sulfuric and nitric acids. The primary source of sulfur oxide is the combustion of fossil fuel for electric power generation, whereas nitrogen oxides are emitted into the atmosphere by combustion of fossil fuels, especially in the engines of cars, trucks, and other transportation system components.[126]

Acid rain damages forests and soils—many forests in Europe and North America receive over twenty-five times the amount of acidity as they would if rain and snow (which are naturally slightly acidic) fell through a pristine atmosphere.[127] Moreover, acid rain destroys the purity of lakes and streams, leaches soil nutrients much faster than normal rain, inhibits the breakdown of dead organic matter and the soil system's extraction of nitrogen from the atmosphere,[128] and damages tree and plant leaves. Less plausible claims are that acid rain is killing forests, corroding city structures, and causing early deaths of 50,000 to 200,000 Americans with respiratory ailments.[129]

Commentators suggest that an obvious solution for acid rain is for utility companies to use low-sulfur Western coal (thereby eliminating 30,000 Eastern mining jobs) and requiring utilities to install smokestack "scrubbers" costing $100 million each (as a result raising electricity bills substantially). Cutting the nation's sulfur dioxide emission by 30% would cost $20 billion, or, in former budget director David Stockman's pithy analysis, about "$6,000 per pound of fish" saved.

The Clean Air Act, moreover, according to scientists and public health commentators, has been a qualified success or failure, notes Michael Weisskopf, in "A Qualified Failure—The Clean Air Act Hasn't Done The Job," appearing in the Washington Post National Weekly Edition, June 19-25, 1989. The act, as administered by the EPA, had greatly reduced lead emissions and carbon monoxide, and it has cut by one-third the 210 million tons of pollution dumped into the air in 1970. Nonetheless, according to Weisskopf, the EPA has failed to implement important parts of the Clean Air Act and has been

too lenient in dispensing concessions and delays.   Critics
assert that the major failures of the act are:

1. Over one-half the population resides in areas where at
   least one of the six deleterious pollutants targeted by
   the Act exceeds standards.

2. EPA standards are too weak to adequately protect the
   nation's ten million asthmatics or the general population with an "adequate margin of safety."

3. Only a few of the hundreds of perilous pollutants
   targeted for control at the source of their emission
   are regulated, in spite of causing cancer, birth
   defects, and genetic mutations.

4. There are no controls on carbon dioxide, a "greenhouse
   gas."

5. There is no standard for acid aerosols, particles that
   transport the most toxic substances to the innermost
   part of the lung.

6. The EPA is not empowered to regulate indoor pollutants;
   EPA and industry spokespersons, however, note the air
   is much cleaner today and that enormous progress has
   been made.

Even though the nation worries about polluted air, construction of electric plants powered by low-pollution "renewable" electricity sources (sunlight, water, steam, and wind,
for instance) will decline sharply beginning in 1990.   From
1,200 megawatts in 1990 (enough energy to power 600,000
homes), the capacity of electric plants brought on line each
year that are fueled by renewable energy sources drops
precipitously to less than 200 megawatts in 1994.   According
to a 1989 research study by the Investor Responsibility
Research Center, reported in "Nation Is Facing a Big Slowdown
In 'Clean' Power," in the August 3, 1989 edition of the Wall
Street Journal, prospects for such "clean" power plants have
been hurt by low prices for the fuels they replace, such as
gas and oil.   According to the study, costs for geothermal
plants are from 4.5 to 10 cents per kilowatt hour; for wind,
7 to 9 cents; for small hydroelectric projects, 4 to 9 cents;
and for solar thermal plants, 12 to 25 cents.   On the contrary, new, natural gas-fired plants, based on current costs
of fuel, can sell power for as little as 5.5 cents a kilowatt
hour.

Water Pollution.   The demands of modern industry and
agriculture and rising levels of population and affluence have
placed unparalleled stress upon fresh water sources.[130] Water
pollution occurs when the natural cleansing action by oxygen
in water is inhibited because of the quantity of wastes
entering that body of water.   Major sources of water pollution
include:

1. Organic materials from sewage, farms, and industries.

2. Chemical runoffs from streets.

3. Acid and mineral drainage from mining.

4. Toxic substances from industry and synthetic.

5. Chemicals in pesticides, plastics, and detergents.

6. Sediments from agriculture and construction.

7. Biological   nutrients,   such   as   nitrogen   in fertilizers.[131]

Until the mid-1950s, responsibility for controlling water pollution, as air pollution, lay primarily with local and state governments.

The EPA controls water pollution principally through the Federal Water Pollution Control Act Amendments of 1972, which mandated federal and state efforts to achieve clean water and eliminate discharges of pollutants into U.S. waters.   Under the amendments, the EPA is empowered to establish a permit system for pollution discharge,[132] and it is illegal to discharge pollutants into U.S. waters without a permit.   The Clean Water Act of 1977 amended the 1972 statute and changed the classification system of industrial pollutants. Moreover, the 1977 act regulates nonpoint sources of pollution such as urban stormwater, agricultural construction, logging runoff, and acid mine seepage, which are difficult to control. Although the EPA has developed uniform national standards to control point pollution, state and local governments have the responsibility of establishing nonpoint source pollution controls because of the variation in soil conditions, climate, and topography that determine nonpoint source pollution.[133]

Samuel Taylor Coleridge's line concerning water every-where without "any drop to drink" has a significant and timely meaning for 1990. A more recent comment by Jacques Cousteau may be even more relevant: "Without water there is no life." The effects of water pollution and population demands could be severe in the 1990s according to Joe Schwartz in an article, "The Real Price of Water," in American Demographics (September 1988), as follows: the gradual decline of agribusiness in Southern California and Arizona and much higher prices for water in the water-rich East.

Of the money the United States expends relating to water supplies, almost 60% ($185 per person in 1979) is used to clean industrial waste water. Unfortunately, water pollution control programs have their incongruities: the EPA's sub-sidies for municipal sewage treatment grants, over $44 billion since 1972, are a huge "pork barrel" and, sadly, there is no solid evidence that the massive outlay has produced cleaner streams or lakes.

Pesticides, Toxic Substances, and Hazardous Wastes. The EPA also regulates pesticides, toxic substances, and hazardous waste disposal. Of the 2.6 billion pounds of pesticides applied annually, 60% are used on agricultural products. Three of the most frequently detected pesticides found on potatoes are DDT, dieldrin, and chlordane, which purportedly were banned years earlier. Since the 1940s U.S. crop losses to insects have doubled, even though pesticide use has increased tenfold. Yet, because of an expanding population and the corresponding decrease in available farmland, pesticides are essential to maintain high crop yields. The 1972 amendments to the Federal Insecticide, Fungicide, and Rodenticide Act (FIFRA) (from which act the EPA has responsibility to preclear certain products) require the EPA to reregister 35,000 pesticides already on the market. The EPA has considered only about three of the 600 active ingredients contained in the 45,000 various commercial products on the market. Consequently, the EPA is not in a position to proffer meaningful conclusions as to the health or environmental effects of the overwhelming number of chemicals in use. Yet, according to the National Academy of Sciences estimates, the following currently legal pesticide chemicals exceed the EPA's "acceptable" rate of one cancer case per million: captafol (with a risk of 594 cases per million), captan (474), and maneb (442).[134]

In 1976 President Ford signed into law the Toxic Substances Control Act (TSCA). The TSCA confers broad and powerful regulatory powers on the EPA to:

1. Prevent unreasonable risks to health and to the environment from chemical substances.

2. Require the chemical industry to develop and report information concerning chemical risks.

3. Control any chemicals with unreasonable risks.

4. Forbid manufacture of new chemicals not proven safe.

5. Regulate details of the manufacture, distribution, use and disposal of commercial chemical products.[135]

Sixty thousand of the seven million known chemicals compounds are in substantial commercial use: under the current regulations, the EPA assumes that a substance can harm human health or the environment until testing indicates otherwise.

During the last decade, government regulations concerning the storage and disposal of hazardous materials have become more stringent. Over 150 million tons of solid waste, including hazardous substances, are annually discarded in the United States. Moreover, between 1950 and 1979, over 1.5 trillion pounds of hazardous waste were deposited in just 3,300 sites in the United States. Common hazardous materials include the toxic or suspected carcinogens vinyl chloride, mercury, lead, PBB, PCB, benzidine, and carbon tetrachloride.[136]

From 60% to 90% of cancers are attributable to environmental components, including exposure to toxic chemicals. According to Karl Grossman, author of The Poison Conspiracy, among the people hardest hit by cancer are those who live near toxic waste dumps, such as Love Canal. Yet, notes Dr. Vernon Houk in the April 1984, issue of Chemecology, if chemicals were completely eliminated, people would still have significant cancer risks "from naturally occurring toxicants that are in our water, are in our food, are in our air." Further, a significant number of dumps that the EPA has identified as substantial risks to human health are directly linked to contaminated groundwater, which is the source of water of about one-half of the U.S. population.

The first effort to solve the hazardous waste problem was market-oriented; industry bore most of the expense. Draconian rules, urged by government regulators, failed. Operators of existing landfill dumps, rather than spend the capital for new improvements mandated by the Resource Conservation and Recovery Act (RCRA) of 1984, closed more than one-third of the dumps. The earlier RCRA of 1976 provides for federal classi- fication of hazardous waste, federal safeguard standards for those who generate and transport it, a tracking system for waste materials, enforcement of standards through permits for facilities that treat, store, or dispose of hazardous wastes, and authorization of state programs to replace federal programs.[137] The newer RCRA of 1984 "prohibits the disposal on land of hazardous wastes unless the EPA determines such disposal will not endanger human health and the environment.

Moreover, the Comprehensive Environmental Response, Compensation, and Liability Act (CERCLA), often termed "Superfund," provides money and authority to the EPA to direct cleanup of abandoned or old waste sites that endanger the public or the environment. Unfortunately, as an EPA admini- strator, Fred L. Smith, notes, allocation of Superfund money is made by "selecting projects based on their political and public relations value and . . . the EPA has often avoided penalizing the real polluters . . ."

The bill coming due for toxic waste cleanup approaches $100 billion. Meanwhile, courts are holding firms, not their insurers, responsible for toxic waste cleanup. In July of 1989, Technicon Electronics and Diamond Shamrock Chemicals were denied insurance coverage, and in December of 1988, a jury found Shell Oil, not its insurers, liable for a $1 billion cleanup of a Colorado site. Some commentators suggest the old "individualist" approach (that holds each individual or entity accountable for his or her own actions) be discarded for a "loss spreading" approach. Loss spreading, according to an article by Amy Dockser, "Corporate Polluters Paying the Price," in the August 1, 1989, edition of the Wall Street Journal, is "based on the premise that everyone shared the benefits of industrialization and everyone must now share its costs." The idea is to create a National Environmental Trust Fund to pay for the cleanup of waste sites where pollution regulations were not violated at the time the waste materials were dumped, with funding to come from a levy on commercial and industrial property-casualty insurance premiums. In other cases, the individual polluter would be liable. Environmental groups and the Bush administration will likely oppose the trust fund initiative because of a stress on individual accountability as a deterrent to future pollution.

In the meantime, communities have resisted the construc- tion of waste treatment plants. The result is that dangerous wastes continue to be sent to injection wells, surface impoundments, and deficient landfills, according to Daniel Mazmanian and David Morell in an article, "The Elusive Pursuit of Toxics Management" appearing in the Winter 1988, issue of

The Public Interest. The authors support less reliance on "uniform rules promulgated by distant federal agencies" and, instead, more flexibility for local initiatives. For instance, New Jersey, which in the late 1970s was notorious for its hazardous waste dumps, has enacted the nation's first mandatory recycling law. The New Jersey statute requires each municipality to salvage 25% of its glass, paper, and other solid waste by 1991, according to a report by Paul Barrett appearing in the Wall Street Journal on July 5, 1988. New Jersey's "spill fund" for toxic cleanups has served as a model for the federal "Superfund," as has its "right to know" law for chemical workers for federal rules. New Jersey also requires toxic waste cleanup by firms before selling their properties. According to Governor (at the time) Thomas Kean, "[W]e've learned you haven't got time to wait for Washington [the federal government to act]."

Other states have taken the initiative as well. Iowa has imposed special taxes on agricultural businesses to clean up drinking water (25% of which is at least slightly contaminated by pesticides).

CONCLUSIONS

A manager's careful thinking concerning ethical and business conduct issues prevents costly mistakes. An understanding of the moral philosophies based on utilitarianism, rights, and duties allows the manager to develop avenues by which to analyze and solve difficult problems. As a locus of power and authority in our modern system, business firms, through any one of the doctrines of business ethics, social responsibility, or social responsiveness, have important, indispensable roles to do more than the minimum the law requires. The extent of that duty beyond the law is subject to interpretation by individual firms and industries.

One focus of social responsiveness is that of protecting the physical environment; the right to a clean, safe environment is considered by many a basic human right. Since the late 1960s, Congress has significantly expanded criminal liability of managers and corporate officials for environmental law violations.[138] Such a right to healthy environment, contrary to some who mask an antibusiness and antifree enterprise mindset behind their fervor for environmental protection, does not mean a discontinuation of long-run economic growth. The business sector's social responsiveness does mean that it must abandon myopic complacency. Wilfred Beckerman, a noted Oxford economist, asserts that economic and technological growth, in fact, enhances human life.

To avoid the stifling and oppressive systems of social control, one ultimate consequence of continued destruction of the environment beyond our ability to cope, business must lead the way in developing the moral resources of self-restraint and respect for human beings. For instance, manufacturers can reduce the amount of waste generated by adopting new processes, recycling waste material, and utilizing new materials.[139] Further, business and society must reduce, where possible, the burning of fossil fuels. For instance, merely improving the efficiency of existing oil and gas furnaces and water heaters

to the fullest cost-efficient extent would save the energy of
4.5 billion barrels of oil; weatherization programs for 53
million oil- and gas-heated homes, .9 billion barrels; and
improving the fuel efficiency of autos and trucks by a
moderate degree, 13 billion barrels.[140] Moreover, the General
Accounting Office (GAO) estimates that a viable market for
purchase and sale of pollution rights could reduce pollution
control costs for many firms by at least 40%.

Another positive step is every firm's performing an
environmental self-assessment to determine compliance with
current law and to seek ways to improve its activities that
may be harming the environment.[141] A May 1989, Opinion
Research poll indicates that Americans are clearly worried
about environmental problems: 80% are very concerned about the
quality of drinking water, nearly 80% about air quality, 66%
about pesticides on food, nearly 60% about ozone pesticides on
food, nearly 60% about ozone depletion, and nearly 50% about
the greenhouse effect. In the same poll, 23% of respondents
noted an illness in their families caused by inferior air
quality, and 19% noted an illness from exposure to hazardous
substances. Firms that brush the tripwire of this public
concern face a wrathful response. Exxon, after the *Exxon
Valdez* grounding and oil spill on March 24, 1989, has been
attacked by consumer groups calling for a boycott of Exxon
products, a local government has cut its ties with the
company, credit card holders have returned their cards, and
the huge company (annual revenues of $88.6 billion) even had
difficulty selling a $110 million issue of two-year bonds.
The spill is likely to diminish Alaskan development opportunities for Exxon and other oil firms. There are undoubtedly
many to blame for the oil spill, including gas hungry American
drivers, but public outrage is focused on Exxon—a fact other
firms must heed.

One constant is certain: public support for a cleaner
environment has grown stronger, even through recessions, in
the twenty-five years from 1965 to 1990. Nonetheless, the
public, not just business, must demonstrate a greater resolve
to pay for the cost of pollution controls. For instance,
President Bush's tough new standards for cleaner air and
water, projected to cost $19 billion if enacted, face two
foes: utility firms and auto manufacturers, on one hand, and
the public on the other. In a May 1989, Opinion Research
poll, although substantial majorities were "very concerned"
about air and water pollution, ozone depletion, and the
greenhouse effect, over one-half of respondents oppose tax
increases to pay for tougher standards, and 67% and 60% oppose
stricter environmental regulations if they would force greater
dependency on foreign oil or eliminate jobs, respectively.
The benefits of an adequately functioning ecosystem are "much
more than matters of dollars and cents," noted a Reagan
administration advisory committee in 1983. That is a thought
that is just as important as the public's specific knowledge
of individual environmental, maladies. The response of
business is just as critical, notes Warren Batts, CEO of
Premark International. "As we enter the '90s, a . . .
[firm's] response to social problems, particularly the
environment, will have a growing, perhaps profound, impact on
its long-term life expectancy," asserts Batts. Toward that

end, Batts continues, "A codified standards of business principles that governs a . . . [firm's] actions will be invaluable in framing an appropriate response."

NOTES

1. Buchholz, Business Environment and Public Policy, 3rd ed. (Englewood Cliffs, NJ: Prentice-Hall, Inc., 1989): 48.
2. Mayne, "The Decline and Fall of Business Ethics", Fortune (December 8, 1986): 66.
3. Bucholz, Fundamental Concepts and Problems in Business Ethics (Englewood Cliffs, NJ: Prentice-Hall, Inc., 1989): 52.
4. Norman, The Moral Philosophers (Atlanta: Clarendon Press, 1983): 1.
5. Goodpaster, Ethics: An Overview, Harvard Business School, Pub. 381-050 (1980): 1.
6. Ibid., 2.
7. DeGeorge, Business Ethics, 2nd ed. (New York: MacMillan, 1986): 15.
8. Powers and Vogel, Ethics in the Education of Business Managers. (Briarcliff Manor, NY: The Hastings Center, 1980): 1.
9. Goodpaster, op. cit., 4.
10. Buchholz, op. cit., 3rd ed., 51.
11. Norman, op. cit., 2.
12. Goodpaster, op. cit., 7.
13. Ibid., 9.
14. Goodpaster, op. cit., 9.
15. Buchholz, op. cit., 3rd ed., 51.
16. Norman, op. cit., 2.
17. Buchholz, op. cit., 3rd ed., 51.
18. Goodpaster, op. cit., 4.
19. Ibid., 5-6.
20. Ibid., 6.
21. Ibid., 9-12.
22. Paine, Approaches to Ethics, Colgate Darden Graduate Business School, Pub. E-020: 4.
23. Ibid.
24. Balancing General Management Responsibilities, Harvard Business School, Pub. 385-154, 1984.
25. Ibid.
26. Goals: The Problem of Balancing Multiple Constituencies, Harvard Business School, Pub. 385-187, 1984.
27. Ibid., 1.
28. Ibid., 2.
29. Ibid.
30. Ibid., 3.
31. Ibid.
32. Ibid., 3-4.
33. Ibid., 4.
34. Ibid.
35. Goodpaster, Ethical Thinking In Business: A Typology, Harvard Business School, Pub. 387-097 (1986): 1.
36. Ibid.
37. Ibid., 2.
38. Ibid., 3.
39. Ibid.
40. Ibid., 4.
41. Paine, op. cit., 6-12.
42. Norman, op. cit., 76-77.
43. Velasquez, Business Ethics: Concepts and Cases (Englewood Cliffs, NJ: Prentice-Hall, Inc., 1982): 47.
44. Goodpaster, Some Avenues for Ethical Analysis in General Management, Harvard Business School, Pub. 383-007 (1982): 5.
45. Buchholz, op. cit., 3rd ed., 56-57.
46. Goodpaster, Some Avenues, op. cit., 5.
47. Sidgwick, The Methods of Ethics, 7th ed. Repub. (Mineola, NY: Dover Publications, Inc., 1966).
48. Norman, op. cit., 77.
49. Paine, op. cit., 11.

50. Ibid.; Moore, *Principia Ethica* (Cambridge: Cambridge University Press, 1903). Chapter V.
51. Buchholz, op. cit., 3rd ed., 57.
52. Norman, op. cit., 95.
53. Kant, *Fundamental Principles of the Metaphysical Ethics*, Abbott Translation, 10th ed., (London: Longmans, Green and Co. Ltd., 1969): 21.; Paine, op. cit., 6.
54. Buchholz, op. cit., 3rd ed., 57.
55. Norman, op. cit., 124.
56. Buchholz, op. cit., 3rd ed., 57-58.
57. Paine, op. cit., 6.
58. Buchholz, op. cit., 3rd ed., 58.
59. Norman, op. cit., 162.
60. Buchholz, op. cit., 3rd ed., 58-59.
61. Hare, *Moral Thinking* (Atlanta: Clarendon Press, 1981).
62. Paine, op. cit., 7.
63. Hare, op. cit., 42.; Ibid.
64. Paine, op. cit., 7-8.
65. Buchholz, op. cit., 3rd ed., 59-60.
66. Ibid., 61-62.
67. Goodpaster, *Some Avenues*, op. cit., 5.
68. Rawls, *A Theory of Justice* (Cambridge, MA: Belknap Press, 1971): 136-137.
69. Buchholz, op. cit., 3rd ed., 62.
70. Rawls, op. cit., 136-142.
71. Paine, op. cit., 8.
72. Buchholz, op. cit., 3rd ed., 62.
73. Rawls, op. cit., 136-142.; Buchholz, op. cit., 3rd ed., 62.
74. Rawls, op. cit., 60.; Buchholz, op. cit., 3rd ed., 63.
75. Paine, op. cit., 8.
76. DeGeorge, op. cit., 78.; Buchholz, op. cit., 3rd ed., 63.
77. Frankena, *Ethics*, 2nd ed. (New York: MacMillan, 1986), 50; Buchholz, op. cit., 3rd ed., 64.
78. Frankena, op. cit., 51.
79. Buchholz, op. cit., 3rd ed., 64.
80. Nozick, *Anarchy, State, and Utopia* (New York: Basic Books, 1974): 150-153; Buchholz, op. cit., 3rd ed., 65.
81. Buchholz, op. cit., 3rd ed., 65-66.
82. Jones, Santag, Beckner, and Fogelin eds., *Approaches to Ethics* (New York: McGraw-Hill, 1962): 52.
83. Maritain, *Moral Philosophy*, (New York: Scribner's Sons, 1964): 40.
84. Paine, op. cit., 12.
85. Gordon and Howell, *Higher Education for Business* (New York: Columbia University Press, 1959): 65.
86. Epstein, "The Corporate Social Policy Process and the Process of Corporate Governance," *American Business Law Journal* 25 (1987): 372-373.
87. Ibid., 373.
88. Ibid., 374.
89. Ibid., 375.
90. Ibid.
91. Bowen, *Social Responsibilities of the Businessman* (New York: Harper & Row, 1953): 6.
92. Eells and Walton, *Conceptual Foundations of Business* (Homewood, IL: Irwin, 1961): 457-458.
93. McGuire, *Business and Society* (New York: McGraw-Hill, 1963): 44.
94. Buchholz, op. cit., 3rd ed., 25-27.
95. Ibid., 27-34.
96. Ibid., 28.
97. Levitt, "The Dangers of Social Responsibility," *Harvard Business Review* 36, 5 (September-October 1958): 41-50.
98. Buchholz, op. cit., 3rd ed., 32-34.
99. Stone, "Corporate Social Responsibility: What It Might Mean, If It Were Really To Matter," 71 *Iowa Law Review*, 1986, 575.
100. Buchholz, op. cit., 3rd ed., 34.
101. Epstein, op. cit., 375.
102. Ibid., 376.
103. Ibid., 377.

104. Ackerman and Bauer, <u>Corporate Social Responsiveness</u> (Englewood Cliffs, NJ: Reston, 1976); and Ibid.
105. Buchholz, op. cit., 3rd ed., 36-39; citing Sethi, "Dimensions of Corporate Social Responsibility," <u>California Management Review</u>, 17, no. 3 (Spring 1975): 58-64.
106. Buchholz, op. cit., 3rd ed., 39-40
107. Stone, <u>What "Corporate Responsibility" Might Really Mean</u>, Harvard Business School, Pub. 382-001, 1975.
108. 42 <u>U.S.C.</u> Sections 4321-4370 (1982).
109. Buchholz, op. cit., 3rd ed. 416.
110. Ibid., 417-419.
111. Ibid., 420-422.
112. Vogel, "The Politics of the Environment," <u>The Wilson Quarterly</u> (Autumn 1987): 51-68.
113. Buchholz, op. cit., 3rd ed., 426-427.
114. Ibid.
115. Lagerfeld, "Coping with Change," <u>Wilson Quarterly</u> (Winter 1988): 117-118.
116. Sagan, "What's The Greenhouse Effect," <u>Our Endangered Atmosphere</u>, ed. McCuen, (Melbourne, FL: McCuen Publications, 1987): 12.
117. Gribbin, <u>The Hole in the Sky</u> (New York: Bantam, 1988): 95.
118. Ibid., 89.
119. Lagerfeld, op. cit., 120-125.
120. Ibid., 89.
121. Ibid., 104-105.
122. Lagerfeld, op. cit., 125.
123. Watson, "Ozone Depletion and the Global Consequences," <u>Our Endangered Atmosphere</u>, ed. McCuen, 82; "Serious Ozone Depletion Is Now Occurring," 90 (Melbourne, FL: McCuen Publications, 1987).
124. Gribbon, op. cit., 143.
125. Lagerfeld, loc. cit.
126. Schneck, <u>Acid Rain</u> (Los Angeles: Tasa Publishing Co., 1981): 13-15.
127. Postel, "Acid Rain Is a Global Threat," <u>The Environmental Crisis</u>, ed. Bach and Hall, (San Diego: Greenhaven Press, 1986): 234.
128. Ibid., 38-41.
129. Vogel, op. cit., 51-68; and Crandall, "Learning the Lessons," <u>The Wilson Quarterly</u> (Autumn 1987): 69-83.
130. <u>The Environmental Crisis</u>, op. cit. 21-22.
131. Buchholz, op. cit., 3rd ed., 429-432.
132. <u>The Environmental Crisis</u>, op. cit., 101-102.
133. Buchholz, op. cit., 3rd ed., 433.
134. Nazario, "EPA Under Fire for Pesticide Standards," <u>Wall Street Journal</u> (February 17, 1989): B-1.
135. Cabot and Fox, <u>The Work of a Regulatory Agency: The EPA and Toxic Substances</u>, Harvard Business School, Pub. 380-081 (Rev. 11/81): 1980.
136. <u>Environmental Quality 1980</u>, Government Printing Office (1988), 217.
137. Penoyer, <u>Reforming Regulation of Hazardous Waste</u> (St. Louis: Washington U. Center for the Study of American Business, 1985), 1; and Buchholz, op. cit., 3rd ed., 442.
138. Mukaitis and Brinkman, "Managerial Liability For Health, Safety, and Environmental Crime: A Review and Suggested Approach to the Problem," <u>American Business Law Journal</u>, 25 (1987), 323; and Abramson, "Government Cracks Down On Environmental Crimes," <u>Wall Street Journal</u> (February 16, 1989): B-1.
139. Freedman, "Firms Curb Hazardous Waste to Avoid Expensive Disposal," <u>The Wall Street Journal</u> (May 31, 1985): 19.
140. Chasis and Speer, "How To Avoid Another Valdez," <u>New York Times</u> (May 20, 1989): 15.
141. Friedman and Giannotti, "How to Perform an Environmental Self-Assessment," <u>The Practical Real Estate Lawyer</u> (November 1987): 53.

2

Balancing Employer and Employee Rights and Responsibilities

INTRODUCTION

The 1990s will continue the new era of employer-employee relations. From 1980 to 1988, 72% of employees who sued their employers for discharging them recovered damages; the awards averaged $582,000.[1] By late 1989 there were 25,000 wrongful discharge suits pending in state and federal courts. Firms must take note of the diversity of developments, especially those in 1989, in the areas of employment at will, privacy, wrongful discharge, whistle blowing, and polygraph testing. For instance, postal workers in Peoria, Illinois, were repeatedly hounded by their supervisor for alledgedly spending excessive time in the bathroom. In protest, the employees wore hats with pictures of toilets to work and were discharged from employment. The employees prevailed in court, with the ruling that their form of protest did not interfere with productivity.

A salesman who had worked for U.S. Steel Corp. for nearly fifteen years was terminated, he claimed, because he had reported to his superiors that steel tubes used under high pressure in the oil extraction industry were a serious danger to the user. When his warnings were disregarded, he related his misgivings to a vice president in sales. As a result, the firm eventually withdrew the tubes from the market, but discharged the salesman. The salesman sued claiming his termination was without cause and against public policy as he was merely protecting the public from an unsafe product. The Supreme Court of Pennsylvania dismissed the lawsuit while asserting, "The law has taken for granted the power of either party to terminate an employment relationship for any or no reason."[2]

Yet, in 1982 Virginia Rulon-Miller, an IBM sales manager who was demoted for dating a sales executive of a competitor, resigned and sued IBM for invasion of privacy and wrongful discharge. A California jury, ruling for Rulon-Miller, awarded her a $300,000 judgment. Earlier, David Edwards, a Citibank employee who complained to top management about what he considered to be irregularities in the handling of currency transactions, lost his lawsuit for wrongful discharge. The court held the complaint groundless because Edwards was a mere employee at will.[3] In 1989 Atari agreed to settle for $12.1 million a lawsuit filed in 1987 in California. Alledgedly,

Atari wrongly administered 15,000 polygraph tests. The settlement is the largest ever in such a case.

In West Virginia an office manager at the First National Bank in Fairmont suspected that the bank was overcharging customers, a violation of state law. Subsequently, a vice president ordered him to add unearned "service charges" to the customer billings. Manager James Harless refused and was discharged. The West Virginia Supreme Court ruled that the doctrine of employment-at-will does not excuse punishment that "contravenes some substantial public policy principle." The court upheld a substantial monetary damages award for Harless against the bank as well as against the vice president who directed the manager to overcharge.

Moreover, in Michigan a representative of Masco Corporation orally promised an employee when hired that he would be discharged only for "just cause." Nonetheless, the company terminated his employment for other than "just cause." The dismissed employee sued and received a damages award of $300,000 for the unjust dismissal.[4] In Maryland an employee who was discharged for refusing to submit to the firm's polygraph examination received $1.3 million as damages.[5]

These examples of successful and unsuccessful lawsuits against firms in the areas of wrongful discharge and invasion of privacy demonstrate a conflict of opinions, but also, in some cases, a shift of balance away from the established doctrines of the omnipotent employer. As a result of the plethora and variety of individual court decisions, as Stanford Law School professor William Gould recognizes, "It is difficult to provide adequate counsel and advice to both employers and employees." The law is neither uniform nor predictable, but firms must be aware of the broader trends in these areas to avoid costly lawsuits and damage awards.

THE EMPLOYMENT RELATIONSHIP: OBEDIENCE, LOYALTY, CONFIDENTIALITY, AND EMPLOYMENT-AT-WILL

The employment relationship is ubiquitous and forms the basis of our economic system. Historically, an employee had little recourse to prevent his or her employer's unfair or damaging acts. Even now, an employee relinquishes considerable autonomy to his or her employer. Most employees accept the firm's unilateral terms without bargaining and conform to the employer's expectation. In fact, the employment-at-will doctrine provides that, in the absence of an explicit contractual agreement to the contrary, an employer or an employee can terminate the employment at any time without reason or notice. Prior to a discussion of the metamorphosis of statutory and judicial responses to this doctrine, it is instructive to review the traditional responsibilities of the employee in our society.

The employee's duties of obedience, loyalty, and confidentiality are essential to the employment relationship and have been recognized as traditional elements in that relationship for centuries. In fact, no enterprise can long survive without the obedience, loyalty, and confidentiality of its employees.

According to Sections 383 and 385 of the <u>Restatement of Agency</u> (summary laws of agency), the employee has a duty to obey the employer's reasonable directions. Further, Section 387 expresses the general principle that "an agent is subject to a duty to his principal to act solely for the benefit of the principal in all matters connected with his agency" and the agent is "also under a duty not to act or speak disloyally . . . except in the protection of his own interests or those of others." Although the agent may act in good faith outside his or her scope of employment even though it injures the principal's business, Section 394 prohibits the agent from acting for "persons whose interests conflict with those of the principal in matters in which the agent is employed."[6]

In addition, an employee is ethically obligated to obey the moral law, as he or she is to conform to civil law. The employee should respect and comply with the employing firm's code of ethics and conduct. Moreover, the employee should treat fellow employees with consideration while refraining from lying or disseminating false information in general. An employee, in addition to fulfilling the terms of his or her express or implicit employment contract, should thoroughly incorporate a consideration of the interests of the firm in his or her work. Managers, in particular, have an important responsibility to nurture a work environment of trust, respect, and assistance—an ambience in which all can effectively work together for the benefit of the firm.

The <u>Restatement of Agency</u>, Section 395, imposes a duty on the employee "not to use or to communicate information confidentially given him by the principal or acquired by him during the course of or on account of his agency . . . to the injury of the principal, on his own account or on behalf of another . . . unless the information is a matter of general knowledge." Except when the employee discloses a crime, he or she generally cannot reveal nonpublic information about the employer gained through the employment. Certainly, protection of free speech is a moral obligation of a free society. This issue is explored further in a later section of this chapter, How the Firm Can Make Whistle Blowing Unnecessary.

These foregoing employment doctrines, so long revered, are undergoing significant transformation. In an age of specialization, an inexorable and powerful trend in the 1990s, it is important that the employee and employer maintain a productive relationship. Trends that include increased numbers of better educated employees have eroded the attitude that supported the duties traditionally owed the employer. Our age is no longer characterized by the preponderance and numbers of manual laborers whose skills can easily be transferred to other enterprises. For example, highly skilled and educated people hold the top 45,000 positions in Exxon, which grew out of Standard Oil, which was founded by two high school dropouts, John D. Rockefeller and Winthrop Aldrich. In today's environment, for the employee, loss of employment translates to anxiety and an often frustrating attempt to match his or her individual skills to those required in an enterprise far different than that of the prior employer. For the employer, replacing a trained employee often results in substantial recruiting and training expense and a plunge in productivity.

One noted writer[7] has emphasized that employees' legal challenges of management increased at least tenfold in the 1970s, due in part to the firm's invasion of the employee's privacy as well as the divided loyalties of employees and the diminished opportunities for the firm's forming binding relationships with employees. In addition, firms that fail to promulgate responsive policies in these areas risk a crippling inability to fully staff critical positions with competent employees. As the rate of labor force growth constricts in the 1990s because of the post baby-boom birthrate decline, firms slow to respond will encounter greatly exacerbated difficulties.

Given this social and economic upheaval, disagreement between employee and employer is inevitable. Management needs to understand the current status of various employment doctrines and to promulgate effective procedures in areas such as termination, due process, privacy, polygraph testing, and whistle blowing, which balance employers' and employees' rights of fair treatment. Firms that are successful in promulgating fair procedures will ensure a stable, loyal, and productive workforce.

EMPLOYMENT-AT-WILL: CURRENT STATUS AND DUE PROCESS

Derived from principles of English law regulating feudal theories of master and servant, the doctrine of employment-at-will asserts that in cases when an employee is hired for an indefinite period without a formal contract that limits the employee's discharge, either party may terminate the employment relationship for any or no cause, moral or immoral, absent an explicit statutory prohibition.[8] Union members usually have contracts that protect against unjust termination; however, the nonunion remainder must rely on statutes that prohibit firings for only a few causes. Moreover, the tide of unionization has been receding: from 33.4% to 16.8% of the civilian workforce since the 1956 merger of the American Federation of Labor and the Congress of Industrial Organizations (AFL-CIO). As of 1985 over 88 million Americans were employed in the private sector. Two million workers not covered by employment contracts or union agreements are terminated, as opposed to millions who are laid off every year; one study estimates 150,000 of these workers are fired without just cause. Further, aside from the National Labor Relations Act of 1935 and Title VII of the Civil Rights Act of 1964, no federal or state statute, save that of Montana, has significantly modified the essential employment-at-will doctrine. Some federal and state courts have held that in limited circumstances other important concerns should take precedence over the empoyer's right to terminate an employee without cause.

The Montana Wrongful Discharge from Employment Act protects workers from arbitrary dismissal but limits their damages awards when they sue their former employers. Under the terms of the statute, nonunion employees without individual contracts cannot be terminated without demonstrating "good cause," which is ultimately determined by the court if a lawsuit contests the firing. In exchange for this protection from arbitrary dismissal, the statute limits an employee's damages to no more than four years of back pay and benefits, bars any recovery for emotional distress, and excludes punitive damages except where the employer acted with fraud or malice. In 1989 the Montana Supreme Court upheld the state constitutionality of the statute. Similar legislation is pending in a number of other states, including Illinois, New York, and California.

One concern that has superseded the doctrine of employment-at-will is that of "public policy," an exception recognized in a majority of states including California, Florida, Illinois, Michigan, New York, and Texas. The public policy exception posits that the firm may not terminate an employee because he or she refuses to engage in an activity that public policy discourages or because he or she takes part in one that public policy encourages. For example, employees discharged for filing workers' compensation benefits,[9] for protesting an employer's unethical or illegal conduct,[10] or for not assisting employees engaged in illegal conduct[11] have successfully sued using the public policy exception to the employment-at-will doctrine.

Nonetheless, other courts have either rejected or so narrowly defined the public policy exception so as to allow a firm's discharging an employee for filing a workers' compensation claim, for excessive absenteeism caused by a job-related injury for which the employee was receiving workers' compensation benefits, for testifying against the employer wherein the employer did not ask the employee to commit perjury, for reporting an employer's dubious accounting practice even though the discharge was allegedly contrary to the internal auditors' code of ethics, and for reporting the employer's air safety violations to the FAA.

Still other courts have denied the employee's claim for damages when discharged for refusing to falsify records pursuant to his or her employer's request, for refusing to engage in the employer's practice of removing identification marks of foreign steel when the employer's customers ordered domestic steel by reason that the Louisiana statute protected only consumers and competition, for testifying truthfully at a wage and hour board hearing, for refusing to promulgate a medical procedure that would cause complications in a terminally ill patient because the nursing code was a personal code, and for refusing to pay invoices of a dubious nature because the employer's illegal act did not violate any right of the employee. Moreover, most courts hold that cases in which an employee is discharged in a manner inconsistent with public policy are actionable in tort, thereby exposing offending employers to punitive damages.

The second principal exception to the employment-at-will doctrine is that of implied contract, recognized by courts in thirty-two states, including Arizona, California, Connecticut, Georgia, Illinois, Maryland, Michigan, Missouri, New Jersey, New York, North Carolina, Ohio, Texas, Washington and Wisconsin, among others. This exception exists when certain specific employer actions, including statements regarding employment security or termination policy, which are communicated to the employee, constitute legally binding employment contracts and that, then, the employee can be terminated only for "cause." Consequently, when an employee receives assurance from the employer of employment as long as his or her tasks are performed satisfactorily, and is fired without cause, an implied employment contract exists.[12]

Yet, on the contrary, courts in other jurisdictions have rejected the employee's claim of implied contract in cases: when termination procedures in the employee's handbook were disregarded, in a similar case when the employee handbook explicitly asserted the policies did not form a contract between the employee and employer, when the employment term was indefinite, and when the salary figure quoted to a subsequently hired employee was annual, not monthly. Usually the employee's providing additional consideration, like relinquishing a prior job to accept the new one, strengthens his or her claim for wrongful discharge.

Still another concern, that of "good faith and fair dealing," is recognized as an exception to the employment-at-will doctrine in seven states,[13] including California, Connecticut, Massachusetts, and Minnesota. Pursuant to this exception, employers may not discharge employees for bad cause or in bad faith if the termination deprives the employee of the benefits of his or her employment agreement. Under the doctrine of good faith, employees facing termination are entitled to expect "full and honest cause or reason, regulated by good faith on the part of the party exercising the power."[14]

Moreover, this good faith penumbra has proscribed disciplinary actions short of discharge that appear to induce the employee's resignation.[15] For example, the courts in a few jurisdictions have found bad faith discharges as exceptions to the employment-at-will doctrine in circumstances: where a firm fired an employee-at-will to avoid paying him promised commissions for work he had successfully completed,[16] and where an employer discharged an employee without notice as required in the employee handbook.[17]

Generally, the courts are divided as to whether the cause of action is grounded in tort or in contract when the good faith and fair dealing exception is recognized at all. Nonetheless, courts in few jurisdictions recognize the good faith and fair dealing exception. Rather, most courts have decreed that requiring good cause for all discharges constitutes an unjustified intrusion in the exercise of managerial discretion. On the few occasions the courts have indeed recognized the good faith exception; the factual situations include the elements that the employer actually prevented the employee from securing payment for past services or realized windfall gains as a result of the employee's efforts.[18]

Other miscellaneous exceptions to the employment-at-will doctrine include the tort of intentional infliction of emotional distress (recognized in four states, including California and New York), which requires an employer's extreme and outrageous conduct that is intended to and directly does cause severe emotional distress. In a 1986 case, a North Carolina court held that the employer's reckless indifference to a coworker's conduct, which caused severe emotional distress to an employee, is actionable under this tort.[19]

Aggrieved, discharged, or harassed employees have utilized two other theories of tort in successful suits against employers: the tort of fraudulently inducing an employee to act to his or her detriment (recognized by courts in four jurisdictions, including Florida and Texas), and the tort of malicious interference with a contractual relationship (supported by courts in eight states, including Alabama, California, Georgia, Illinois, North Carolina, and Oregon). In the employment context, the former tort embodies three essential elements: the employer must knowingly make false statements or must make them with reckless disregard of the truth; the employer must make them with the intent to induce the employee's action; and the employee must have relied on the false statements to his or her detriment. Hence, Union Pacific Railroad employees, induced by the company to reveal their knowledge of a company supervisor's misappropriation of funds with the assurance that there would be no reprisal, successfully sued when they were harassed, threatened with transfer, or fired.[20]

The tort of malicious interference with contractual relationships manifests the following elements in the context of employment discharge: the defendant (more likely a supervisor, coworker, or subordinate) must be aware of a valid contract and, further, "must maliciously and intentionally induce a breach of the contract that results in damages." In Powers v. Delnor Hospital,[21] an employee received unsatisfactory appraisals of her work based on dishonest statements made by her supervisor. As a result of her termination because of the false information, the aggrieved employee successfully brought suit against the employer.

The farrago of conflicting decisions has created enormous confusion. With upward of 10,000 such wrongful termination suits filed per annum, firms must institute internal grievance procedures and adhere to the guidelines set forth later in this chapter to avoid the ethical and legal quicksand of angry employees' retaliation.

EMPLOYMENT PRIVACY

After the employment-at-will area, privacy is the most dynamic and rapidly developing section of employment law. The concept of privacy as an individual right actionable through the tort of invasion of privacy has its public genesis in an 1890 Harvard Law Review article authored by Samuel D. Warren and Louis D. Brandeis.[22] The employer's warranted or unwarranted intrusion and the employee's desire to be left completely alone in job-related and nonjob-related matters have resulted in substantial legal and social conflict. An employee, at home, before and after working hours, enjoys well-established privacy rights to be free from arbitrary search and seizure of his or her papers and possessions. As an employee in the workplace, however, he or she enjoys no such similar rights.

In Chapter 3, testing and screening for drug use, alcohol abuse, AIDS and genetic predisposition, and the delicate balancing of the conflicting rights are discussed. Other privacy issues include the scope of employee job applications, personnel records, monitoring of employee conversations, physical intrusions such as locker searches, and polygraph testing. All of these issues comprise one of two basic privacies: that of "information privacy," the interest in controlling the collection, administration, use, and disclosure of information regarding employment; and the second, that of "behavior privacy," the interest in engaging in activities free from the employer's regulation or surveillance at and beyond the workplace.[23]

Obviously, the employer needs to collect employment information to effectively manage his or her firm. Decisions about hiring, training, security, compensation, promotion, and retirement require extensive data collection and maintenance. Employing firms have a concern that their actions avoid conflict with the various statutes requiring and proscribing record-keeping, information disclosure, and other employment privacy concerns. Often these statutes and their accompanying case law conflict. In particular OSHA, Title VII, and other federal acts impose specific record-keeping responsibilities. On the other hand, certain federal and state statutes seek to protect privacy: the Freedom of Information Act[24] exempts certain confidential information, such as personnel and medical files, from public disclosure. Further, the Privacy Act of 1974[25] empowers an individual to request the correction, amendment, or deletion of personnel information, and take action if the request is denied.

Additionally, various states have enacted privacy statutes regulating states' and local agencies' collection, preservation, use, and disclosure of information regarding individuals. The statutes have responded to privacy issues including the following: protection of whistle blowing, disclosure of credit information, employee access to personnel files, and prohibiting an employer from inquiring about a job applicant's or employee's arrests, convictions, communicable diseases, smoking, political preference, and psychological matters.[26]

Judicial protection of employment privacy is grounded in constitutional, tort, and contract theories. The federal government and some states recognize a constitutional right to be free from intrusion or to enjoy personal privacy. Many of the tort causes of action available to aggrieved or wrongfully discharged employees such as fraudulent misrepresentation, infliction of emotional distress, and interference with contractual relationship are available to provide privacy protection.

Also, other tort doctrines of invasion of privacy, defamation, false imprisonment, and disclosure of employment records rest as well in the aggrieved employee's legal arsenal. Invasion of privacy requires public disclosure of the employee's private facts. Information in personnel files, whether accurate or not, like test scores, reprimands, salary, and performance evaluations, are "private facts." Further, defamation is comprised of the publication of an untrue statement that exposes a person to contempt, hatred, or ridicule. An employer that communicates reasons for an employee's discharge or a negative job performance evaluation has provided grounds for legal action; normally, however, employers enjoy a privilege to communicate in good faith in response to legitimate inquiry within certain information channels.[27]

According to Prosser, author of <u>Handbook of the Law of Torts</u>, 4th ed. (1971), false imprisonment occurs when the employer or agent restrains the employee's movement, usually to search or interrogate the employee. Under the tortious maintenance of employment records theory, the employer violates his or her duty of care in maintaining employment records and references in a reckless manner.

Last, employees have successfully sued under causes of action grounded in contract. In this regard, the employee usually has designated any of the following as the basis for his or her violated right of privacy: oral or written employment contracts, employment policies, and collective bargaining agreements.[28]

Guidelines for the Firm Regarding Employment Privacy

Privacy guidelines, when internalized in the firm's operations, significantly reduce the possibility of disputes with employees, project an image of respect for the employees and to the public, and provide a means for resolving disputes within the firm, thus obviating the necessity of further encumbering federal and state privacy legislation. Areas of primary concern that the firm must address are employment information collection, maintenance and internal use, employee access to information, disclosure of employment information to third parties, and employee lifestyle in and beyond the workplace. Although protecting the employee's privacy, the following guidelines[29] do not hinder a firm's operating efficiency, prevent access to relevant information, or inhibit accurate record-keeping.

1. The firm should collect and maintain in personnel files only job-related facts about applicants or employees. This required procedure usually eliminates data such as criminal charges without convictions, hearsay, gratuitous notes about an employee's ability, and previous addresses.

2. Employment information sources such as blood tests, fingerprinting, physical examinations, and work area surveillance and photographing are valid collection methods because the scope is job-related. Firms should greatly restrict or eliminate intelligence or personality tests, however.

3. Employment information should be collected only through reliable methods, which should preserve the dignity of the applicant or employee.

4. The firm should never interview third parties without the applicant's or employee's prior knowledge. Further, the firm should inform the applicant or employee of any background investigation before its promulgation.

5. The firm should classify as confidential every employee's personnel file.

6. Disclosure of personnel file information should be for routine use only with each such use evaluated as to whether it is consistent with the decision for which it is applicable. For instance, a manager preparing an employee's performance evaluation has no need to review the employee's financial history.

7. The firm should allow access to selected portions of the employee's personnel file only on a strict "need to know" basis.

8. The firm should allow the employee's access to employment information to correct and supplement it.

9. The firm should periodically purge outdated employment information at least three years old. The employee's consent should be required to destroy information less than three years old.

10. The firm should severely curtail or eliminate random disclosures of employment information unless an employee consents to the dissemination. Consequently, the firm should provide credit agencies and landlord no more than basic facts such as whether the employee does work for the firm.

11. The firm should permit no communication of gratuitously negative opinions to a prospective employer of an employee who is to be or has been terminated.

12. The firm should provide to any terminated, demoted, or transferred employee a written and complete statement of the reason for the sanction.

13. The firm should allow no one to examine an employee's files, desk, or locker in his or her absence, except a senior manager who believes that one of these physical spaces contains information required for a management decision that must be promulgated in the employee's absence.

14. The firm's regulation of the employee's lifestyle (e.g., dress and grooming, smoking, social contacts, and employment opportunities) should be reasonable and specifically related to the employee's position. Constraints should be imposed only if it is in the firm's business interest.

WHISTLE BLOWING, POLYGRAPH TESTING, AND THE BILL OF RIGHTS

How the Firm Can Make Whistle Blowing Unnecessary

Historically, differences of opinion between a firm and its employees were resolved privately, within the organization. If the employee disagreed on conscience grounds with the firm's decision, the proper course was resignation.   Now, however, the modern employee often chooses an alternative: speaking out on matters of conscience while attempting to change the organization from within.[30]

Authorities have expressed support and opposition to whistle blowing. Specifically, a number of commentators have posited that employees should have undivided loyalty to the firm.   "Ideally," wrote Paul R. Lawrence in his 1958 work, Organizational Behavior Patterns, a Case Study of Decentralization, "We should want one sentiment to be dominant in all employees from top to bottom, namely a complete loyalty to the organizational purpose."

On the other hand, Professor Thomas I. Emerson observed in his important work, The System of Freedom of Expression, that a "system of freedom of expression that allowed private bureaucracies to throttle all internal discussion of their affairs would be seriously deficient."   Moreover, another legal scholar, Phillip I. Blumberg, has predicted that whistle blowing "will become an area of dynamic change in the corporate organization. . . ."[31]

Whether muckraker, scoundrel, traitor, or modern-day Martin Luther, the whistle blower is a ubiquitous fact.   More often, employees are deciding to expose their firms' defective products, pollution, and corruption.   There is a great danger in stifling critics and dissent within an organization. Without dissent, old policies become dogma, not mere procedures, ripe for beneficial modification or elimination.

Employees in public organizations have substantial legal rights to voice dissent, firmly grounded in First Amendment guarantees of free speech.   Dissident employees facing reprisals in private organizations receive protection from the courts under some circumstances, usually through the public policy or another exception to the employment-at-will doctrine discussed earlier in this chapter.

Realizing that much whistle blowing occurs because the firm is unresponsive to the employee's early warnings, a firm can take several steps, as follows, to make whistle blowing unnecessary.[32]

1. The firm should establish an "open door" policy by streamlining its grievance procedures to allow employees to receive speedy and sympathetic hearings.
2. The firm should emphasize through policies, codes, and employee handbooks that employees have freedom to express their views, controversial or not.
3. The firm should recognize that allowing dissent, even that not currently protected by law, may be in the best interest of the firm's future, and by squelching a whistle blower the firm is inviting negative publicity.

4. The firm should communicate to its employees a tolerance of dissent and an abiding respect for each employee's principles and individual conscience.
5. The firm should realize that its relationship with society includes not just business considerations but also a commitment to promulgate an ethical, responsible climate in which each employee is a respected actor.

The Ban on Polygraph Tests, and Alternatives

The polygraph is an instrument that seeks to verify the truth and is reasonably accurate, so advocates assert.[33]   Although critics[34] have attacked the device as intrusive and inaccurate, its use burgeoned—as late as 1988, over 10,000 examiners conducted 2 million polygraph examinations. In 1988 about 300,000 law-abiding citizens failed polygraph tests and were then assumed to be poor employment risks, and, hence, lost a chance of employment.

Then, effective December 27,1988, Congress enacted the Employee Polygraph Protection Act, which almost completely bans polygraph testing in the private sector while exempting federal, state, and local governments from its provisions. Further, the 1988 act allows the federal government to test by polygraph private individuals who are engaged in activities related to national security. In 1988 the federal government administered polygraph tests to at least 150,000 Americans. Moreover, according to the act, Public Law 100-347, an employer may test an employee in "connection with an ongoing investigation involving economic loss or injury . . . such as theft, embezzlement, misappropriation, or an act of unlawful industrial espionage or sabotage." There are conditions to such usage: (1) "the employee has access to the property that is the subject of the investigation," and (2) the employer executes a statement to the examinee prior to the test setting forth the particularity of the incident in question and the basis for testing.

In addition, the 1988 act does not prohibit use of a polygraph test on prospective or current employees by an employer authorized to manufacture, distribute, or dispense certain controlled substances. Moreover, some types of security guard, armored car, or security alarm firms are exempted as well.

The act is expected to reduce by 80% the per annum number of polygraph tests administered prior to its enactment. Others[35] estimate that the new law will lead to a sharp increase in internal retail theft, which already costs retailers $40 billion per year. Further, employers turn to other forms of security: using undercover detectives, increased employee training, rewarding exposure of dishonest employees, installing electronic security systems, undertaking extensive background investigations of prospective employees, and use of psychological testing. In addition, more employers are screening prospective employees through handwriting analysis. Some experts claim such an analysis can accurately define a person's personality, suitability for a job, and addictive tendencies. Critics contend that it is not a useful tool.

Polygraph Guidelines after the Act[36]

1. The firm should eliminate completely pre-employment testing or confine its use to those certain specific circumstances, allowed in the act.

2. The firm should confine polygraph testing to employees who are reasonably suspected of sabotaging the firm's property, of committing a serious crime on the firm's property, or of stealing the firm's or another's property in the workplace; and to those employees who have access to information and other data, the nondissemination of which is deemed in the national interest.

3. The polygraph test should be terminated immediately if the employee refuses to continue.

4. The polygraph examiner should never ask questions in a manner designed to needlessly intrude on or degrade the employee.

5. The polygraph examiner should not pose questions concerning political beliefs, sexual preference or behavior, opinions or beliefs about unions or other labor organizations, opinions or beliefs about racial matters, or religious beliefs or affiliations.

6. The polygraph examiner should not test any employee who is suffering from a medical or psychological condition, or who is receiving any treatment that might cause abnormal responses during the examination. A medical doctor's or licensed psychologist's written letter will be sufficient to prove one of these exempting conditions.

7. The firm should provide the employee, prior to testing, a written statement signed by an executive detailing the foundation for the firm's reasonable suspicion that the employee was involved in the activity under investigation and a list of all questions to be asked during the test.

8. The firm should provide the employee to be tested reasonable notice of the location, time, and date of the test, together with notification that the employee may consult legal counsel during the examination. Further, the firm should indicate the nature of the tests and devices to be used, and whether the testing room contains observation devices such as a camera or two-way mirror, and whether a tape recording will be made.

9. The firm should allow the employee to make a tape recording of the process—a privilege the firm can also exercise. Notice must be given of intent to tape record.

10. The firm, at the examination site, should notify the employee that the latter does not have to submit to the test as a condition of employment and that any employee statement during the examination and the test results can be used as a reason for sanctions, including discharge.

11. Within a reasonable time after the test results are fully evaluated, the firm should confer with the tested employee before any adverse employment action, reveal the test results, provide the employee with a transcript of the examination, and any conclusion rendered as a result of the test.

12. The firm and the examiner should not disclose the polygraph examination results to anyone except the employee examined or his or her agent, the employer, and a court of law or government agency if properly subpoenaed or ordered.

13. The polygraph test itself should not be less than one and a half hours in duration, and the examiner should not administer more than five polygraph tests in one day.

14. The firm should incorporate these policy guidelines in appropriate internal publications and other vehicles of dissemination to all employees.

Guidelines Concerning Wrongful Discharge Suits, Due Process, and the Bill of Rights

Conflicting decisions regarding the firm's right to terminate and wrongful discharge have created an environment of uncertainty. Employees, especially the mushrooming body of professional and middle management, have attacked the employment-at-will doctrine. Firms that institute guidelines may well avoid a work environment hamstrung by a freshet of interfering legalities.

1. The firm should create internal systems that establish clear and consistent procedures for terminating or otherwise punishing employees. The firm should be especially concerned that all procedures are grounded in fundamental due process rights.

2. The firm should establish a bill of rights for its employees incorporating these guidelines. (Guidelines in employment privacy, polygraph testing, and making whistle blowing unnecessary appear elsewhere in this chapter.)

3. The firm should allow each employee who feels he or she has been sanctioned for asserting any right in the bill of rights to receive a fair hearing before a neutral tribunal or arbitrator. The findings of the hearing should be transmitted to the firm's management and to the employee.

4. The firm should establish a first-resort grievance procedure whereby employees have the right to discuss a concern with a small number of executives or managers.[37]

5. The firm, as an alternative to item 4, can establish "employee assistance officers," as Bank of America designates them. These officers confidentially receive

employee complaints and confer with the employee and his or her supervisor and manager to solve the difficulty. Further, another alternative is the "open door" procedure in which employees submit questions and concerns about individual and broader issues for written managerial response.   This system also preserves the employee's anonymity.

6. The firm should eliminate words such as "permanent," "career path," "job security," "partnership track," and "long-term growth" in its advertisements, job applicant interviews, and employee handbooks.   The firm can use qualifiers such as "usually" and "in most cases" in its personnel manuals.   The firm should consider using other precautions, including a form to be signed by new employees declaring that the firm can terminate employment at any time, with or without good cause.   Courts have varied in their interpretation of such disclaimers, but the common thread of those disclaimers upheld by courts includes the following elements:
   a. The firm requires prospective employees to acknowledge by signing in writing that they serve at the will or pleasure of the employer.
   b. There should also be a disclaimer placed prominently in the employment handbook manual or code. It must be clear, explicit, conspicuously placed, and distinguished to negate any reliance by an employee of a representation in the employee handbook.
   c. The disclaimer, moreover, must contain language that the handbook, manual, or code contains no promises; that, regardless of what the handbook, manual, or code provides, the employer promises nothing and remains free to change wages and working conditions without consulting anyone or receiving anyone's agreement; and that the employer continues to maintain the absolute right to terminate anyone with or without good cause.
   d. The disclaimer contained in the employer handbook or code should clearly indicate that no one, except a specified vice president, can change the at-will employment. Sears and General Motors have effectively used disclaimers.   Nonetheless, there is no guarantee that their validity will be upheld, given the dynamic interpretation by the courts.

7. When the firm first contemplates firing a troublesome individual, the manager responsible for the decision should review the firm's personnel policies and discuss relevant questions with personnel managers.[38]

8. After completing guideline 7, the manager should discern whether any oral or written statement has been made to the troublesome employee that a court may construe as an implied employment contract.

9. If the manager determines that no basis for an implied contract exists, he or she should decide whether the employee could persuasively argue that the reason for termination is not the firm's economic necessity or the

employee's incompetence or inadequacy but reprisal. The firm's retaliation might, for instance, be directed against the employee for an act that may come within the purview of the public policy exception—for instance, if the employee complained about an illegal firm practice or a health hazard, or opposed an invasion of privacy.

10. If no case for retaliatory discharge exists, the manager may terminate the troublesome employee. However, if such a case does exist, the manager should consult legal counsel who specializes in the field and ascertain, with the assistance of said counsel, whether the court of local, state, or federal jurisdiction attaches significance to a self-serving motive or discharge and how broadly it interprets "public policy."

CORPORATE RESPONSE

The response of the well-managed firms that participated in author Manley's year-long study on the erosion of the employment-at-will and the need to balance the firm's and employees' rights and responsibilities is noteworthy. Bank of America, for example, has formulated a disclosure code to provide all information requested by that firm's employees, and it maintains an "open line" for confidential complaints and a "hot line" for responses to oral questions and complaints. At Polaroid, an employee-elected committee regularly hears grievances alleging unfair treatment. Although the committee's decisions are advisory, Polaroid management rarely overrules them. The aggrieved employee, further, can appeal the decision to an independent arbitrator.[39]

Control Data has established the Employee Advisory Resource to investigate over 600 employee complaints per month and provide counsel to troubled employees. Citibank has established a multistep Problem Review Procedure, under which aggrieved employees attempt to solve any difficulty with their supervisors. Citibank's many level appellate process includes review by the supervisor's manager, the division director, and ultimately a five-member review board.

CONCLUSIONS

Courts and society have increasingly recognized employee rights of due process in termination and discipline cases as well as employment privacy. Moreover, the number of states in which courts support management's unqualified prerogative to discipline and discharge at-will employees and to intrude upon employees' privacy rapidly is diminishing. Business firms' responses have varied primarily along two avenues: the first is a defensive attempt to preserve all management powers through a rigidly prescribed and regulated work environment. Whereas this plethora of precautions avoids some litigation, the inherent source of the disquiet, a climate that inhibits employee commitment and trust, remains unchanged.

Other business firms recognize that the late twentieth-century employee is more sophisticated, educated, and skilled

than his or her early or midcentury forbears. Intense
competition and changing technology in 1990 are causing
employers to listen to their employees, who are likewise
demanding to be heard. Surveys, like that in 1989 by Wyatt,
a consulting firm, demonstrate that participative management
is a positive trend. For many firms, such management involves
formal and informal communication: from written reports on
pay and performance to audits of employee attitudes and
values, as well as breakfast meetings to mine employees for
suggestions. Moreover, these progressive companies have
implemented grievance or arbitration procedures that provide
due process to their employees. By preserving the individual's sense of dignity, the firm faces fewer destructive
lawsuits and concomitant litigation expense and enjoys
enhanced employee commitment, and better public and community
relations. Moreover, the firm substantially benefits from an
early warning system that alerts the company to corruption,
discontent, and potentially disastrous scandal.[40] The
development of an informed and loyal workforce, reinforced to
report wrongdoing, is likely to improve the firm's profitability.[41]

The time is ripe, perhaps overripe, for firms to realis-
tically examine the statutory and judicial erosion of employer
rights and the apparent signs of increased employer liability
in the 1990s. Perhaps the most important reason for firms to
react positively to employees' new expectations is that
concepts such as privacy and due process are esteemed values
in our society-at-large. Incorporating guidelines contained
in this chapter balances the firm's prerogatives to manage and
employees' rights to enjoy such values in the workplace.

NOTES

1. Copeland, "The Revenge of the Fired," Newsweek (February 16, 1987):
   46-47.
2. Geary v. U.S. Steel Corporation, 319 A. 2d 174, and see Summers,
   "Protecting All Employees Against Unjust Dismissal," Legal Issues in
   Doing Business, Harvard Business Review (1983): 76.
3. Ewing, "Your Right to Fire," Legal Issues in Doing Business, Harvard
   Business Review (1983): 70.
4. Ebling v. Masco Corporation, 292 N.W. 2d 880 (1980).
5. Moniodis v. Cook, Md. Ct. Spec. App. 883 (1985).
6. Blumberg, "Corporate Responsibility and the Employee's Duty of Loyalty
   and Obedience," Oklahoma Law Review (August 1971).
7. Ewing, "Due Process: Will Business Default," Legal Issues in Doing
   Business, Harvard Business Review (1983): 61.
8. Bakaly, Jr. and Grossman, Modern Law of Employment Contracts:
   Formation, Operation and Remedies for Breach (Orlando, FL: Harcourt
   Brace Jovanovich, 1983). Hames, "The Current Status of the Doctrine
   of Employment-at-Will," Labor Law Journal (January 1988): 19. These
   publications form part of the basis for this discussion of employment-
   at-will.
9. Smith v. Piezo Technology and Professional Administration, 427 So 2d
   182 (Florida, 1983).
10. Brown v. Physicians Mutual Insurance Co., 679 SW 2d 836 (Kentucky,
    1984); Sheets v. Teddy's Frosted Foods, 427 A 2d 385 (Connecticut,
    1980); and Palmateer v. International Harvester Co., 421 NE 2d 876
    (Illinois, 1981).

11. Vermillion v. AAA Pro Moving and Storage, 704 P2d 1360 (Arizona, 1985); Tameny v. Atlantic Richfield Co., 164 Cal. Reporter 839 (California, 1980), Delaney v. Taco Time International, 681 P2d 114 (Oregon, 1984); and, Cordle v. General Hugh Mercer Corp. 325 SE 2d 111 (West Virginia, 1984).
12. Ebling v. Masco Corp., 292 NW 2d 880 (Michigan, 1980).
13. Hames, "The Current Status of the Doctrine of Employment-at-Will," Labor Law Journal (January 1988): 27.
14. Pugh v. See's Candies, Inc., 116 Cal. App. 3d 311, 171 Cal. Rept. 917 (1981).
15. Heckser and Sonnenfeld, Individual Rights: The Challenge to Employment-at-Will, Harvard Business School Publication #486-060, 1985.
16. Maddaloni v. Western Massachusetts Bus Lines, Inc., 438 NE 2d 351 (Massachusetts, 1982).
17. Gates v. Life of Montana Insurance Company, 638 P2d 1063 (Montana, 1982).
18. Hames, op. cit., 32.
19. Hogan v. Forsyth Country Club Co., 340 SE 2d 116 (North Carolina, 1986).
20. Mueller v. Union Pacific Railroad, 371 NW 2d 732 (Nebraska, 1985), and see Hames, op. cit., 29-30.
21. 481 NE 2d 968 (Illinois, 1985), and see Hames, op. cit., 29.
22. "The Right to Privacy," Harvard Law Review 4 (1890): 193.
23. Belair, "Employee Rights in Privacy," 33 N.Y.U. Conf. Lab. 3 (1980): 3-4, as cited in Decker, "Employment Privacy Law for the 1990's," Pepperdine Law Review 15 (1988): 551, 562.
24. 5 U.S.C. Section 552 (1982).
25. Ibid., Section 552a (1982).
26. Decker, op. cit., 568-569.
27. Ibid., 571.
28. See Ibid., 573.
29. Author Manley has created or adapted these guidelines based on his knowledge of the area and of the examination of "Employment Privacy Law for the 1990's," by Decker in the Pepperdine Law Review, and the IBM standards. The author is unaware of any firm that has devoted more energy to developing a balanced policy regarding employment privacy than IBM.
30. Walters, "Your Employees' Right to Blow the Whistle," The Business of Ethics and Business edition, Harvard Business Review (1986): 138.
31. Ibid., 142.
32. Ibid., 143.
33. See Barland, "The Case for the Polygraph in Employment Screening," Ethical Issues in Business (Englewood Cliffs, NJ: Prentice-Hall, 1988): 319.
34. Lykken, "The Case Against the Polygraph in Employment Screening" Ethical Issues in Business (Englewood Cliffs, NJ: Prentice-Hall, 1988): 323.
35. Singer, "Employers Assay Ban on Polygraphs," New York Times (January 1, 1989): 12.
36. A number of state statutes and the thorough SCANA Corporation Administrative Manual section on polygraph testing form the basis for many of the guidelines on polygraph testing; see especially Cal. Lab. Code Section 432.2 (West Supp., 1988); Conn. Gen. Stat. Section 31-51g (1987); Mich. Comp. Laws Ann. Sections 37.201-.208 (West, 1985); and Pa. Cons. Stat. Ann. Section 7321 (Purdon, 1982).
37. See Hecksher and Sonnenfeld, op. cit., for the basis of guidelines 4, 5, and 6.
38. For the genesis of guidelines 7, 8, 9, and 10, see Ewing, op. cit., 70.
39. Ewing, op. cit., 61.
40. Heckscher and Sonnenfeld, op. cit., 6, 8.
41. Decker, op. cit., 579-580.

3

Drugs, Alcoholism, AIDS, and Genetics in the Workplace

INTRODUCTION

The illicit use of drugs and alcohol on the job has become nearly as common as the coffee break. The pervasive influence of drug and alcohol consumption in the workplace has been widely noted. According to Bureau of Labor Statistics data released in 1989, 11.9% of the 3.9 million American private sector employees who were tested for drugs tested positive. In 1989 investigators found high levels of alcohol in the blood of the *Exxon Valdez* captain as well as a Coast Guard radar operator after the ship grounded, spilling 240,000 barrels of oil into Prince William Sound in Alaska. Canadian sprinter Ben Johnson was stripped of his gold medal won at the Seoul Olympics in 1988 for having tested positive for an anabolic steroid. Moreover, within two hours of employment at the Chevron Harris nuclear plant, an undercover investigator purchased cocaine from a fellow employee; after a few months' investigation eight employees were arrested for selling narcotics at the plant. Further, at least fifty train accidents from 1975 to 1983 were attributed to drug or alcohol abuse. *Time* magazine quoted Dr. Howard Frankel, medical director of Rockwell's space shuttle division, who estimated that at least 20% of the workers at the final assembly plant of the space shuttle were intoxicated by alcohol or drugs.[1]

Alcoholism and drug abuse cost American business billions of dollars annually—about $800 for every employee. The annual loss in productivity alone resulting from drug abuse is from $34 billion[2] to $60 billion,[3] and, from alcoholism, in excess of $50 billion.[4] Other estimates place the annual cost to American society at $136 billion. There are further substantial, less easily quantified losses due to medical expenses, theft, poor decision-making at all levels, accidents and injuries, adverse effects on employee morale, wasted material, work errors, poor product quality, and replacement and training. In a late 1988 survey, Substance Abuse in the Work Force by Mercer Meidinger Hansen, Inc., human-resource executives, mayors and governors and other respondents almost unanimously describe the problem as "very significant." Yet, only 22%, up from 8% in 1983, view drug and alcohol abuse as a "very significant" problem in their own firms. To highlight the fight against illegal drugs, former President Reagan insisted two years ago that his urine and that of his Cabinet members and vice president be tested for the presence of illicit drugs. President Bush's antidrug strategy unveiled in September 1989 requires testing of federal employees and asks other employers to promulgate tests "where appropriate." By late 1989 well over one-fifth of all private-sector employees worked for firms that had established drug testing programs.

As a result of the deleterious effects of drugs and alcohol abuse, and since drug and alcohol testing is legal in the private sector, firms are attacking illegal drug use and alcohol abuse by implementing physical testing and employee assistance programs. Of America's largest firms, including one-half of Fortune 500 firms, 49% have either or both of these programs. IBM, for example, which President Bush has mentioned as a model for drug screening, began testing all applicants in 1984, and in 1986 tested all employees with "unexplained changes in behavior" in the workplace. Over 25% of employers of recent college graduates screen job candidates and another 20% intend to begin such testing. In addition, in three 1989 opinions, the United States Supreme Court ruled that the federal government, as well as railroads and airlines, may require drug testing under certain circumstances.

Related issues are AIDS and genetic screening in the workplace. AIDS continues to spread; by the beginning of 1989 nearly 80,000 cases had been reported in the United States. The epidemic has raised a number of questions to which a business firm must effectively respond. Nearly 58% of respondent firms in one 1988 survey indicate that a case of AIDS has occurred among employees or dependents covered by company health plans. Moreover, President Bush's August 1989 agreement with congressional leaders to expand Title VII's protection against discrimination to 37 million disabled Americans and people ill with AIDS or infected with the virus provides new challenges to firms. Yet, according to a Foster Higgins survey in August 1988, 62% of respondents did not intend to establish an AIDS policy by the end of 1989. As a result of not having an effective AIDS policy, a Norfolk, Virginia, fast-food chain is being sued for discrimination by Michael Wolfe, a pizza maker. Wolfe complained that he felt ill, triggering rumors he might be afflicted with the AIDS virus; his employer terminated him. In addition, genetic screening is a means of testing individuals to determine the presence of any heritable traits that would predispose them to occupational illness.

Guidelines are needed to assist firms in the adoption and administration of such programs. Strict adherence to these guidelines is necessary to safeguard the employer from lawsuits and the employee from abuse.

ILLICIT DRUG USE AND ALCOHOLISM

A controlled substance is any depressant, stimulant, hallucinogen, cannabinoid, or narcotic defined as such by the Drug Enforcement Administration (DEA) of the U.S. Department of Justice. Some of these drugs are legal when prescribed by a physician. Testing for controlled substances is designed to reveal commonly abused drugs such as amphetamines, marijuana, hashish, cocaine, heroin, and codeine. According to proponents, drug testing increases employee safety, health, and efficiency, reduces the escalation of product and services costs typically transferred to the consumer; attacks the power of organized crime; and reduces society's demand for illicit drugs. Even private athletic associations have reported favorable results. For instance, Dr. Robert Dugal, a member of the International Olympic Committee medical commission reported in August 1989, that drug-testing procedures used at the Olympics and other major sporting events for the last two decades have effectively eradicated short-term use by athletes, leaving only the careless athlete, such as Ben Johnson, to be detected. Dugal warned that a year-round, short-notice testing program was necessary to eliminate drug use. Detractors, on the contrary, assert that there is little research to support the claim that drug testing is a deterrent to abuse. In fact, critics contend, such testing may drive drug users to alcohol, and that testing, especially random tests, have a deleterious effect on employee morale.

Dr. Michael Walsh of the National Institute on Drug Abuse indicates that approximately 23 million of the 56 million Americans who have tried marijuana still use it and 6 million of 22 million who have tried cocaine continue the practice. Although there is some indication that illicit drug use had declined slightly since 1986,[5] it remains a staggering problem. Obviously, given these figures and the steady increase in the number using drugs in the last two decades, a significant number of America's workforce are drug users. In fact, in 1982 officials estimated that 3-5% of the American workforce regularly used illicit drugs, a figure that has since grown. Other estimates are that over 11 million employees abuse controlled substances and alcohol. Moreover, drug use while working has increased. The Cocaine National Help Line in 1986 revealed that 69% of those calling admitted they regularly worked under the influence of cocaine.

Alcohol, on the other hand, is society's favorite recreational drug and, not coincidentally, the most abused substance in America. Alcoholism, which afflicts 10-12 million Americans, is one of the leading killing diseases; 80% of all violence in the home is alcohol related, and 50% of vehicular fatal accidents involve the use of alcohol. In fact, there are more alcohol-related accidents than those caused by all illegal drugs combined. Approximately one of every ten employed persons is an alcoholic. Each year, 25,000 people die of cirrhosis of the liver. Alcoholism, which has been recognized as a medical disease by the American Medical Association since 1956, is often treated behaviorally but is not defined as a controlled substance by the DEA. Interestingly, illegal drug use is usually classified as a behavioral malady, yet treated medically.

Employer Response: Implementation of Drug and Alcohol Testing Programs

Employee testing is not a new occurrence. Employers have utilized testing for a long time to determine an employee's or applicant's intelligence, attitude, or honesty. Now, the emphasis in testing is the confirmation of behavioral, not psychological, aberrations.   Tests of this nature include medical screening for illegal drug use.[6]   The increasing popularity of drug testing extends to private sector employers, as well as the government.

Firms cite four primary reasons for instituting drug screening programs.   First, to achieve higher productivity, firms must act to minimize substance abuse since abusers are considerably less productive than sober fellow workers.   The average substance abuser is ten times more likely than a nonuser to be late or absent, 2.5 times more likely to have absences of eight days or more, three times as likely to cause an injury on the job, and five times more likely to file a worker's compensation claim.   Further, substance abusers generally have more expensive health care needs and necessitate more disciplinary sanctions.   These factors escalate the cost of labor, an avoidable increased expense that the firm transfers to the consumer in the form of higher product and service costs.

A second reason cited by firms to support drug testing is the expansion of the liability of employers for the actions of their employees.   Traditionally, under the doctrine of respondeat superior,[7] the employer may be held liable for the negligent actions of an employee that were authorized by the employer, or for negligence in dealing with or selecting an employee.   In a pregnant expansion of respondeat superior, the Texas Supreme Court in Otis Engineering Corporation v. Clark[8] found that it was the duty of an employer to control an intoxicated employee who was off duty.   In Otis a machine operator was dismissed early because his intoxication was deemed by the firm to be a safety hazard.   The Otis supervisor escorted the employee to his vehicle and asked him if he were able to drive.[10]   After responding that he was indeed competent, the employee was involved in a fatal accident, which killed him and two occupants of another vehicle.   The court maintained that the families of the two victims could sue the firm under a wrongful death action, even though the intoxicated employee was off duty and not acting within the scope of his employment.

Another area of expansion of the firm's liability is in the issue spectrum surrounding workplace safety.   The Occupational Safety and Health Act (OSHA) requires that each employer "shall furnish to each of his employees employment and a place of employment . . . free from recognized hazards that are causing or are likely to cause death or serious physical harm to his employees."[9]   Consequently, a firm's failure to respond to an employee's drug or alcohol abuse may breach the firm's duty.   Employers argue that drug testing allows them to protect the health and safety of all employees as well as to prevent substance-related accidents.

A third factor specified by firms to reinforce their drug testing is the lingering effects of illegal drugs.   The principle that what an employee does in off-duty time is inconsequential and not a subject of disciplinary action has been subverted.   One study clearly indicates that, long after the sensation of marijuana intoxication has passed, airplane pilots perform poorly in flight-simulated landings.   Obviously, the marijuana that had been ingested by the pilots in the experiment adversely affected their ability to perform cognitive tasks and complex behavior at least twenty-four hours later. This fact presents a strong argument against those who assert that drug tests are unfair because they demonstrate mere use and not always present intoxication.

Finally, employers are necessarily concerned about the security of their firms. Substance abusers are more likely to steal the firm's assets and sell confidential information. In a sensitive industry such as defense contracting, a drug abuser may also be vulnerable to blackmail, since loss of security clearance by reason of a narcotics felony conviction would cost the abuser his or her employment.[10]

Drug testing in the public sector has expanded since the implementation of the army's Drug and Alcohol Abuse Prevention and Control Program, which began in 1972 and tested over 4 million service personnel in its first fourteen months. Testing programs have since included employees of the federal government, the other three military branches, the coast guard, and a number of federal administrative agencies, including the Federal Bureau of Aviation, the Central Intelligence Agency, and the Federal Bureau of Investigation. In two cases decided in 1989, the U. S. Supreme Court accorded the federal government broad discretion in imposing drug testing on both private employees and government workers involved in public safety or law enforcement. The Supreme Court ruled in Skinner v. Railway Labor Executives' Association (Case No. 87-1555) that the federal government may require drug testing of workers who occupy sensitive and safety-related jobs but did not respond to the question of widespread, random testing of government workers. Also, in National Treasury Employees Union v. Von Raab (Case No. 86-1879), the Court decreed that U.S. Customs Service workers seeking transfer or promotion to positions that involve intercepting narcotics traffic, carrying guns, or handling classified material may be required to submit one-time-only tests for drugs even though there exists no probable cause of use or level of individualized suspicion.

In a third case, Consolidated Rail Corporation v. Railway Labor Executives' Association (Case No. 88-1), the Supreme Court held that railroads and airlines, as Conrail, under the Railway Labor Act, may include drug tests in periodic physicals required of workers without collective bargaining. The case arose as a result of Conrail's announcement on February 20, 1987, that "urinalysis drug screening would be included henceforth as part of all periodic and return-from-leave physical examinations." The railroads underscored the need for drug testing by reference to the Chase, Maryland, railroad accident in 1987 that killed seventeen and injured 174. The engineer and brakeman were found to have been using marijuana. Studies cited by the railroads estimated 25% of railroad employees consume alcohol on duty. Further, in 1989 the National Labor Relations Board (NLRB), which governs workers outside the railroad and airline industries, held that unionized employers must bargain with unions when they wish to establish drug and alcohol testing of current employees. Employers, however, can test job applicants for drug and alcohol use without first bargaining with the unions.

Although a majority of business firms have not implemented drug and alcohol testing programs, there is a pronounced trend to testing.   In 1983 only 3% of U.S. companies employed drug testing of any kind.   By January of 1989, however, more than a third of all American firms had established testing programs covering   millions   of   workers.   According   to   the   survey Substance Abuse in the Work Force, 50% of respondents' firms conduct   pre-employment   drug   testing;   29%   test   current   employees.   Only 27% of respondents endorse random drug sampling of their employees, however.

Many consider a resolute antidrug stance as essential to controlling the nation's drug problem.   Arthur P. Brill, Jr., a staff member of the President's Commission on Organized Crime, reflects this attitude toward employee substance abuse: "This is not a rights issue, because drugs are illegal.   There is no legal right to take them."[11]   Further, Richard L. Lesher, president   of   the   U.S.   Chamber   of   Commerce,   describes   the business sector's use of testing to curtail drug use: "Our message is simple.   If you do drugs, you don't work . . . We have no alternative but to commit ourselves to this cause and to see it through."[12]   In addition, the President's Commission on Organized Crime in a March 1986 report encouraged wider use of testing: "Government and private sector employers who do not already require drug testing of job applicants and current employees   should   consider   the   appropriateness   of   such   a testing program."

As a consequence, companies that have implemented medical screening programs to detect drug use include ALCOA, AT&T, DuPont, Ford Motor Company, Federal Express, IBM, Greyhound Lines, Exxon, Mobil, the New York Times, Capital Cities/ABC, Northeast Utilities, Shearson Lehman, TWA, Lockheed, and United Airlines.   These private firms primarily use urinalysis to detect the use of amphetamines, barbiturates, cocaine, and marijuana.

The Variety and Results of Drug Testing Programs

Whom and when employers test vary significantly among firms. The firm may require tests of all job applicants, all employees as part of scheduled physical examinations, those employees suspected of drug use, employees about to be promoted, those who have been involved in accidents, or all employees on a random basis.   Some programs, such as ones administered by the U.S. Customs Service, test only those who are employed in critical positions.   By 1986, 29% of Fortune 500 firms used pre-employment drug screening tests and 26% performed drug tests on employees under certain circumstances.

For   instance,   Kidder,   Peabody   &   Company,   a   prominent invest-   ment   bank,   established   a   comprehensive   testing program.   All   Kidder   employees   are   tested   periodically. Kidder protects the employee's rights through reconfirmation by further testing if results are positive and by a procedure that allows the employee to explain or challenge tests.   At Salomon Brothers, another investment bank, all newly recruited personnel undergo testing.

The dramatic reduction in drug abuse within the U.S. military is an indication of the positive results of testing. There is little doubt that testing by private firms has reduced the deleterious effects of abuse in the workplace as

well. Such programs have protected the health and safety of
innocent employees from the actions of drug abusers.   As
accident rates decrease, liability insurance premiums also
decrease.   Decreased absenteeism and better judgment enhance
product quality while lowering costs of production.

For instance, Southern Pacific Railroad reported substantial decreases in on-the-job injuries through its drug testing
program.   In 1985 the firm disclosed that accidents resulting
from human error had been reduced by over 70% from the
previous year. Moreover, after Southern Pacific Transportation Company instituted postaccident testing in 1984, the
firm's rate of railroad accidents dropped from 22.2 for every
million miles in 1983 to 2.2, according to a <u>Wall Street
Journal</u> article by David Wessel on September 7, 1989.   Also,
some studies, including one by the U. S. Postal Service's in-
house psychologist Jacques Normand, have found pre-employment
drug testing to be a significant predictor of an employee's
reliability.   Those postal workers who tested positive for
drug use were absent 41% more often and were terminated 38%
more often than those workers who did not test positive.
Following institution of a drug testing program at its Vogtle
nuclear plant, Georgia Power Company disclosed a tenfold
descent in injuries to just one-half per 200,000 working hours
in 1985.[13]

Types of Tests and Potential Problems

For the purposes of drug testing, virtually all employers,
whether private or public, use urine testing.   Whereas blood
tests are the sole convenient, reliable means to detect
intoxication, urinalysis is the prevalent testing mode for
three reasons: (1) the nature of the intrusion required by a
urine sample is less invasive than that in a blood sampling,
(2) the residue of drugs remains in the excretory system long
after the effect of the drug has disappeared, and (3) the
commonly used urine tests are inexpensive, can be administered
by nontechnical personnel, and yield results in a few minutes.
The two most commonly used urinalysis tests are the enzyme
multiplied immunoassay test (EMIT) and the gas chromatography-
mass spectrometer test (GC/MS).

The EMIT, the most widely used urinalysis by employers,
has been criticized for several reasons.   First, the test
cannot determine when the drug was ingested or the intoxication level at the time of testing.   Second, experiments by
the National Institute of Drug Abuse found that from 5% to 20%
of EMIT results are false.   Despite assertions by the Syva
Corporation, the manufacturer of the EMIT, that the test is at
least 97% accurate when properly administered, Northwestern
University studies indicate that 25% of the employer-admin-
istered positive test results are inaccurate.   "False positives" occur most often when untrained personnel using
incomplete procedures administer the test.

Also, even if administered correctly, the EMIT may yield
a "false positive" by mistaking legal substances or body
illnesses for illegal drugs as a result of "cross-reactivity."
For example, the painkiller ibuprofen, present in numerous
nonprescription cold medicines, as well as kidney or bladder

dysfunction, can trigger a false positive reading. Other legal substances that the EMIT may mistake for a variety of illegal drugs are aspirin, Contac, and Nyquil. In addition, the test may confuse poppy seeds with opiates such as heroin, and herbal teas for cocaine. Moreover, the similarity between the chemical composition of a chemical derivative of marijuana and of the pigment melanin, which naturally occurs in high levels in Hispanics and Blacks, might also cause "false positive" results. Of course, the EMIT may also fail to identify those subjects who have ingested illegal drugs by registering "false negative" readings.

On the other hand, the GC/MS test, which must be performed in a laboratory, is more reliable.[14] In fact, an EMIT positive result corroborated by GC/MS testing is exceptionally reliable. Even though the GC/MS test requires a greater time to receive results, its use significantly reduces the chance of error in a firm's drug testing program.

Nevertheless, any test will only be as accurate as the standard of care in observing strict processing procedures. Instrument malfunction and human error (sample mislabeling, dirty equipment, incorrect collection, and failure to preserve urine samples at proper temperatures) account for error in laboratories. For example, the Centers for Disease Control reported as much as a 60% "false positive" error rate in its nine-year study of thirteen independent laboratories.

Legal Issues in Drug and Alcohol Screening of Applicants and Current Employees

Firms defend their use of drug testing by asserting that it will almost surely ensure a safe workplace and that, legally, the doctrine of employment-at-will provides them the authority to impose any conditions upon the employment relationship as long as that condition does not violate an employment contract or statute that specifically restricts that prerogative. Nonetheless, drug testing often clashes with the job applicant's or employee's interests.

Job applicants are much more likely to be tested than employees. The pre-employment physical examination is customary in our society. There is no legal requirement to inform the applicant that he or she is being tested for drug use, that he tested positively, or that she was not hired because of the positive result. Job applicants simply do not have the vested employment rights of current employees. Firms may establish freedom from using illegal or abusing legal drugs as a condition of employment for job applicants.

Current employees have more expansive rights regarding drug testing by private employers. What prerogatives exist are grounded in the employee's common law rights in contract or tort law. The firm's improper drug screening may occasion employee causes of action as invasions of privacy, defamation, wrongful discharge, and intentional infliction of emotional distress.[15]

Privacy. Invasion of privacy is an issue relevant to drug screening in both private and public sectors. Although the Fourth Amendment right to privacy does not apply to the private sector, a business firm's employee may still rely on tort causes of action that protect his or her privacy. A few states[16] have specific constitutional provisions extending a right of privacy to citizens, but the common law right to privacy is recognized in almost every state.[17] The employee terminated for refusal to submit to an alcohol or drug screening or for the results of the test may assert a specific privacy invasion claim, "intrusion upon seclusion." The employee must demonstrate that the intrusion is highly offensive and objectionable to the reasonable person. This action, however, is unlikely to be successful because private sector employees are under no compulsion to submit to the testing. Even the employer's disclosure of private facts about the employee's test results does not violate the right of privacy in most cases, especially when the dissemination of the results was within the firm.

Defamation. An employee has a cause of action if the employer communicates false information about the employee's drug or alcohol use to a third person, which injures the employee's reputation. Generally, an employer may communicate information in good faith to someone who has a legitimate interest in the information even if the information is false.[18] In one case, a Texas appeals court upheld a damage award in a defamation suit brought by an employee against his firm. When the employee fainted at work, the firm's surgeon administered a drug test to determine if a drug caused the fainting. The test results indicated the presence of methadone. The employee was suspended and discharged, even though subsequent tests revealed no methadone or other drug in his system. The appellate court upheld the jury verdict, which awarded the employee compensatory and punitive damage because the firm's officials made false statements that the employee was a narcotics user "when they knew better."

Wrongful Discharge. Many states have enacted statutes that provide exceptions to the general rule of employment-at-will—that an employment contract of indefinite duration can be terminated legally by either the employer or employee at any time. Courts have split on whether codes of employee conduct or handbooks constitute a binding contract. Consequently, without a breach of contract, the prerequisite for a terminated employee's filing a wrongful discharge action is that the discharge be coupled with a violation of public policy. The public policy can be statutory or nonstatutory. Currently, San Francisco has enacted a municipal ordinance severely proscribing drug testing in the workplace. In no other jurisdiction has a state court found terminations resulting from failure to submit to testing or arising from the test results to be against public policy.

Emotional Distress. An employee who has been discharged because of failure to submit to testing or due to the results may also bring an action alleging that the discharge caused severe mental distress. Legal recovery requires certain elements: the employer's intentional or reckless infliction of severe emotional distress in an extreme and outrageous manner that causes the employee distress that is so severe that no reasonable person could be expected to endure it.

Guidelines for the Firm's Testing

A firm that wishes to balance its interests against those of the employee should implement specific practical guidelines in its drug or alcohol testing program in the areas of justification, procedure and implementation.

1. The firm should examine the goal sought to be achieved by the program. Rehabilitative, as opposed to strictly punitive, programs are preferable, as is conducting any testing in conjunction with employee assistance programs. Rehabilitation of drug users or alcohol abusers is considerably more cost-effective than hiring and training replacements. Employer-employee relations, especially important in the 1980s and 1990s, are enhanced as well. Moreover, whereas employers of nonunion employees have almost unlimited authority in testing, courts and arbitrators have ruled that an employer cannot institute a blanket, random testing program when employees have a collective bargaining representative. In that case, the employer must negotiate the testing with the collective bargaining agent.

2. The firm should consider the nature of the enterprise and the employee's tasks and duties. There should be a direct nexus between the testing and a business or job-related necessity. For instance, protection of firm property, improving productivity, enhancing workplace safety, reducing health and liability insurance premiums, and improving the quality of the firm's products are important reasons for testing. Moreover, as all employees and managers should be responsible for maintaining an illicit drug- and alcohol-free work environment, the firm should emphasize that their well-being is harmed by abuse on the job.

3. The firm's consideration of a different threshold of testing based on reasonable suspicion is helpful. Under this procedure, when a supervisor has reasonable cause to suspect drug or alcohol use, the firm may test. Some firms, including Rockwell International, apply this lower threshold procedure to employees in "sensitive positions."

4. The firms should establish clear policies and rules regarding the sale, use, or possession of alcohol or illegal substances in the workplace. Prohibited substances and the sanctions for violation of the regulations should be clearly communicated to all employees. The entire policy should be in writing and should be created by a cross section of employees who volunteer their services in the codification. Further,

the policy should be included in collective bargaining agreements and in employment contracts.

5. Ensuring that the policy is available to job applicants as well as current employees demonstrates to all that due process through adequate notification is a principle of the firm.

6. Establishment of an oversight committee to implement the regulations and suggest changes cultivates an institutional commitment and signals all employees that the firm is serious about administering the program judiciously. The committee membership should include, among others, management representatives, employee representatives, and health care professionals with experience in substance abuse.

7. Management and supervisory personnel should be thoroughly trained in implementation of the program, such as detecting drug or alcohol-impaired performance. Possible early warning signs of controlled substance or alcohol abuse include: abrupt change in mood or attitude, sudden resistance to direction at work, unexpected or sudden decline in work quality or attendance, impaired relations with coworkers who are friends, unusual loss of temper, escalated borrowing from coworkers, theft at work, and an amplified secrecy about one's actions. Specific symptoms of alcoholism include: the smell of alcohol or breath deodorants on an employee's breath, red eyes, flushed face, hand tremors, and loss of coordination. Further, pronounced controlled substance abuse exhibits certain manifestations as well: disorientation, lethargy, dilated or constricted pupils, and poor distance or time perception. The firms should also educate all employees regarding symptoms of alcohol or drug abuse and what procedures to adopt when they discern such symptoms. Management and supervisors should carefully document evidence of such impaired performance.

8. The firm should generally promulgate testing only when probable cause, business necessity, or reasonable suspicion exists. Documentation from field personnel in regular contact with the employee should form the basis for testing. The foundation for suspicion should be articulable facts.

9. If random testing is used, as it should be with employees in inherently dangerous jobs and in those related to public safety, randomness of selection must be assured—this process removes any arbitrariness in the selection process.

10. Employees should be notified of the date and time of testing. The notice should typically be from one to four days, because the EMIT test will usually be negative if five days have elapsed between illegal drug use and the test.

11. At the time of the testing, the employee should be allowed to complete a form through which the employee discloses his or her use of prescription (with a note from the prescribing physician) and nonprescription drugs within the prior month. This information should be sealed and examined by laboratory personnel only if the test results are positive.

12. Testing should be conducted by reputable independent laboratories. Any information that is not illegal drug or alcohol related should be maintained as strictly confidential.

13. The employer should substitute a gown for the employee's clothing to maintain dignity. No access to personal items, including clothing or pocketbooks, should be allowed. The testing officer should listen for and never observe urination.

14. An identification number and date, not the employee's name, should be affixed to the sample in the presence of the employee, who should signify in writing that the container number and his or her assigned testing number are identical.

15. If an EMIT positive is recorded, a GC/MS should be used to confirm the EMIT finding before any disciplinary action. Test results should be released only to those persons who have a significant need to know them.

16. The employee should have an opportunity, at the firm's expense, to have the sample retested and confirmed by an alternate method at a licensed independent laboratory and to rebut or explain the results.

17. A clear warning and an opportunity to complete a rehabilitation program should be communicated to any employee whose positive reading on the EMIT is confirmed by the GC/MS.

18. Any disciplinary action must be based on the way in which the employee's substance use or alcohol abuse affects his or her job performance or on the violation of specific, disseminated company regulations that prohibit the use, possession, or sale of alcohol or illegal drugs on the firm's property.

19. If the employee's conduct does not improve after procedures 1–17, above, and after a reasonable time following the warning that he or she will be terminated if conduct does not improve, the employee may be discharged.

20. The firm should redesign jobs that are either stressful or boring; alcohol and drug abuse are related to these job types.

21. The firm should vigorously enforce safety standards on the job.

22. The firm should establish an Employee Assistance Program (EAP) to assist troubled employees.

23. The firm should praise employees for efforts in promoting and maintaining alcohol and drug abuse-free environments, accident-free days, and low absentee rates.

24. Above all, the firm should treat employees with respect and follow a fair program while realizing that the military spends approximately $10,000 to discover and discharge one controlled substance abuser.

Employee Assistance Programs

Employer responses to an employee's positive drug finding vary from punitive measures to requiring that employee's mandatory attendance in counseling programs. Approximately 25% of firms that test currently employed persons habitually discharge any employee whose urinalysis confirms illegal drug use. The majority of firms that test, however, encourage or require treatment for substance and alcohol abuse. The trend today is clearly toward identifying, educating, and treating the chemically dependent person, and over 56% of the largest 1000 firms listed in Fortune have established programs aimed at assisting alcoholic and drug using employees. This early identification most effectively occurs at the workplace.

An Employee Assistance Program (EAP) is an effective method to address the personal problems of employees. There were 5,000 such programs in 1983, and the number has significantly increased to 8,000 in 1985 as firms realize the social and economic benefits of rehabilitation. Firms such as Northwestern Bell and Adolph Coors provide company financed counseling programs or the cost of employee enrollment in employee assistance programs to treat alcohol or drug addiction or counsel abusive employees. U.S. News and World Report has indicated that other firms such as Digital Equipment and DuPont encourage employees to enter counseling and intensive assistance programs without fear of further sanction.

According to a 1987 American Medical Association study, firms have discovered that EAPs usually comprise an efficient approach to reducing alcohol- and drug-related job-performance problems. Specifically, the EAP rehabilitation approach is usually less expensive than the cost of training new employees or of ignoring the problem. Moreover, such programs in place have increased the morale of the firm.

Another important consideration for those firms with EAPs in place and those debating the merits of establishing them is the growing concern of skyrocketing health care costs. Alcoholism or drug abuse, if left untreated, inevitably results in serious illness that requires expensive treatment, including long-term hospitalization. The firm ultimately absorbs the cost of such long-term treatment through higher insurance premiums and more frequent disability claims.

Certain standards enhance the performance of an EAP or similar firm program. A written policy statement on alcoholism and illegal drug use should definitively set forth deleterious effects of abuse and the firm's response and sanctions if troubled employees fail to cooperate. The organizational position of the program should be at the management level and the support staff should combine administrative and clinical skills. Other key success factors include educating and communicating to employees and their families the merits of the program, maintaining a comprehensive resource file concerning providers of services, and instituting a periodic program review and evaluation to assure that the program is addressing the employees' needs.

AIDS AND GENETIC PREDISPOSITION

AIDS: The Scope and Cost[19]

Acquired Immune Deficiency Syndrome, which has so far afflicted one in 4,200 Americans, is not the first sexually transmitted disease to stir concern and controversy. During the late 1800s about one in ten persons contracted syphilis. Unlike syphilis, however, there is presently no cure for AIDS, which is caused by the HIV/LAV virus. Approximately one-half of those who have been diagnosed as having AIDS have died. About one-half of the U.S. cases of AIDS have involved persons living in the large metropolitan centers of San Francisco, Los Angeles, and New York.
One-and-a-half-million Americans are infected with the HIV/LAV virus. From 20% to 45% of those currently infected will develop AIDS or AIDS-related complex (ARC) within five years. The first U.S. case was documented in 1981; by March of 1987 more than 31,000 cases had been reported and over 18,000 deaths were attributed to AIDS, which radically transforms the structure of the human immune system, rendering the body unable to defend itself against infection. By the end of January 1989, the infectious disease had killed over 35,000 Americans of the 80,000 infected; 275,000 to 450,000 people will suffer full-blown AIDS symptoms by 1993. By 1991 AIDS will likely become the leading cause of death for Americans 25 to 44 years of age, with 2 million people having been exposed to the virus.
The AIDS virus is transmitted through sexual contact, by exposure to infected blood, by organ transplantation from a virus-infected donor, and to newborn infants from infected mothers. According to the Centers for Disease Control guidelines published November 15, 1985, health care workers, personal service employees, food service workers, and other workers with AIDS do not create health risks to fellow employees or the public. Moreover, AIDS is not spread by casual, nonsexual contact.

Cost of AIDS. Illness imposes a variety of pecuniary and nonpecuniary costs upon society. The impact of AIDS on the nation's economy is staggering. The cost of medical care for the (lower estimate) 270,000 cumulative AIDS cases by 1993 is approximately $22 billion.[20]   Blue Cross and Blue Shield estimates that its expenses in treating AIDS patients will rise to $150,000 per patient, and the total cost will exceed what that insurance company expends for all other health care claims.

In addition to personal medical costs, there are substantial nonpersonal costs. Federal spending on AIDS education and research increased from $234 million in 1986 to over $910 million in 1988. The estimated cost of foregone earnings due to AIDS-caused disability or premature death implies a loss of between $146 and $168 billion. In addition, as the AIDS epidemic spreads and continues to be concentrated regionally, the crush on the nation's health care will intensify. Eventually, the nation's taxpayers will bear the burden.

AIDS Testing. As has been noted, screening processes are often controversial because such tests threaten the interests of those tested. The AIDS tests currently in use detect the presence of antibodies to the virus, not the virus itself. This antibody testing comprises two stages: the first, a simple and inexpensive test called Enzyme Linked Immunosorbent Assay (ELISA), and the second, the Western Blot test, for those samples that test positively under ELISA. Some estimates indicate as few as 10% of positive ELISA results among low incident groups are true positives. Unfortunately, the Western Blot test does not eliminate all false positives. On the other hand, among populations having a high incidence of infection, there exists a greater risk of false negative testing results. Clearly, there is no infallible test.[21]

Response and Guidelines in the Workplace Concerning AIDS. A telephone poll conducted in 1988 by Georgia Tech's Center for Work Performance Problems indicates that AIDS has created tremendous management challenges for American business firms.[22] Among the respondents, 37% indicated that they would not share tools or equipment with a coworker suffering from AIDS; 66% expressed grave reservations about using the same bathroom; 40% were concerned about eating in the same cafeteria with persons with AIDS. More telling, 42% responded that it is likely that people who claim to have various illnesses are really concealing AIDS infections.

Responding to such fears, the Citizens Commission on AIDS, an advocacy group representing major U.S. employers, has endorsed a set of principles that would protect the rights of employees with the disease and bar employer testing for antibodies to the virus.[23] Endorsers include AT&T, ITT, Chemical Bank, Johnson & Johnson, IBM, Time Incorporated, Girl Scouts of the U.S.A., and Warner Lambert. The guidelines reject job applicant AIDS screening and call for protecting the confidentiality of employee medical records and implementing AIDS education programs for employees.

The General Accounting Office, the congressional watchdog over the executive branch, has formulated a policy on AIDS.[24] The only one of its kind in the federal government, the policy includes key elements:

1. Being AIDS-free is not a condition for hiring or for continued employment.

2. An AIDS-diseased employee is under no obligation to disclose the condition to a GAO manager.

3. GAO efforts to help an employee ill with AIDS should be the same as the efforts to help employees with other life-threatening diseases.

Firms that Wish to Screen and Relevant Legal Issues. If a firm refused to hire, terminated, or placed special restrictions on AIDS victims, and the medical community termed such action to be unnecessary, the firm would likely face costly lawsuits. An employer that unconditionally refuses to employ anyone with AIDS violates federal and state handicap discrimination laws.[25] Interestingly, OSHA, the ubiquitous intervenor, does not indicate what tests may not be administered.

Nevertheless, a firm can likely refuse to employ those who are too sick to do the job, as protections of disabled persons are not yet absolute under state or federal laws. Basically, an employer has such a legal defense of "job-relatedness"—if a protected applicant or a current employee cannot satisfactorily perform the job tasks. For example, this defense would normally be successful if the AIDS-infected person cannot work regularly. The firm may determine the AIDS-infected employee cannot perform the essential functions of the job. Pursuant to the Vocational Rehabilitation Act and many state statutes that require reasonable accommodation for the handicapped, the employer should attempt to restructure the job or reassign the employee to a less physically demanding position.

A number of potential defenses appear to be unavailable to the employer who does not hire an AIDS-infected applicant or terminates an employee with AIDS. These include concern that AIDS will be transmitted in the workplace, that employees will refuse to work with someone who has AIDS, providing care for AIDS-infected employees that is too expensive for the firm to bear, and the cost of training an employee who may likely die or be unable to work within a year or two, or less. A handicap is not job-related if by reasonable accommodation the impairment can be eliminated; thus a disabled person is qualified and the handicap cannot be the basis for an adverse employment decision. In such cases, the firm should abide by the finding of the employee's physician or physician retained by the firm.

Further, the firm's working conditions may pose a health risk to an AIDS-diseased employee because of susceptibility to opportunistic infections and diseases from contagious fellow workers or of danger to a noninfected employee from an AIDS victim. An employer has an affirmative duty pursuant to the General Duty Clause of the OSH Act to "[f]urnish to each of his employees employment . . . [that is] free from recognized hazards . . . likely to cause death or serious physical harm to his employees . . ." Moreover, an employee has a right not to work in an unsafe workplace. Although OSHA and the National Labor Relations Board recognize an employee's right to refuse to work in dangerous, hazardous, or life-threatening environments, AIDS is not transmitted through casual contact, according to current medical opinion, and would not form the

basis generally to avoid work.   Rather, it appears that
ignorance and prejudice do not comprise "good faith" objections.   These questions, as the one concerning the AIDS
victim's physical ability to perform job tasks, must be
resolved on an individual basis.

President Bush and congressional leaders agreed in August
1989 to support legislation that will extend the protection of
Title VII of the 1964 Civil Rights Act to disabled persons,
including those Americans with the virus or ill with AIDS.
Such legislation, when enacted, will provide federal protection for the disabled against job discrimination.   The law as
proposed will first apply to private employers of twenty-five
persons or more, but eventually it would cover employers with
a minimum of fifteen employees.   These employers, then, will
not be legally able to dismiss or refuse employment to
qualified persons because those people have AIDS or they test
positive for the HIV virus.   Presently, disabled persons are
protected under the Rehabilitation Act of 1973, which prohibits discrimination by federal agencies and by employers
receiving federal funds.

Consequently, if a firm employs a testing program and
discovers antibodies to AIDS in certain workers, it must
proceed according to the above guidelines.   Further, the firm
must follow the same precautions enunciated in the earlier
section concerning drug and alcohol screening to avoid
lawsuits based on common law remedies in tort and contract
law, especially invasion of privacy.   Predictive screening to
determine who is likely to develop AIDS is even more unreliable.   Neither the presence of ARC nor seropositivity in a
person through a screening test necessarily indicates that the
person has or will have AIDS.   Still, firms that wish to test
should follow additional safeguards: (1) the firm should
require every job applicant or employee being tested to
execute a consent form, (2) the firm should ensure that the
consent is informed and the person has an understanding of the
social and medical natures of an HIV infection, (3) the firm
should refer those who test positively for HIV to counseling
to help them deal with the repercussions and to prevent the
spread of the virus, and (4) the firm must maintain positive
test results as absolutely confidential.

Genetics: The Scope

In American laboratories, many biologists have embarked on a
$3 billion project to transcribe the genetic assembly and
operating manual for the human body.   The goal is to obtain
the over three billion letters of genetic instructions that
direct the human body's functioning.   In the process,
scientists will seek ways to detect and predict thousands of
genetic components of hypertension, depression, diabetes,
heart disease, alcoholism, Alzheimer's disease, and cancer.

The effort, known as the Human Genome Project, seeks to
link every instruction in a person's complete set of genes
(genome) to one of the body's functions.   By understanding the
process, scientists will be able to ascertain the diseases and
conditions to which a person is susceptible.   The use of this
knowledge raises momentous issues in every fact of a person's

life and augers limited job selection, matched marriage partners, and variable costs of insurance based on a person's proclivity to develop a particular disease.

Genetic Testing: Screening and Monitoring. A number of incentives exist for employers to genetically test applicants and current employees. Medical and business ethics reinforce the basic concept that people should not be exposed to hazardous conditions. OSHA has implemented this principle through regulations concerning the workplace. In addition, one author has specified the advantages of medical screening: reduction in civil liability, absenteeism, sick leave, turnover, health insurance and workers' compensation costs, and the maintenance or enhancement of the firm's goodwill.[26]

Genetic testing is comprised of genetic screening and genetic monitoring. Genetic screening is a one-time testing to ascertain whether a person has any heritable traits that would predispose him or her to an occupational malady, exemplified by testing to determine genetic error in metabolism (thalassemia). In 1983 the Office of Technology Assessment (OTA) determined that there was an insufficient correlation between certain genetic traits (i.e., sickle cell trait) and enhanced susceptibility to occupational illness to warrant screening.[27] Typically, firms focus genetic screening on job applicants.

Genetic monitoring, on the other hand, serves a universally praised function by periodically examining the body fluids of employees to determine chromosomal damage from exposure to toxic materials in the workplace such as vinyl chloride and benzene. Although in its technological infancy, genetic monitoring offers benefits in establishing safe exposure levels and protecting employee safety.[28]

Genetic screening is essentially the assessment of a future health status. The firm considers whether a person's biochemical or chromosomal genetic character and composition are likely to influence his or her ability to perform job tasks in the future. Conversely, examinations that test vision, hearing, and controlled substance abuse measure current health status and, specifically, whether the applicant or current employee, with reasonable accommodation, can safely and efficiently discharge the indispensable tasks of the employment.

Other types of predictive screening, similar to genetic screening, include: (1) evaluation of general health status by considering past illness and current clinical testing, (2) appraising behavioral factors, including diet, tobacco, drug, and alcohol usage; lifestyle activities; and psychological factors (a type of screening discussed in prior sections of this chapter), (3) assessing innate characteristics, uncontrollable by the applicant or employee, such as sex, race, age, and family health history, and (4) examining medical status relative to past occupational exposures, a process that includes detecting reactions to chemicals and chromosomal changes through genetic scanning.[29]

Predictive screening, although valuable to the firm, presents scientific difficulties. For example, a person may not actually develop a genetically heritable malady suffered by that person's parent. Factors such as diet and obesity are relevant to the development of certain types of cancer but not to others.   Further, any prediction is speculative; medical screening offers health forecasts two and three decades in the future. As long as it is aware of these inherent short-comings, the firm averts unwarranted dependence on predictive screening as the sole indicator of fitness for particular employment.

Application of genetic screening, although helpful, may suffer serious impediments through lawsuits brought pursuant to Title VII of the 1964 Civil Rights Act.   Many genetic markers evaluated in genetic screening are assigned more heavily to certain ethnic and racial groups. To overcome the possible legal challenge to this disparate impact of genetic testing, the firm must satisfy the business necessity or job-relatedness threshold.   In this regard, in one Title VII lawsuit challenging genetic-related employer action, the Fifth Circuit upheld a decision to terminate an employee with sickle cell anemia. In a contrary decision, a 1980 Equal Employment Opportunity Commission (EEOC) decision held that a similar termination contravened Title VII.[30]

CONCLUSIONS

The use by business firms of testing to determine controlled substance abuse, alcohol abuse, the presence of the AIDS virus, HIV, and genetic damage or predisposition is expanding inexorably.   Critics of testing argue that the concomitant invasion of privacy, a right described by Justice Brandeis as the "right most valued by civilized man,"[31] is an insidious by-product of testing.   Testing is naturally intrusive and certainly can be abused by overreaching employers.   Studies indicate a potential for inaccurate and unreliable results. In addition, many consider testing to be a quick fix for a complex penumbra of social problems.

Nonetheless, the firm does have the right to expect that its employees will be reasonably productive and not inhibit the safety of the workplace. Proper testing programs for drug and alcohol abuse have produced numerous benefits, including improvements in employee morale, work quality, productivity, and accident and absence rates.

Firms should necessarily regulate testing for illegal drugs, alcoholism, AIDS, and genetic damage and predisposition in accordance with standards and guidelines articulated in this chapter.   In addition, this self-regulation should include:

1. Elimination of all ill-conceived tests after an audit of existing tests.

2. Establishment of a testing committee with a mission to weigh the often-competing interests of the firm and the employee.

3. Ensuring the dignity of the employee at all times.

4. Assurance of the highest reliability of the tests used and the utmost confidentiality of the results.

5. Avoidance of the misconception that testing is an effective substitute for education and, in the case of alcoholism and controlled substance abuse, for rehabilitation.

6. Establishing or allowing access for employees to assistance programs.

7. Avoiding the redirection of emphasis on reducing workplace hazards to mere control of exposed or ill workers.

8. Close monitoring of the dynamic development of the law of testing to fully comply with statutes and case law.

Self-regulation in this manner will likely preserve the firm's testing right and attendant benefits as well as the employee's dignity.

NOTES

1. Hamm, "Mandatory Drug Testing: Balancing the Interests," _Arizona Law Review_ (1988): 297, in which were cited _Business Week_ and _Time_ articles.
2. National Institute on Drug Abuse survey citation in "Screening for Drug Use: Technical and Social Aspects," Grabowski and Lasagna, _Issues in Science and Technology_ (Winter 1987).
3. English, "Getting Tough on Worker Abuse of Drugs; Alcohol," _U.S. News and World Report_ (December 5, 1983): 85.
4. Abramowitz and Hamilton, "Drug Testing on Rise: Corporate Concern Up But Abuse is Down," _Washington Post_ (September 21, 1986) D1, col. 1.
5. Research Triangle Institute, _Economic Costs to Society of Alcohol and Drug Abuse and Mental Illness: 1980_ (1984): 6.
6. "The Ruckus Over Medical Testing," _Fortune_ (August 19, 1985): 57.
7. _Restatement (2d) of Agency_, 212–218 (1957); see also Prosser and Keeton, _The Law of Torts_, 5th ed. (St. Paul, MN: West, 1984), 568–577.
8. 668 S.W. 2d 307 (Texas, 1983).
9. 29 _U.S.C._, Section 654 (a)(i)(1982).
10. Castro, "Battling the Enemy Within," _Time_ (March 17, 1986): 52–53.
11. Hoffer, "A New Focus on Drugs," _Nation's Business_ (December, 1986): 57.
12. Ibid, 58.
13. Ungarola, "Mandatory Drug Testing in the Workplace, Protect Safety, Not Drug Abuse," _American Bar Association Journal_ 34 (1986): 34 .
14. Englade, "Who's Hired and Who's Fired," _Student Lawyer_ (April 1986): 23.
15. Rothstein, "Screening Workers for Drugs: A Legal and Ethical Framework," _Empl. Rel. L.J._ 11 (1985–86): 433.
16. See the constitutions of Alaska, Arizona, California, Florida, Hawaii, Illinois, Louisiana, South Carolina, and Washington.
17. See Prosser and Keaton, _The Law of Torts_, Section 117; see also the California Constitution, Article I, Section 1.
18. _Restatement (Second) of Torts_, Section 594 (1977).
19. Baker, _A.I.D.S.—Everything You Must Know About Acquired Immune Deficiency Syndrome_ (Saratoga, CA: R&E Publications, 1983), 9. Symptoms include chills, rapid weight loss, extreme fatigue, swollen lymph glands, shortness of breath, diarrhea, and infections that do not heal normally.

20. Bloom and Carliner, "The Economic Impact of AIDS in the United States," Science (February 4, 1988): 604-609; see also Morgan and Curran, Public Health Report #101,459 (September-October 1986).
21. See Bayer, Levine and Wolf, "HIV Antibody Screening: An Ethical Framework for Evaluating Proposed Programs," J.A.M.A. 256 (1986): 1768, as cited in Kleiman, "AIDS, Vice, and Public Policy,"   Law and Contemporary Problems 51 (Winter 1988): 329, and discussion: 329-333.
22. "Georgia Tech Poll Finds AIDS Fears in Workplace," Wall Street Journal (April 4, 1988): 14.
23. "Employers Back Rights Guidelines for AIDS Victims," Wall Street Journal (February 18, 1988).
24. "When Fear of AIDS Freezes an Agency," Washington Post (February 4, 1988): A-21.
25. Leonard, "Employment Discrimination Against Persons with AIDS,   U. Dayton L. Rev. 10 (1985): 681.
26. Rothstein, op. cit., 675.
27. Ibid, 679.28.Ibid, 679-680.
29. Ibid, 676-677.
30. Ibid, 680, which cites Smith v. Olin Chemical Corporation, 555 F. 2d 1283 (5th Circuit 1977) and EEOC Dec. No. 81-8, 27 Fair Emplt. Prac. Cas. (BNA) 1781 (1980).
31. Olmstead v. United States, 277 U.S. 478 (1928) (Brandeis, J., dissenting).

4

Preventing Sexual and Nonsexual Harassment in the Work Environment

INTRODUCTION

Despite much progress in breaking down employment barriers, employees, primarily women, still encounter discrimination on the job in the form of sexual harassment. What is more, sexual harassment is likely to occur in white, as well as blue, collar employment. Men, too, have been harassed, and will be more prone to sexual harassment as greater numbers of women occupy supervisory and managerial positions. Homosexual harassment also occurs, with distressing consequences to the victim. In fact, according to a survey by Venture, a publication for small business owners, 62% of women recounted sexual harassment in the workplace, as did 38% of the men, two-thirds by other men. Sexual harassment, nonetheless, usually involves men harassing women. Since the most significant change in the labor market in the late 1980s has been the influx of women (60% of persons entering the labor force were women) and because by the year 2000 over 66% of new entrants will be women, the problem of sexual harassment will be exacerbated.

Recently, in one firm's meeting of department heads, male managers tossed a prophylactic back and forth while offering provocative comments, even though two female department heads were present. Moreover, at the Boston office of Goldman Sachs, a leading investment banking firm, Kristine Utley was the only female sales associate in the money market department. Utley charged the firm's environment as "hostile, intimidating, and sexist" in a suit filed in December 1987. According to Utley, the sexual harassment at Goldman included firm memos that announced the hiring of new female employees, with each memo containing a photograph of a naked pinup. Utley also described literature routinely circulated at Goldman containing jokes. "Why beer is better than a woman," an example of the literature, included the rejoinder, "A beer doesn't get jealous when you grab another beer" and "a beer always goes down easy."

Some observers consider sexual harassment as tantamount to "corporate rape" and point to the multitude of cases in which male supervisors have offered jobs and promotions to women as inducements for sex favors. In other situations, women experience coercion to submit to men's demands for sexual favors or risk losing employment. Catherine Broderick, a Securities and Exchange Commission lawyer, proved in court that her superiors frequently awarded promotions and salary increases to women with whom they had sexual relationships. A federal court agreed and found the affairs created an offensive work environment. As a result, in 1988 the court ordered the SEC to award Broderick several promotions and retroactive salary increases; the total settlement was $145,000.

For others, the harassment takes the form of a hostile, abusive workplace, with or without a demand for sexual favors. Deborah Katz, a Herndon, Virginia, air traffic controller suffered verbal taunting on the job—she was referred to as "the cow" and "the bitch." Although Katz prevailed in her sexual harassment suit in 1983 against the Department of Transportation, she recounts the difficulty of returning to the workplace: "It's like being sent back to your parents after a court finds they abused you sexually."

Firms that refuse to eliminate sexual harassment face lawsuits, disastrous public relations, negative publicity, and loss of business. A 1989 Forbes survey indicates that in California, settlements for sexual harassment cases average $300,000. For instance, Fallon McElligott's flip response to a woman who alleged sexist advertising directly caused the loss of a major client. In October of 1988, Neala Schleuning, the female director of Mankato State University's women's center, termed as "negative stereotypes" Fallon McElligott's advertisement about "Dynasty," the television program, which placed over photos of three female stars the headline, "Bitch, Bitch, Bitch." The agency responded to Schleuning's criticism by sending her a photograph of a naked African boy with his face pressed against the rear of a cow and the suggestion that the woman would "be able to deal with these people in the same firm, evenhanded manner."[1]

When US West received a copy of that and subsequent regrettable correspondence by the ad firm, it terminated the firm, which had worked for US West since the latter's founding in 1983, from the estimated $10 million renewal of its corporate ad business. Other Fallon McElligott clients, including Federal Express, Continental Illinois Bank, Lee Jeans, and Porsche USA, expressed no plans to drop the firm but certainly could if the ad firm commits subsequent improprieties. "We just overreacted and used bad judgment," explains a chastised Patrick Fallon.

NATURE AND SCOPE OF THE PROBLEM

Sexual harassment is a widespread problem that exists in every type of employment. In 1985, 7,273 sexual harassment complaints were filed with the Equal Employment Opportunity Commission (EEOC) for review, a prerequisite before a plaintiff can file a federal court action under Title VII of the 1964 Civil Rights Act. A 1988 Wall Street Journal survey of sex discrimination complaints filed with the EEOC specifies that 9% involved sexual harassment.

Further, in a survey of federal employees,[2] 42% of the 694,000 women and 15% of the 1,168,000 men indicate they have experienced some form of harassment. Moreover, a U.S. Navy study released at approximately the same time reports that over one-half of the navy women interviewed responded that they had been subjects of sexual harassment.

Other reports estimate that at least 49% of working women in various occupations have experienced sexual harassment and 51% of women have been victims of or witness to sexual harassment on the job.   In a November 1976 Redbook/Harvard Business Review survey, 90% of the women who responded to a questionnaire reported that they had "experienced one or more forms of unwanted attention on the job."[3] Numerous other more recent studies report varying levels of sexual harassment: 42% in a BNA survey of members of its Personnel Policies Forum; over 50% of females and nearly 40% of males in a Los Angeles County survey; and 42% of women and 15% of men in a Merit Systems Protection Board Study.   Incidence of sexual harassment is a problem abroad as well: the authors of "Sexual Harassment in the Workplace—Women Defend Themselves" estimate that 25% of West German working women have been subjects of sexual harassment.

In 1980 Harvard Business Review conducted another joint survey with Redbook on the issue.   One finding from HBR subscribers is that the respondents believe that sexual harassment is a serious matter: 10% have witnessed or been told of a situation in their firms to the effect that a person who has refused sex has received a poor evaluation or similar detriment.   Other major survey findings include: sexual harassment is perceived as an issue of power, with a supervisor's behavior as more threatening than a coworker's even in exactly similar situations; men and women disagree on the frequency of sexual harassment while agreeing in general on what that harassment comprises; lower level managers are much more aware of sexual harassment occurrences than mid- or high-level managers; most view the EEOC guidelines on sexual harassment as reasonable; and 73% of respondents are in favor of company policies against harassment, but only 29% work in firms where such policies have been promulgated.

Moreover, although persons usually agree that certain extreme circumstances constitute sexual harassment, there is a wide divergence of perceptions in less obvious cases.   For instance, in the Harvard Business Review survey,[4] 87% of the respondents believe the following description indicates sex abuse: "I have been having an affair with the head of my division.   Now I've told him I want to break it off, but he says I will lose out on the promotion I've been expecting." Other circumstances elicited similar judgments: 90% believe a boss's pinching or patting an employee when she enters his office is sexual harassment and 78% label as harassment an employee's receiving a poor evaluation from her supervisor after refusing to have sex with him.

On the other hand, in the same Harvard Business Review survey, views on less extreme behavior evidenced a supervisor/coworker disagreement on what constituted sexual harassment.   For instance, in the following described situations, when the term "a man I work with" is substituted for "supervisor," the rate of those describing the act as sexual harassment decreases, often significantly: (1) "Whenever I go into the office, my supervisor eyes me up and down, making me feel uncomfortable. (This is, or possibly is, harassment, say 76%, up from 69% when "a man I work with" is used instead of "supervisor."); (2) "My supervisor starts each day with a sexual remark. He insists it's an innocent social comment." (It is harassment, or possibly is, say 90%, but 86% say it is harassment when "man I work with" is used in the description.); (3) "Every time we meet, my supervisor kisses me on the cheek." (Sixty-seven percent believe this circumstance is, or possibly is, co-worker harassment. (This is labeled harassment by 80%, but 67% say it is, or possibly is, coworker harassment when "the man I work with" is used.); (4) "My supervisor asked me out on a date. Although I refused, he continues to ask me." (Whereas 61% consider this as coworker harassment or possible harassment, if "the man I work with" is used, 87% view it as such when "supervisor" is used.)

In all cases, the perceived gravity of the harassment depends on who is making the advance (supervisor or coworker), the degree of apparent serious intent, and the victim's understanding of the consequences of either responding positively or negatively. Further, there is a striking difference in the perception between men and women as well as upper level and lower level managers. For example, 66% of men and 63% of high-level managers "agree or partly agree" with the assertion, "The amount of sexual harassment at work is greatly exaggerated," whereas only 32% of women and 44% of lower level managers agree."[5] Nonetheless, according to the overwhelming weight of studies and surveys, sexual and other harassment is a pervasive problem. Moreover, workforce demographics and increasing sensitivity are elements that suggest greater liability for business firms unless they effectively address sexual and other harassment on the job.

THE COSTS OF PERCEIVED SEXUAL HARASSMENT

Catherine MacKinnon, in her book, Sexual Harassment of Working Women, rejects the argument that sexual harassment should be dismissed as harmless incidents of natural attraction. She recognizes that the problem is one of perception, "[T]he near-universal response of authoritative men—employers and husbands . . . to women's complaints of sexual harassment is to consider them personal incidents" (p. 83). Certainly, people who have contrasting frames of reference could scarcely be expected to easily define or resolve the problem.

The cost of sexual harassment in monetary and personal terms is staggering. The federal government, a civil service study expounds, spent an estimated $267 million from 1985 to 1987 as a result of harassment to replace employees who left work permanently, to pay sick leave for absences, and to compensate reduced productivity. The cost in the private sector is much greater.

Most telling, however, are the grave physical, psychological, and economic effects on the victims. The most common manifestations of the psychological injury include: increased stress and feelings of "powerlessness, fear, anger, nervousness"[6] sometimes leading to complete emotional breakdown. According to a 1979 Working Women's Institute study, 96% of sexual harassment victims surveyed displayed psychological symptoms such as anger and fear, and 12% sought psychological therapy. The physical effects include nausea, headaches, loss of appetite, fatigue, and often substantial weight change—effects that 63% of the participants in the Working Women's Institute survey experienced.

Further, sexual harassment poses a serious threat to a woman's economic advancement. The harassed worker faces conflict and stress every day—factors that tend to inhibit anyone's job effectiveness. If the harassed worker remains on the job, the stress may continue with expected negative effects on job performance. Conflict of this nature diminishes an employee's ambition and decreases job satisfaction. The employee may be forced to resign or be terminated because of refusing to submit to demands for sex or quit because of offensive working conditions.[7] The collective implications of the physical, emotional, and economic results of sexual harassment are devastating. Clearly, no employee, male or female, should suffer such assaults to individual dignity as a condition of employment.

TITLE VII: DEFINITIONS AND STANDARDS OF EMPLOYER LIABILITY

The federal courts have recognized sexual harassment in the workplace as a form of employment discrimination prohibited by Title VII of the Civil Rights Act of 1964. Under Title VII, only employers may be held liable for sexual harassment in the workplace, no matter the identity of the actual offender. The term "employer" refers to a person engaged in an industry affecting commerce who has fifteen or more employees and any agent of such a firm. Moreover, as of 1990 many states and local governments have outlawed sexual harassment in anti-discrimination statutes and ordinances.

Sexual harassment defies exact definition because of the substantial number of ways it is manifested. Nonetheless, several authors have proposed plenary definitions of sexual harassment. It has been defined as "the unwanted imposition of sexual requirements in the context of a relationship of unequal power,"[8] and, "any attention of a sexual nature in the context of a work situation which has the effect of making a woman uncomfortable on the job, impeding her ability to do her work or interfering with her employment opportunities."[9] Examples of sexual harassment under these definitions include: criticizing or commenting upon another's body; unsolicited kissing, squeezing, pinching, or grabbing of another's body; unsolicited propositions; suggestions or demands for dates or sexual activity; placing in the work environment an obscene picture; derogatory jokes; staring; ogling; any unsolicited touching; and forced sexual activity.[10]

Sexual harassment[11] is defined by the EEOC as: Unwelcome sexual advances, requests for sexual favors, and other verbal or physical conduct of a sexual nature . . . when (1) submission to such conduct is made either explicitly or implicitly a term or condition of an individual's employment, (2) submission to or rejection of such conduct by an individual is used as the basis for employment decisions affecting such individual, or (3) such conduct has the purpose or effect of unreasonably interfering with an individual's work performance or creating an intimidating, hostile, or offensive work environment.

The EEOC guidelines do not have the binding force of substantive law because they are promulgated by an agency, not Congress. Nonetheless, courts seriously consider them in their rulings. Types 1 and 2 above comprise traditional sexual harassment, also known as quid pro quo harassment, which involves "a demand for sexual favors in return for the promise of some benefit to the employee, such as a promotion, or the threat of some punishment, such as discharge or demotion."[12] The type of person who harasses is one who can reward, punish, or blackmail the employee. Under current law, only supervisors and managers can commit quid pro quo sexual harassment.

Type 3, on the other hand, describes the harassing environment that, relatively, has been more recently recognized by the courts. Such harassment creates a hostile, intimidating, or offensive work environment, and differs from the first and second types, because employment benefits are not necessarily threatened, as coworkers as well as supervisors can commit the harassment, and as this particular harassment requires a number of actions over a period of time.

Whereas the employer is generally vicariously liable for quid pro quo harassment, most courts have established a stricter standard for "hostile environment" cases. In the latter situation, the employer will not be held liable unless th employer knows, or should have known, of the coworker harassment and took no remedial steps to obviate it. Courts have focused on two criteria to assess employer liability in hostile environment cases: the type of harassment and the managerial level of the offender. Courts that focus on the nature of the harassment as the operative criterion usually hold that the employer should not be vicariously liable because the supervisor's power as a manager does not assist him in creating the hostile environment. On the contrary, courts that emphasize the managerial level of the offender generally hold the employer vicariously liable for the verbal, visual, or physical misconduct of the supervisor that actually created the hostile or offensive working environment.[13]

The major division among the courts today, however, relates to the standard of employer liability for hostile work environments created by supervisors. In contrast, under quid pro quo harassment, the employer's vicarious liability derives from the fault of the employee (supervisor or manager), regardless of whether the employer was actually aware of the harassment. In a landmark case, a federal circuit court held that a supervisor who harassed an employee had acted within the scope of his employment, and ruled that "respondent superior does apply here" because "the action complained of was that of a supervisor, authorized to hire, fire, discipline or promote, or at least to participate in or recommend such actions, although what the supervisor is said to have done violates company policy." [Emphasis added][14]

The unique factual composition of many sexual harassment claims render such cases difficult to adjudicate. Sexual advances in the workplace may be perceived as natural attraction. Whereas quid pro quo sexual harassment is easily recognizable because of the demanded tradeoff and direct economic consequences, the hostile environment type is not. The same actions can be perceived as offensive to women but harmless to men.

Concluding whether particular conduct is actionable sexual harassment can be based either on an objective or subjective standard. An objective test would seek to answer whether an ordinary employee would have been offended by the particular conduct in question. Under a subjective test, the uniqueness of the sensitivities of the alleged victim would be weighed.[15] Moreover, many court decisions have applied a judicial standard stricter than that of the EEOC guidelines. For instance, although the guidelines suggest that a single incident could be sexual harassment of any type, the courts usually require evidence of a pattern of harassment and that the pattern of conduct be severe or pervasive. Consequently, even a pattern of offensive conduct or speech does not necessarily form the basis for a Title VII action. In one case, a federal district court held that a male supervisor's vulgar language and the display of erotic posters of women by male coworkers did not constitute a hostile working environment to the detriment of a female office employee.[16]

Title VII Remedies and Relief: Cases Leading to Meritor

The first legal claims of sexual harassment as a form of job discrimination arose in the mid-1970s and the women plaintiffs were unsuccessful. In <u>Miller v. Bank of America</u>,[17] the court required a demonstration that an employer's policy "imposes or permits consistent, as distinguished from isolated, sex-based discrimination on a definable employee group" as a precondition for a Title VII violation. In <u>Miller</u>, a bank employee alleged that her supervisor discharged her when she refused to be sexually cooperative. In <u>Corne v. Bausch & Lomb</u>,[18] clerical workers claimed that their supervisor's continuous verbal and physical sexual advances effectively coerced them to resign their employment. The <u>Corne</u> court determined the sexual advances to be a "personal proclivity," not sufficiently related to the workplace context.

The landmark decision in the case of <u>Williams v. Saxbe</u>[19] held that a claim of sex discrimination is demonstrated when a male supervisor retaliates against a female employee who refuses his sexual overtures. The <u>Williams</u> court also noted the supervisor's actions created a job place environment that discriminates on the basis of gender. In a later case, another court found a Title VII violation by an employer when a supervisor made a sexual proposition, even when he did not carry out the threat of punishment.[20] Moreover, <u>Rogers v. EEOC</u>[21] was the first case to recognize a legal cause of action based on a discriminatory work environment. In that case, a Hispanic plaintiff established a violation of Title VII by proving her optometrist employer created an offensive workplace environment through the optometrist's segregating the patients. A decade later, the 11th Circuit concluded in <u>Henson v. City of Dundee</u>[22] "that a hostile or offensive atmosphere can, standing alone, constitute a violation of Title VII."

One of the broadest interpretations of sexual harassment has resulted from the ruling in <u>McKinney v. Dole</u>.[23] McKinney, the female plaintiff, alleged that her male supervisor prevented her from leaving her office by twisting her arm. The employer of the supervisor argued that there were no sexual connotations to the action. Nonetheless, the court upheld McKinney's legal right to bring suit under a sexual harassment theory and ruled that any unequal treatment that would not occur except for the sex of the employee could "if sufficiently patterned or pervasive, comprise an illegal condition of employment under Title VII."

The Meritor Decision: Relief and Inadequacy of Relief under Title VII

The Supreme Court unanimously acknowledged for the first time a cause of action under Title VII for sexual harassment in 1986 in <u>Meritor Savings Bank, FSB v. Vinson</u>.[24] The Court clearly established in <u>Meritor</u> that Title VII protection extends beyond economic or tangible discrimination to noneconomic discrimination in a hostile or offensive work environment.

In 1974 Mechelle Vinson was hired to work at a branch office managed by Sidney Taylor, a vice president of Meritor Savings Bank. She was eventually promoted to assistant branch manager as a result of an excellent job performance but was discharged in 1978 for excessive use of sick leave. During her employment after her training period, Vinson later testified at her sex harassment trial that she agreed to have sex with Taylor because she feared losing her job if she refused. Vinson claimed over "the next several years she had intercourse with Taylor forty to fifty times," was fondled at work by him, and even sexually assaulted by him.

Vinson, further, related that she did not report the harassment incidents to Taylor's supervisors or lodge a formal grievance through the bank's established complaint procedure because she feared Taylor. Although Taylor had no power to employ, discharge, or promote employees at the branch, he could offer recommendations for such actions. Taylor denied all of Vinson's material allegations. The bank denied knowledge of, or authorization for, Taylor's alleged misconduct.

In <u>Meritor</u>, the Supreme Court recognized that a cause of action for sexual harassment existed when that harassment was "sufficiently severe or pervasive to alter the condition of the victim's employment and create an abusive working environment." Consequently, not all workplace sexual harassment is violative of Title VII if that harassment does not meet the "severe and pervasive" or the "altering of workplace" requirements. After dismissing the assertion that voluntary sexual relations is a proper defense, the Court pointed to the critical question as being whether the sexual activities were "unwelcome." In essence, the Court maintained that voluntary actions can be unwelcome and, hence, actionable under Title VII. The Court, however, asserted that a complainant's sexually provocative speech or dress "is obviously relevant" in determining whether "she found particular sexual advances unwelcome."

Nonetheless, the Supreme Court in Meritor rejected the lower court's holding that employers are strictly liable for their supervisors' sexual harassment.   The Court thereby refused to endorse the prior EEOC guidelines that urged strict liability for employers.   In lieu of the standard of strict liability, the Court adopted the newly constructed EEOC position that agency principles be considered by lower courts as a standard for employer liability.   Moreover, the Supreme Court in Meritor rejected the bank's view that employers are not liable when employees fail to avail themselves of clearly established employer grievance procedures against sexual harassment.   The Court did not define precisely what behavior constitutes sexual harassment, instead referring to the vague EEOC guidelines.

The Meritor decision failed to clarify or remedy a number of issues.   The Supreme Court did not precisely define what actions do or do not constitute sexual harassment; nor did the Court address the inadequate remedies under Title VII.   When an employer is held liable for illegal sexual discrimination, under Title VII the court may enjoin the employer's discrimination and "order such affirmative action as may be appropriate, which may include, but is not limited to, reinstatement or hiring of employees, with or without back pay . . . or any other equitable relief as the court deems appropriate." The court also may award the plaintiff a reasonable attorney's fee.   Equitable relief under Title VII is limited to tangible losses: reinstatement, back pay, lost employment benefits, and attorney's fees—relief that has meaning primarily to victims of quid pro quo harassment.   Victims of work environment discrimination have the incommensurate remedies of injunctions and attorney's fees.   Moreover, Title VII does not allow the victim compensatory or punitive damages—for lost earning capacity or for nonmonetary harm such as severe emotional distress or physical harm.   Consequently, many successful Title VII plaintiffs procure rather hollow victories.

In addition, there is an extremely short statute of limitations within which the Title VII claim must be brought, or it is forever barred.   Last, the statute applies only to employers with fifteen or more employees; hence, harassment victims in smaller firms receive no protection under Title VII, although most states have enacted antisexual harassment statutes that apply to firms of every size.

Remedies Beyond Title VII

Firms should be aware that even when relief is not available or desirable through Title VII, the victim of sexual harassment has a wide choice of other legal causes of action,[25] one or more that may fit the victim's circumstances: tort law, equal protection under the constitution, statutory law, breach of contract, and criminal law.

Historically, traditional tort causes of action were the only vehicles for legal reparation for sexual harassment victims before the courts extended Title VII protection to prohibit this type of discrimination.   Tort recovery includes the possible recovery of both compensatory and punitive damages—awards that respond to the physical, monetary, and psychological harm done the victim.   Tort actions offer the additional advantages over Title VII lawsuits of less complex procedures, the right to jury trial, and a longer statute of limitations within which to file the claim.   Nonetheless, sexual harassment is not yet recognized as an independent tort; a sexually harassed plaintiff must prove the elements of a recognized tort to recover. Battery, for instance, requires contact with the plaintiff.   Assault, on the other hand, requires the plaintiff's imminent apprehension of offensive or harmful conduct. If the plaintiff has experienced or anticipated physical contact, then recovery is possible. However, verbal abuse generally is not actionable under battery or assault torts unless the victim demonstrates circumstances that caused the plaintiff's reasonable apprehension of imminent contact.[26]

Most states allow damages recovery for misconduct that causes severe emotional distress. Restatement (Second) of Torts defines this tort as follows: "One who by extreme and outrageous conduct intentionally causes severe emotional distress to another is subject to liability for such emotional distress, and if bodily harm to the other results from it, for such bodily harm."[27] This tort's efficacy is limited in sexual harassment suits because many harassment acts, to a jury, are more irritating than outrageous. For instance, pestering has been held not sufficiently outrageous to trigger the applicability of the emotional distress tort. Further, there is no recognized definition of "outrageous conduct." Nevertheless, the threat of economic coercion in sexual harassment has been the basis of successful legal claims under the tort of infliction of emotional distress.[28] In one such case, Howard University v. Best, a female professor claimed that a male dean's unrequited sexual advances caused her termination of employment.   The court rejected the limp assertion that such conduct was a "social impropriety" and found the conduct outrageous. Yet, in other jurisdictions the courts have held that sexual harassment is not outrageous conduct.[29]

Furthermore, in an invasion of privacy suit, the plaintiff must demonstrate an expectation of privacy. The Restatement (Second) of Torts, Section 21, defines this tort as an invasion, "physically or otherwise, upon the solitude or seclusion of another or his private affairs or concerns . . . if the intrusion would be highly offensive to a reasonable person." Basically, all quid pro quo sexual harassment is an invasion of privacy because it usually is accompanied by the offending party's demands and questioning of the victim. Under this theory, a victim has stated a claim for invasion of privacy by allegations that her supervisor had called her at home and made unseemly remarks about her sexual life.[30]

A claim of interference with contractual relations, moreover, only protects the plaintiff against the action of a third party, assuming a contract between the plaintiff and an employer.[31]   The plaintiff must show that a supervisor or coworker, by sexual harassment, procured the plaintiff's discharge.[32] In every event, this tort theory requires proof of economic harm as psychological damages are absolutely excluded, it does not apply to the termination of employees at will, and it precludes recovery against the employer.

An employee who is terminated from employment as a result of sexual harassment may have a remedy under a tort or contract theory of wrongful discharge. Courts have found an express or implied contract for continued employment in employee handbooks, even without an otherwise express contract.[33]

Tort recovery, then, offers numerous avenues for a sexually harassed victim. The victim can recover compensatory and punitive damages for injury to her personal interests—formidable weapons in any lawsuit. Nonetheless, the victim cannot recover against the employer—rather, only against a coworker or a supervisor unless that harassing employee or supervisor was acting within the scope of his employment, a highly unlikely circumstance given the definitions of the various tort theories.

The public employment employee has an additional remedy that is not extended to private sector employees—equal protection of the federal Constitution's Fourteenth Amendment. In Bohen,[34] a 1986 case, the court found that sexual harassment of the female plaintiff violated the equal protection clause. In that case, the plaintiff, a female dispatcher with a fire department, suffered repeated acts of sexual harassment in the form of hands pressed against her crotch and lewd language from coworkers and her supervisor. The court held: "Forcing women and not men to work in an environment of sexual harassment is no different than forcing women to work in a dirtier and more hazardous environment than men simply because they were women." Additionally, the Bohen court defined the scope of equal protection by asserting that a "single, innocent, romantic solicitation which inadvertently causes offense to its recipient is not a denial of equal protection."

Also, the sexually harassed victim may find a remedy in state antidiscrimination statutes,[35] criminal statutes ranging from battery and self-exposure to rape; and the private civil action under the Racketeer Influenced and Corrupt Organization Act (RICO).[36] The civil cause of action derived from RICO is grounded in activities indexed in the criminal provisions of RICO. In one such case, the plaintiff alleged that coworkers' continual sexual harassment hounded her to terminate her employment. The union shop steward had attempted to coerce her purchase of raffle tickets, even though the act constituted extortion under a state statute. The court upheld the plaintiff's cause of action under RICO.[37] In another case the court ruled that an allegedly sexually harassed plaintiff had standing to sue under RICO.[38]

OTHER WORKPLACE HARASSMENT

Nonsexual harassment in the workplace can be as demeaning, insidious, and destructive as sexual harassment. It inhibits productivity and morale growth and should never be tolerated. Examples of such harassment are: the use of profane, abusive, or demeaning language; disorderly conduct such as fighting; causing physical harm to another; intimidation; any activity or speech that disrupts other employees; slurs or jokes in bad taste; and any activity or speech that discriminates against any employee on the basis of race, color, religion, sex, national origin, ancestry, marital status, age, disability, or veteran status.

Title VII and other statutory and constitutional protections have been extended to victims of nearly every type of nonsexual harassment, which are comparable to sexually offensive environment cases because, unlike quid pro quo harassment, the supervisor or manager does not use authority to demand some act from the employee. Courts, moreover, have recognized that certain harassment does not influence an employment term, condition, or privilege so as to be actionable under Title VII.[39] For instance, in Rogers v. EEOC,[40] a federal court held that a "mere utterance of an ethnic or racial epithet which engenders offensive feelings in an employee" may not sufficiently change the offended employee's condition of employment so as to violate Title VII.

In cases of harassment under Title VII based on race, national origin, or religion, the courts generally impose vicarious liability on the employer for the supervisor's harassment. Specifically, the courts impute liability, in cases of a supervisor's or manager's misconduct, to the employer, based on the supervisor's acting within the scope of "his duties as supervisor"[41] or as an agent of his employer.[42] However, when a coworker is the perpetrator of racial or religious harassment, the courts generally apply a knowledge standard and often deny liability if that employer has taken prompt remedial action to quash the harassment.

1989 SUPREME COURT DECISIONS

Supreme Court decisions in 1989 limited an 1866 statute as the basis for lawsuits against racial harassment in the workplace.

In Patterson v. McLean Credit Union (Case No. 87-107), the Supreme Court ruled that Title 42 U.S.C. Section 1981 (originally enacted as part of the Civil Rights Act of 1866) does not apply to claims of racial harassment in the workplace. The Court held that "[r]acial harassment relating to the conditions of employment is not actionable under Section 1981, which provides that '[a]ll persons . . . shall have the same right . . . to make and enforce contracts . . . as is enjoyed by white citizens,' because that provision does not apply to conduct which occurs after the formation of a contract and which does not interfere with the right to enforce established contract obligations." The Court specifically indicated that it was not, in this case, overruling its 1976 decision in Runyon v. McCrary (427 U.S. 160), in which the Court ruled that Section 1981 "prohibits private schools from excluding children who are qualified for admission, solely on the basis of race." Moreover, the Court indicated that Section 1981 may still serve as the basis for job discrimination suits if they are based on an interference with the right to make a contract.

Justice Anthony Kennedy, author of the Patterson opinion, indicated that workers who allege harassment, as McLean, may bring suits under Title VII of the Civil Rights Act of 1964. Section 1981 is an attractive vehicle for employment discrimination lawsuits because prevailing plaintiffs can collect damages rather than the back pay limited by Title VII. In addition, Section 1981 also circumvents Title VII's more restrictive time limits for filing suit, as well as the more rigid procedural requirements that Title VII discrimination suits first be filed with the Equal Employment Opportunity Commission (EEOC).

In Jett v. DALLAS Independent School District (Case No. 87-2084), moreover, the Court ruled that a white football coach, whom a federal jury determined had been racially harassed and discriminated against by the school's black principal, could not bring suit against their joint employer (Dallas Independent School District). The Court held that, to recover under 42 U.S.C. Section 1981, a public employee must demonstrate that the discrimination resulted from "official policy or custom."

GUIDELINES TO PREVENT SEXUAL AND OTHER HARASSMENT

Sexual and other harassment claims are ripe for abuse. According to labor lawyer William C. Bruce, "Sexual harassment cases are . . . difficult to disprove because there are usually no witnesses other than the complainant and the protagonist." Consequently, because employers are "squeamish about the publicity," an unscrupulous plaintiff can achieve a quick settlement and destroy another person's career.[43]

The EEOC guidelines declare that "prevention is the best tool for the elimination of . . . harassment." Firms should abide by the following guidelines to protect their employees, supervisors, and managers, and their reputations, in an era of rising numbers of sexual and other harassment claims:

1. The firm should provide a work environment free from all types of harassment, and the chief executive officer should, in a reasoned and dignified manner, disseminate throughout the firm his or her commitment to this goal.

2. The firm should thoroughly identify offensive behavior, epithets, insults, and verbal abuse; specifically cite examples of prohibited acts; and definitively declare that sexual harassment and nonsexual harassment are forbidden in the workplace.

3. The firm should incorporate the definition and examples of item 1, above, in a comprehensive written policy statement in personnel manuals, codes of ethics and conduct, posted notices, and circulated memoranda. The policy's protective purview should include customers, suppliers, and visitors.

4. The policy should include sanctions against employees violating the policy. This policy section should catalog varying degrees of punishment depending on the category and frequency of the harassing conduct.

5. The firm should establish and periodically update educational workshops with the tone of education and prevention to explain the policy, the implementation, and the administration of the reporting procedures under the policy to all employees, including management. Consciousness-raising seminars can effectively inform managers and supervisors of the consequences of their misconduct. The firm can use commercially prepared videos, such as "Shades of Gray," produced by Learning International. Merck, for instance, has provided funds for production of helpful materials by an outside group.

6. The firm should thoroughly explain the antiharassment policy to all new recruits in periodically updated training sessions.

7. At all employee meetings, educational workshops, and training sessions, managers and compliance officers should encourage employees to pose serious questions about the policy and to report any complaints of sexual or other harassment.

8. The firm should assign responsibility of the antiharassment program to a high-level person—a vice president or ranking assistant to the chief executive officer. The firm's reporting and grievance procedure should be strictly confidential to encourage reporting of all incidents of harassment. The firm should identify trustworthy supervisors, personnel officers, and an outside person or ombudsman to receive and investigate complaints. When employers are dedicated to a viable grievance system with effective sanctions and mediation exercises, the employee finds less need to file a sex or other discrimination suit, and the courts are less likely to find the employer liable.[44] A complainant should not be required to address his or her grievances to a superior.

9. Upon receiving a complaint, the firm should direct its compliance officer, ombudsman, or other person or persons comprising the grievance committee, often with the help of the firm's lawyer, to conduct an immediate and thorough investigation. The investigation should include questioning the employee who filed the grievance, the employee against whom the grievance is raised, and any other employees. The more complete the investigation, the more likely a clear decision can be reached.

10. If the investigation reveals that there was sexual or other harassment, the firm's remedial measures should include, at a minimum, removal of the employee from the work area and disciplining of the harasser. The courts have sustained a number of the firm's sanctions, including termination of the harasser's employment. In all cases, those who determine the sanction should consider the nature of the harassment as well as the

totality of circumstances surrounding the harassment, including the reputation of the harasser.

For instance, first-time harassers could receive a written caution that a more severe penalty will be levied if the offensive conduct is not abandoned. A second-time abuser would receive suspension without remuneration, and a repeated violation would draw a discharge.

11. If the investigation verifies no credible evidence of harassment after the accused employee denies the complaint, the accused should be considered innocent, and the accused's employment file should be purged of that accusation of sexual or other harassment.

12. The firm should not deviate from the established policy and procedure, although it should periodically review and modify it, if necessary.

13. The firm should ensure that it treats all employees alike and require that all employees, including managers, strictly adhere to the firm's policy.

14. The firm should allow the complainant the first option, prior to submitting the complaint in the formal procedure, of informally writing a private letter that details the offensive conduct to the alleged offending party. This step should be taken after a confidential conference with an appropriate officer who is on the committee described in item 8, above. A confrontation by letter has many positive benefits:[45]   third-party intervention in harassment cases often polarizes the parties involved; the offended and offender have an opportunity to see things the same way; the offender, perhaps wrongfully accused, has an opportunity for defense by responding; the offended party allows the offending party a warning and a chance to make amends; the offended party has an opportunity to halt the harassment without provoking a public counterattack; and the offended party can demonstrate that he or she took all reasonable steps to halt the offender's conduct prior to the filing of a grievance.

15. The firm should take reasonable steps permanently to eliminate in the work environment not only the overt acts of discrimination and harassment, but also those customary patterns of behavior and cultural stereotyping that limit opportunities for certain of society's groups.

16. The firm should promote employee access to social workers, psychologists, psychiatrists, and employee assistance personnel. The counseling should be available for offending and offended parties.

17. The firm should stimulate healthy peer relationships among women employees.

18. The firm should consider instituting, as a constituent part of its code of conduct, the principle that all sexual relationships between supervisors and their subordinates are conflicts of interest.[46] If the consenting subordinate is trading sexual favors for advancement, the interests of management are jeopardized. Further, knowledge of the existence of consenting relationships between superior and subordinate has a disquieting influence as well on the morale of other employees. A company's prohibition of this type also affords a diplomatic way for persons to avoid becoming sexually involved. Moreover, consenting relationships between senior and junior persons often end; the tension that remains can poison the work environment.

Finally, a company policy against sexual relationships between supervisors or managers and their subordinates may allow women who advance to be perceived as doing so on merit, and protect the integrity of mentoring relationships. If a romance were to develop, the firm could simply transfer the managerial or supervisory responsibility for that junior person to another supervisor or manager.

CONCLUSIONS

Many legal remedies are available to the sexually or non-sexually harassed employee. Courts, arbitrators and commentators continue the expansion of the definition of all types of harassment, including sexual harassment. As the law of harassment expands, so will new theories of recovery. The firm's sole prophylactic against liability is prevention. In promulgating and observing the foregoing guidelines, the firm serves its interest in that a harassment-free work environment enhances greater productivity. Further, the firm is spared expensive lawsuits and negative publicity that adversely impact selling its goods and services and recruiting talented persons of all races and sexes who want to be assured that everyone has an opportunity for success.

Clearly, consumers, especially females, are becoming more knowledgeable of firms that are sensitive to women—as evidenced by the 1988 book, The Best Companies for Women. The authors selected Avon as one of fifty-two preferred firms, partially because it terminated a male employee for sexual harassment.

Sexual and other forms of harassment undermine the entire concept of the firm: the hiring and promoting of all persons of merit to produce the highest quality products and services. Many firms have underemphasized the importance of preventing workplace harassment, often with seriously detrimental effects. Yet, it is management's responsibility to address the growing problem of workplace harassment, which robs the self-confidence, efficiency, and morale of a substantial portion of the workforce.

NOTES

1. Gibson, "Fallon McElligott Lose a Major Client Over 'Stupid' Reply to Sexist Ad Charge," <u>Wall Street Journal</u> (January 14, 1989): 10.
2. <u>Merit Systems Protection Board Report on Sexual Harassment in the Federal Workplace</u>, cited in "Sexual Harassment: Some See It . . . Some Won't," <u>When the Executive is a Woman</u> edition, <u>Harvard Business Review</u> (1981): 49.
3. Safran, "What Men Do to Women on the Job: A Shocking Look at Sexual Harassment, <u>Redbook</u> (November 1976): 149.
4. "Sexual Harassment: Some See it . . . Some Won't": 54-60.
5. Ibid., 51.
6. <u>Sexual Discrimination in the Workplace</u>, 1981; Hearings Before Senate Committee on Labor and Human Resources, 97th Congress, 1st Session (1981), 524.
7. Goodman, "Sexual Harassment: Some Observations on the Distance Travelled and the Distance Yet to Go," 10 <u>Cap. U.L. Review</u>: 456, note 1 (1981).
8. MacKinnon, <u>Sexual Harassment of Working Women</u> (1979): 1.
9. Vermeulen, "Comments on the Equal Employment Opportunity Commission's Proposed Amendment Adding Section 1604.11, Sexual Harassment, to Its Guidelines on Sexual Discrimination," <u>6 Women's Rts. L. Rep.</u> 286 (1980).
10. Andrews, "The Legal and Economic Implications of Sexual Harassment," <u>N.C. Cent. L.J.</u> 14 (1983): 119.
11. 29 <u>C.F.R</u> Section 1604.11(a) (1987).
12. McCulloch, <u>Termination of Employment: Employer and Employee Rights</u> Section 10, 103, at 10, 107 (1984).
13. Anderson, "Employee Liability under Title VII for Sexual Harassment after <u>Meritor Savings Bank v. Wilson</u>," <u>Columbia Law Review</u> 87 (1987): 1258, 1262-1263.
14. <u>Miller v. Bank of America</u>, 600 F. 2d 211 (9th Cir. 1979), 213.
15. Rizzolo, "A Right with Questionable Bite: The Future of 'Abusive or Hostile Work Environment' Sexual Harassment as a Cause of Action for Women in a Gender-Biased Society and Legal System," <u>New England Law Review</u> 23, 263 (Summer 1988): 268-269.
16. <u>Rabidue v. Osceola Refining Co.</u> 584 F. Supp. 419 (E.D. Mich., 1984).
17. 600 F. 2d 211 (9th Cir. 1979).
18. 390 F. Sup. 161 (D. Ariz., 1975).
19. 413 F. Supp. 654 (D.D.C. 1979).
20. <u>Bundy v. Jackson</u>, 641 F. 2d 943 (D.C. Cir. 1981).
21. <u>Rogers v. EEOC</u>, 454 F. 2d 234 (5th Cir. 1971) cert. denied, 406 U.S. 957 (1972).
22. 682 F. 2d, 902 (11th Cir. 1982).
23. 765 F. 2d 1129 (D.C. Cir. 1985).
24. 106 S. Ct. 2399 (1986).
25. Dworkin, Ginger, and Mallor, "Theories of Recovery for Sexual Harassment: Going Beyond Title VII," 25 <u>San Diego Law Review</u> (1988): 125, and Schoenheider, "A Theory of Tort Liability for Sexual Harassment in the Workplace," 134 <u>University of Pennsylvania Law Review</u> (1986): 1461.
26. <u>Restatement (Second) of Torts</u>, Section 31 (1965).
27. Ibid., Section 46(1) (1965).
28. <u>Harvard Univ. v. Best</u>, 484 A. 2d 958 (D.C. 1984), and <u>Shaffer v. National Can Corp.</u>, 565 F. Supp. 909 (E.D. Pa. 1983).
29. See <u>Hooten v. Pennsylvania College of Optometry</u>, 601 F. Supp. 1151 (E.D. Pa., 1984).
30. <u>Rogers v. Lowes L'Enfant Plaza Hotel</u>, 526 F. Supp. 523 (D.D.C. 1981).
31. <u>Restatement (Second) of Torts</u>, Section 766 (1979).
32. <u>Kyriazi v. Western Electric Co.</u>, 461 F. Supp 894 (D.N.J., 1978).
33. "Employee Handbooks and Employment-at-Will Contracts," <u>Duke Law Journal</u> (1985): 196, and <u>Monge v. Beebe Rubber Company</u> 114 N.H. 130, 316 A. 2d 549 (1974).
34. <u>Bohen v. City of E. Chicago</u>, 799 F. 2d 1180 (7th Cir. 1986).
35. E.g. <u>Wis. Stat. Ann.</u> Section 111.39(c) (West, 1985); <u>Pa. Stat. Ann</u> tit. 43 Section 926(b)(Purdon, 1986); and <u>Mich. Comp. Laws Ann.</u> Section 37.2801 (West, 1985).
36. 18 <u>U.S.C.</u> Sections 1961-68.

37. Hunt v. Weatherbee, 626 F. Supp. 1097 (D. Mass., 1986).
38. Acampora v. Boise Cascade Corp. 635 F. Supp. 66 (D.N.J., 1986).
39. Henson v. City of Dundee, 682 F. 2d 897 (11th Cir. 1982).
40. 454 F. 2d 235 (5th Cir. 1971), cert. denied, 406 U.S. 957 (1982).
41. Calcote v. Texas Educational Foundation 578 F. 2d 95, 98 (5th Cir. 1978) for racial harassment.
42. Compston v. Borden, Inc. 424 F. Supp 157 (S.D. Ohio, 1976).
43. Machlowitz and Machlowitz, "Preventing Sexual Harassment," ABA Journal (October 1, 1987): 78-80.
44. Ferguson v. E.I. DuPont de Nemours & Co., Inc. 560 F. Supp. 1172. (D. Del., 1983).
45. Rowe, "Dealing with Sexual Harassment," When the Executive Is a Woman, Harvard Business Review, (1981): 155; see also, Collins and Blodgett "Sexual Harassment . . . Some See It . . . Some Won't", op. cit., 47.
46. Rowe, "Dealing with Sexual Harassment," 158.

5

Equal Employment Opportunity and Nondiscrimination on the Basis of Sex, Race, Age, and Disability

INTRODUCTION

In the 1988 movie, <u>Working Girl</u>, Sigourney Weaver heads a mergers and acquisition department of an investment banking firm. In reality, only fifteen women are among the 599 managing directors in America's five most prominent investment banks. Yet, the 1980 U.S. Census revealed for the first time that white males do not comprise a majority of the nation's workforce, as women and minority men make up 51% of the job market.

Certainly, Ann Hopkins understands the vagaries of promotion in a male-dominated world. In 1978 Hopkins was hired as a manager in the Washington office of Price Waterhouse, the prominent nationwide accounting firm. She was nominated four years later for promotion to partnership, and for good reason: she had cultivated new business to the extent of $34 to $44 million and, in the preceding year, had billed more hours than any of the other eighty-seven candidates for partnership. Partners who refused her a partnership promotion criticized her as "macho" and harsh to coworkers. Hopkins countered that she was the victim of male stereotyping. "To be difficult to work with is somewhat in the eyes of the beholder," she says. "We had difficult jobs to do." The Supreme Court heard oral arguments in November 1988, and ruled in 1989 that employers sued for sex discrimination must demonstrate that they would have made the same decision without any bias, but need only present a moderate amount of evidence as proof. The lower federal court, which had earlier determined bias by Price, now must rule based on the new, lesser burden on the employer.

On the other hand, white males have experienced discrimination as a result of affirmative action programs. Philip and Paul Malone, rejected by the Boston Fire Department because of low scores on their 1975 exams, were subsequently hired in 1977 after submitting new applications containing false racial information. On the new applications, the identical twins declared that they were black and were consequently hired under an affirmative action program despite much lower exam scores than the passing grade for whites. The fair-haired, fair-skinned Malones were terminated after ten-year careers because an investigation deemed their claim to minority status "phony."

For a half-century, Paul Johnson worked diligently as a farm boy, a roustabout laying pipeline in Kansas, and a roughneck in the Texas oil fields. "All my life, I've believed you work hard enough for something, you're going to get it," Johnson reflects. "Now I learn that belief means nothing." Johnson, appointed as a Santa Clara County roads dispatcher, lost his job when the county roads director instead hired Diane Joyce after acquiescing to pressure from the local affirmative action office. Reflecting on the loss of his reverse discrimination suit[1] in the Supreme Court in 1987, Johnson declares bitterly, "The white male is in serious danger."

Other historic Supreme Court decisions have held that states and municipalities could use laws and ordinances that ban discrimination in public accommodation to compel private organizations to admit women to membership. The most symbolic cases effectively directed the Jaycees (1984), Rotary International (1987), and exclusive New York clubs (1988) to discontinue their practices of barring women. "The last bastion of white male power will be forced to throw in the towel," observes Donald Lenhoff of the Women's Legal Defense Fund.

Yet, the concept of equal opportunity is an ideal component of the free enterprise model. The positive growth of any economy results from enhancing and using the abilities of all persons to their fullest extents. Merit, many assert, not irrelevant factors such as race, sex, religion, or national origin, is the most important consideration in society's system of distributing economic rewards. Under a meritorious system, the best performers and competitors should capture the spoils.

This concept has the prerequisite that all persons have an opportunity to demonstrate their merit. Unfortunately, a substantial number of persons did not realize this opportunity because of racial, religious, gender, age, or disability characteristics. As a result, the government passed laws to end discrimination that prevents members of society from having an equal chance at available employment and the training and experience necessary to fully pursue economic opportunities.[2] As a consequence, when a twenty-five-year-old receptionist in Nebraska was discharged because her 40-inch bust was distracting to coworkers and a left-handed checkout clerk who refused to change to right-handed computerized key punching was terminated, they won damages and other relief in court based on employment discrimination. Moreover, by the late fall of 1989, with strong support from President Bush and acceptance by the U. S. Chamber of Commerce, Congress appears ready to pass a sweeping proposal, the Americans With Disabilities Act, which would virtually eliminate discrimination against disabled persons in the workplace and in public accommodations.

This chapter explores the plethora of federal statutes, executive orders, and regulations that prohibit employment discrimination because of age, race, color, sex, religion, national original, disability, or status as a veteran (Vietnam). From an analysis of 1989 developments, and in light of the pros and cons of affirmative action, and the doctrine of comparable worth, effective guidelines are offered for firms that wish to strengthen or establish affirmative action programs.

ATTACK ON DISCRIMINATION BY EXECUTIVE ORDERS AND ACTS OF CONGRESS

In American politics, it seems few problems are actually resolved. In the case of discrimination, the government has attacked on many fronts.

Executive Orders

Two executive orders, promulgated prior to the historic civil rights acts of the 1960s and 1970s, presaged the later major public policies and upheaval. In 1941 President Franklin D. Roosevelt issued Executive Order 8802, which prohibits racial discrimination by firms working under federal contract and established the Fair Employment Practices Committee, with weak policing powers. Employers and unions were required "to provide for the full and equitable participation of all workers in defense industries, without discrimination because of race, creed, color, or national origin." The order resulted in substantially increased employment opportunities for minorities and women, until demobilization.

Two decades later, President John F. Kennedy executed Executive Order 10925, which requires government contractors to act affirmatively to ensure that minorities are treated equally regarding job opportunities. The order created the Equal Employment Opportunity Commission (EEOC) and empowered it to investigate complaints and enforce a prohibition on discrimination by federal contractors. The Office of Economic Opportunity was empowered to administer ten separate programs (including Job Corps and Vista) to increase economic opportunity.

On August 28, 1963, 200,000 blacks marched in Washington, D.C. for "jobs and freedom." Subsequently, the Economic Opportunity Act was enacted in 1964 to attack unemployment and illiteracy.

The Civil Rights Act of 1964

The landmark response to employment and other discrimination, however, was the Civil Rights Act of 1964,[3] an omnibus statute that provided the first federal fair employment practices law. The act makes it unlawful employment practice to fail to employ or to terminate or otherwise discriminate against an individual regarding his or her compensation, conditions, terms, or privileges of employment because of race, color, religion, sex, or national origin. The act forbids discrimination not only by an employer, but also by a labor union or employment agency. The conditions, terms, and privileges of employment include fringe benefits, training, retraining, and other educational programs. Further, under the 1964 act, it is unlawful to limit, segregate, classify, refer, assign, or promote an employee in any way that contributes to the deprival of that person's employment opportunities or adversely affects his or her status as an employee because of race, color, religion, sex, or national origin.

Two other characteristics of the Civil Rights Act of 1964 are noteworthy. First, the act assigned implementation of the statute to the EEOC but invested in that agency no power to enforce it. The EEOC could only investigate, mediate, and recommend legal action to the Justice Department. Second, Title VII of the act prohibits preferential treatment of persons against whom discrimination is directed. That unambiguous language provides that nothing in the act requires "an employer . . . to grant preferential treatment to any individual or to any group because of the race, color, religion, sex, or national origin of such individual or group on account of an imbalance which may exist in such employment as compared with the total or percentage of such persons . . . ."[4]

The 1964 act was passed only after a long and divisive legislative fight and it marked the first time that a U. S. Senate filibuster had been terminated by cloture vote (71-29) on a civil rights bill. Nonetheless, the statute was the law of the land, and, most important, President Lyndon B. Johnson vigorously supported it. After delivering an appeal to end bigotry, Johnson indicated that he would unequivocally enforce and observe the Civil Rights Act of 1964: "I'm not going to let them build up the hate and try to buy my people by appealing to their prejudice."

In 1965 President Johnson issued Executive Order 11246 (later amended by 11375), which prohibits discrimination based on race, color, religion, sex, or national origin by all primary contractors and subcontractors who have federal contracts greater than $10,000. The order directs them, regardless of their previous behavior, to promulgate "good faith" affirmative action programs for the hiring and job training of minorities. "Affirmative action" was created but not defined. Revised Order 4[5] eliminated much of this ambiguity by requiring contractors (with fifty or more employees and federal contracts of over $50,000) to create written programs that identify female and minority underutilization, together with goals and schedules to correct the 1964 Act's underutilization.

The Equal Employment Act of 1972

Despite the passage of the monumental 1964 Civil Rights Act, unemployment still affected women far more severely than men, and blacks to a far greater extent than whites. In 1971, for instance, unemployment among women twenty years and older was 5.7% compared to 4.4% among men in the same age range. The rate of black unemployment, 9.9%, was nearly twice as great as the white employment rate, 5.4%.

The 1972 Equal Employment Opportunity Act amended and broadened the coverage of Title VII of the 1964 Civil Rights Act. The 1972 act authorizes the EEOC to implement and enforce Title VII provisions through court action. Title VII now sanctions conduct by the following employers: labor unions with at least fifteen members, private and public employment agencies, private and public educational institutions, private employers of at least fifteen persons, and joint labor-management committees that direct training programs. Those firms that do not attain these threshold standards and are, hence, excluded from the broad reach of federal laws, probably fall within the jurisdiction of state laws against discrimination.

Executive Order 11625 and Other Important Acts

In 1971 President Richard M. Nixon issued Executive Order 11625, at 3 C.F.R. 616 (1971), and that directive became a major catalyst for development of minority business enterprise programs. The Secretary of Commerce was directed to establish certain goals to encourage businesses "owned or controlled by one or more socially or economically disadvantaged persons . . . from cultural, racial, chronic economic circumstances or background."

Moreover, the Equal Pay Act of 1963 bans sex discrimination in remuneration for equal work in jobs under similar working conditions and that require equal effort, skill, and responsibility. As a result of the statute, firms are prohibited from reducing wage rates to symmetrize pay between the genders. Presently, protected individuals comprise executive, administrative, and professional employees, and employees subject to the minimum wage requirements of the Fair Labor Standards Act.[6] In the first nine years after its enactment, $55 million was awarded as compensation for wage inequities.

The Age Discrimination in Employment Act, as amended, is designed to protect persons between the ages of forty and seventy years against employment discrimination in hiring, termination, and promotion practices. Specifically, an employer commits an illegal act when:

1. The employer fails to hire or otherwise discriminates against any individual in the protected age bracket regarding that person's compensation, conditions, terms, or privileges of employment because of his or her age.

2. The employer reduces the wage rate of any employee in order to comply with the act.

3. The employer limits, classifies, or segregates employees in the protected age bracket in any way that deprives or tends to deprive any such employee of any employment opportunities because of age.

4. The employer indicates in employment advertisements or otherwise any limitation, preference, specification, or discrimination regarding the protected age group.

5. The employer discriminates against any job applicant or current employee because that person has opposed action prohibited by the act.

The Age Discrimination in Employment Act sanctions employers (of at least twenty employees), employment agencies,
and labor unions (of at least twenty-five members). Nonetheless, employers or firms may discriminate where age is a bona
fide occupational qualification of the job. Moreover, an
employer may observe the terms of a seniority system or
benefit plan (insurance, pension, retirement) without violating the statute, except that the benefit plan may not excuse
the failure to employ any individual in the protected age
bracket. Last, the employer may discipline or discharge a
person in the age bracket for good cause, provided age is not
a factor.[7]

Americans are retiring earlier than ever before: 70% now
cease employment before their sixty-fifth birthday. Further,
according to Brad Edmondson, who comments in "Inside the Empty
Nest" in the November 1987 issue of American Demographics, the
percentage of men between the ages of fifty-five and fifty-
nine who work has dropped to 79% in 1986 from 89% in 1979. By
2020 the fifty-to-sixty-four age group will comprise 59
million Americans. Hence, the statute may be more useful in
the future. Moreover, research indicates that workers in
their fifties and sixties function intellectually as well or
better than workers in their thirties, and that older workers
are more dependable and have better attendance than younger
employees.

The Vocational Rehabilitation Act of 1973 and the Vietnam
Era Veterans Readjustment Assistance Act mandate federal
contractors to affirmatively act to hire and promote qualified
handicapped and disabled and qualified veterans of the Vietnam
era. The Rehabilitation Act states:

> No otherwise qualified handicapped individual . . .
> shall, solely by reason of his handicap, be excluded
> from participation in, be denied the benefits of, or
> be subjected to discrimination under any program or
> activity receiving Federal financial assistance or
> under any program or activity conducted by any Execu-
> tive Agency.[8]

For purposes of the Rehabilitation Act, a "handicapped
person" is one "who has a physical or mental impairment which
substantially limits one or more of such person's major life
activities, has a record of such an impairment, or is regarded
as having such an impairment."[9] In the last few years,
several federal courts, including the Supreme Court, have held
that a contagious disease can be a handicap within the meaning
of Section 504 of the Rehabilitation Act thereby enhancing the
possibility that AIDS will eventually be included as a
handicap within the act.[10]

Furthermore, as of late fall 1989, Congress appeared
likely to pass the Americans With Disabilities Act, a proposed
statute strongly supported by President George Bush. The act
includes the following provisions: (1) discrimination against
a disabled person qualified for a job would be banned regarding employment, discharge, or workplace conditions, (2) public
places and new buses must permit access to the disabled, and
(3) telephone systems must provide electronic-typing linkage
to voice services for people with a hearing disability.

Businesses would be required to modify the workplace to allow a qualified, though disabled, person the opportunity to work.

Moreover, the Pregnancy Discrimination Act of 1978, found at U.S.C. Section 2000e-(K)(1982), further amended Title VII, and it proscribes employment discrimination against pregnant women. Among other prohibitions, employers cannot refuse to employ or terminate a woman solely because she is pregnant. Employers are prohibited from establishing a mandatory leave for a pregnant woman unless such leave is based on her inability to work; employers cannot deny reinstatement rights to the woman who is on leave for pregnancy-related purposes.

Section 1981 of the 1866 Civil Rights Act, found at 42 U.S.C., is an effective vehicle for pressing employment discrimination claims. Courts have historically construed Section 1981 as a civil rights statute that allows blacks (and whites, in reverse discrimination suits) to institute legal action against any contractual partners, including employers, who have discriminated against them. In a case involving an assistant professor of Arab ancestry whose lower court lawsuit for tenure denial is slowly working its way to the Supreme Court, the Court has recently broadened the coverage of Section 1981 to include suits for discrimination based on ancestry as well as race. The Court examined the section's legislative history and ruled, "Congress intended to protect from discrimination identifiable classes of persons who are subjected to intentional discrimination solely because of their ancestry or ethnic characteristics. [emphasis added]" The statute is much more favorable to plaintiffs than Title VII because, unlike Title VII, Section 1981 allows a jury trial and punitive, as well as compensatory, damages to plaintiffs. Nevertheless, the Supreme Court in a 1989 decision, Patterson v. McLean Credit Union (No. 87-107), limited the applicability of Section 1981 by decreeing that its coverage does not extend to lawsuits alleging racial harassment on the job, after hiring. The Patterson ruling may well adversely impact the claim of the aforementioned assistant professor of Arab ancestry because the tenure denial likely occurred after employment.

IMPLEMENTATION ISSUES

Affirmative Action, Preferential Treatment, and Reverse Discrimination

Equal opportunity implies that everyone has an equal chance to obtain a job or promotion. Affirmative action, on the other hand, has as its object the achieving within a certain time a composition within the major occupational categories that reflects that of the relevant external labor market. Affirmative action implies a set of result-oriented procedures designed to considerably accelerate the achievement rate of equal employment opportunity. Affirmative action programs establish goals, usually quotas, and time frames by which to accomplish the goal of equal employment opportunity.[11] Preferential treatment benefits minority group members as a whole, not just identified victims of discrimination.

Because of the conflicting rights of employer, disadvantaged employee, and passed-over majority groups, affirmative action is often a zero-sum process. Because affirmative action programs are implicitly redistributive, often at the expense of innocent employees, they are controversial and produce animosity within nonminority groups. According to professors Schotter and Weigelt of New York University in a recent article in Business and Society Review titled "The Benefits of Equal Opportunity," affirmative action programs attempt "to compensate groups for their high cost of effort by changing the rules of the tournament to favor them."

Reverse discrimination occurs when an equally or more qualified nonminority, usually a white male, is passed over for employment or promotion, which benefit is actually awarded to a racial or sexual minority group member. In the first fifteen years after the enactment of Title VII of the 1964 Civil Rights Act, the utility and legality of remedial numerical goals[12] and timetables[13] were recognized by federal courts. Thereafter, instances of reverse discrimination were less tolerated as the courts extended Title VII's protective penumbra to white males and within Title VI in the Bakke decision, and struck preferential treatment under certain circumstances.

Affirmative action can operate on four distinct levels.[14] The first, pure nondiscrimination, embodies a willingness to treat in employment matters the sexes and races the same. Some critics consider this particular approach to be insensitive to the deleterious effect of past discrimination. Further, this level of affirmative action may not significantly increase minority and female employment in nonstereotyped positions. The second level of affirmative action comprises a concerted effort to expand the number of minority and female applicants and employees; however, the firm hires or promotes based entirely on merit.

The third and fourth types of affirmative action programs entail preferential hiring and the use of quotas, respectively. Preferential hiring involves the firm's systematic favoritism of minorities and females in hiring and promoting decisions. Last, the quota system includes specific numerical goals for minority and female hiring and promoting, and the necessary means to realize those goals.

Nathan Glazer, in "The Affirmative Action Stalemate," appearing in The Public Interest, discussed the substantial opposition to and inequity of the principle of racial quotas or group rights. He lamented the fact that "moving against it would appear to black leaders, and to other blacks, as an attack on their interests and their well-being." An activist federal judge almost a decade ago offered an opposite opinion. In an article, Judge Skelly Wright called for the wholehearted embrace of remedial employment, "It is time . . . to admit that the Constitution and the Civil Rights Act permit us to remedy the wrongs of the past . . . to abandon the abstractions of 'color blind' theory and admit that there can be no such thing as a 'color blind' approach to achieving racial equality . . . "[15] It is time, Wright continued, "to concentrate our efforts on ensuring that the remedies we construct are humane and effective, that they respect, so much as is possible, the rights of all." Supporters of compensatory programs argue that race or sex, the characteristic held to be irrelevant when blacks or women are mistreated, is not the basis for remedial compensation. The real basis is the wrongs that blacks or women have suffered and the special needs they have. The second component of the argument for compensatory programs is that claiming race is irrelevant to whether someone should be mistreated is not incompatible with claiming that race is relevant to whether someone should be helped. Different issues are involved—what is relevant to one issue can be irrelevant to the other.[16]

Another author supports the idea that the issue of deciding whether to allocate a penalty or loss is a different one from deciding whether to allocate a subsidy: "It is a verbal gimmick to elide past prejudice with preferential treatment." A benefit "is obviously dissimilar to a penalty, a beneficiary different from a victim, although both fit under the discrimination rubric."[17] Blacks and women, the argument continues, have suffered because of economic exclusion and, consequently, are entitled to preferential treatment. Because white males have profited from these past wrongs, they should make amends.

Critics of preferential treatment (and reverse discrimination) point out difficulties in that policy: it is inconsistent, because either discrimination is illegitimate or it is not; it licenses discrimination, often against innocent persons; and third, it is unfair.[18] Moreover, a person's "race or ancestry could serve as a justifying basis for special benefits only if having this race or ancestry was, in itself, a special merit which deserved reward or special lack which required compensation . . . unless one is prepared to return to racist and aristocratic principles, one must deny that one's race or ancestry is in itself a matter of special merit or special lack." Therefore, "one must deny that race or ancestry, in itself, can serve as a justifying basis for a program of special benefits."[19] Others argue that only the specific individuals who actually discriminated against women and minorities should suffer economic reparation and that those restitutions should be extended only to those minorities and women who have actually experienced discrimination. In other words, to these critics, preferential treatment (and reverse discrimination) is the wrong penalty at the wrong time directed against innocent groups whose only indiscretion is being or not being born into a certain racial or gender group.

The most consequential issue in 1990 regarding equal rights in employment is the concept of comparable worth. This doctrine, which has its roots in the 1963 Equal Pay Act, is far removed from the notion of equal pay for equal work. Sean DeForest, in his Personnel article, "How Can Comparable Worth Be Achieved," defines comparable worth as a "concept requiring equal pay for employees whose work is of comparable value even if their jobs are totally different from each other." The Bennett Amendment to Title VII of the Civil Rights Act of 1964 clarifies the relationship between that act and the 1963 Equal Pay Act.

DeForest summarizes the arguments against and in favor of comparable worth. Women comprise much more of the part-time labor force than men; hence, there is a discrepancy in earnings. Women also choose jobs that pay less and have shorter careers to bear and raise children. These factors explain much of the reason that, in early 1989, women were earning on average only 60% of men's income. Further, tampering with wages established by the law of supply and demand violates an underpinning of our economic system. Moreover, the cost in establishing a comparable worth policy is prohibitive. One respected consulting firm places the cost at more than $320 billion and a resulting increase in inflation of 10%. The increased cost of wages, argue critics, would decrease productivity and devastate American competitiveness in world markets. Last, there is no practical program for implementing a policy of comparable worth. A comparable worth approach would foster an avalanche of discrimination lawsuits and cause severe competition and dislocation between the sexes.

Proponents contend that, although the nondiscriminatory factors above do contribute to disparity in earnings, discrimination against women exists to the equivalent of 29% to 43% of male earnings. Other studies, they claim, reinforce this finding—that a portion of the wage disparity is discrimination-fueled. Supporters of a comparable worth policy believe a widespread modernizing of job evaluation systems would be beneficial to society and serve as the vehicle for equitably assigning worth to jobs. Implementing comparable worth programs would offer important benefits. Women and their families would realize a higher living standard. Local governments and business would attract higher quality persons of both sexes and enjoy increased productivity from committed employees.

In 1981, although expressly stating that it was not endorsing the comparable worth doctrine, the Supreme Court ruled in County of Washington v. Gunther that female jail patrons, who received only 70% of the salary of male guards, had suffered discrimination even though the jobs were dissimilar. Presently, at least a dozen states have enacted statutes requiring public and private employers to pay equally for comparable worth; another two dozen are considering such statutes.

Developments in Applying Civil Rights Laws to Affirmative Action in Employment

Over the first decade and a half following the enactment of the 1964 Civil Rights Act, the Supreme Court regularly refused to hear cases that presented challenges to the numerical remedies.[20] The Court developed new doctrines in other cases to support affirmative action. In perhaps the most significant Title VII decision, the Supreme Court in Griggs v. Duke Power Co.[21] focused on the visible effects of discrimination. In Griggs, the Court announced the disparate impact theory, hailed by Eleanor Holmes Norton, 1977-81 chairperson of the Equal Employment Commission, as "the most important concept in modern employment discrimination work." The theory holds that a business practice that is neutral on the surface, but which disproportionately excludes job applicants or employees from previously excluded groups, cannot be used if that business practice is not job related, regardless of the employer's lack of intent to discriminate unless it is a business necessity. In Griggs, the effect of requiring employees for certain jobs to score at a certain level in a general intelligence test and a mechanical comprehension test was discriminatory because blacks were excluded by test standards that were not job related.

The Supreme Court first addressed the merits of affirmative action in 1978 in Regents of University of California v. Bakke,[22] and affirmative action in employment in 1979 in United Steelworkers of America v. Weber.[23] Earlier, in 1976, the Supreme Court had ruled in McDonald v. Santa Fe Transportation Co. that Title VII barred racial discrimination against whites on the same standards as applicable to blacks.[24] In Santa Fe, two white workers had been terminated when they appropriated company property, whereas the black involved had not been discharged.   The Supreme Court declared such asymmetrical treatment illegal.

In Bakke, a bare majority of five justices endorsed the notion of considering race in medical school admissions, but the five were divided on the constitutionality of the particular program that had excluded Allan A. Bakke, a white male applicant, while admitting minority applicants whom the university had rated as substantially below Bakke.   In the second majority opinion in Bakke, the Supreme Court (another bare majority of five) decreed that the special admission program for minority students at the University of California at Davis violated Title VI of the 1964 Civil Rights Act, which forbade racial discrimination, and ordered Bakke's admission. Under Bakke, quotas based entirely on race where no previous discrimination is found are unconstitutional.

In Weber, decided the next year (1979), the Court conferred affirmative action a broader sanction as it declared that Title VII did not bar private employers and unions from voluntarily reserving a specified percentage (in this case, 50%) of positions in training programs for blacks.   The affirmative action plan, the Supreme Court declared, "rectified old patterns of racial segregation and hierarchy," even though Weber, a white male, had been excluded from a training program for higher paying skilled jobs.   The Court specifically noted that the voluntary program would end when the percentage of black skilled workers approximated the percentage of blacks in the local labor force.

In 1980 the Court upheld in Fullilove v. Klutznick[25] the constitutionality of a minority business enterprise statutory provision that required that 10% of federal funds for local projects be reserved for minority contractors.   In 1984, in Firefighter's Local Union No. 1784 v. Stotts,[26] the Court struck a lower court order that required that race override seniority regarding layoffs so a specified degree of black employment would be maintained. The Court held that the lower court's order was contrary to Title VII's expressed protection of bona fide seniority systems. Section 703(h) of Title VII provides:

Notwithstanding any other provision of this subchapter, it shall not be an unlawful employment practice for an employer to apply different standards of compensation, or different terms, conditions or

privileges of employment, pursuant to a bona fide
seniority . . . system . . . provided that such
differences are not the result of an intention to
discriminate because of race, color, religion, sex or
national origin . . . .

Since the closely divided Bakke and Weber decisions, the
Supreme Court has not adopted consistent positions on affirmative action.   In 1986 and 1987 the Court receded from the
broader implication of Stotts in four cases and did not end
the confusion over which particular affirmative action
programs are constitutional.   In Wygant v. Jackson Board of
Education,[27] the Court ruled unconstitutional a school board
policy of laying off white teachers before less senior
minority teachers to preserve the affirmative action balance.
Nonetheless, in Local 28 of Sheet Metal Workers Association v.
E.E.O.C.,[28] Local Number 93 v. City of Cleveland,[29] and United
States v. Paradise,[30] the Supreme Court upheld the challenged
affirmative action plans.
    In Sheet Metal Workers, the Court upheld an order by the
EEOC that required a union, found to have discriminated in the
past against Hispanics and blacks, to reach a numerical goal
(29%) of minority members.   In Cleveland, it validated a
public employer's voluntary affirmative action plan challenged
by nonminorities.   The City of Cleveland had agreed in a
consent decree to reserve a fixed number of planned promotions
for minority firefighters and to forbid the use of seniority
points as the only factor in determining promotions.   The
Court rejected the contention of the firefighters' union that
the consent decree violated Title VII.   In Paradise, the Court
decreed that courts could order employers to temporarily use
strict quotas in hiring and promotion to remedy "egregious"
historic discrimination against blacks.   Hence, Sheet Metal
Workers and Paradise established the doctrine that government
agencies and the courts can order unions and employers, guilty
of past discriminatory acts, to adopt quotas.   When layoffs
were at issue, Wygant posited the exception to the doctrine.
    It was not until Johnson v. Transportation Agency, Santa
Clara County[31] in 1987 that the Court decided whether quotas
could withstand constitutional scrutiny if no record of past
discrimination existed.   In Johnson, the Court upheld an
affirmative action plan voluntarily adopted by the California
county's transportation agency.   Among 238 skilled craft
positions, not one had ever been held by a woman.   The
temporary plan's goal was to fill a certain percentage (36%)
of those skilled jobs with women to reflect the female
composition of the area labor market.   Diane Joyce was hired
even though her interview score was marginally lower than that
of Paul Johnson, a white male, who had also applied and who
eventually sued.   Under Title VII, the ruling decreed that a
voluntary affirmative action program was legal when there was
"a conspicuous imbalance in traditionally segregated job
categories," even though the transportation agency had no
prior record of discrimination.
    Nonetheless, a recent decision may limit the thrust of
Johnson.   In January 1989 the Supreme Court struck as unconstitutional a Richmond, Virginia, ordinance that assigned 30%
of all that city's construction subcontracts to minority

firms.   The Court in Richmond v. J. A. Croson Co., 488 U.S.
(1989) declared any government program that favors one race
over another to be "highly suspect" and subject to "strict
scrutiny." The Richmond City Council had adopted a set-aside
requiring at least 30% of the dollar amount of city construction contracts to be subcontracted to businesses at least 51%
owned by American citizens who are "Black, Spanish-speaking,
Orientals, Indians, Eskimos, or Aleuts."   Croson, a white-
owned firm, was the only bidder for a particular project; the
only minority supplier of fixtures submitted a bid well over
market price.   Croson lost the contract because the city
refused to raise the contract price (to cover the over market
fixtures bid) or waive the requirements of minority preference.   Justice O'Connor's opinion found that the set-aside
plan "denies certain citizens the opportunity to compete for
a fixed percentage of public contracts based solely on their
race." For such an affirmative action program to be constitutional, the government promulgating such a program must prove
that there is a history of identifiable prior discrimination
against the group favored in the program and, even if there is
such discrimination, a racial set-aside must be the remedy of
last resort.   The Court found no record of identifiable
discrimination against minority contractors.   The Supreme
Court indicated its concern about "the danger that a racial
classification is merely the product of unthinking stereotypes
or a form of racial politics." The Richmond ruling did not
outlaw special consideration of race and gender by government
agencies—only set-asides that do not first prove actual
discrimination against the groups benefited by the set-aside.
The government may still utilize affirmative action measures
that do not classify by race.
     The Richmond decision, moreover, will not necessarily
jeopardize affirmative action in private enterprise.   According to Juan Williams, in his article concerning Richmond,
appearing in the Washington Post National Weekly Edition,
February 27-March 5, 1989, a 1985 Fortune survey reveal that
95% of the chief executive officers polled use numerical goals
to gauge the progress of minorities and women in their firms.
In addition, 90% indicate that their firms employ affirmative
action to meet "corporate objectives unrelated to government
regulation." Donald McHenry, former U.N. ambassador, noted
this affirmative action tone when he observed that "most of
the Fortune 500 companies I know of took the initiative on
this one because they decided it was good business."

Other Important 1989 Supreme Court Decisions

Other 1989 U.S. Supreme Court decisions narrowed the scope of
civil rights laws regarding employment discrimination and
affirmative action. In Wards Cove Packing Co. v. Atonio (No.
87-1387), the Court interpreted the Civil Rights Act of 1964,
which bars discrimination in public and private employment.
Wards Cove held that claims that a firm's employment policies
have a discriminatory effect cannot be proved by merely
comparing the number of minorities in one type of job to the
number of whites in another. Rather, such comparisons must be

made to the broader labor market and plaintiff—workers bear the burden of discrediting the employer's justification of its employment policies. To avoid any sinister pressure toward quotas, Justice Byron White, author of the majority opinion in Wards Cove, wrote that a minority employee must demonstrate the requirement under attack (for example, a high school education) actually produces the objectionable result (fewer numbers of minority in a job type). Any other practical option, noted White, would coerce the employer's adoption of racial quotas—"a result that Congress expressly rejected in drafting Title VII."

Moreover, in Martin v. Wilks (No. 87-1614), the Court held that white firefighters in Birmingham, Alabama, were not barred from challenging as reverse discrimination a court-approved affirmative action plan, to which they were not parties, agreed upon by employers and minority or women employees. The Court opinion by Chief Justice Rehnquist refers to the "deep-rooted historic tradition that everyone should have his own day in court," in granting white fire-fighters their right to challenge the preferential promotion of allegedly less qualified black firefighters.

In Lorance v. AT&T Technologies, Inc. (No. 87-1428), in a majority opinion by Justice Antonin Scalia, the Court held that employees' claims that a seniority system discriminates by sex or race must be filed when the system is established, even if the bias was not apparent then. The Court, further, held in Public Employees Retirement System of Ohio v. Betts (No. 88-389) that federal law prohibiting age discrimination in employment does not preempt employers making distinctions based on age in employment benefit plans, such as disability, insurance, and pensions. Rather, the plaintiff, according to the opinion written by Justice Anthony Kennedy, to prove illegal discrimination under the Age Discrimination in Employment Act of 1967, must demonstrate that the reduced benefits have resulted from "an intent to discriminate in some non-fringe benefit aspect of the employment relation."

In addition, the Supreme Court determined in Patterson v. McLean Credit Union (No. 87-107) that an 1866 civil rights statute (42 U.S.C. Section 1981), which preserves all cit-izens' equal rights to make and enforce contracts, does not apply to lawsuits alleging racial harassment at work. Nor does the same statute allow lawsuits alleging employment discrimination against local governments, unless the bias is based on official policy, according to the Court in Jett v. Dallas Independent School District (No. 87-2084). In that case a black administrator discriminated against a white school employee and demonstrated a bias in favor of hiring less-qualified black workers. Nonetheless, Jett could not bring a lawsuit against the school district because the administrator's actions were not based on official local government policy, although Jett did recover from the black administrator.

Last, in Price Waterhouse v. Hopkins (No. 87-1167), the Supreme Court determined that an employer sued for sex discrimination may avoid liability by demonstrating that "it would have made the same decision in the absence of discrim-ination" by a "preponderance of the evidence," rather than the rigorous standard of "clear and convincing evidence." Ann

Hopkins sued Price Waterhouse under Title VII of the Civil Rights Act of 1964 charging discrimination against her on the basis of sex in its partnership decisions. The court of appeals upheld the district court's ruling in Hopkins' favor. The Supreme Court remanded the case to the court of appeals for further proceedings based on the lesser burden.

These fine judicial distinctions about the parameters of affirmative action and discrimination are irritating to managers and union leaders alike, with good reason. "There is no single conception of the permissible scope of affirmative action that commands the respect of five justices . . . there appear to be no fewer than six different viewpoints . . . the outcome emerging from the confluence of distinctive viewpoints that happen to overlap on the facts of a particular case."[32]

Nevertheless, Paradise and Johnson clarified the voting pattern of the justices and the doctrinal basis to uphold reasonable affirmative action, until the 1988-89 Court term.

Justice Kennedy, who replaced the usually pro-affirmative action Justice Lewis Powell on the Supreme Court, is a libertarian conservative who is discomfited by affirmative action's emphasis on group rather than individual rights. In thirty-one decisions rendered by five to four margins, Kennedy deserted the conservatives only twice, and he provided the needed fifth vote to restore constitutional protections to property rights and economics liberties, after a hiatus of fifty years. Kennedy has also joined a bare majority to curb the excesses of applications of affirmative action and civil rights laws. Justice O'Connor, usually more conservative than former Justice Powell, has emerged as the pivotal vote in social issues, including civil rights.

In its 1989 decisions, the Court is not suddenly allowing discrimination, but, rather, making quotas harder to justify or to force employers to establish them. In the 1988-89 term, O'Connor sided with conservatives in all the civil rights rulings that have made it moderately more difficult to prove discrimination, and she authored the Richmond decision. Nonetheless, the principle of stare decisis may be a moderating prophylactic to any volte face from the affirmative action doctrine and the conservative margin is so slender that the five conservative justices merely undermine, rather than overturn, liberal precedents. The conservatives, moreover, focus on the letter, not the spirit, of civil rights statutes. In essence, that doctrine is that a court or government agency can order quotas in affirmative action in limited circumstances. Voluntary quotas, however, can be promulgated and upheld without a showing of prior discrimination except in government-created minority set-asides, which require a showing of past discrimination. In the case of layoffs, seniority systems prevail over quota systems.

GUIDELINES FOR ESTABLISHING A COURT-PROOF AFFIRMATIVE ACTION PROGRAM

Title VII suits based on alleged violations of the law prohibiting discrimination in employment because of race, color, religion, sex, or national origin have been litigated since 1965. Executive orders requiring affirmative action predate the 1964 Civil Rights Act. Penalties for violation include monetary damages as well as the firm's public embarrassment and possible loss of consumer loyalty. The firm's development or improvement of a comprehensive voluntary affirmative action program is an important step in avoiding the predicaments that lead to expensive litigation. Elements of an effective plan include: survey and analysis of the firm's existing employment structure, thorough examination of all descriptions and classifications, conscientious development of goals and timetables, effective and imaginative recruiting, and a comprehensive inventory of the skills of existing employees.[33]

Survey and Analysis

The firm's first task is to survey the existing employment structure to ascertain the presence of minorities and women by location, department, and job description and classification. Then the firm should determine where minorities and women are clustered, excluded, or underutilized—based on reasonable expectations because of the presence of the protected groups in the labor market, usually local (standard metropolitan statistical area).

Examination of Job Descriptions and Classifications

If the survey above reveals job classifications and descriptions drawn with insufficient precision, then the firm should immediately redraw them. The firm should establish prescribed qualifications and wage scales based on business grounds and ensure that barriers to minorities and women are not present. Irrelevant qualifications or ones that exceed the requirements of the job have fueled many successful Title VII cases.

Conscientious Development of Goals and Timetables

The firm should correct exclusion and underutilization of protected groups by establishing measurable and realistic numerical goals (hiring and promoting) and timetables by which the exclusion and underutilization are remedied. Goals in this usage are distinct from quotas, which are often court ordered to redress past discrimination. The affirmative action program should contain no self-critical statements, because they are discoverable in any subsequent litigation.

Effective Recruitment

The firm can imaginatively recruit minorities and women to fill excluded and underutilized classifications. Systematic record-keeping effectively describes the flow of minority and women job applicants as well as employees seeking promotions. Job application forms should be separate from information about race and sex. The EEOC mandates that any employment testing have a high correlation between exemplary test performance and success on the job for which the testing is promulgated. In this regard, an industrial psychologist can design a test so that job-relatedness can be established.

Inventory of Skills of Current Employees

A comprehensive skills inventory of current employees establishes a baseline for training and development programs. The firm learns about the skills of its employees—helpful in seeking qualified employees to fill higher level positions. In this manner, a firm can chart job mobility and create training programs to develop all employees, including, of course, minorities and women.

Other Guidelines

In addition to the foregoing guidelines and standards and others apparent in this chapter's discussion, the following guidelines[34] are helpful:

1. The firm's management should be vigorously committed to the entire program.

2. The firm's direct responsibility for establishing an equal employment opportunity policy must be firmly understood by every employee.

3. An outside consultant can serve as a prod in accomplishing the first and second guidelines (above).

4. The affirmative action policy requires a thorough implementation and feedback system to be effective. The firm should carefully devise such a system.

5. The firm's personnel director or similarly designated manager should monitor and approve all actions involving employees.

6. The firm should establish an Equal Employment Opportunity Department with the following responsibilities:
   a. All contracts with and approvals of information submitted to a government agency.
   b. Coordination of the firm's programs.
   c. Interpretation of EEO laws, regulations, statutes, and executive orders with the assistance of the firm's legal counsel.
   d. Dissemination of the firm's EEO policy and guidelines to all employees.

7. The firm should select, hire, assign, train, transfer, promote, lay off, and compensate employees on the basis of ability and other meritorious qualification without discrimination because of race, color, religion, age, national origin, or ancestry.

8. The firm should not discriminate against any qualified job applicant or employee because of a mental or physical handicap or status as a disabled or Vietnam era veteran.

9. The firm should affirmatively act to remedy any deficiency in its equal employment opportunity and affirmative action program. In so doing, the firm will continually evaluate the utilization of minorities, females, physically, or mentally handicapped individuals, and disabled or Vietnam era veterans.

10. The firm should establish result-oriented goals and schedules to eliminate underutilization of minorities and females throughout the firm's organization.

11. Instituting goals never implies that the firm must hire unqualified applicants. Numerical goals are expressly or impliedly subject to the availability of qualified minority applicants.

12. Further, the firm must not limit, segregate, or classify employees in any manner that tends to deprive any individual of employment opportunities or adversely affect any person's status as an employee because of race, color, religion, sex, national origin, or ancestry.

13. The firm must ensure that no job is classified as "male" or "female" and assume that any person who is qualified for a job must be seriously considered for it.

14. The most common issues that prompt sex discrimination complaints as a percentage of the total complaints are: discharge, 27%; terms and conditions of employment, 13%; sexual harassment, 9%; wages, 9%; pregnancy, 7%; promotion, 5%; and hiring, 4%.[35] The firms should ensure their antidiscrimination program is court-proof in these areas.

15. The firms must avoid sexual or racial stereotyping in any oral or written description of an applicant or employee. Further, the firm must root out evident sexism or racism, whether conscious or otherwise, in any evaluation process.

16. The firm should act to eliminate grants or denials of employment or of advancement in employment based upon grants or denials of sexual favors. Any harassment of any kind in the work environment is prohibited.

RESULTS AND RESPONSES BY FIRMS

Minority and female employment rights and mobility have undergone a sea-change as a result of changing attitudes and civil rights statutes, rulings, and regulations.   A quarter of a century after the release of the dismal findings of the Presidential Commission chaired by Otto Kerner, black America had made many significant economic advances. Of blacks aged twenty-four and older, 64% had completed a high school education, up from 30% in 1968. Black families with two parents who are employed in two jobs earn, as an average, 85% as much as white families with two incomes, up from 73% in 1968. Two-thirds of the nation's 30 million blacks earn at least $10,000 annually.[36]

A majority of blacks "have fared quite well" during the 1980s, according to Joseph Perkins, a Wall Street Journal editorial writer. In his article "Boom Time for Black America," which appeared in the 1988 summer edition of Policy Review, Perkins determined from economic data that black business persons have been extraordinarily successful. Estimates by economist Andrew Brimmer are revealing: black businesses sold goods and services totaling $18.1 billion in 1987, contrasted with $12.4 billion in sales in 1982. Black businesses grew at an average annual rate of 7.9%, much higher than the 5% average annual rate of growth of all American corporations. Further, many large black businesses, like TLC Beatrice, Johnson Publishing, and Philadelphia Coca-Cola Bottling, eschew reliance on government measures or set-asides for minority businesses. Blacks are also increasing their presence in the management of American firms. The EEOC reports that the number of black managers and officers in corporations with at least 100 employees increased from 165,000 in 1980 to 215,000 in 1985.

Since the recession ended in 1982, black employment has increased by 24.9%, twice the rate of white employment and the best-ever five-year job increase for black Americans. By 1987 the black employment rate had grown to "record levels" of 56% compared to 49% in 1982. Employed blacks have increased from 9.2 million in 1982 to over 11.5 million by early 1988. Black families' median income rose 46% faster than white families from 1981-86. A significant number of blacks are moving up the economic ladder: since 1981 the percentage of black families in the highest income bracket—$50,000 in 1986 dollars—has increased to 8.8 from 5.1. In 1985 nearly a million black families earned at least $40,000; 300,000 other black families earned between $35,000 and $40,000. Further, the unemployment rate of black teenagers, considered the least employable of workers, is presently at 34%, one of the lowest rates in a decade. Still, despite the gains, the unemployment rate among blacks remains twice as high as that of the entire workforce. Murray Friedman, vice chairman of the Civil Rights Commission, believes America has entered a "post civil rights era" and should "focus more energy on jobs, the development of middle-class skills for minority underclasses, and economic growth in the years ahead."[37]

Furthermore, since 1960 women have flooded America's workplaces, not as consumers but as "value adders" to firms. Whereas only 42% of women worked in 1960, over 66% do today. Horst Stipp, author of "What is a Working Woman?" in American Demographics (July 1988), relates that a 1987 Roper opinion survey of women yielded interesting results. Only 26% of women over sixteen years of age had not worked in the prior two years and had no work plans. The survey also indicates that only 7% of women between eighteen and forty-nine years of age are continuously nonworking.

According to Harvard Business School professor Regina Herzlinger, in 1986, 30% of managers, 16% of lawyers, 20% of doctors, 40% of programmers, and 40% of accountants and auditors were women.   In 1986, 83% of the female officers in the Fortune 500 were at vice presidential or higher levels, from 35% in 1980.   In 1986, 33% of those receiving MBAs and 14% receiving engineering degrees were female—a substantial increase from the 2% level in 1966.   In 1984, 3.5 million self-employed women owned 2.8 million firms—28% of all U.S. companies.[38]

Despite the aforementioned gains in traditionally male-dominated occupations, women remain underrepresented in science, engineering, and full professorships.   Nonetheless, in 1985 women received about one-half of master's and bachelor's degrees and over one-third of doctoral degrees. The average working husband still earns over twice what his employed wife does.   In 1986 women from the company vice president's level higher still earned about one-half as much as male executives at that level.   The gains are impressive, but women still are concentrated in traditional women's occupations, which provide less wages.   This wage disparity should narrow considerably, because for women the stay-at-home role is becoming more unpopular; only 20% of women aged eighteen to forty-nine indicate that their ideal lifestyle is that of homemaker or mother.

Yet, in spite of the changes concerning rights and roles of women in our society, the "intellectual double standard" of women's having bias for male performance as superior to their own in certain professions remains.[39]   In an article, "Management Women and the New Facts of Life," appearing in the January-February 1989 issue of the Harvard Business Review, Felice Schwartz offers a two-track career plan for women.   The plan suggests relegating many working mothers to a less demanding career path, whereas firms would single out women who set aside family demands for fast track.   To reduce their losses in training women only to lose them to motherhood, firms must find a method to segregate "career" women from "career and family" women.   Critics have replied that two-thirds of the new workers in the labor force of the 1990s will be women; if firms sideline working mothers, it will be counterproductive.

Sun Microsystems and General Motors

A number of firms, including Sun Microsystems and General Motors, have instituted impressive affirmative action programs that assist minority businesses.   Sun Microsystems has directed its purchasing department to develop relationships with disadvantaged business concerns.

General Motors earmarked $44.5 million for the five years following 1983 for a variety of educational programs for minorities and women.   Substantial assistance has flowed to programs like the Native American Science Education and the Michigan Hispanic Scholarship Fund.   The General Motors Minority Supplier Development Program is the largest of its

kind in America.   Through it, potential minority suppliers
receive training and consulting to aid them in securing GM's
business.   In 1987 GM purchased $902 million of materials and
services from 1,500 minority suppliers.   GM's subsidiary,
Motor Enterprises, Inc., provides start-up capital to
establish new minority businesses.   GM assists and trains
minority persons to acquire and operate auto franchises and by
February 1988 there were 198 minority-owned and operated GM
dealerships.   The firm spends over $7 million annually for
advertising in minority newspapers, magazines, and radio and
television stations.   Further, it has instituted two programs
to encourage participation of minorities in the insurance
industry.   GM also formed the Women in Management Advisory
Committee in 1980 to encourage the success of women within the
firm.   The committee assists in recruiting women and in
addressing women's issues.

CONCLUSIONS

In 1989 morally and legally, it is widely accepted that a
person has a right not to be discriminated against.   Whereas
1,000 employment discrimination class action claims were filed
in 1976, fewer than fifty were filed in 1988.   Barry
Goldstein, an NAACP legal defense attorney, attributes the
decrease in cases filed to the 379 federal judges—half the
federal judiciary—that President Reagan appointed.   These
judges are more likely to reject claims of race and sex
discrimination.   According to Goldstein, the lawyers "fear
that the likelihood of winning is much less."
       Although the courts may not be the sheltered, safe harbors
they once were, minority members and women also have received
and continue to receive substantial assistance from American
firms' affirmative action programs. Most important, attitudes
of the white male group are much more receptive to full
minority and female economic participation.   Business firms
have been among the most stable American institutions during
the last decade in support of preferential hiring.
       Although Title VII in 1989 is older than the National
Labor Relations Act at the time of enactment of the Taft-
Hartley Act, no similar statutory reaction to it has tran-
spired.   In fact, Title VII has been strengthened by amendments such as the Pregnancy Discrimination Act.   Title VII is
now a mature statute with little left for the federal
judiciary to decide. The Supreme Court has not been willing,
despite its more conservative composition, to abandon the
remedial statutory interpretation of Title VII to protect
minorities and women against employment discrimination.
       The Court's decisions and the threat of future employment
discrimination suits are reminders to firms to stay the course
in overcoming employment discrimination.   The business
community welcomes stability of interpretation and enforcement. Voluntary affirmative action often serves the interests
of both minority and female employees and employers.   For
minority and female employees, forbearance from bringing
lawsuits and acceptance of firms' voluntary affirmative action
programs relieve them of the difficulties of proving historic
discrimination. For employers, promulgating court-proof plans

avoids litigation costs and potentially substantial monetary damages. In all such cases, comity between the firm and its employees is enhanced. While providing assistance to minority members, firms should give more than scant attention to the problems of innocent bystanders, usually white males, whose promotions or chances of jobs may be at stake. Moreover, advocates of quotas or apologists for minority underperformance often immediately and impulsively focus on discrimination as the explanation for individual disadvantage or injury, thereby overlooking other innocent causes. For example, people of any race or sex who steal from their employers or who are incompetent should have their employment terminated.

NOTES

1. Johnson v. Transportation Agency, Santa Clara County, 107 S. Ct. 1442 (1987).
2. See Buchholz, Business Environment and Public Policy, 3rd ed. (Englewood Cliffs, NJ: Prentice-Hall, 1989), 314-348, for a discussion of the concept of equal employment opportunity.
3. See especially Title VII, 42 U.S.C. Sections 2000e to 2000e-17 (1982), as amended by the Equal Employment Opportunity Act of 1972, Pub. L. No. 92-261, Sections 2-11, 13-14, 86 Stat. 103 (1972).
4. Title VII, 42 U.S.C. Section 703(j) (1982).
5. Issued by the Office of Federal Contract Compliance in 1970.
6. Buchholz, op. cit., 318-319.
7. Goodyear's anti-discrimination and personnel policy.
8. 29 U.S.C. Section 794 (1982).
9. 29 U.S.C. 706(7)B (1982). The definition is further refined by regulations of the Department of Health and Human Services.
10. School Board v. Airline, 107 S. Ct. 1123 (1987).
11. Buchholz, op. cit., 328.
12. Local 28, Sheet Metal Workers' International Ass'n v. EEOC, 106 S. Ct. 3037, Note 28 (1986), and Firefighters' Local Union No. 1784 v. Stotts, 467 U.S. 612-613 and Note 10 (1984).
13. Uniform Guidelines on Employee Selection Procedures, 29 C.F.R. Section 1607.17(3)(a) (1986).
14. Seligman, "How Equal Opportunity Turned Into Employment Quotas," Fortune (March 1973): 162, and Buchholz, op. cit., 327.
15. Wright, "Color-Blind Theories and Color-Conscious Remedies," U. Chicago L. Rev., 47 (1979): 245.
16. Nickel, "Classification by Race in Compensatory Programs," Ethics, 84 (1974): 146.
17. Green, "Reparation for Blacks," Commonwealth 90 (June 1969) 359.
18. Gross, "Is Turn About Fair," Journal of Critical Analysis vol. 5 (January-April 1975).
19. Nickel, op. cit., 149.
20. EEOC v. American Tel. & Tel. Co., 556 F. 2d 167 (3d Cir. 1977), cert. denied sub nom. Communications Workers of Am. v. EEOC, 438 U.S. 915 (1978); Detroit Police Officers' Ass'n v. Young, 608 F. 2d 671 (6th Cir. 1979), cert. denied, 452 U.S. 938 (1981); and, United States v. United Bhd. of Carpenters, Local 169, 457 F 2d 210 (7th cir.), cert. denied, 409 U.S. 851 (1972).
21. 401 U.S. 424 (1971).
22. 438 U.S. 265 (1978).
23. 443 U.S. 193 (1979).
24. McDonald v. Santa Fe Transportation Co., 427 U.S. 273 (1976).
25. 448 U.S. 448 (1980).
26. 467 U.S. 561 (1984).
27. 476 U.S. 267 (1986).
28. 106 S. Ct. 3019 (1986).
29. 106 S. Ct. 3063 (1986).
30. 107 S. Ct. 1053 (1987).

31. 107 S. Ct. 1442 (1987).
32. Gottesman, "No Legal Certainty Yet on Affirmative Action," <u>Nat'l L.J.</u> (August 11, 1986): S-8.
33. Chayes, "Make Your Equal Opportunity Program Court-proof," <u>Harvard Business Review: Legal Issues in Doing Business</u>: 93.
34. Many of these guidelines are adopted from the chapter's text and from the thorough nondiscrimination section in Goodyear's code.
35. McCarthy, "Supreme Court to Rule on Sex-Bias Case," <u>Wall Street Journal</u> (June 14, 1988): 37.
36. Zinsmeister, "Black Demographics," <u>Public Opinion</u> (January-February 1988), as cited in <u>Wilson Quarterly</u> (Summer 1988): 21.
37. Friedman, "Job Statistics Reveal Good News in Race Relations," <u>Wall Street Journal</u> (December 15, 1988): 32.
38. Herzlinger, "Problems Aren't Dancing on the Glass Ceiling," <u>Wall Street Journal</u> (February 17, 1988): 28.
39. Seymour and Voss, "Equality for Women?" <u>Business Horizons</u> (November-December 1989): 10.

6
Workplace Safety, Consumer Protection, and Product Quality

INTRODUCTION

In the 1970s and 1980s, safety in the workplace and consumer protection became serious national issues in the United States. The over 94 million American workers comprise an essential and valuable national resource. Although occupational injuries are usually traumatic events whose causes are easily recognized as work related, occupational illnesses are much more complex, as it is often not apparent that an illness is caused by a specific workplace hazard.[1] Moreover, the etiology of many diseases, including cancer, is not well understood. Yet, each year an estimated 11,000 people die and over 2 million suffer injuries or illnesses as a result of accidents or exposure to hazards in the workplace.[2]

Since the Industrial Revolution (late eighteenth century) and the use of power machinery, workers have been exposed to an increasing variety of safety and health hazards, from electrical shock to carcinogenic or toxic chemicals and elements. For example, a June 1989 report by the University of North Carolina School of Public Health indicates a high rate of stillborn and underweight and early deliveries by women married to men involved in certain industries—certain exposures such as benzene may have an adverse effect on male sperm. Workplace dangers are not a recent phenomenon: occupational illnesses such as "brass chills from zinc poisoning," "painter's colic" from lead poisoning, and "grinder's consumption" from dust inhalation were present a century and a half ago. Moreover, from 1960 until 1970 the rate of manufacturing accidents increased over 26%.[3] The first presidential report concerning Occupational Safety and Health Act (OSHA) indicated as many as 100,000 deaths and 390,000 disabling diseases projected per annum due to hazardous substances such as asbestos, lead, carbon monoxide, and cotton dust.[4] For instance, projections are that at least 350,000 people will die from asbestos-related cancer over the next four decades.

Moreover, the economic and social costs of workplace injuries and illnesses are staggering. For example, economic losses from workplace accidents have increased from $8 billion in 1970, to $30 billion in 1982, $38.4 billion in 1986, and $42.4 billion in 1987. Researchers point to employee turnover and overtime, both signs of a healthy economy, as the culprits. Occupational injuries and illnesses pose additional serious problems: the physical and emotional trauma of the injured or ill workers and their families, higher employer costs because of more expensive insurance premiums and production delays, and society's loss of income and the products represented by absent workdays.[5]

In 1970 in response to the reported 14,000 worker deaths and 2.5 million worker injuries and disabilities, a bipartisan Congress enacted the Occupational Safety and Health Act to preserve the nation's human resources and assure safe and healthful working conditions. For nearly two decades the OSH Act has regulated the technology and workplace practices of employers, an altogether new governmental function and intrusion. The act comprises one of a constellation of laws and regulations, often conflicting, that address most occupational safety and health concerns.   In 1989, for example, as a result of OSHA's rules requiring an employer to inform workers if they have been exposed to hazardous chemicals, Lockheed Corporation agreed to pay $1.5 million in fines to settle charges that it violated safety and health standards at its Burbank, California, plant. In addition, as part of the settlement, Lockheed agreed to correct unsafe or unhealthy work practices in all of its plants.

Likewise, in 1989 Secretary of Labor Elizabeth Dole acted to allow OSHA implementation of needed regulations, such as those protecting people who work in storage vessels and railroad tank cars, which had been proposed but neglected for a decade. In addition, acting OSHA head Alan McMillan, while waiting for the expected late 1989 Senate confirmation of President Bush's nominee for OSHA head, Gerard Scannell, has pursued more vigorous rule-making and enforcement.

Furthermore, producers, vendors, and consumers two millennia ago operated pursuant to the accepted Roman maxim of caveat emptor, "let the buyer beware."   Whereas consumers until this century were generally competent to exercise purchasing decisions, modern mass production and marketing of numerous complex products have required a concomitant system of consumer protection.[6] For example, there are more than 200 different kinds of toothbrushes available in the marketplace today.[7]   Consumerism and consumer protection experienced a renaissance in the 1960s, caused by an avowed need to redress the imbalance between vendors and consumers.   Yet decades later, consumers still distrust business: a public opinion survey indicates that only 19% of the respondents agree that business attempts to strike a fair balance between profits and the public interest.[8]

Despite the blessings of modern technology, the quality and safety of products must be closely monitored by business firms and by government. For instance, notable 1988 events include: two ex-Beech-Nut nutrition officials were found guilty of marketing apple-flavored sugar water that was labeled as pure apple juice for babies, and the Consumer Product Safety Commission and the Justice Department revised a settlement with manufacturers of all-terrain recreational vehicles to require them to fund $8.5 million in advertising the vehicles' potential safety hazards. Aequitron Medical Inc. divulged plans to recall as many as 5,000 machines used to monitor heart and respiration rates of infants at risk for

Sudden Infant Death Syndrome because some machines had faulty alarm systems.   In addition, Bristol-Myers agreed with the Food and Drug Administration to recall the remainder of 200 million doses of the anticholesterol drug, Questran, because it was contaminated with small quantities of a pesticide during the production process.   Moreover, Eastman Kodak revealed that batteries it claimed would last ten years *won't*, and consequently Black and Decker is recalling thousands of flashlights and terminating shipments of a new line of smoke detectors that carried the Kodak battery, the Ultralite 9-volt.

Further, in July 1989 the FDA announced that it would ban red dye No. 3, the only known waterproof red food dye—the one that keeps cherries red in fruit cocktail cans—because an individual may have as much as a one in 100,000 chances of getting thyroid cancer or other forms of cancer from it. Whereas the FDA typically fields tampering threats or complaints (280 in 1988 and 760 in 1987, often related to cyanide), the worst case since the cyanide Tylenol poisoning of 1982 occurred in March of 1989 when the FDA imposed a ban on all Chilean fruit.   FDA inspectors, pursuant to a phone threat in Santiago, Chile, found cyanide on Chilean grapes being unloaded from the *Almeria Star* docked in North Philadelphia.

Later in 1989 the Environmental Protection Agency banned the use of Alar on apples because of its threat to cause cancer.

In 1990 the FDA, in the wake of the Supreme Court's 1989 Webster abortion decision, will decide whether RU-486, a drug that sloughs a fertilized egg from the wall of uterus, can be marketed.   In the late summer of 1989 the FDA, headed by Commissioner Frank Young, requested several companies, including Squibb and Dow Chemical, which complied, and Sandoz, which has not, to cease promotion of milk suppressants for new mothers who do not breast feed their babies.   From late June through September of 1989 the FDA moved to revoke its approval for thirty generic drugs and suspended another 141 compounds, as a result of its investigation of whether generic drugs achieve results comparable to brand name products in the face of some firms' falsified bioequivalency data.

Today, the consumer relies on laws and regulations for protection against poor quality, hidden defects, and product flaws that can be harmful and, occasionally, deadly.[9] Although the basic agenda of consumerism may change, the movement will continue to have a significant impact on the business sector, as business firms are increasingly bearing more of the costs associated with defective or deleterious products.[10]

WORKPLACE HEALTH AND SAFETY

The Occupational Safety and Health Act of 1970

The underlying purpose of the Occupational Safety and Health Act (OSHA) of 1970[11] is "to assure so far as possible every working man and woman in the nation safe and healthful working conditions . . ."   A bipartisan Congress intended OSHA to serve as a comprehensive plan to decrease the incidence of employment-related illness, injury, and disease[12] by authorizing the establishment of health and safety standards, providing mechanisms for enforcing those standards, and protecting employees who complain of unsafe working conditions.

The statute was a powerful response to the fact that 14,000 workers had died and about 2.5 million had been injured in job-related accidents in 1970[13] and to the National Safety Council estimate that economic loss from work-related accidents totaled $8 billion.[14]   Moreover, prior to the enactment of the OSH Act, most state regulation had proved to be inadequate to the task of improving the health and safety of the workplace; criticism included wide variation in state statutes' coverage and enforcement.[15]   To fill the void of inaction, Congress established the Occupational Safety and Health Administration (OSHA), located in the Department of Labor, with broad legislative and executive powers to establish and enforce standards related to health and safety in the workplace through workplace inspections, citations, and monetary penalties; to institute required record-keeping procedures for employers to implement; and to collaborate with the states in developing their health and safety programs.

In addition, Congress also created the National Institute for Occupational Safety and Health (NIOSH),[16] an agency in the Department of Health and Human Services that conducts research to promulgate health and safety standards and regulations through OSHA, provides education and training programs, and can inspect workplaces and gather evidence and testimony from employers and employees.   Further, the suggestion for a standard or regulation, usually promulgated under the OSH Act through an administrative rule-making procedure, can emanate from OSHA, a union, or an interested party (employer or employee), as well as NIOSH.

The OSH Act also created the Occupational Safety and Health Review Commission (OSHRC), an independent agency consisting of three commissioners appointed by the president and forty-five administrative law judges, whose mission is to dispose of appeals from employers concerning violations and penalties resulting from OSHA inspections.   An administrative law judge hears the appeal, and resulting appellate decisions can be appealed to the full commission, and likewise its decision to the U.S. Court of Appeals and, if the high court grants certiorari, to the U.S. Supreme Court.

The OSH Act has broad coverage, regulating all employers, regardless of their size, who are engaged in a business affecting commerce,[17] unless the employer falls within a category expressly excluded from the act's coverage.   For instance, local, state, and federal government[18] employees are covered under separate provisions, and workplaces regulated under other federal laws, such as the Coal Mine Health and Safety Act,[19] are excluded from the OSH Act.   Yet, even with the exclusions, the act empowers OSHA to regulate well over 5 million workplaces.   Further, in order to design and enforce its standards, OSHA has a staff of greater than 2,300 persons, second in size only to the Environmental Protection Agency among social regulation agencies.[20]

Setting Standards and the Resultant Problems. The OSH Act authorizes the secretary of labor to create enforceable health and safety standards and provides procedures for their promulgation. Standards are defined as "legally enforceable regulations governing conditions, practices, and/or operations of the regulated institutions to assure that certain objectives [defined by congressional legislation] of the regulator can be achieved."[21] Specifically, a health or safety standard assures healthful and safe workplaces, according to the Department of Labor. Unlike the National Labor Relations Act, which lists proscribed practices, the OSH Act contains merely a general duty[22] clause and certain health and safety standards that have the force of law. Moreover, the secretary of labor's interpretation of standards has "great weight . . . as long as it is one of several reasonable interpretations."[23]

There are two basic OSH Act standards: (1) "national consensus standards," primarily authored by the American National Standards Institute (ANSI) and the National Fire Protection Association (NFPA), and, (2) "permanent standards," which may be new or revised standards.[24] National consensus standards relate to subjects such as machine guards, fire extinguishers, and electrical groundings, whereas permanent safety standards apply to particular industries and comprise four primary classifications: agriculture, maritime, construction, and general industry. Health standards, on the other hand, pertain to particular substances, such as lead or benzene, with which employees may be in contact.[25]

The secretary of labor must publish the proposed regulation, which is usually subject to the provisions of the executive order mandating a cost-benefit analysis, in the <u>Federal Register</u>, and, thereafter, interested parties can comment or object within thirty days, upon which objection a hearing is held. Within sixty days after the hearing, if the secretary still wishes to proceed, the standard is issued. Any employer adversely affected by a new standard may challenge it in the appropriate federal circuit court of appeals, and such legal action does not stay the effect of the standard, which the circuit court of appeals will uphold "if [the standard is] supported by substantial evidence in the record considered as a whole."[26]

Often unwieldy under the best of circumstances, the completion of rule-making procedures requires twenty-two separate steps. Under limited circumstances, OSHA can establish emergency temporary standards that take immediate effect and remain in place until replaced by a permanent standard. Such emergency standards arise from circumstances in which employees face grave danger as a result of exposure to toxic substances or agents or of new hazards posing a serious safety difficulty. Like permanent standards, emergency temporary standards can be challenged in the appropriate court.[27]

OSHA has issued standards of medical surveillance that require employers to monitor employee health and take corrective actions if health difficulties arise, as well as standards that limit toxic substance levels to which employees can be exposed. In some cases, like lead exposure, OSHA can even establish standards that require the removal of employees from the workplace.[28] Further, the Supreme Court has established that OSHA cannot regulate with the goal of creating an "absolutely risk-free workplace," but, rather, has to accept some risks that are small, and, further, must consider whether "the risk from a toxic substance [can] be quantified sufficiently to enable the Secretary [of Labor] to characterize it as significant in an understandable way."[29]

OSHA's reliance on standards has been criticized by commentators on a number of grounds:[30]

1. Workplaces and the concomitant hazards are not uniform, and, therefore, safety standards cannot be written with sufficient specificity to accommodate the various, unique conditions of the over 5 million workplaces in this country.

2. OSHA's standards eliminate only one-fourth to one-third of work injuries because a substantial number of hazards are work-specific, and therefore uncontrollable by standards.

3. Many safety professionals have concluded that, in fact, workers' behavior is the primary determinant of accidents, whereas OSHA standards misguidedly emphasize capital equipment to eliminate hazards.

4. Dangerous conditions and elements in the workplace vary continuously because of constant changes in technology.

5. Because of the substantial length of time required for final promulgation, many standards are outdated.

6. Standards have little meaning without inspections and penalties for deviations; since inspections are highly labor-intensive with expensive logistical costs, it is extremely difficult to improve the productivity of inspectors through mechanical devices.

7. Rather than discovering ways to reduce unsafe working conditions, inspectors are induced to concentrate on employers' compliance with standards, even though the very concept of inspections relies on a representative sample of observations, and the standards themselves necessitate subjective, instead of objective, interpretations.

8. According to one commentator, OSHA regulations have not been particularly effective in modifying business firms' incentives to invest in safety because the expected penalties for noncompliance are negligible and because the expenses to achieve compliance with regulations and standards are substantial.[31]

In the end, critics assert that OSHA has not had a significant effect on safety.[32]

Nonetheless, in response, Gerard Scannell, President Bush's nominee for OSHA chief, has indicated that he will likely propose, after Senate confirmation in late 1989, greater criminal fines for egregious employer violations, acceleration of and inclusion of unions in OSHA's rule-making process, and promulgation of a motor vehicle safety standard to protect on-the-job drivers. Clearly an activist, Scannell, as director of standards for OSHA in the 1970s, supervised the promulgation of regulations that serve as the nucleus of present-day standards.

In fact, the workplace of the 1990s, although considerably more productive, is more dangerous. The National Safety Council recently related that in 1987, the latest year for such government statistics, job-related disabilities climbed 16% to 70,000 and job-related illnesses and injuries increased 5% overall and 12% in the manufacturing sector.

Enforcement. OSHA health and safety officers' inspections comprise the first layer of enforcement. These inspections measure compliance with established national standards. OSHA undertakes four types of investigations or inspections as follows in order of priority: (1) inspections of imminent dangers, (2) investigations of catastrophes and fatalities, (3) investigations of complaints, (4) general or programmed inspections, and (5) repeat inspections of workplaces cited for allegedly serious violations. Reinspection occurs after an inspection by an OSHA compliance officer, and (if the compliance officer does not issue the citation immediately following the inspection) following OSHA's subsequent mailing to the employer a clear and thorough description of the violation, the standard broken, and, finally, a responsible time within which the employer must abate the violation.[33] Whereas approximately 86% of all inspections are of a general category, complaint inspections comprise 9% of the total.[34]

The total of inspections has risen or fallen based on the approach or emphasis of the particular presidential administration: 80,800 inspections in 1975 and 90,300 in 1976 as a result of the Nixon and Ford administrations' emphasis on general inspection; a one-third drop to the 57,200-63,400 range as a consequence of the Carter administration's elimination of the less-productive aspects of inspection and enforcement; and the present level of inspections, less than 70,000 annually, because of the conscious targeting of inspections by the Reagan and Bush administrations.[35] The present rate of inspection translates into less than one inspection for every two centuries for a particular business, and the number of employees covered by inspections decreased from its apex of 8.1 million in 1976 to 2.9 million in 1983.[36]

Furthermore, whereas the one explicit limitation on the scope of an OSHA inspection is "reasonableness,"[37] the Supreme Court in Marshall v. Barlow's Inc.[38] held Section 8(a) of the OSH Act unconstitutional as to the authorization of business inspections without a warrant. Nonetheless, any employer who permits entry without a warrant waives the right to insist upon that warrant.[39] However, in the case of imminent danger or a fatality, the OSHA inspection is based on probable cause and no warrant is required.[40] In addition, the Supreme Court has decreed that the Barlow's decision does not require a warrant provided an OSHA official serves a subpoena in the business facility's public area, and the Eighth Circuit Court of Appeals has ruled that no warrant is required when an OSHA official merely seeks to obtain records that the business, pursuant to regulation, is required to maintain.[41]

Violations and Sanctions. During the inspection, the OSHA inspector attempts to identify violations of OSHA standards, and in determining compliance, the inspector can only consider technical feasibility, based on general technical knowledge, of the employer's conforming to standards.[42] In 1977 after OSHA attempted to eliminate its pursuit of trivial violations, the number of OSHA violations dropped precipitously. Whereas the average inspection results in less than two citations for violations of OSHA standards, a greater emphasis on violations that pose serious threats to worker health has resulted in health standards violations comprising one-third of total standards violations.[43]

Moreover, although annual penalties have never exceeded $26 million, they are presently in the $6 million range. OSHA assesses penalties based on the category of violation: (1) an "other than serious violation" (one that probably would not cause serious physical harm or death) carries a proposed, but discretionary, penalty of $1,000 per violation and can be reduced, (2) a "serious violation" (where there exists substantial probability of serious physical harm or death) has a mandatory penalty of $1,000 per violation and can also be adjusted to a lesser amount, (3) a "willful violation" (one that the employer intentionally and knowingly commits) has a fine of $10,000 per violation and may be adjusted downward, and if the willful violation has resulted in death, the punishment includes a court-imposed penalty of not more than $10,000 or incarceration for up to six months, or both, and, (4) a "repeated violation" carries a fine of up to $10,000 for each violation.[44]

Whereas annual OSHA penalties total approximately $6 million and average only $57.00 per violation, workers' compensation premiums exceed $10 billion, and higher wages generated by attendant work risks comprise $69 billion.[45] In addition, OSHA penalties are minuscule compared to the costs of compliance: regulations proposed between 1975 and 1980 have a compliance cost of $100 to $500 billion. In the opinion of one commentator, based on these figures, penalties offer little deterrence, and penalties have no significant impact on employers, who now may decide to avoid remedial actions until actually inspected.[46]

Record-Keeping. The OSH Act of 1970 requires employers to promulgate and maintain records of work illnesses and injuries. These records serve numerous functions, including the following: they form a basis for reliable illness and injury rates; they assist employers in identifying those factors that cause workplace illness and injuries; and the records help compliance officers in their inspection and investigation procedures.[47] The two types of employee records that employers must prepare and maintain are: the Log and Summary, which classify illness and injury incidents, and, the Supplementary Record, which provides for the documentation of supplementary information concerning every recordable illness and injury. All cases of occupational illness must be recorded on the Log and Summary if they result in medical treatment, transfer to another job, unconsciousness, restriction of motion or work, one or more forfeited workdays, or death.[48]

One of the more controversial changes in OSHA requirements was the 1981 introduction of records inspections in which the OSHA inspector examines the employer's lost workday accident rate for the prior two years, in most instances, and for the past three years for very small employers.[49]   A formal inspection results if the rate is above the national manufacturing rate of lost workdays.[50]

Employer and Employee Rights and Responsibilities Regarding the OSH Act.[51] Under the OSH Act, employers are charged with certain responsibilities and invested with certain rights. Besides those already mentioned in this chapter, employer duties include: (1) providing a workplace free of recognized hazards that are likely to cause employees serious physical harm or death, (2) gaining knowledge of mandatory OSHA standards and providing copies to employees, (3) facilitating employees' awareness of OSHA, (4) providing medical examinations when OSHA standards require, (5) abating cited violations within prescribed time periods, (6) informing employees of their rights and responsibilities, (7) providing present and former employees or their agents with access to the Log and Summary, and (8) avoiding any discrimination against employees who properly exercise their rights under the act.[52] Such responsibilities are designed to reduce injuries and illnesses. For example, by fully informing off-shore oil workers about hazards and educating employees about how to work safely over a two-year period by use of a video tape, Chevron reduced its recordable injury rate by one-half and saved $2.3 million.[53]

Important rights of employers include: (1) receiving advice and off-site consultation from OSHA, (2) receiving the compliance officer's identification and reason for inspection during visit, (3) receiving an opening and closing conference with the compliance officer, (4) contesting the notice of citation and proposed sanction, (5) having a role in developing health and safety standards, (6) petitioning for temporary or permanent variances from standards for just cause, (7) receiving assurance that the confidentiality of trade secrets observed by a compliance officer during inspection will be maintained, and (8) petitioning NIOSH for information on whether any workplace substance has potential toxic consequences in the concentrations in use in the employer's workplace.[54]

Whereas OSHA does not cite or sanction employees for breaches of their duties, each employee is expected to obey the standards, regulations, rules, and orders under the OSH Act pertaining to his or her own work conduct.[55] Among these responsibilities are the following duties: (1) reporting hazardous work conditions to his or her supervisor, (2) reporting any injuries or illnesses to his or her supervisor, and (3) cooperating with any OSHA compliance officer who is conducting an inspection.[56]

Employee rights include the following: (1) requesting exposition from the employer regarding workplace health and safety hazards and procedures in case of accident or exposure to a toxic substance, (2) requesting an OSHA area director's inspection of the workplace if hazards or violations of OSHA standards are thought to exist, (3) being assured of anonymity if the employee files a written complaint, (4) having an employee representative accompany the OSHA compliance officer during inspection, (5) receiving a closing discussion with the compliance officer following the inspection, (6) receiving timely notification of the employer's petition for variance from an OSHA standard and the right to testify at any subsequent hearing, and (7) submitting comments or information to OSHA regarding the issuance, revocation, or modification of OSHA standards.[57]

Employers apparently have more responsibilities than rights, and employees more rights than responsibilities. Refusal of employees to comply with health and safety measures is not an employer defense; consequently, the employer is responsible for such matters as employees' wearing safety equipment like hard hats and earplugs.[58] Moreover, employers, corporations, and officers are subject to criminal prosecution for work-related deaths and injuries under various state penal codes, as well as the criminal sanctions of the OSH Act for workplace health and safety violations.[59] For example, Film Recovery Systems, Inc., managed a silver recycling plant in Illinois in which workers utilized a cyanide wash process to recycle and separate the silver from used x-ray film. Many of the workers, primarily illiterate Polish and Mexican immigrants, regularly suffered physical irritation or headaches and, in February 1983, an employee died of acute cyanide toxicity.

Pursuant to an Illinois penal statute[60] that provides that a person can be convicted of murder if he (or she) knew that his action or inaction created "a strong probability of death or great bodily harm" to the victim, three FRS executives were found guilty of murder, while Film Recovery and Metallic Marketing Systems, Inc., which owned one-half of FRS stock, was convicted of involuntary manslaughter and fourteen counts of reckless conduct.[61] The trial court held that the executives had known the cyanide was hazardous and also that workers were experiencing symptoms associated with cyanide poisoning, but had both failed to warn the employees of the dangers or provide adequate safety equipment.[62]

Another Texas case resulted in the criminal conviction of Joseph Tantillo, president of Sabine Consolidated, Inc., for negligence when two company employees were killed after the walls of a twenty-seven-foot trench collapsed and buried the men. The court decision found that Tantillo had demonstrated a disregard of the basic safety needs, as the trench walls allegedly were not adequately supported.[63]

The OSH Act, hence, provides criminal sanctions for violations of OSHA standards[64] if the employer's violation is willful and causes death. Moreover, the employer must breach a specific OSHA rule or standard, not merely the OSH Act's general duty clause.[65] Violation of the act's general duty clause results only in civil, not criminal, sanctions.[66] Because it is an administrative agency, OSHA may not impose a criminal sanction, but, instead, must refer the case to the Department of Justice (DOJ). Historically, OSHA has invoked the criminal provisions infrequently, and through October of 1987 had referred only forty-two criminal cases to the DOJ.[67]

Furthermore, the issue of whether workers may themselves reject unsafe assignments without employer retribution was decided in <u>Whirlpool v. Marshall</u>, 100 S. Ct. 883(1980).   A number of employee rights are "inferred" from the OSH Act's broad mandate to provide hazard-free working environments.[68] For example, in <u>Whirlpool</u>, two maintenance employees refused to walk on a wire screen suspended at a high altitude above the plant floor, even though so directed by their company supervisor.[69]   The Supreme Court determined that an employee is legally protected when refusing a task of such a nature that "a reasonable person under the circumstances then confronting the employee would conclude that there is real danger of death or serious injury," and, in addition, "there is insufficient time to eliminate the danger through resort to the regular enforcement channels."[70]   Nonetheless, the high court decreed that employers are under no legal duty to pay workers who refuse to carry out assigned tasks.[71]

Another issue concerns the OSHA Right to Know Law, whose purpose is to ensure that employers "receive information and training to allow them to handle hazardous substances safely."[72]   Such types of hazardous materials include: corrosives, carcinogens, highly toxic materials, irritants, and chemicals that affect body organs.[73] Those who support the right-to-know nature of this law maintain that, in order to adequately safeguard the employee's knowledge in the work-place, employers observe a duty to disclose health hazards information to employees as well as an obligation to provide health and safety records to employees.[74]

Specifically, OSHA rules require manufacturers and importers of certain substances, examples of which are identified above, to properly label such substances and to train employees to handle them safely.   Once a chemical is deemed a health hazard, the firm must prepare Material Safety Data Sheets (MSDS) by listing the name of the chemical, the physical and health hazards, appropriate exposure levels, measures for safe handling, and emergency treatment pro-cedures, together with the name and address of the person who prepared the MSDS.[75] Moreover, the employer must insure that each chemical container bears a label that will adequately inform employees of the nature of the substance and any hazardous effects.[76]

In addition, employers must promulgate training manuals and implement and record training programs, including tailored education for special risk groups such as women of childbear-ing age, temporary employees, and workers with health restrictions.[77]   In addition, under the Toxic Substances Control Act, the Environmental Protection Agency has imple-mented an expansion of the hazard communication program for some chemicals that are not included in the hazard communica-tion standard.[78] Typically, the Right to Know rule preempts all state statutes regulating like matters in the manufactur-ing sector;[79] however, preemption does not apply when the rationale for the state statute is different than the "object and purpose" of the federal standards on toxic chemicals.[80]

The Toxic Substances Control Act of 1977

The Toxic Substances Control Act (TSCA), a prophylactic approach to provide healthy and safe work environments, became effective on January 1, 1977. The TSCA provides the Environmental Protection Agency (EPA) with broad authority to regulate the manufacture, import, processing, distribution, use, and disposal of chemical substances."[81] Although the TSCA excludes certain chemicals such as drugs, cosmetics, pesticides, food additives and, tobacco products from coverage,[82] the act encompasses approximately 60,000 chemicals manufactured for commercial use and several million research and development chemicals.[83] The act's scope is vast as there are over 7 million known chemical compounds, with over 1,000 new chemicals produced each year.[84]

The thrust of the TSCA is that government should determine whether a substance can harm human health or the environment before it is commercially introduced.[85] The EPA is empowered through the TSCA to review information concerning the risks of new chemicals before their import or manufacture to determine whether those chemicals should be admitted, controlled, or prohibited access to the open market.[86] Moreover, the act also protects employees from employer discrimination when an employee has or is about to initiate a proceeding under the act, testifies in a related hearing, or participates in any manner in such a proceeding.[87]

The TSCA controls access to the market of potential chemical risks in a number of ways. First, no person may manufacture a new chemical substance or an existing chemical "for a significant new use," without submitting to the EPA a notice of intention to do so at least ninety days prior to commencement of such manufacture or processing.[88] Almost every TSCA review includes a discussion and determination of "unreasonable risk," which is not specifically defined in the act and, instead, is prescribed by a balancing test that "consider[s] the environmental, economic, and social impact" finding as to risk.[89] The act requires that, prior to TSCA regulatory action, the EPA must enter specific findings in the regulatory record as to unreasonable risk to human health or the environment.[90] If the EPA administrator believes an unreasonable risk exists, after reviewing the manufacturer's submission of required information, including any test data, regardless of age or results, that administrator may issue a proposed order to prohibit or limit the manufacture, processing, distribution in commercial use, or disposal of such substance.[91]

In addition to imposing work environment controls on new chemical substances that may present an unreasonable risk, the EPA may promulgate regulations to address risks of existing chemicals.[92] These regulations may require manufacturers of existing substances to conduct tests on these chemicals if: the substance may present an unreasonable risk or there may be substantial environmental or human exposure to the chemical; there is insufficient information to predict the environmental or health effects of the substance; and the testing is required to develop that information.[93] If the EPA determines that some type of control of an existing chemical is required, the agency can limit or prohibit manufacture, processing, or

distribution of the substance in commerce; require use
restrictions or bans; mandate informative labeling; prescribe
notice or record-keeping requirements; or establish disposal
requirements.[94]

Remedial Approaches to Healthy and Safe Workplaces: Worker's Compensation and Tort Litigation

The upheaval of the Industrial Revolution was characterized by
the movement in the nineteenth century of vast numbers of
persons from the relative tranquility of their homes, where
they practiced their cottage industries, to huge, often unsafe
factories.[95] Germany in 1884, England in 1897, and various
states of the United States in the first two decades of the
twentieth century responded to the alarming number of worker
injuries by establishing a compensation program.[96]

Before the enactment of worker's compensation statutes, the
only recovery recourse for injured employees was grounded in
suits based on employer negligence.[97] Employers had powerful
defenses such as the doctrines of assumption of risk,
contributory negligence, and fellow servant. As a consequence, courts typically decreed that an injured employee
assumed the customary risks associated with a work occupation,
and could recover damages only if it could be demonstrated
that the employer was negligent, that the employee had not
contributed to the injury through personal negligence, and
that none of the employee's fellow workers contributed to the
injury through their negligence.[98]

Worker's compensation, based on no-fault principles, "is
designed to provide an adequate and efficient remedy to
relieve the economic and social consequences arising from
employment related injury and illness."[99] An additional
feature of worker's compensation is the active involvement of
insurance companies that have been instrumental in directing
the companies toward accident prevention programs that lower
accident rates and severity, and, hence, insurance premiums.[100]

Although the states have enacted a variety of worker's
compensation statutes, there are certain common elements,
among them: (1) compulsory application of the worker's compensation doctrine to certain, specific employment, (2) benefits benefits based on the employment, not fault, (3) benefits
awarded pursuant to a schedule of death or the type of injury,
with the recovery derived from the injured or decedent
employee's level of earnings, (4) exclusive employer liability, (5) compulsory insurance or proof of insurance on the
employer's part, and (6) agency or commission, not judicial,
administration of the worker's compensation statutory
procedure.[101] In addition, the benefits scheduled in the
worker's compensation statute comprise the sole and exclusive
remedy an injured employee has against his or her employer and
certain other persons or entities, including fellow employees
and the employer's insurer,[102] with minor exceptions discussed
later in this chapter.

As long as the worker's injury is traumatic, the worker's
compensation system functions effectively; however, difficulties arise when occupational factors allegedly have caused
chronic illness or disease, because the relationship between

the work and the injury is not as easily established.[103] Critics of the efficacy of applying worker's compensation laws in such nontraumatic injury cases posit a number of objections:

1. The long latency period between exposure and symptoms increases the employee's difficulty in proving work relatedness or bringing action before the applicable statutes of limitation bar recovery.

2. The possibility of synergistic effects of multiple exposures that are occupational and nonoccupational complicates the determination of liability and damages.

3. The mobility of the American workforce often prevents employees from identifying the specific exposure(s) that caused the injury or disease.

4. Even the most recent and advanced epidemiology and toxicology studies of chemicals and working environments are deficient, thereby complicating the proof process.

5. In some states there is no recovery for partial disability, and in others, recovery lies only for partial disability, not death or total disability.

6. Some worker's compensation statutes place limits on compensable medical costs that may be unrealistically low for prolonged illness due to occupational disease.[104]

Moreover, the worker's compensation system has been severely criticized by the National Commission on State Worker's Compensation Laws, which notes that less than one-half of the states' statutes meet even one-half of the Labor Department's recommendations for state systems, including more widespread coverage of occupational diseases.[105]

A second remedial approach to healthy and safe workplaces—tort litigation that circumvents the exclusive remedy of worker's compensation—is an anathema to employers.[106] Certain tort theories, significant encroachments on the exclusive remedy principle, have increased employers' liability exposure. First, the contribution or indemnification theory allows the entity or person successfully sued by the injured employee to receive a contribution from the employee's employer if that employer is successfully sued by the manufacturer as a result, for example, of the former's negligent maintenance or operation of the equipment by which the employee suffered injury. Hence, in Dole v. Dow Chemical Co.,[107] the court allowed an indemnification action against the employer by a third party chemical company when an employee died while cleaning the employer's grain bin that had been fumigated by a toxic substance manufactured by the chemical company.[108]

A second theory that employees have used to skirt the exclusive remedy doctrine in worker's compensation statutes is an expanded form of intentional tort,[109] which is an exception

to many state worker's compensation statutes.[110]   Under this
theory, the injured employee can sue the employer for the
latter's intentional act that results in the harm.   However,
the different state standards regarding the type of conduct
that fits the exception ranges from, on one hand, something
approaching criminal intent where the employer knowingly
intended to cause harm to the employee[111] to, on the other, a
willfully reckless misconduct that could reasonably lead to
employee injury.[112] This intentional tort theory has nurtured
successful litigation, with its permitted claims for pain and
suffering and punitive damages, as a circumvention of the
exclusive remedy doctrine woven in the worker's compensation
statutes.

In cases in which employees of asbestos manufacturers
allegedly have contracted asbestos-related disease, plaintiff's lawyers have established intentional tort as an
exception, as in McDaniel v. Johns-Manville Sales Corp., 487
F. Supp. 714 (N.D. Ill. 1978), and other cases.[113]   In
McDaniel, it was ruled that the employer's failure to warn
employees of asbestos hazards comprises the torts of misrepresentation, fraud, and conspiracy to deceive, which
thereby establishes the intentional harm exception.

Other plaintiffs' lawyers have successfully applied the
intentional tort theory and its various permutations in cases
involving other chemical substances, as well.[114] Nonetheless,
many courts have rejected the expansion of the intentional
tort theory as an exception to the exclusive remedy doctrine.[115]

Yet another doctrine, dual capacity, has provided a
vehicle, in addition to the indemnification and intentional
tort exceptions, for circumventing the exclusive remedy
doctrine.   As Professor Larson notes in his treatise, The Law
of Worker's Compensation, under the doctrine of dual capacity,
an "employer may become a third person, vulnerable to tort
suit by an employee, if—and only if—he possess a second
persona so completely independent from and unrelated to his
status as an employee that by established standards the law
recognizes it as a separate legal person." [116]   The basis for
the dual capacity doctrine is the employee's right to sue a
third party tortfeasor regardless of the existence of the
worker's compensation remedy.   Examples include: when a
hospital employee sues the hospital for malpractice resulting
from treatment the employee received as a patient,[117] and when
an employee truck driver sues the employer tire manufacturer
for injuries suffered from an on-the-job tire blowout.[118]   As
of 1987 only California, Illinois, Michigan, Montana, and Ohio
had adopted the dual capacity doctrine.[119]

Employer Guidelines: Warning Employees About Hazards

In addition to the suggestions made in this chapter, employers
should adhere to the following guidelines:[120]

1. Employers should ascertain that every hazard warning
   uses easily understood language and pictographs and
   accurately depicts the actual degree of the hazard.

2. Such warning signs should be highly visible to affected employees and the employer should utilize on-the-job safety training to reinforce the meaning and intent of the sign.

3. The signs should be constructed of metal, plastic, or other durable materials and be positioned, with letters of sufficient size and highly readable color combinations, so that persons who have less than perfect eyesight can read them.

4. Employers should avoid wording on the warning sign that is so technical or ambiguous that employees of ordinary intelligence and knowledge cannot understand the warning's import. Toward this end, employers should promulgate a test to determine the number of illiterates they employ. Obviously, employers should determine that all employees, including illiterates, comprehend the warnings.

5. Employers should utilize "signal words" that readily convey the nature and extent of the danger associated with the hazard. The signal words "warning," "caution," and "danger" denote three distinct degrees of danger and should be used with their companion colors, orange, yellow and red, respectively.

6. The warning signs should also contain text that describes the specific danger (for instance, "radiation," "high voltage"), together with information concerning how to avoid the particular hazard.

7. Employers should maintain accurate records concerning the date and location of posted warning signs, the timing and nature of safety instructions, and memoranda of the employees' comprehension of such warnings.[121]

8. Employers that do not employ safety professionals should retain outside counsel to ascertain that all warnings comply with industry or OSHA standards.

GOVERNMENT AGENCIES AND CONSUMER PROTECTION

In the 1960s and 1970s, as a result of public concern and the consumer movement, Congress passed consumer protection statutes that created new agencies or added new powers to old agencies at an unprecedented rate.[122] Under the Reagan and Bush administrations, consumer organizations have not had the influence they exercised in earlier decades. "Things are a lot different from the days when Ralph Nader could rely on general outrage to get things done," notes the former director of Congress Watch.[123] Nonetheless, the legislation already enacted offers powerful protection to consumers.

Federal Trade Commission. The Federal Trade Commission was established in 1915 pursuant to the Federal Trade Commission Act (FTCA) of 1914[124] to ensure "vigorous, free and fair competition in the marketplace." Five commissioners, appointed by the president for terms of seven years, administer the act. The focal point of the FTC's consumer protection responsibility is Section 5 of the FTCA, which empowers the commission to protect consumers against "unfair methods of competition" in commerce.[125]

In addition, the Magnuson-Moss Warranty-Federal Trade Commission Improvement Act of 1975 amended Section 5 so that the FTC can now sanction "unfair methods of competition in or affecting commerce, and unfair or deceptive acts or practices in or affecting commerce," which activities are illegal.[126] The Magnuson-Moss Act was a response to, among other matters, the 1969 estimation by Senator Philip Hart, chairman of the Senate Subcommittee on Antitrust and Monopoly, that approximately 25%, or $200 billion per year, of the spent consumer dollars receive products or services of no value.[127] In 1983 Congress amended Section 5 to extend FTC jurisdiction to "unfair or deceptive acts or practices in commerce."

The commission has statutory authority to prevent any general restraint of trade in interstate commerce; deceptive or false advertising of consumer goods and other deceptive or unfair practices; and activities that tend to lessen competition or create a monopoly, including price discrimination and various acquisitions and mergers.[128] Three major bureaus of the FTC have unique responsibilities: the Bureau of Economics provides statistical and economic analyses to the other bureaus, the Bureau of Competition investigates and prosecutes restraint of trade violations, and the Bureau of Consumer Protection promulgates consumer protection, for example, in advertising practices, credit procedures, marketing abuses, product and energy information, and product liability.[129]

The FTC has long issued interpretative trade practice rules ("industry guides") that, as they appear in Subchapter B of Title 16 of the Code of Federal Regulations, describe acts or practices in a particular industry that the commission considers violations of the "unfair or deceptive acts or practices" prohibition in Section 5.[130] Whereas trade practice rules do not have the force and effect of law, "trade regulation rules," on the contrary, delineate specific activities proscribed by the FTCA, and breaches are considered violations of the statutory provision from which the regulation rule is derived.[131] The FTC's power to promulgate trade regulation rules, which the FTC had decided to exercise in 1962, was upheld in National Petroleum Refiners Association v. FTC,[132] a case in which the trade regulation rule involved provided that failure to display gasoline octane ratings on service station pumps would constitute a "deceptive practice," and, hence, violate Section 5. Under the Reagan and Bush administrations, the FTC shed its activist role and has emphasized individual consumer protection cases while deemphasizing broad rule-making authority.[133]

The Magnuson-Moss Act also significantly increases the FTC's remedies,[134] for prior to that act, the only procedure available to enforce Section 5(a) of the FTCA was a cease-and-desist order. Under such a procedure, prior to the FTC's issuance of a complaint and notice of hearing regarding a suspected Section 5(a) violation, the involved party can consent to a formal cease-and-desist order, or the party may informally agree to discontinue the questionable practice. Before the enactment of the Magnuson-Moss Act, the FTC could merely seek punishment of the violation of the cease-and-desist order, whether agreed to formally or decreed by the commission following testimony and the administrative law judge's recommendation.

Congress added significant sanctions: first, Section 408 of the Alaska Pipeline Act authorizes the FTC to obtain temporary restraining orders and preliminary injunctions of actual or threatened violations of any provision of any law administered by the FTC.[135]   The penalty for violation of cease-and-desist orders increased from $5,000 to $10,000. Second, Magnuson-Moss amended Section 5(m)(1) of the FTCA to impose civil sanctions for a first violation when the offending party knowingly violates a trade regulation rule, or when a party knowingly violates a cease-and-desist order issued against a third party.[136]   Moreover, the amended act also authorizes the FTC to seek damages in behalf of those injured by unfair or deceptive actions or practices, under certain circumstances, where a reasonable person would have known that the action or practice was dishonest or fraudulent.[137]

Consumer Product Safety Commission.   Of an estimated 35 million Americans annually who suffer injuries involving the use of consumer products, approximately 110,000 are permanently disabled and 30,000 are killed, at an economic cost of $5.5 billion.[138]   To reduce the number and severity of such accidents, Congress enacted the Consumer Products Safety Act (CPSA) of 1972[139] and the Consumer Product Safety Commission (CPSC) to administer the act.   The commission, like the FTC comprised of five members appointed for seven-year terms by the president, is empowered to issue and enforce safety standards relating to "safe performance, composition, contents, design, construction, finish, or packaging of more than 10,000 consumer products."[140]   Its mission is "to protect the public against unreasonable risks of injury associated with consumer products."[141]

A decision to promulgate a mandatory safety standard is normally based on data for injuries and deaths related to the product.   Lawrence Kushner, a CPSC commissioner from 1973 to 1977, explains: "The number and severity of the injuries, coupled with the expectation that a technically and economically feasible standard can be developed to reduce them, are the determining factors."[142]

Further, the Consumer Product Safety Commission has authority, in case of a potential danger in a product's use, to require that the product be "marked with or accompanied by clear and adequate warnings or instructions,"[143] and "may declare that the product is a banned hazardous product," if the commission deems "the public is not adequately protected."[144]   In addition, the CPSC is responsible for initiating and monitoring the recall of hazardous products; assisting industry in developing voluntary safety standards; helping consumers evaluate the comparative safety of products; conducting research and developing testing procedures for unsafe products; collecting, analyzing and publishing injury and hazard data; and assisting in reconciling federal, state, and local product safety laws and enforcement.[145] The commission can direct a manufacturer, distributor, wholesaler, or retailer to recall, repair, or replace any product the commission determines to be unreasonably dangerous.[146] Products exempted from the act's provisions include: tobacco and tobacco products, food, firearms, motor vehicles and equipment, certain boats, pesticides, aircraft, drugs, and cosmetics.[147] The CPSC, for example, in issuing over twenty standards, has regulated lawn mowers, matchbooks, baby cribs, bicycles, and children's sleepwear.

Since 1973 the CPSC has promulgated well over 1,300 recalls or other corrective actions related to more than 200 million products.[148] The CPSC does not, in order to recall or ban hazardous products, have to promulgate the rule-making process.   Recent CPSC ban and recall actions have addressed various products including: roller skates, electric drills, asbestos-containing hairdryers, scuba equipment, refuse containers, and thermostats.[149]   In the estimation of Kip Viscusi of Duke University, however, there is no "clearcut evidence of a significant beneficial effect on product safety from CPSC actions."[150] Given the fact that there has been no downward shift in poisoning rates after the advent of safety caps, Viscusi asserts: "The more general ramification of these results is that technological solutions to safety problems may induce a lulling effect on consumer behavior . . . [and] that failure to take [individual actions] . . . into account will result in regulations that may not have the intended effect."[151]

Moreover, Lawrence Kushner has pointed out the CPSC's inability to formulate safety requirements that are technically as well as economically feasible when the proposed standard requires the manufacturer to develop the subject product's manufacture or design beyond the state of the art.[152] The lack of innovation-forcing requirements in the standards can be cured, Kushner asserts, by encouraging interested parties to submit a "full-size, working prototype of the product in which the identified hazards had been reduced or eliminated."[153] Each producer who proffered a prototype would also estimate its retail cost and effectiveness in reducing or eliminating the hazards, and the CPSC would seek an offer to develop a standard with the optimal combination of safety and cost.[154]   Such a procedure, posits Kushner, "should substantially reduce the troublesome uncertainties about technical feasibility and cost" and "encourage small, innovative companies [manufacturers with small market share have little influence on the standards which in fact emerge] to demonstrate their designs."[155]

Any person who violates a Consumer Product Safety Commission ruling may be fined from $50,000 to $500,000 and incarcerated for up to one year. Further, the federal courts are empowered to enter an injunction against activities that violate the commission rules or orders.   The "tattletale" section of the act requires manufacturers, wholesalers, distributors, and retailers to report any known serious product safety deficiency or defect to the CPSC within twenty-four hours.[156]   Specifically, Section 15 of the Consumer Products Safety Act requires a subject firm to notify the CPSC that its product: (1) fails to comply with any applicable product safety standard, or (2) contains a defect that "could create a substantial risk of injury to the public, and hence presents a substantial product hazard."[157]   The Consumer Product Safety Amendments of 1981 mandate that the commission's advance notice of any proposed rule must request the development of a voluntary standard by interested parties. If the voluntary standard appears likely to eliminate or adequately reduce the risk of injury, and substantial compliance is probable, the CPSC must defer to the voluntary standard.[158]

National Highway Traffic Safety Administration. Congress enacted the National Highway Traffic and Motor Vehicle Safety Act (NHTMVSA) of 1966 and created the National Highway Traffic Safety Administration (NHTSA) to establish standards for motor vehicle safety. Later legislation authorized the NHTSA to set vehicle safety, fuel economy, and emission standards.[159]   The NHTSA is headed by an administrator appointed by the president and confirmed by the Senate; six associate administrators serve the administrator.

Among the regulatory activities of NHTSA, which is based within the Department of Transportation, are the following: establishment and enforcement of mandatory average fuel economy standards for new vehicles; regulation of safety performance for new and used motor vehicles and equipment; investigation of auto safety defects and directing manufacturers to correct such defects; establishment of standards for auto crash ratings and bumpers; enforcement of the uniform national maximum speed limit; and administration of the federal odometer law.[160]

In setting safety standards, the NHTSA focuses on the statistically greatest hazards and considers the number of accidents and injuries the standard is likely to eliminate. The agency has ordered manufacturers to include safety features such as seatbelts, safety windshields, steering columns that can absorb impact, high-mounted stoplights, and dual brake systems.[161]   Further, the agency must also contemplate the cost of compliance with the standard.[162]

Similar to the Consumer Product Safety Commission, the NHTSA can promulgate a recall of hazardous products. Manufacturers are required to report motor vehicle safety defects and any failure to comply within five days of their discovery. In response to such information, or as a result of its independent investigations, the NHTSA can require a recall, even for defects not covered by an established standard.[163]

Americans spend approximately $15 billion each year in attempts to make vehicles and roads safer. John Semmens, an economist with the Arizona Department of Transportation, asserts that since the passage of the NTMVS Act of 1966, government planners have been obsessed with an "engineering model." This model, Semmens and fellow critic Dianne Kresich emphasize, assumes that all safety problems can be solved by strict standards or refined design, and such ill-advised emphasis actually creates as many safety dilemmas as it eliminates.[164]   Highway death rates rose in population terms from 19.1 per 100,000 persons in 1925 to 19.3 in 1986. These critics of the NHTSA posit that "[p]sychology [driver's awareness of risks] may be more important than technology" in enhancing highway safety.[165]

The Food and Drug Administration. Food and drug laws have long been essential elements in civilized societies: early Egyptian law dictated the proper handling of meat; Greek and Roman laws prohibited short measures for grain and cooking oil and adding water to wine; and in the Magna Carta in 1215, England's King John asserted that there would be only one measure of wine, ale, and corn.[166] Moreover, the Industrial Revolution's concomitant increased use of chemicals, such as harmful food colors containing lead and arsenic, was the catalyst for enactment by the British Parliament in 1860 of the first general nationwide food law of modern times.[167]

The U.S. Food and Drug Administration (FDA) is an agency within the Health and Human Services Department (HHS), and the basis for its authority is the Food and Drug Act of 1906 and subsequent acts such as the Food, Drug, and Cosmetic Act of 1938, the Public Health Service Act of 1944, the 1968 Radiation Control for Health and Safety Act, the Fair Packaging and Labeling Act of 1966, and the Drug Price Competition and Patent Restoration Act of 1984.[168] The FDA's purpose is to "protect the public against impure and unsafe foods, drugs, and cosmetics, and to regulate hazards involved with medical devices and radiation."[169]

The Federal Food, Drug, and Cosmetic Act (FFDCA) of 1938, the most "important and far-reaching law enforced by the FDA," had as its catalyst the elixir sulfanilamide fatal poisonings in 1937 of 107 people, mostly children. Diethylene glycol, similar in substance to a chemical used as antifreeze, was the deadly solvent that liquefied the sulfa drug, sulfanilamide. Public outrage led to congressional passage of the FFDCA of 1938,[170] which closed many loopholes and included specific requirements that were educational and preventive in design. As a result, the FDA is empowered to require testing before a product is marketed.

The FDA regulates "the composition, quality, safety and labeling of food, food additives, colors, and cosmetics"; establishes standards for safe limits of radiation exposure; develops programs and standards relating to veterinary drugs; develops standards and regulations for proper manufacturing practices for medical devices; develops the composition, safety, quality, efficacy, and labeling of all drugs for human use; and regulates and sets standards for the development, manufacture, testing, and use of biological products.[171]

Under present law, all new drugs require proof that they are safe and effective before the FDA, specifically its Bureau of Drugs, approves their marketing.[172] Chemists, pharmacologists, physicians, statisticians, microbiologists, and other Bureau of Drugs staff members thoroughly analyze and assess every new drug application. The sponsor of a new drug has the responsibility for developing data that demonstrates the safety and efficacy of the drug and must also provide evidence to the bureau's satisfaction that sufficient controls will be established by the sponsor to ensure appropriate purity and quality of the new drug.[173] In addition, the FDA may order the removal of certain ingredients from the market as, for example: tribromsalan, removed from drugs and cosmetics because it causes extra sensitivity to light, and zirconium from aerosol deodorants because of possible damage to lung nodules,[174] and in 1988 stomach acidifiers, which purported to aid digestion by adding hydrochloric acid to the stomach, as unsafe and ineffective.

Critics contend that the FDA's cumbersome and lengthy approval process has inordinately delayed public access to needed drugs, such as those used against AIDS, and the huge amount of paperwork and filing and long waiting period has unduly burdened drug manufacturers and inhibited innovation.[175] For example, the average period for clinical study and agency approval of a new drug increased from 2.7 years in 1966 to 6.6 years in 1973. In addition, the number of applications for clinical study fell by more than one-half from 1963 to 1976.[176] Pharmaceutical firms have significantly reduced their basic research, whereas the cost of discovering and developing a new drug since 1960 has risen over eighteen times, half of which is attributed to the FDA requirements.[177]

In response to criticism, that the FDA's excessively conservative approach rejects good drugs and, in any case, causes unnecessary delays, the FDA revised the new drug approval process in February 1985. The result is the New Drug Application (NDA) Rewrite, similar to the reform proposal first published in 1982, which: (1) reduces the amount of supporting data required for an NDA, (2) institutes a policy for accepting foreign data in approving new drugs, (3) establishes new deadlines for FDA review during the evaluation process, and (4) institutes procedures for the accurate and timely apprising of drug sponsors of their application status.[178] Agency estimates of the benefits of these changes include 200,000 more prescriptions per year because of speedier approval of therapeutically significant new products, reduction of the average review time for new chemical entities from twenty-one to nineteen months, a decrease from twenty-seven to twenty-one months for NDA review of standard products, and an elimination of $5.7 million in filing costs for drug sponsors, and simultaneous review by different FDA departments.[179] Secretary Heckler of Health and Human Services termed the rewrite "the most important change in FDA drug regulation in twenty years."[180]

Under the Reagan administration, the FDA also established a "fast track" system that gives priority to those drugs that offer therapeutic advantages over drugs already in the marketplace. For example, in 1984 the FDA approved twenty-two new drugs, all novel chemical entities. Two of them, Trental and Pentam 300, are considered by the FDA to offer substantial therapeutic advantages.[181] In addition, the FDA has allowed AIDS patients to have access to experimental drugs such as Compound Q. The FDA and top researchers hope to enhance the safety of such drugs by cooperating with the research and testing efforts of those infected with AIDS and the doctors who treat them.

These measures to accelerate the approval process, though generally welcome and beneficial, have resulted in some serious problems due to lack of scrutiny. For instance, the FDA was severely criticized for its faulty surveillance of drugs after agency approval in the case of Zomax, a popular

painkiller, and Draflex, an arthritis remedy.[182]   Such difficulties publicly embarrassed the FDA and stifled other
proposed reforms to deregulate the approval process.[183]

In another area fraught with controversy, the FDA, under
the Delaney Clause, is required to prohibit the use of any
particular additive that induces cancer in humans or animals.
The Delaney Clause is comprised of three separate provisions
that apply restrictions on three classes of food constituents:
food   additives,[184]   color   additives,[185]   and   animal   drug
residues.[186]   The FDA is empowered by the "general safety"
clause of the Food, Drug, and Cosmetic Act to take any action
available under the Delaney Clause.   Although Congress,
through the Delaney Clause, has attempted to determine
regulatory policy by enacting a rigid statutory standard, the
FDA has determined that the Delaney Clause "implicitly allows
the addition of cancer-causing substances in trivial amounts
that pose at most only a negligible risk of harm."[187]   For
example, the FDA has allowed the use of methylene chloride to
decaffeinate coffee.

Two years after the Delaney Clause was adopted in 1958 to
govern substances added to food, Congress enacted a similar
premarket method of approval for colors added to drugs, foods,
and cosmetics.[188]   In the area of color additives as well, the
FDA recognizes the triviality exception.   Following the
"triviality doctrine," the FDA in 1986 gave final approval to
permanently allow the colors Red Number 19 and Orange Number
17 for use in externally applied cosmetics, even though each
color induced cancer in test animals.[189]

In determining that it thus has the inherent authority to
disregard literal terms of the Delaney statute when the matter
is de minimis, the FDA relied on the two opinions[190] of Judge
Leventhal that applied the de minimis doctrine.[191]   In one of
the two decisions, Alabama Power Co. v. Costle, the D.C.
Circuit Court asserts that "[u]nless Congress has been
extraordinarily rigid, there is likely a basis for an
implication of de minimis authority to provide exemption when
the burdens of regulation yield a gain of trivial or no
value."[192]

In approving the two color cosmetic additives noted above,
the FDA found the risks from using the cosmetics trivial
because they were well below the one-in-a-million lifetime
risk used by the FDA as a threshold.[193]   Thus the FDA established the same standard of risk it has used in assessing the
safety of color and food additives that have carcinogenic
constituents.   Although the risk of one color was less than 1
in 19 billion and the other was below 1 in 9 million,[194] the
D.C. Circuit Court of Appeals, in Public Citizen v. Young,[195]
ruled that even though the colors presented a trivial risk of
cancer, the de minimis exception conflicts with the "natural,
almost inescapable" reading of the Delaney Clause.[196]

The assumptions underlying the Delaney Clause have changed
since its enactment: the universe of detectable chemicals
"added" to food is much more vast than that contemplated by
legislators in 1958, and significantly greater numbers of food
ingredients have been proven carcinogenic than expected.[197]
Moreover, the FDA learned from the congressional rebuke when
the agency invoked the Delaney Clause in its proposed banning
of saccharin in 1977 that some food ingredients enjoy a

preferred status.[198]   The FDA proposal to ban saccharin triggered a rapid response from Congress, which quickly acted to preempt implementation of the ban; a moratorium has been reenacted on four occasions.[199]   A second axiom of the saccharin experience and the Delaney Clause is the difficulty in establishing rigid principles—one reason why Congress so frequently delegates discretion to federal agencies.[200]   A final lesson of the saccharin episode, moreover, is that Congress, in refusing to revise the Delaney Clause, has transferred the difficulties in dealing with the literal application of the Delaney Clause to the FDA administrators.[201]

Despite the dysfunction caused by Congress' explicit, yet imprudent, expression of will in the Delaney Clause, it has demonstrated an incapacity for allowing the FDA to utilize risk assessment in evaluating and regulating carcinogens.[202] Former Surgeon General C. Everett Koop notes: "It worries me greatly, but the facts don't seem to help much . . . [when] people . . . have an inappropriate sense of what is dangerous . . . [when] you translate the weight and time it takes a laboratory rat to develop bladder cancer to a 200-pound man drinking Fresca [which contains artificial sweeteners], it comes out about two bathtubs full each day. People dropped Fresca in a minute, but they continue to smoke."[203]   Yet, a person in the United States is thousands of times more likely to perish because of an auto or household accident than of cancer caused by manufactured pesticides in human food.[204]

PRODUCT LIABILITY AND TORT REFORM

The scope of business responsibility for the design, production, and distribution of its products has increased exponentially.   Each year 20 million Americans suffer injuries, including 30,000 deaths, in consumer products incidents, and 5 million persons are injured and 30,000 killed in vehicular accidents. The odds against escaping an injury at home, at work, or at the steering wheel are thus surprisingly low for the average American family of four—"an injury every four years or so."[205] Moreover, insurance costs doubled in 1985 for 40 percent of the U.S. Chamber of Commerce members, with nearly a fourth of these firms realizing premium increases of over 500%.[206]

Every year approximately 110,000 product liability cases are filed, and from 1974 through 1983 product liability suits in federal district courts increased from 1,579 to 9,221.[207] The number of product liability suits filed in federal district courts between 1974 and 1981 expanded at an average annual rate of 28%, over three times faster than the average annual growth of civil lawsuits filed in federal courts.[208] There were 401 million-dollar or greater verdicts in 1984 alone, with the average verdict now over $1 million.[209]

A basic element in the insurance crisis is the magnitude of the underwriting losses in the property and casualty insurance industry as well as the extreme difficulties underwriters encounter in predicting future losses so that they can establish adequate premiums to compensate the losses.[210]   Two basic factors in this insurance and product liability crisis are the substantial change in legal doctrines that effectively expands liability and the award of punitive or exemplary damages—exposing manufacturers to unprecedented risks. The law of products liability is "that body of common and statutory law permitting money reparation for the substandard conduct of others resulting in product-related injury to the injured party's person or property."[211] This body of law, the distillate of over seventy years of decisional law that originally protected manufacturers earlier in this century, has shifted far from the original stance that manufacturers and vendors are liable for damages only when (1) they have been negligent or unreasonably careless concerning a product, or (2) they have breached an express or implied warranty.

The judicial birth of the product liability doctrine occurred in 1916 in MacPherson v. Buick Motor Co.,[212] in which the New York Court of Appeals held that the manufacturer of any product capable of serious harm, if uncarefully made, owes a duty in the design, inspection, and fabrication of the product to the immediate purchaser and all others who might foreseeably be in contact with the product.[213] The MacPherson doctrine, now accepted by all American courts, is the direct descendant of the tort principle that an individual who sustains loss to his or her person or property as a result of another's breach of a cognizable duty of care may recover damages for that injury.[214] Prior to the court's recognition of the liability doctrine of the standard negligence theory, manufacturers could be held liable only if they failed to exercise reasonable care to make the subject product safe for those consumers who were reasonably expected to use the product.

In addition, prior to the use of the product liability doctrine, the only remedy, other than negligence, by which a plaintiff could recover from product injuries or loss was under the theory of express or implied warranty, which is concerned with the quality, performance, or safety of the product, not the prudence or negligence of the seller.[215] An express warranty relates to the seller's material representation of performance, effectiveness, or safety of the product, and a breach of that representation forms the basis of the suit for damages. Moreover, an implied warranty, breach of which is actionable, can arise: (1) unless expressly disclaimed, upon the sale of a product by a merchant of such products that the product is considerably similar in quality, performance, and safety to similar products sold in general (an implied warranty of merchantability), or (2) when the buyer expresses to the seller a need for a product for a specific and special application (an implied warranty of fitness for a particular purpose).[216]

For certain types of facts, such as damages caused by wild animals or sickness caused by unwholesome foodstuffs, the common law did permit the injured party to recover damages without being required to prove that the defendant's conduct was negligent.[217] The introduction in 1963, however, of the doctrine of strict liability in tort for the sale of "defective" products that are "unreasonably dangerous" to the consumer[218] radically altered the products liability jurisprudence.[219] In Greenman, a man was injured while using a power tool in his home workshop. Under the theory of strict tort liability, which is broadly similar to liability for breach of an implied warranty of merchantability, the basis for the cause of action is the safety of the product, not the conduct or prudence or imprudence of the seller.[220]

In addition, in 1965 the American Law Institute promulgated Restatement (Second) of Torts, Section 402A, "Special Liability of Seller of Product for Physical Harm to User or Consumer," which has been adopted by a majority of American jurisdictions.[221] This strict liability remedy requires no showing of negligence by the seller and, further, recognizes liability for any seller of a product "in a defective condition unreasonably dangerous to the user or consumer or his property." The rationale supporting this strict liability doctrine, according to tort law commentator William Prosser, is "a social philosophy which places the burden of the more or less inevitable losses due to a complex civilization upon those best able to bear them, or to shift them to society at large."[222]

As a consequence of the strict liability doctrine, to recover damages the plaintiff merely needs to establish that the product caused the injury and that a defect in design or construction or the product's operating instructions and safety warnings render it unreasonably dangerous or hazardous to use.[223] For instance, even the consumer's negligent use of the product may not be an adequate defense as when the mother of a fourteen-year-old son recovered substantial damages from his intentional inhaling of the freon propellant from a Pam container.[224]

In addition, other extensions of the strict liability doctrine have simply jettisoned as flotsam the revered legal principles of causation, fault, negligence, contributory negligence, and assumption of risk. For example, the Beshada v. Johns-Manville Corp.[225] decision, rendered by the New Jersey Supreme Court, establishes that there may be no mitigating circumstances on which a manufacturer may rely to avoid strict liability. In Beshada, the court struck the "state-of-the-art" defense; the defendant companies had demonstrated that they were unaware of the dangers of asbestos when they marketed the product and that such dangers could not have been discerned with the then-available scientific techniques.

Critics point out that the consumer ultimately pays for the higher insurance premiums and cost of manufacture through increases in product prices. According to one researcher, "Out of every dollar paid by consumers to cover the relevant liability costs, less than fifty cents . . . are returned to the consumers in benefits. Most of the rest [of every premium dollar] . . . goes to pay the lawyers, adjusters, and the like."[226] Another substantial cost to society is the companies' hesitation due to potential legal liability in introducing innovative products or expanding into new markets.[227] This inhibition damages American competitiveness and entrepreneurship, thereby assuring a lower standard of living for American consumers.

Added to the manufacturer's uncertainty that it may be liable for product hazards about which it could not possibly have known at the time of the product's introductions are the unfairly large and disproportionate awards of punitive or exemplary damages, as critics charge, especially in "mass tort" cases such as asbestos litigation. The concept of awarding damages in excess of actual loss has its roots in the Code of Hammurabi (200 B.C.).[228] Usually applied to intentional or conscious conduct involving behavior beyond negligence, exemplary damage became a tool to punish and deter reprehensible conduct.[229] The early American case of Coryell v. Colbaugh, reflecting the reasoning for allowing punitive damages in the English common law cases of Huckle v. Money[230] and Wilkes v. Wood,[231] explained the basis of punitive damages as not compensatory but, on the other hand, established to "give damages for example's sake, to prevent such offenses in the future . . . "[232]

Nonetheless, critics do not have to defend Johns-Manville's unconscionable withholding of evidence of the asbestos damage to workers and users, or A.H. Robbins' officials continuing to market the Dalkon Shield when they knew the product was not only dangerous but potentially deadly to attack certain aspects of exemplary damages awards.[233] Critics and defenders alike specify the weaknesses in the tort system relating to awards of exemplary damages: (1) "the unbridled pursuit of exemplary damages in mass tort cases could conceivably cause the tort system to fail in its primary compensatory purpose"[234] because the first successful plaintiffs exhaust the available funds, and (2) too vague jury instructions and a jury's fundamental lack of ability because "[j]urors . . . simply cannot fathom the intricacies in meaning and subtle connotations . . . for measuring reckless or wanton conduct."[235]   Other critics assert that exemplary damages, aside from any arguments concerning unfair or excessive economic results, are "quasi-criminal" penalties without the safeguards of criminal procedure.[236]   Advocates answer that exemplary damages' punishment and deterrence are necessary complements to an inadequate criminal justice system.[237]

The issue of punitive damages as unfair and excessive has been the subject of important 1989 federal court decisions. Recently, a New Jersey federal court dismissed a lawsuit involving exemplary or punitive damages as a violation of the due process clause of the Fourteenth Amendment.[238]   Another substantial argument against such damages, that they are contrary to the excessive fines clause in the Eighth Amendment, failed in Browning-Ferris v. Kelco Disposal, a case decided in 1989 by the United States Supreme Court.[239]   The Court held that the Eighth Amendment guarantee against "excessive fines" does not in any way limit punitive damages awarded in private, civil lawsuits; however, the Court suggested that such damages may violate the "due process" guarantee, an issue to be decided in some future case. Moreover, the Court refused to hear several challenges to large punitive damage awards against Metromedia Inc. ($14 million), Goodyear ($4 million), and General Host Corporation ($10 million).

In addition, some state courts have recently questioned the wisdom of allowing punitive damage awards in cases where the plaintiffs have alleged breaches of "good faith and fair dealing."   These contract-type disputes cut across a wide range of cases in employment, insurance, and lender fields. The California Supreme Court, for example, congruent with the state's consumers' initiative Proposition 103, which rolled back vehicle insurance rates, has eliminated lawsuits by employees seeking damages for wrongful discharge in most instances, and it overturned a landmark 1979 ruling that permitted consumers far-ranging power to sue insurers for bad-faith actions involving the latters' handling of insurance claims. The California high court expressed concern over the "potentially enormous consequences [of extending punitive damages to wrongful discharge cases] for the stability of the business community," in the ruling, Foley v. Interactive Date Corporation. Moreover, in 1988 the Oklahoma Supreme Court, which previously had upheld punitive damage awards against insurance companies' bad-faith breaches of contract, refused to allow the availability of punitive awards in commercial loan transactions.

Reformers, concerned about the growth of a litigious society, have suggested the establishment of a uniform product liability law and other reforms in the tort system. The challenge, as noted by Gordon Malott, chairman and CEO of FMC, is "to ensure standards that are understandable by manufacturers, equitable to product makers and users alike, and uniformly interpreted by courts and juries nationwide. . ."[240] The thrust of many of these reformers is to avoid what they term is the march toward automatic compensation; "liability without defect, similar to . . . 'no-fault' [liability] . . . [where] the injured consumer would be automatically compensated after [merely] showing he had been injured by the product."[241] Malott suggests the following standards to address this matter: (1) a negligence-based standard to judge the adequacy of product design and proper suitability of warnings, (2) the presumption that a product that conforms to government safety requirements is reasonably safe, (3) a limitation on liability for design or manufacturing defects to a specific time period, and (4) the assignment of liability and damages based on a system of comparative responsibility.[242]

Another commentator suggests further reforms in developing a reasonable system of liability: (1) a reasonable burden of proof on the plaintiff to demonstrate that the subject product actually caused the damage, (2) a limitation on lawyers' contingency fees to a reasonable approximation of the work actually performed, and (3) a requirement that damage awards be predominantly grounded in actual economic loss, and a limit on the amount of additional awards for intangible injuries.[243] A reform bill containing some of these features died in the Senate at the end of the 1986 session.[244]

With the apparent stalling of a congressional bill, many states in 1986 instituted significant steps to limit liability claims,[245] including: abolishment of joint and several liability for noneconomic damages (California), limiting punitive damages (Kansas), and allowing periodic payments for awards exceeding $250,000 (New York). Even advocates of the present tort system of products liability suggest two procedural changes. First, the court should allow full disclosure of the defendant's economic condition in all cases of exemplary damages, and evidence regarding the impact of an exemplary damages award on the defendant's future financial affairs. Second, in mass tort cases, the trial should be bifurcated: in the first stage the jury would determine

liability for compensatory damages. In the second stage, the
same jury should then consider "all relevant evidence of
future claims and the economic condition of the defendant,"
which would protect wealthy defendants from prejudice during
the liability portion of the trial.[246]

Even in the absence of regulation and a product liability
system that has eased the injured consumer's burden of proof,
firms have a substantial incentive to manufacture quality
products. First, the culture of the designer and engineer
demands attention to safety considerations. In addition,
consumer choices among various manufacturers and products
often hinge on those consumers' knowledge of the quality and
safety of producers and products.[247] According to John Young,
CEO of Hewlett-Packard, "In today's competitive environment,
ignoring the quality issue is tantamount to corporate
suicide."[248] In Made in America: Regaining the Productive
Edge, a 1989 book by MIT's Commission on Industrial Productivity, the author's central conclusion is that America has
lost its productive edge because, inter alia, there is a
tendency to pay too little attention to excellence in product
and manufacturing design.[249] Moreover, other studies indicate
that enhancing product quality increases profitability[250] by
reducing costs of labor, work in process and inventory, and
warranty and liability claims, and improving the utilization
of product equipment and tools.[251]

Like quality leaders Hewlett-Packard, IBM, Walt Disney,
and Procter & Gamble, firms have experienced sales and market
share benefits from improved product quality: increases of
market share at a rate five or six times greater than firms
whose product quality declined.[252] Moreover, changes in
product quality have the strongest correlation to changes in
market share, compared to the modest or nonexistent correlation of advertising and price change, respectively.[253]

Successful firms have identified several factors in
achieving the use of product quality as a competitive
strategy: (1) unqualified support of top management,
(2) quality as a key element in the firm's overall strategy,
(3) employees convinced that concern for quality is an
important characteristic of their jobs, (4) quality standards
that are established and measured, (5) product quality defined
from the consumer's perspective, and (6) a companywide system,
not just that of quality inspections in the manufacturing
process, but of quality improvement that links all functional
departments in providing defect-free work to the next user.[254]
Today's complexity of products requires top-level efforts to
assure continued pressure to inculcate safety and quality
considerations at all points in the production stage,[255] and in
most cases, to develop a formal, written safety and quality
policy.[256]

CONCLUSIONS

The reasons for continued striving to protect the safety of
the workplace are obvious. Even after nearly two decades of
OSH Act enforcement, estimates of the annual number of deaths
and disabling injuries range from the Bureau of Labor
Statistics (BLS) estimate of 5.75 million employees to the

National Institute of Occupational Safety and Health (NIOSH) tally of more than 10 million.[257]   Beyond fulfilling certain moral responsibilities, businesses such as Chevron have discovered that cost savings outweigh safety program expenditures.

Critics of present OSHA policies recognize numerous inherent benefits and the legitimacy of OSHA's purpose in enhancing workplace safety and have suggested basic reforms to improve OSHA's efforts to promote such safety, including greater flexibility in standards design and more stringent enforcement of those standards.[258]   Just as important, however, labor and management must cooperate to promote a safe and healthy work environment.   In the end, it is individual attitudes and psychology, as much as safe equipment and work areas, that reduce accidents.   Moreover, commentators view the quiltwork of laws and legal doctrines that address health issues, including the OSH Act, TSCA, worker's compensation, and tort legal systems, as causing "often duplicative, unnecessary and inconsistent regulation and litigation, which does not serve to further the interests of either employers or employees."[259]

Consumer protection as discussed in this chapter refers to a substantial number of laws, regulations, guidelines, and activities whose purpose is to regulate business and protect consumers from unsavory or unfair practices in the marketplace.[260]   This concept is not novel, for builders and architects in ancient Babylon were admonished to carefully design and construct their products,[261] and the Bible reinforced that concern for protection: "When thou buildest a new house then thou shalt make a battlement for thy roof, that thou bring not blood upon thine house if any man fall from thence."[262]   Nonetheless, the industrial-age hazards posed by machines with rotating, gearing, cutting, and shearing motions to shape wood and metal caused so many injuries by the midnineteenth century that legislatures in Europe and America, their attention riveted to these perils, enacted protective legislation.   In a desire to receive fair treatment, the American public supported the creation of a huge bureaucratic infrastructure to assist in the administration of the new laws.

Despite the creation of these numerous, intrusive laws and government agencies that regulate business conduct, the American public is increasingly dissatisfied with the marketplace.[263]   As one commentator noted in 1989, "Increasingly, people see grave risks in the most basic elements of their lives: their food, their water, even the air they breathe."[264]   These public concerns and pressures have no doubt influenced legislatures and the nation's jurisprudence to expand the scope of product-related injuries for which business firms now face damages.   The application of strict liability has radically increased the costs of product liability; the substantial change and expansion of liability has caused confusion among business firms.   Ultimately, these increased costs are paid by consumers, in higher product and services charges and in the lack of innovation and entrepreneurship of the nation's firms.

Moreover, whereas some commentators consider consumerism as in a decline stage of its life cycle, others believe that the movement is in a "mature, active stage."[265]   In any case, the proper response of business firms should be their institution of product safety and quality and risk-reduction programs that enhance product quality and control legal liability. One commentator suggests that business firms adopt a strategy of combining purchaser-oriented marketing, active consumer affairs departments, and selected cooperative enterprises with external consumer protection organizations.[266] Certainly, aside from regulations and laws, the rising consumer expectations and global competition of the 1990s are powerful catalysts for firms to emphasize, as have Polaroid, Ford, and Hewlett Packard, product quality and safety as key factors in a successful competitive strategy.[267]

NOTES

1. Buchholz, Business Environment and Public Policy, 3rd ed. (Englewood Cliffs, NJ: Prentice-Hall, 1989), 349.
2. Mason, "OSHA's Hazard Communications Standard," Vital Speeches (December 1, 1986): 118; see also National Safety Council, Accident Facts (1986).
3. Buchholz, op. cit., 353.
4. Foulkes, "Learning to Live with OSHA," Harvard Business Review (November-December 1973): 58.
5. Anderson, Buchholz and Allam, "Regulation of Worker Safety Through Standard-setting: Effectiveness, Insights, and Alternatives," Labor Law Journal (October 1986): 731.
6. Hemphill, The Consumer Protection Handbook (Englewood Cliffs, NJ: Prentice-Hall, 1981), 3-5.
7. Ibid., 4.
8. Bloom and Greyser, "The Maturing of Consumerism," Harvard Business Review (November-December 1981): 133.
9. Hemphill, loc. cit., 3-5.
10. Bloom and Greyser, op. cit., 130.
11. 29 U.S.C. Sections 651-678 (1982).
12. Marinelli, "Worker Protection and The Law of the Occupational Safety and Health Act," Suffolk University Law Review 21 (1987): 1053.
13. Marinelli, op. cit., 1053, citing S.Rep.No.1282, 91st Cong., 2nd Sess. 54 (1970).
14. Insurance Information Institute, Facts Book, Property Casualty, Insurance Facts, 1984-85 Edition (New York, 1985), 84, as cited in Anderson et al., op. cit., 731.
15. Buchholz, op. cit., 352.
16. 29 U.S.C. Section 671(a)(1982).
17. Ibid., Section 652(5)(c)(1982).
18. Ibid., Section 652(5)(1982).
19. Ibid., Section 653(b)(1).
20. Viscusi, "The Structure and Enforcement of Job Safety Regulation," Law and Contemporary Problems, 49, 4 (Autumn 1986): 133.
21. Anderson et al., op. cit., 734.
22. Marinelli, op. cit., 1053-1054.
23. Ibid.
24. Ibid., 1058-1059.
25. Buchholz, op. cit., 355.
26. 29 U.S.C. Section 655(f)(982), as cited in Marinelli, op. cit., 1060.
27. Buchholz, op. cit., 356-357.
28. Marinelli, op. cit., 1060.
29. Industrial Union Department, AFL-CIO v. American Petroleum Institute, 448 U.S. 607 (1980), as cited in Marinelli, op. cit., 1061.
30. Anderson et al., op. cit., 735-737.
31. Viscusi, op. cit., 527-528.
32. Ibid., 528.
33. Buchholz, op. cit., 358.
34. Viscusi, op. cit., 135.
35. Ibid.
36. Ibid., 136.

37. Marinelli, op. cit., 1056.
38. 436 U.S., 325 (1978).
39. Marinelli, op. cit., 1057, citing Southern Ind. Gas & Elec. Co., [1972, Rev. Comm.] O.S.H. Dec.(CCH) 15,328 (September 29, 1972).
40. Marinelli, op. cit., 1057.
41. Ibid., 1058, citing Donovan v. Lone Steer, Inc., 464 U.S. 416 (1984) and Donovan v. Union Packing Co., 714 F. 2d 840 (8th Cir. 1983).
42. Viscusi, op. cit., 138.
43. Ibid., 138-141.
44. Buchholz, op., cit., 358.
45. Viscusi, op. cit., 139.
46. Ibid., 139-140.
47. Buchholz, op. cit., 359.
48. Ibid.
49. Viscusi, op. cit., 140.
50. Ibid.
51. Buchholz, op. cit., 360-361 for a thorough description. This material is taken from that source.
52. Ibid.
53. McGuire, "Hazards in the Workplace," Trial (June 1988): 24.
54. Ibid.
55. Ibid.
56. Ibid.
57. Ibid., 361.
58. Buchholz, op. cit., 371.
59. 29 U.S.C. Sections 657, 666.
60. Ill. Ann. Stat., Ch. 38, para. 9-1(a), (Smith-Hurd, 1979), as cited in Kolodziej, "Pursuit of the Corporate Criminal," Boston College Law Review 29 (March 1988): 467.
61. Film Recovery Sys., Nos. 83-11091, 84-5064, as cited in Kolodziej, 467.
62. Ibid.
63. Buchholz, op. cit., 372.
64. 29 U.S.C. Section 666(e),(f) (1982).
65. Ibid., Section 666(e) (1982), as cited in Kolodziej, 471.
66. Ibid., 472.
67. Ibid., 473.
68. Buchholz, op. cit., 372.
69. Ibid., 373.
70. Ibid.
71. Ibid.
72. Fed. Reg. 53,821, 53,283 (1983), as cited in Marinelli, op. cit., 1063.
73. Marinelli, op. cit., 1063.
74. Buchholz, op. cit., 373.
75. 29 C.F.R. Section 1919.1210 (g)(2)(1985), as cited in Marinelli, op. cit., 1063.
76. Ibid., Section 1910.1210 (f)(4)(1982).
77. 15 O.S.H. Rep. (BNA) 1008-09 (March 6, 1986), as cited in Marinelli, op. cit., 1064.
78. 16 O.S.H. Rep. (BNA) 1061 (March 11, 1987), as cited in Marinelli, op. cit., 1064.
79. 29 C.F.R., Section 1910.1200(a)(2)(1985), as cited in Marinelli, op. cit., 1064.
80. West Virginia Manufacturers Association v. West Virginia 714 F. 2d 308 (4th Cir. 1983), as cited in Marinelli, op. cit., 1065.
81. Stillman and Wheeler, "The Expansion of Occupational Safety and Health Law," Notre Dame Law Review 62 (1987): 980.
82. Idem., citing 15 U.S.C. Section 2602(2)(1982).
83. Buchholz, op. cit., 436.
84. Ibid.
85. Ibid.
86. Ibid.
87. 15 U.S.C. Section 2622 (1982).
88. Stillman and Wheeler, op. cit., 983.
89. 15 U.S.C. Section 2601(c)(1982).
90. Stillman and Wheeler, op., cit., 982.
91. Buchholz, op. cit., 437.
92. Stillman and Wheeler, op. cit., 984.

92. Stillman and Wheeler, op. cit., 984.
93. Environmental Protection Agency, The Toxic Substances Control Act (Washington, DC: EPA, 1976), 2, as cited in Buchholz, Business Environment and Public Policy, 3rd ed. (Englewood Cliffs, NJ: Prentice-Hall, 1989), 437.
94. Buchholz, op. cit., 438.
95. Stillman and Wheeler, op. cit., 971.
96. Ibid, 969.
97. Ibid, 971.
98. Blackburn, Klayman, and Malin, The Legal Environment of Business: Public Law and Regulations (Irwin, 1982), 476-477.
99. Ibid.
100. Buchholz, op. cit., 352.
101. Stillman and Wheeler, op. cit., 971.
102. Ibid., 972, citing Ill. Ann. Stat., Ch. 48, para 138.5(a) (Smith-Hurd, 1986).
103. Ibid., 972.
104. Ibid., 971-973.
105. Buchholz, op. cit., 352.
106. Stillman and Wheeler, op. cit., 1003.
107. 30 N.Y. 2d 143, 282 N.E. 2nd 288, 331 N.Y.S. 2d 382 (1972), cited in Stillman and Wheeler, op. cit., 1004.
108. Stillman and Wheeler, op. cit., 1004.
109. Ibid.
110. 96 A.L.R. 3d., 1064, (1979).
111. Evans v. Allentown Portland Cement Co., 433 Pa. 525, 252 A. 2d 646 (1969) and Castleberry v. Frost-Johnson Lumber Co., 283 S.W. 141 (Tex. Civ. App. 1926), as cited in Stillman and Wheeler, op. cit., 1005.
112. Stillman and Wheeler, op. cit., 1005.
113. See also Martin v. Granite City Steel, 607 F. Supp. 1430 (S.D. Ill. 1985).
114. Blankenship v. Cincinnati Milacron Chems., Inc.. 69 Ohio St. 2nd 608, 433 N.E. 2nd 572, cert. denied, 459 U.S. 857 (1982), as cited in Stillman and Wheeler, op. cit., 1006.
115. Footnote 196, as cited in Stillman and Wheeler, op. cit., 1006.
116. 2A Larson, The Law of Workman's Compensation, Section 72.81 (1982), as cited in Stillman and Wheeler, op. cit., 1006.
117. Duprey v. Shane, 241 P. 2d 78 (Cal. App. 1951), affirmed, 39 Cal. 2nd. 781, 249 p. 2d 8 (1952); and Panagos v. North Detroit General Hospital, 35 Mich. App. 554, 192 N.W. 2d 542 (1971).
118. Mercer v. Uniroyal, Inc., 49 Ohio App. 2d 279, 361 N.E. 2nd 492 (1976).
119. Stillman and Wheeler, op. cit., 1007.
120. McGuire, op. cit., 24.
121. Ibid.
122. Buchholz, Fundamental Concepts and Problems in Business Ethics (Englewood Cliffs, NJ: Prentice-Hall, 1989), 213.
123. Saddler, "Consumer Groups Try to Keep Earlier Gains as Their Power Wanes," Wall Street Journal (December 31, 1986): 1.
124. The Act was passed in 1914; the FTC was empowered in 1915.
125. Epstein and Nickles, Consumer Law, 2d ed. (St. Paul, MN: West Publishing Co., 1981), 12.
126. Ibid., 14.
127. Nader, editor, The Consumer and Corporate Accountability, (Orlando, FL: Harcourt, Brace, Jovanovich, 1973), viii.
128. Buchholz, Business Environment and Public Policy, op. cit., 382.
129. Ibid., 381.
130. Epstein and Nickles, op. cit., 14.
131. Ibid.
132. 482 F. 2d 672 (D.C. Cir. 1973).
133. Buchholz, op. cit., 383.
134. Epstein and Nickles, op. cit., 16.
135. Ibid., 18.
136. Ibid., 19.
137. Ibid., 20.
138. Hemphill, The Consumer Protection Handbook, (Englewood Cliffs, NJ: Prentice-Hall, 1981), 88.

139. Public Law 92-573, as cited in Hemphill, op. cit., 88;   see 16 C.F.R. 1512 (1985).
140. Hemphill, op. cit., 90.
141. Petty, "The Consumer Product Safety Commission's Promulgation of a Bicycle Safety Standard," Journal of Product Liability 27 (1987).
142. Kushner, "Product Safety Standards and Product Innovation Too," Harvard Business Review (July-August 1980): 36.
143. Public Law 92-573, Section 7(a), as cited in Hemphill, op. cit., 90.
144. Ibid.
145. Buchholz, op. cit., 384.
146. Ibid.
147. Ibid.
148. Ibid., 386.
149. Viscusi, op. cit., 529.
150. Ibid., 553.
151. Ibid.
152. Kushner, loc. cit.
153. Ibid., 37.
154. Ibid., 38.
155. Ibid.
156. Epstein and Nickles, op. cit., 90.
157. 15 U.S.C.A. Sections 2064(a) and (b) (1975) as cited in Madden, "Post-Manufacturing Obligations," Products Liability, 2nd ed., (St. Paul, MN: West Publishing Co., 1988), 109.
158. Buchholz, op. cit., 386.
159. Federal Regulatory Directory, 5th ed. (Congressional Quarterly, Inc., 1986), 766.
160. Ibid.
161. Ibid.
162. Buchholz, op. cit., 387.
163. Ibid., 390.
164. Wilson Quarterly (Summer 1988), 46.
165. Ibid.
166. Janssen, "The U.S. Food and Drug Law: How It Came; How It Works," Food Drug Cosmetic Law Journal 35, 3 (March 1980): 132.
167. Ibid.
168. Federal Regulatory Directory, op. cit., 319.
169. Buchholz, op. cit., 387.
170. FDA Consumer 22, 9 (November 1988), 28.
171. Federal Regulatory Directory, op. cit., 320-321.
172. Farley, "How FDA Approves New Drugs," FDA Consumer 21, 10 (December 1987-January 1988): 7.
173. Ibid., 7-14.
174. Ibid., 12.
175. Federal Regulatory Directory, op. cit., 323.
176. Buchholz, op. cit., 396-397.
177. Ibid., 397; see also, "The Hidden Cost of Drug Safety," Business Week (February 21, 1977): 80, and Grabowski and Vernon, The Regulation of Pharmaceuticals: Balancing the Benefits and Risks, (Washington, DC: American Enterprise Institute, 1983), 23-48.
178. Federal Regulatory Directory, op. cit., 322.
179. Ibid., 322-323.
180. Ibid.
181. Ibid.
182. Buchholz, op. cit., 400.
183. Ibid.
184. 21 U.S.C. Section 348 (1982).
185. Ibid., Section 376 (1982).
186. Ibid., Section 360(b)(1982).
187. Gilhooley, "Plain Meaning, Absurd Results and the Legislative Purpose: The Interpretation of the Delaney Clause," Administrative Law Review 40, 2 (Spring 1988): 267.
188. Ibid, 271. See also 21 U.S.C. Section 376 (1982).
189. Listing of D&C Orange No. 17 and Red No. 19, 51 Fed. Reg. 28,331 and 28,346 (1986).
190. Monsanto v. Kennedy, 613 F. 2d 947 (D.C. Cir. 1979), and Alabama Power Co. v. Costle, 636 F. 2d 360 (D.C. Cir. 1979).
191. Gilhooley, op. cit., 274.
192. 636 F. 2d 323, 360-364 (D.C. Cir. 1979).

193. Fed. Reg. 50, 51,551, 51,555-556 (1985).
194. Gilhooley, op. cit., 274.
195. 831 F. 2d 1108 (D.C. Cir. 1987).
196. Stillman and Wheeler, "The Expansion of Occupational Safety and Health Law," Notre Dame Law Review 62 (1987), as cited in Gilhooley, 275.
197. Merrill, "FDA's Implementation of the Delaney Clause: Repudiation of Congressional Choice or Reasoned Adaptation to Scientific Progress?" Yale Journal on Regulation 5 (1988): 1, 12-18.
198. Ibid., 31.
199. Saccharin Study and Labeling Act, Public Law No. 95-203, 91 Stat. 1451 (1977).
200. Pierce, "The Role of Constitutional and Political Theory in Administrative Law," Texas Law Review 64 (1985): 469, and Gilhooley, 301.
201. Merrill, op. cit., 32 (1988).
202. Ibid., 87.
203. Specter, "Fear of Frying," The Washington Post National Weekly Edition (May 15-21, 1989): 9.
204. Ibid.
205. Kolb and Ross, Product Safety and Liability (New York: McGraw-Hill, 1980), 4.
206. Buchholz, op. cit., 400.
207. "Unsafe Products: The Great Debate Over Blame and Punishment," Business Week (April 30, 1984): 96.
208. Malott, "Let's Restore Balance to Product Liability Law," Harvard Business Review, reprint 83311, 51; see also Glaberson and Farrell, "The Explosion in Liability Lawsuits Is Nothing But a Myth," Business Week (April 21, 1986): 24.
209. Ibid.
210. Buchholz, op. cit., 401.
211. Madden, "Post-Manufacturing Obligations," Products Liability, 2nd ed., (St. Paul, MN: West Publishing, 1988), 1.
212. 217 N.Y. 382, 111 N.E. 1050 (1916).
213. Madden, op. cit., 1.
214. Brown v. Kendall, 60 Mass. 292 (1850).
215. Madden, op. cit., 2.
216. Ibid., 3.
217. Malott, op. cit., 52.
218. Greenman v. Yuba Power Products, Inc., 59 Cal. 2d 57, 27 Cal. Rprtr. 697, 377 P. 2d 897 (1963).
219. Madden, op. cit., 3.
220. Varady v. Guardian Co., 153 Ill. App. 3d 1062, 106 Ill. Dec. 908, 506 N.E. 2d 708 (1987).
221. Madden, op. cit., 19.
222. Prosser, Handbook of the Law of Torts (St. Paul, MN: West Publishing, 1955), 317.
223. See Malott, op. cit., 52.
224. Ibid., 54.
225. Ibid., 55; see also Leibman, "Liability for the Unknowable," Business Horizons (July-August 1982): 35.
226. Malott, op. cit., 56.
227. Ibid.
228. Demarest and Jones, "Exemplary Damages as An Instrument of Social Policy: Is Tort Reform in the Public Interest?" St. Mary's Law Journal 18 (1987): 798.
229. Ibid., 799 citing 1 Belli, Modern Trials, Sections 16.1-16.3 (2d ed. 1984).
230. 95 Eng. Rep. 768 (K.B. 1763), as cited in Demarest and Jones, op. cit., 800.
231. 98 Eng. Rep. 489 (K.B. 1763), as cited in Demarest, Ibid.
232. 1 N.J.L. 77 (1791), as cited in Demarest and Jones, op. cit., 800.
233. Brodeur, Outrageous Misconduct: The Asbestos Industry on Trial (1985) and Mintz, "At Any Cost: Corporate Greed, Women and the Dalkon Shield," The Progressive (November 1985): 20; see also Demarest and Jones, op. cit., 806-808.
234. Demarest and Jones, op. cit., 811.
235. Sales and Cole, "Punitive Damages: A Relic That Has Outlived Its Origins," 37 Vanderbilt Rev. (1984) 1117, 1137-1138.

236. Note 70, <u>Harvard Law Review</u> 517, 524 (1957), as cited in Demarest and Jones, op. cit., 816.
237. Owen, "Civil Punishment and the Public Good," 56 <u>S. Cal. L. Rev.</u>, 103 (1982), as cited in Demarest and Jones, op. cit., 819.
238. <u>Wall Street Journal</u> (March 20, 1989), 14.
239. Ibid.
240. Malott, op. cit., 56.
241. Bennigson and Bennigson, "Product Liability: Manufacturers Beware!" <u>Harvard Business Review</u> (May-June 1974): 132.
242. Malott, op. cit., 57.
243. Copulos, "An Rx for the Product Liability Epidemic," <u>Backgrounder: The Heritage Foundation</u> (May 15, 1985): 8-9, as cited in Buchholz, <u>Business Environment and Public Policy</u>, 402-403.
244. Buchholz, op. cit., 403.
245. "What Some States Have Done to Limit Liability Claims in Their Courtrooms," <u>Wall Street Journal</u> (August 1, 1986): 10.
246. Demarest and Jones, op. cit., 831-832.
247. Eads and Reuter, "Designing Safer Products: Corporate Responses to Product Liability Law and Regulation," <u>Journal of Products Liability</u> 7 (1984): 265.
248. Shetty, "Product Quality and Competitive Strategy, <u>Business Horizons</u> (May-June 1987): 46.
249. Rowen, "Strategy for Success," <u>The Washington Post National Weekly Edition</u> (May 22-29, 1989): 5.
250. Buzzell, "Product Quality," <u>The PIMS Letter on Business Strategy</u> 4 (1978), 3; and see Peters and Waterman, <u>In Search of Excellence: Lessons from America's Best Run Companies</u> (New York: Harper and Row, 1982), as cited in Shetty, op. cit., 48.
251. Shetty, op. cit., 49.
252. Ibid., 50.
253. Ibid.
254. Ibid., 51-52.
255. Eads and Reuter, op. cit., 265.
256. McGuire, op. cit., 68.
257. Buchholz, op. cit., 349-350.
258. Viscusi, op. cit., 150.
259. Stillman and Wheeler, op. cit., 1009.
260. Steiner and Steiner, <u>Business, Government and Society: A Managerial Perspective</u> (New York: Random House, 1980), 273-274.
261. Roberts, "The Origins of Product Safety," <u>Journal of Products Liability</u> 7 (1984): 19.
262. Deuteronomy, XXII:8.
263. Bloom and Greyser, op. cit., 132.
264. Specter, op. cit., 9.
265. Bloom and Greyser, op. cit., 132-133.
266. Ibid., 136.
267. Ibid., 139.

7
Protecting the Firm's Proprietary and Confidential Information

INTRODUCTION

In the 1980s the United States and other industrial economies increasingly relied on knowledge, rather than natural resources or commodities, to add value to their products and services. Knowledge-intensive industries, in contrast to traditional resource-based businesses, developed at a fissionable rate.[1] Development, use, and protection of this knowledge are the prime success factors for firms in the 1990s. As a result, proprietary information is the "new gold of the market place,"[2] according to S.R.I. International's Donn Parker. In this regard, firms, whether large or small, should anticipate the need for protection against misappropriation of their intellectual property, including patents, copyrights, trademarks, confidential business information and trade secrets.

Often, maintaining success for a firm depends on preserving its unique and exclusive practices and ideas. These assets, including the firm's proprietary technology, are vital resources for any company to maintain old and cultivate new products and markets. To one learned commentator, such proprietary information comprises the "company jewels."[3] Yet, thefts of trade secrets, one form of intellectual property, alone cost American firms $20 billion dollars a year, according to August Bequai, counsel to the American Society for Industrial Security.[4] Difficulty arises when a key employee leaves the firm's employ to accept a position with a competitor firm. There is a tendency, often realized in subsequent action, for that employee to divulge to his or her new employer the former firm's customer lists, secret formulas or processes, or computer software.

In 1982 as a result of a sting operation involving FBI agents posing as IBM employees and accepting bribes, IBM filed suit against Hitachi, other Japanese and American firms, and two former IBM employees, alleging theft of trade secrets and confidential information. According to FBI affidavits, Hitachi had paid over $600,000 for stolen information concerning IBM's technology.[5] As a consequence of the settlement, IBM secured the right to inspect Hitachi's new products to determine that Hitachi was not using IBM's protected proprietary information. In other cases, firms use the prospect of a job to pump information from eager applicants during interviews."[6] In another instance, as a result of the 1986 suit against former chairman and cofounder, Steven Jobs, for infringing on the firm's proprietary information, Apple received permission to inspect new computers of Jobs' firm NEXT before they are marketed. Further, DuPont was the victim of ingenious industrial espionage when a photographer took photos from a plane of that firm's plant being built to house its secret process for producing methanol.

Protecting, as IBM and Apple have, such competitively advantageous information is important, because developing intellectual property is expensive and time-consuming. Moreover, intellectual property protection, whether by patent, copyright, trademark, trade secrecy law, or restrictive covenants, encourages innovation, because firms can have a reasonable assurance that they will earn an adequate return on investments after developing that proprietary information. In fact, an economic system based on free enterprise relies upon innovation and ingenuity. In addition, "[f]airness and honesty in business competition is fostered by the principle that creating a unique idea giving one an advantage over one's competitor gives rise to a right to prevent others from taking and using the idea."[7] Too often, firms neither understand the protection afforded them nor do they effectively utilize covenants not to disclose or compete, which comprise an effective prophylactic recourse to prevent use or disclosure of intellectual property.

Although the process of identifying and protecting intellectual property appears obvious at first blush, an examination of what has and has not gained protected status suggests the complexity of that very process. For instance, computer programs that design class rings, a high-efficiency particulate air-filter process, many customer lists, a franchisor's business forms, and a labor-estimating manual of 57,000 entries have not gained legal validation as trade secrets. On the other hand, a computer software program relating to a management system for oil dealers, a software prompter for television, and a financial accounting system reporting requirements of school districts have attained trade-secret status.

Obviously, the firm must understand the fine distinctions so it avoids reliance on an intellectual property it cannot protect. At any rate, proprietary and other information is the currency of competition—and this fact is true for business firms of every size in every industry, whether service or manufacturing. For example, Coca-Cola Company understands the gravity of protecting its intellectual property. According to Robert A. Keller, senior vice president and general counsel, the firm keeps the written version of its formula for Coca-Cola in a security vault at the Trust Company of Atlanta, and the vault can be opened only by a resolution of the board of directors. Only two persons in the firm know the formula and oversee the actual preparation of the product, and they are never allowed to fly on the same airplane.[8]

Intellectual property comprises a vital resource for firms and can be classified as patents, copyrights, trademarks, confidential business information, or trade secrets. The basis of patent (as well as copyright) protection emanates from Article 1, Section 8 of the U.S. Constitution, which holds: "The Congress shall have power . . . to promote the progress of science and useful arts, by securing for limited times to authors and inventors the exclusive right to their respective writings and discoveries."

According to Union Carbide's chief patent counsel, Thomas I. O'Brien, "Patents are an incentive to invention, an encouragement to investment in the commercialization of new technology, and a promoter of technology transfer both within the country as well as to and from other countries."[9] Patents are issued by the U.S. Patent and Trademark Office and comprise three specific types of intellectual property: utility, plant, and design. A patent does not grant the inventor exclusive rights to practice the invention of the patent—to make, use, or sell the patent.[10] On the contrary, if the inventor wishes to maintain the secrecy of the invention, that person or firm can thereby exclude others from using the invention. Moreover, the inventor has a "negative right" to exclude another from constructing or employing the invention in return for placing the information in the public domain.[11] In addition, the patent holder may grant for a certain consideration, as a royalty payment, a license to another to make, use, or sell the patented invention as Union Carbide has done with its patented process for manufacturing polyethylene. As a result, about one-quarter of the world's polyethylene production employs the Union Carbide proprietary process.[12]

The patent owner must police the marketplace to determine any unauthorized use. The patent owner can recover damages from or gain an injunction against the infringer. A willful infringer, including a firm that has exercised care in attempting to determine whether its action constitutes a patent infringement, can suffer punitive as well as treble damages.[13]

A utility patent is issued to "protect new, useful processes, devices, or inventions" for a seventeen-year term and that process, service, or invention, to be patentable, must satisfy a number of requirements. Specifically, it must fall within one of following classes: manufacture, machines, composition of matter, and processes; and it must be new, useful, and nonobvious. Only the actual inventor may apply for patent protection, although the inventor often transfers the patent, after issuance, to a business firm. The laborious process of securing a patent can comprise two or more years; during the application process, the invention obtains a "patent pending" status and the government is prohibited from revealing the invention.[14]

A plant patent is obtainable for a seventeen-year term to protect any new variety of plant that the applicant can reproduce in an asexual manner. A design patent protects nonfunctional characteristics of useful objects for three, seven, or fourteen years. A design patent must satisfy the following prerequisites: it must be aesthetically appealing and not dictated only by utilitarian or functional concerns, and the design must be novel, nonobvious, and embodied in an article of manufacture.[15]

Copyright protection, a species of intellectual property, is exclusively federal and exists in an original work of authorship that is established in a tangible medium of expression from which it can be comprehended.[16] Copyright protects the expression against copying and other specific acts; however, copyright does not protect a method of operation or an idea. The distinction between idea and expression defines the "boundary between the domain of the patent and that of copyright."[17] Copyright protection, which extends for a term of fifty years after the death of the creator, allows authors and artists the exclusive right to print, copy, sell, and distribute their intellectual and artistic creations. The subject of copyright includes books, pantomimes, and choreographic works, plays, movies, recordings, paintings, prints, maps, ornamental designs of useful objects, and sculptures. Copyright laws specifically include plans, ideas, systems, methods, and devices.[18]   The purpose of copyright, according to the Supreme Court in its 1985 decision in Harper and Row Publishers, Inc. v. Nation Enters 105 S. Crt. 2218, is to "increase and not impede the harvest of knowledge."

Generally, a trademark, first used by members of medieval Europe merchant guilds, is a distinctive mark of authenticity, whether a name, symbol, device, or configuration, through which the product of a particular manufacturer or the vendible commodity of a merchant may be differentiated from those of others.[19]   Three other types of protected marks are: service marks such as "Holiday Inn;" certification marks such as the "Real" seal on dairy products or the "G" symbol on movies; and collective marks used by members of an association or the like, such as "American Bar Association."   To maintain trademark and other mark protection, an owner must use it and prosecute any infringement. Among those unprotectable terms are generic terms, even though formerly a trade name, which refer to the general class of the product, such as zipper, aspirin, and escalator.

Confidential business information, though less secret than a trade secret, has been accorded protection by the courts. One important requirement, in order for the firm or person to demonstrate that the information falls within the rubric's protection, is that the information has been confidentially disclosed with the clear understanding that it is confidential.   Even though the information is within the public domain, if the recipient of that information reaps any value from his or her disclosure of it, he or she may be liable for damages under the legal theory of unjust enrichment.[20]   The courts have, in some cases, found a duty on the part of the recipient of an idea to transfer the already existing patent covering that idea to the inventor even though the recipient had searched for the idea in existing patents and had purchased that patent from a third party patent holder. In such cases, the courts have ruled that the confidential nature of the relationship between the inventor and the recipient precludes the latter's enrichment at the expense of the former.[21]

TRADE SECRETS

A commonly accepted definition of trade secret is "any formula, pattern, device, or compilation of information which is used in one's business, and which gives him an opportunity to obtain an advantage over competitors who do not know or use it." A trade secret may be a formula for a chemical compound, a process of manufacturing, treating, or preserving materials, a pattern for a machine or other device, or a list of customers,"[22] together with a pattern, program, or technique.[23] Whereas a business with a trade secret can receive protection against unauthorized disclosure or use, there is no concomitant right against another's independent development or valid reverse engineering, which is an analysis of the product to discern secrets of its manufacture, structure, or operation.[24]

Unlike a patent, a trade secret does not provide a specific term monopoly against others' usage, and to have any protection, the trade secret owner must take reasonable measures to maintain the secrecy of the subject information. However, the trade secret itself may or may not be patentable; trade secrecy is merely an alternative to patents as a form of legal protection. Coca-Cola, for example, maintains its cola recipe as a trade secret because, unlike that of trade secrets, patent protection would expire after seventeen years. Trade secret protection, entirely controlled by state law, has enveloped information about a welding process, a formula for pressurized shaving lotion, a tape recorder, a storage system for materials, a brick used to line cement kilns, a process for manufacturing compressed cotton bath sponges, and a scrap metal recovery process.[25]

In 1987 the Supreme Court reaffirmed the critical importance of protecting business information: "Confidential information acquired or compiled by a corporation in the course and conduct of its business is a species of property to which the corporation has the exclusive right and benefit . . . ."[26] Courts and commentators have composed several tests to determine whether particular information constitutes a trade secret. Under all of the tests, however, the plaintiff has to carry a substantial burden to prove that the information or knowledge is, in fact, a trade secret. The most common test is that appearing in the Restatement of Torts, Section 757, comment b(1939), which lists six factors as follows:

1. The extent to which the information is known outside of [the] business.

2. The extent to which it is known by employees and others involved in the business.

3. The extent of measures taken by the holder of the alleged trade secret to guard the secrecy of the information.

4. The value of the information to the holder and to his or her competitors.

5. The amount of effort or money expended by him or her in developing the information.

6. The ease or difficulty with which the information could be properly acquired or duplicated by others.

A trade secret, however, does not need to be so novel as to qualify as a patent. The secret to be protectable must have commercial value, even if never marketed or used outside the firm, and it must be generally unavailable to persons beyond the group selected by the owner of the secret to trust with its use or knowledge.   Further, the information, to qualify as a trade secret, must be in continuous use; this requirement eliminates information that has a fleeting value such as a bid for a job.[27]

The test for the third factor in the Restatement standard is based on reasonableness, and, toward this end, "[t]he owner of a trade secret must take reasonable precautions to protect its secrecy" and that degree of secrecy "need not be absolute" but "be such that it would be difficult for others to obtain the information without using improper means."[28]   Whereas the rule in a few jurisdictions requires absolute secrecy, the reasonableness standard, the majority view, has as its rationale: "Reasonable precautions against predatory eyes we may require, but an impenetrable fortress is an unreasonable requirement . . . "[29]   Moreover, in the landmark case, E.I. du Pont de Nemours & Co. v. Christopher, the court placed a burden on the defendant, the employee who misappropriates the trade secret, to refrain from employing improper methods to discover the trade secret.[30]

Another often-cited test, in addition to the Restatement measure, is the one that appears in Aetna Bldg. Maintenance Co. v. West, 246 P. 2d11, (Cal. 1952).   The elements of the Aetna test are:

1.   The employee possesses trade or business secrets or confidential information not readily available to others.

2.   The employee, with intent to injure, solicits the customers of his or her former employer in a competitor-business.

3.   The customers are preferred customers whose trade is profitable, and knowledge of whom is confidential and a trade secret.

4.   A single concern is usually patronized by a customer and the names of customers are secret.

5.   There is an established business relationship between the customer and the former employee that normally continues.[31]   Other tests, such as Hollingsworth,[32] are adaptations of Aetna.

Uniform Trade Secrets Act

A third standard of establishing a "trade secret" is provided by the Uniform Trade Secrets Act,[33] which a number of states, including California, Connecticut, Delaware, and Minnesota, have adopted.   That act defines a trade secret as information, including a pattern, formula, program, device, method, technique, or process, that (1) derives independent economic value, actual or potential, from not being generally known to, or readily ascertainable by proper means by, competitors, and

(2) that is the subject of efforts that are reasonable under the circumstances to maintain its secrecy.[34] Although the Restatement only implicitly recognizes certain information as a trade secret, the act clearly establishes that a trade secret can be information. Moreover, the act definition appears sufficiently broad to encompass negative information as well—data that indicates what ideas or designs are undesirable or not feasible—and it covers single-event information, such as status reports, which the Restatement excludes by requiring instead that the secret be in continuous use.[35]

The act recognizes two basic types of misappropriation of trade secrets: (1) misappropriation through improper means, and (2) the voluntary disclosure or use of another's trade secret by one who used improper means to acquire the knowledge of the secret or knew or should have known that his or her knowledge was derived from someone who had used improper means or owed the owner of the secret a duty to maintain secrecy, or acquired it under circumstances that gave rise to a duty to maintain secrecy.[36] Misappropriation by improper means includes, among others, theft, misrepresentation, bribery, breach or the inducement of a breach of duty to maintain secrecy, and espionage through electronic or other means.[37]

The legal remedy for the improper appropriation of a trade secret is grounded in the tort theory of conversion. Courts are divided as to whether trade secret disputes are within the purview of a property right or confidential relationship duty. The most frequently sought legal remedy is that of injunctive relief. When the plaintiff seeks a preliminary injunction, the court generally employs the common law test as follows:

1. Whether the employer has demonstrated a reasonable probability of success on the merit—whether a trade secret appears to exist.

2. Whether the plaintiff will suffer irreparable harm without injunctive relief.

3. Whether granting a plaintiff preliminary relief, in the form of an injunction, will cause even greater harm to the employee.

4. Whether granting preliminary relief serves the public interest.[38]

The court may enjoin an employee from misappropriating a trade secret whether or not he or she has executed a restrictive covenant or contract.[39] The employee may also be liable in tort for damages, especially in cases where he or she has enjoyed a confidential relationship with the plaintiff and has received a trade secret and benefitted by its use. The plaintiff may sue the new employer, to whom the employee has transmitted the trade secret, under theories of tortious interference with a contract, unfair competition, or misappropriation of a trade secret.[40] Damages may include damage to business and goodwill as well as lost profits.[41] Although trade secret protection has generally existed in state civil common law, more than twenty states, including New York and

California, have enacted trade secret criminal statutes as well.

The Uniform Trade Secrets Act, adopted by a number of states, provides for injunctive and monetary relief for the misappropriation of trade secrets.[42] Under the act, the court can enjoin either actual or threatened misappropriation of a trade secret, compel affirmative acts to protect a trade secret such as the return of documents, and condition future use of a trade secret upon payment of a royalty when an injunction appears unreasonable.[43] Damages for actual losses as a result of the misappropriation also lie under the act, as well as any unjust enrichment not calculated in the actual losses portion of the damages. Actual damages recovery covers that time period in which the misappropriation occurs but in which no injunction to prohibit the misappropriation has been issued.[44] The act provides for punitive damages, limited to an amount that is twice the award of actual damages and unjust enrichment, for "willful and malicious" misappropriations. The act also authorizes an award of attorney's fees to the prevailing party in situations in which the losing party acts in a reprehensible manner.[45]

Other Remedies

Other remedies exist for misappropriation of trade secrets. The federal Racketeer Influenced and Corrupt Organizations Act (RICO) (discussed in Chapter 12 and used by IBM in its suit against Hitachi) is attractive because it allows the recovery of treble damages and attorney's fees.   Under RICO, the plaintiff must prove that the defendant's alleged misappropriation of the trade secret is part of a pattern of racketeering in or affecting interstate commerce in which the defendant was involved, with resulting injury to the plaintiff's business or property.[46] Often, plaintiffs use state unfair competition statutes as the basis for lawsuits.   To prevail under this legal theory, the employer must prove the subject information is a trade secret; a third party obtained the trade secret through deceptive, unfair, or illegal means; and the employer suffered harm by the imminent or actual disclosure or use of the trade secret.[47] Under a breach of trust theory, the court may find that the employment relationship is confidential and that the employee has a duty not to act against the employer's interests, regardless of whether there exists an employment contract.[48] An employer can successfully prevail under a breach-of-contract theory, whether the contract is oral or written or whether it is implied from the totality of circumstances, if it can establish that the former employee, not the employer, breached an express or implied contract, and the employer suffered damages as a result.[49]

In addition, because the firm's directors or officers generally must satisfy higher standards of loyalty than other employees, a director or officer may be liable to the firm if it appropriates an opportunity in the firm's line of business that the firm had the ability and expectancy to pursue.[50] Related legal theories are those of inducing a breach of contract and interference with a prospective business advan-

tage.   Under the inducing a breach of contract theory, if a
new employer solicits an employee to abandon his or her prior
employment, the harmed former employer may, as IBM, recover
damages.   To prevail under intentional interference with a
prospective economic advantage, the plaintiff firm must
demonstrate that it suffered damages because the defendant
intentionally and unjustifiably disrupted the plaintiff's
economic relationship, of which the defendant had knowledge,
with a third party, which would have resulted in a future
economic benefit to the plaintiff.[51]   In a few states, the
plaintiff firm, from whom the defendant has allegedly misappropriated a trade secret, can prevail under a legal theory
of negligent interference with a prospective economic advantage if the harm to the plaintiff was foreseeable, and the
defendant intended the transaction to affect the plaintiff.[52]

Protecting the Firm's Computer Software: Advantages and Disadvantages of Trade Secret and Copyright Protection In General

Computer software is the information that runs the computer's
machinery (hardware).   In 1983 the world software market was
$18 billion, of which the U.S. share was 70%.[53]   That market
has increased significantly since, at an average annual rate
in excess of 25%. Any firm that invests in the development of
its own computer software for sale or internal use obviously
is entitled to have it legally protected, since development
costs are often significant.

State trade secret protection safeguards computer software.[54]   In Kewanee Oil Company v. Bicron Corp., the Supreme
Court stated: "The maintenance of standards of commercial
ethics and the encouragement of invention are the broadly
stated policies behind trade secret law."[55]   Clearly, then, a
firm that invents computer programs has safe harbors in which
to protect its development.   Moreover, in Tandy Corp. v.
Personal Micro Computers, Inc.,[56] the court determined that the
1976 Copyright Act[57] extended federal copyright protection to
computer software.   Later, the Computer Software Copyright Act
of 1980[58]amended the 1976 act and added a definition of
"computer program" and defined the exclusive rights of
copyright holders of computer programs.

Consequently, any firm must determine whether to employ
trade secrecy or copyright to protect the computer software
that it has developed.   There exist advantages and disadvantages for each form of legal protection, generally and
specifically as they relate to computer software.   Trade
secrecy advantages[59] include: its clear applicability over the
broad range of program representations; its protection of
underlying ideas and information against both unauthorized use
and improper disclosure; its protection of a broad range of
subject matter (e.g., a program as well as a flow chart); the
immediacy of its protection from its creation; the potentially
indefinite duration of its protection; the probable reduction
of improper use because the owner-firm normally has a generally complete knowledge of those licensed to use the trade
secret (software); and the availability to the owner firm of

preliminary relief (e.g., injunction against use or dissemination) in any lawsuit.

Disadvantages[60] of trade secrecy protection are numerous, too. This form of protection is ill-suited to information (e.g., computer software) that is characterized by broad proliferation. In addition, trade secret protection is not particularly suited to induce others to develop compatible programs; it is constantly subject to an immediate loss of protection through disclosure, and its secrecy is difficult to maintain. Last, there is no treaty that establishes international reciprocity regarding trade secrets.

The numerous advantages[61] of copyright protection include the following: copyright protection has prospered in an environment of significant proliferation, and this intellectual property right is not diminished by infringement or proliferation; it is suitable for inducing third party creation of compatible programs, because it can allow full disclosure without divestment of the intellectual property right. Copyright protection, although relatively inexpensive, uncomplicated, and rapid to obtain, has an extraordinary duration (e.g., for works created after 1977, the protected term is the author's life plus fifty years). Additionally, copyright, as a body of federal law, usually dominates state law in conflict situations in conformity to the supremacy clause of the U.S. Constitution, Article VI, Clause 2. Also, in copyright suits the plaintiff frequently secures preliminary relief, such as injunctions to prevent infringement; and multilateral treaties provide for reciprocal treatment of nationals of signatory nations.

Copyright disadvantages[62] include: copyright does not prevent the owner of a copy from renting or selling it; the Copyright Act indicates that copyright does not protect the basic algorithms of a program; and in the noncommercial climate of computer usage, it is difficult to restrain copyright infringement.

Often, especially in the case of computer software, it is advisable to simultaneously protect the firm's proprietary information through trade secrecy and copyright. Copyright, which "extends to tangible forms of an author's expression, complements trade secret law, which protects the author's underlying ideas."[63] Moreover, copyright also provides a safety net in the event of dissemination of the trade secret (software). The firm should guard against the divestment of trade protection when copyright is obtained by securing the confidentiality of the trade secret. Nonetheless, together trade secret and copyright provide the software owner with greater protection than either alone.[64]

EMPLOYEE CONTRACTS

Precautions to Protect Confidential Information, Prevent Competition, and Establish Ownership of Inventions

Under the common law, it is not necessary for an employer to rely on a written agreement with an employee to protect the firm's confidential information and trade secrets, since there often exists an employee duty not to use or disclose the

firm's confidential information.[65] Yet, restrictive covenants
not to compete and not to disclose provide additional protection to employers. The importance of such covenants not to
compete is illustrated in a case[66] in which a firm developed
a materials handling system for sale to General Motors.
Following a successful marketing campaign of the product to
GM, key firm employees departed to create a competitive firm
and offered an automated system to GM. The court disagreed
with the former firm's contention that the departed employees'
knowledge of the decision makers at GM was a protectable trade
secret. The firm, though, could have protected itself against
exploitation by obtaining covenants not to compete.[67]

Covenants not to compete, although disfavored and strictly
construed as an infringement on free competition and trade,
are enforceable if the employer gives consideration to the
employee in exchange for the latter's promise not to compete.
Most jurisdictions consider new or continued employment as
adequate consideration, whereas a few, as in Pennsylvania,
require that contracts executed after employment has begun be
supported by some change in the status of the employee, such
as a promotion or pay raise.[68]

The contract not to compete must be reasonable in three
regards to be enforceable: the restraint against the employee
must be no greater than what is necessary to protect the
employer in some legitimate business interest, the restraint
must not be unduly harsh (primarily from the point of view of
the period the covenant operates and its geographic scope) in
curtailing the employee's legitimate efforts to earn a liveli-
hood, and whether the common or statutory law of the jurisdiction, specified in the covenant or determined in litigation
that applies to the contract's enforcement, holds the restraint against the employee as violative of public policy.[69]

Courts enforce covenants not to disclose the firm's
confidential information, because the former employee is under
a duty, regardless of a contract, not to disclose or use "in
his new employment . . . special skill, technique, or the
like, knowledge of which [the employee] confidentially
acquired in his earlier employment."[70] The courts usually
restrict the limitation against a former employee's use of
confidential information to the time discovery of the information could be reasonably made using lawful means.[71] Normally,
to be upheld as the noncompetition agreement, the covenant not
to disclose confidential information must contain reasonable
chronological and geographic limits; the information the
employer seeks to protect must be confidential; and the
contract restriction must be reasonably necessary for the
protection of a legitimate proprietary interest.[72] Since the
use of an express contract in these instances is always
preferable to a contract implied in law, the firm should be
very careful to draft restrictive contracts that will pass
court scrutiny.

Guidelines For Drafting Convents Not To Compete Or Not To Disclose

Guidelines are appropriate in drafting covenants not to
compete and not to disclose:[73]

1. The firm should carefully draft the agreement, ascertain that the information protected is indeed confidential, reduce time and geographic limitations to a minimum, and name in the contract the most favorable jurisdiction with which it has sufficient legal contacts to enforce the agreement.

2. The firm should require restrictive covenants to be executed only by those employees who possess skills or knowledge that, if used by a competitor, could injure the firm's legitimate business interest.

3. The firm should require the selected employees to execute the restrictive covenants contemporaneously with first employment.

4. The firm may wish to provide for forfeiture of future benefits, provided such forfeiture does not violate the Employment Retirement Income Security Act (ERISA), together with a broad remedies provision.

5. The firm should provide written notification regarding employee rights under the appropriate state statutes.

6. The firm should make certain that the employment policy manuals are consistent with the restrictive covenants.

7. The firm may wish to provide for the less formal and expensive, but speedier, arbitration process.

PROTECTING THE FIRM'S RIGHTS IN INVENTIONS AND PATENTS

Patents of inventions can provide a firm with profitable and exclusive positions in its most important processes and products and generate income from licensing of the patents derived therefrom, according to Union Carbide's chief patent counsel, Thomas O'Brien. For instance, Union Carbide annually files over 1,200 patent applications and has over 21,000 patents and patent applications worldwide. No matter what its size or market, almost every firm must address the issue of employee inventions.

In the 1890 decision, Solomons v. United States, [74] the Supreme Court, in grappling with the issue of employer and employee rights concerning inventions, distinguished two circumstances of employee inventions: those made by employees whose job task is to invent and those promulgated by employees in general, noninventive employment while using the employer's property. Without a specific agreement, an employer's rights are derived from the employee-inventor's employment status, which is determined by state law. [75]

The employer has the burden of demonstrating that the employee-inventor's status, determined in part by the employer's expectations, requires him or her to assign the resulting patent to the employer. First, when an employer hires an employee to invent a specific thing, there is an implicit obligation on the employee's part to assign any resulting patent from an invention to the employer—even one from an invention created without any employer assistance.[76] Neverthe-less, if the employee can prove that the invention is not related to his or her assigned duties, or to the employer's business and research, the employee is not required to assign the patent for the invention.[77]

Second, an employee employed to generally use his or her inventive skills, as opposed to being assigned either to invent a specific thing or to solve a particular problem, owes no patent resulting from his or her invention.[78] Nonetheless, in the Dubilier[79] decision, the Supreme Court held that an employer may own a patent resulting from the invention of an employee hired generally to exercise his inventive skills, provided: the inventor created the invention during hours of employment; the invention is within the employer's scope of business; or the employer assigned tasks similar to those performed in the invention process to the inventor.[80]

The third type of employee, one who is not hired to invent, does not implicitly agree to assign any patent resulting from his or her invention, even when he or she creates that invention through employment.[81] Nonetheless, when the employee uses the employer's resources in creating the invention or when the employer promotes the invention with a reasonable expectation of royalty-free use, the employer may have a nonexclusive license to use the invention. The employer's royalty-free nonexclusive, nontransferable license, termed a "shop right," exists for the life of the patent, whether the employment ends in the meantime, and allows the employer to use, manufacture, and sell products embodying the patent within its normal range of business.[82]

Because the common law, explained above, can be vague and arbitrary, it "has proven unsatisfactory to both employers and employees and has to a considerable extent been supplanted by contractual arrangements."[83] The courts usually strictly construe these employment contracts that allocate patent rights and supersede the common law against the employer. The majority of states allow contracts in which the employee-inventor, in consideration of regular salary, has a binding obligation to assign inventions to the employer, and cooperate in disclosing inventive activity and in patent prosecution activities.[84] Of course, the parties may limit the agreement to inventions made in the course of the inventor's research or work. On the other hand, they may include all inventions, even those unrelated to the employee's work, or even those created independently during the employment term or for a certain period after the employee leaves his or her employ-ment.[85] The courts attempt to "balance the perceived in-equities in bargaining position between employers and em-ployees, and to limit inventions covered by employment agreements to those in which the employer has a legitimate and justified business interest."[86]

In an expected response to the uncertainty of court interpretation and the resulting lack of uniformity in the interpretation, a number of states, such as California, Illinois, Washington, Minnesota, and North Carolina, have enacted statutes that limit the scope of an employer's right to own inventions created by an employee outside the firm's business on his or her own time without use of the firm's time or resources.[87]

Guidelines: Reasonable Steps to Protect the Firm's Proprietary Information and Trade Secrets

Affirmative action to safeguard trade secrets may prevent misappropriation and, hence, lawsuits. In addition, in any lawsuit that seeks redress because of misappropriation, the steps that the firm takes to protect the secrecy of the information is often the touchstone of the success or failure of the firm's case, and any such policy places the employee on notice of the obligation to preserve the secrecy of the information.

1. Regardless of its size, the firm should review all proprietary information to determine its importance, and the firm should establish and disseminate a written policy relating to secret and other proprietary information. The policy should include a general discussion of what constitutes proprietary information, examples of how the information can be misappropriated, and the firm's security system. The firm should periodically audit the policy to effect necessary modifications in the program and to demonstrate reasonable steps to preserve confidentiality in case of litigation.[88] The firm should consider the standard practices of firms in its industry.[89]

   The firm should appoint an audit group to establish and monitor the proprietary information program. These individuals should be trustworthy persons with a demonstrated record of commitment to the firm. For example, the American Tobacco Company has limited access to a tobacco formula to only twenty employees. The firm's legal counsel, an engineer (if the proprietary information is complex), and a member of the firm's security staff are valuable members of any audit committee.

2. The firm should disclose secret information only to those employees who have need of it for particular tasks or duties.

3. The firm should inform those trusted employees that the information is a trade secret and instruct them not to disclose the secret to others. Those employees should have an opportunity to suggest means to improve security.

4. The firm should label every proprietary information "top secret" or "confidential" and with prohibitions against its distribution outside of the firm. Proprietary information includes trade secrets and the following: technical documents, blueprints, and manufacturing information that reveal formulas, designs, or general "know-how."

5. The firm's audit committee should review every communication (e.g., speech, technical paper, article, and interview) by key employees and those having access to the secret information to co-opt any voluntary or

negligent disclosure of proprietary information. Additionally, the firm should caution any of its employees who attend trade conferences to be cautious in their formal or informal communications.

6. The firm should employ any of the following measures regarding securing its place of business where the trade secret is used: locks, guards, fences, displayed notices of the proprietary information or trade secret, utilization of the trade secret in an area geographically segregated or removed from the remainder of the plant, barriers or privacy screens around the area where the firm uses the trade secret, displays of false ingredients to confuse observers, and use of a paper shredder to dispose of recordings of formulas, computations, and inventories.[90]

Notice of the proprietary information or trade secret use and of the employees' obligations should appear on bulletin boards in firm newspapers or circulars, and in computer systems. In addition, trade secrets and other proprietary information, when possible, should be locked in files. The firm should employ special security measures to restrict access to any computer system in which proprietary information is stored. When transmitting computer data, firms should encode or scramble transmissions over telephone lines.[91]

7. The firm should take the following steps in dealing with the firm's employees: covenants not to compete and nondisclosure agreements (see Exhibit A at the end of this chapter);[92] fully investigating the trustworthiness of any potential employee, especially one whose task requires physical proximity to the use of the trade secret; causing the departing employee to acknowledge the trade secret in a termination interview and document; and requiring that each employee in the area of the trade secret use display a security or access badge.[93] The firm should request that employees not discuss proprietary information outside of the restricted area. Inquiry as to any potential employee's background should include a determination of whether that applicant was exposed to trade secrets or confidential information, and how he or she honored those confidences. In addition, the firm should consider dividing the secret process into several steps, as one firm accomplished with its poultry seasoning product, and, hence, restricting the number of employees familiar with the complete process. There should be a control system in which employees record the use, as a in sign-out procedure, of confidential documents.

8. The firm should establish a program for the protection of inventions and patents developed by the firm. In this regard, the firm should require every employee to execute Exhibit B (see later in this chapter).[94] Union Carbide has established an impressive, thorough policy

to protect its ownership of inventions and the patents developed by its employees. Toward this end, Union Carbide, according to Thomas O'Brien, the firm's chief patent counsel, employs extensive invention disclosures, guidelines for laboratory record-keeping, invention assignments, and confidentiality agreements.

9. In regard to nonemployees, such as visitors and repairmen, the firm should promulgate the following precautions: visitor screening, visitor logs and schedules, passes, requiring visitors to be accompanied by company escorts, a security policy relating to tours, denial of access to competitors or the press,[95] and barring of cameras and tape recorders. Firms should establish confidentiality agreements with suppliers, manufacturers, purchasers, or licensees to whom it may disclose confidential information. Firms should determine that such third parties have their own security systems that adequately protect the firm's confidential information while in the third party's possession.

10. The firm should summarily refuse to consider any outside ideas before receiving a full waiver from the submitter of the idea, since a number of ideas conceived by inventors are trade secrets. Legal recovery has occurred in such cases, when disclosure is not perfected, on the legal theory of misappropriation of a trade secret or breach of a confidential relationship, especially when the firm has encouraged the submission of the idea.[96]

11. The firm should refrain from inducing any employee to divulge trade secrets or confidential information of former employers.

12. The firm should be prepared to authorize lawsuits to recover damages for any misappropriation of a trade secret. In so doing, the firm establishes a deterrent to future misappropriation.

13. The firm should require a new employee to enter patent or confidential information contracts by which the latter assigns all rights to the firm of anything that employee may invent. Such an agreement places the employee on notice that he or she will have exposure to the firm's proprietary information. The agreement should include the warning that the employee's subsequent use of the proprietary information for his or her own purpose will be a breach of the firm's confidentiality. Moreover, the agreement should contain a general description of the areas the firm considers to be proprietary.

14. The firm should require each visitor in laboratory and manufacturing areas to enter a written agreement that

he or she will maintain the confidentiality of any proprietary information to which he or she is exposed.

15. The firm should educate every director, executive, manager, supervisor, and employee regarding what areas comprise proprietary knowledge and what do not. The firm should schedule annual meetings for all employees to remind them of the critical need to maintain the secrecy of the firm's proprietary information.

16. The firm should require every existing employee, no matter what access he or she has to proprietary information, to execute an annual agreement[97] acknowledging that he or she has access to proprietary information, that the firm is adequately safeguarding that proprietary information, and that he or she will immediately report to the firm any unauthorized use or disclosure of that proprietary information. Moreover, the agreement should define the trade secret information which it covers.

17. The firm's general counsel should debrief every departing employee who has been exposed to the firm's proprietary information.[98] At the meeting, the general counsel should provide the employee with oral and written reminders of the latter's obligation to maintain the confidentiality of the firm's proprietary information. The firm should require the employee to surrender any technical notebooks or memoranda, keys, and any lists or devices that are the firm's property. Moreover, the firm should require the employee to execute, in the presence of the general counsel, an acknowledgement (see Exhibit C later in this chapter)[99] of the specific nature of the employee's continuing obligation for preserving confidentiality. The firm's general counsel should advise the departing employee's new employer, in writing, of the employee's continuing obligation to preserve the confidentiality of the firm's proprietary information.

18. In the few jurisdictions, such as California and Michigan, that do not enforce postemployment noncompetition agreements, the firm should consider entering a legitimate postemployment consulting contract with important employees as a means of preventing those employees' employment with a competitor.

19. The firm should send letters after the exit interview reminding every former employee that he or she is prohibited from disclosing confidential information to the new employer. However, liability arises if the letter threatens the former employee's new employment, as when the new or potentially new employer terminates or refuses to establish the employment because of fear of a lawsuit initiated by the former employer-firm.[100]

CONCLUSIONS

In the competitive national and international climate of the 1990s, corporate managers must acquire and preserve advantages over competitors. Managers' ability to create and protect commercially sensitive information has a direct bearing on the firm's profitability. Further, by preserving such assets the firm is able to provide employment to others and is encouraged to search for further proprietary information.

As discussed in this chapter, proprietary information is not confined to technology, but, rather, includes any information useful to the firm—from customer lists to pricing policy. Firms have resorted to industrial espionage and the hiring of competitors' key employees to garner other firms' family jewels. In fact, the two leading causes of information losses are ubiquitous domestic and international piracy and employee mobility.[101] Further, whereas reverse engineering is a legal and unpreventable form of determining the inner workings of a competitor's product, a firm's tight control of its proprietary information will protect those secrets that reverse engineering does not reveal.

Litigation to protect the firm's proprietary information disrupts the operations of the firm, diverts management attention, and is expensive and time-consuming. By safeguarding its trade secrets and confidential information and the selective use of employee agreements—invention and patent assignments, together with covenants not to compete or disclose—the firm can eliminate much of the uncertainty of litigation. Still, the firm should balance its legitimate needs against employees' rights to mobility. Extraordinary measures to restrict employees may have a chilling effect on the development or maintenance of harmonious employer-employee relations.

Any effective protection plan, reduced to a written policy, includes an audit of what information is a trade secret. The firm should not wait to promulgate an effective, comprehensive program until a misappropriation or controversy over employer-employee rights occurs. The guidelines proffered in this chapter provide an audit protection framework and help a firm optimize, not merely maximize, the firm's security measures. A well-administered program to protect the firm's intellectual property is not, however, a guarantee that misappropriation will never transpire; however, it lessens the risk of loss and the damage when misappropriation does occur. Toward this end, the firm must have the support of its employees to effectively administer its policy. Employee loyalty is the best protection a firm can have against the loss, disclosure, or misuse of its intellectual property.[102]

EXHIBITS

EXHIBIT A.   Confidentiality and Assignment Agreement

This CONFIDENTIALITY AND ASSIGNMENT AGREEMENT is entered into on _____19____ by Company and _____ _____(Employee.)

The parties acknowledge that:

A.   Company's business is the development, marketing, and selling of _____; and

B.   Company wishes to employ Employee, and Employee wishes to be employed by Company;

In consideration of Employee's employment by Company and the mutual promises stated in this agreement, the parties agree as follows:

1. <u>Employment</u>

   The company agrees to employ Employee, and Employee agrees to be employed by the Company as a _____ _____ (title or position), and in such other positions as Company may assign, on the terms set forth below. Employee's duties will include _____ _____ and other duties as may be assigned by Company. Employment may be term- inated at any time by the Company with or without cause.

2. <u>Outside Employment</u>

   While in the Company's employment, Employee agrees to devote all of his or her business time and services to the business and interests of the Company and not to hold other employment or engage in any other business enterprise which is in competition with the Company.

3. Conflicting Obligations

By working for the Company, Employee will not breach any agreement with or duty to a former employer regarding its secret or confidential information or the assignment of inventions. Employee will not disclose to the Company or use for its benefit any secret or confidential information belonging to others.

4. Confidentiality

During the course of employment by the Company, Employee will learn about or become aware of a variety of information related to the Company's business that is secret or confidential. This information is of great value and importance to the success of the Company's business.

It is impossible to identify all forms of information that are secret or confidential. Examples of secret or confidential information are:

- Computer program designs and passwords
- New product ideas and prototypes
- Engineering techniques, schedules, and proposals
- Customer lists and sales data
- Vendor lists and cost data
- Employee files and salaries
- Manufacturing techniques and costs
- Production statistics
- Current and projected marketing and sales statistics and studies
- Pricing and profit information

Employee understands that the above list is not exhaustive and agrees that other information that concerns the Company's products and competitive business position is also secret or confidential. Such information is secret or confidential until it is publicly disclosed by an authorized officer of the Company or until it comes into the public domain in some other lawful manner.

Duty Not to Disclose. In order to protect the Company's secret or confidential information, Employee promises not, without prior written approval by an officer of the Company, to directly or indirectly use or disclose to any other person or business entity the Company's secret or confidential information. Employee further promises to take all reasonable precautions to protect against the negligent or inadvertent disclosure of the Company's secret or confidential information to any other person or business entity.

Duty to Return. Upon termination of employment, Employee further agrees to return to the Company all documents and materials received from or created for the Company, including, but not limited to, those documents and materials containing or relating to secret or confidential information.

5. Assignment of Inventions and Works of Authorship (California)

Employee will promptly disclose and will, and hereby does, assign fully to the Company all inventions, works of authorship, improvements, developments, and discoveries that relate in any manner to the present or prospective business or research of the Company.

Inventions mean discoveries, concepts, and ideas, whether patentable or not, relating to any present or prospective product, service, business, research, and development of the Company. Works of authorship mean all forms of original expression fixed in any tangible medium.   Examples of works of authorship include graphics, audio-video works, computer programs, software, firmware, designs, and musical notes and records.

Upon the Company's request, Employee will sign all papers the Company considers necessary or advisable to patent any invention or improvement or register any copyright. Employee agrees to take these steps both during and after employment.

The above provision does not apply as described below:

Any provision in an employment agreement that provides that an employee shall assign or offer to assign any of his or her rights in an invention to his or her employer shall not apply to an invention for which no equipment, supplies, facility, or trade secret information of the employer was used and which was developed entirely on the employee's own time, and (a) which does not relate (1) to the business of the employer, or (2) to the employer's actual or demonstrably anticipated research or development, or (b) which does not result from any work performed by the employee for the employer. Any provision that purports to apply to such an invention is to that extent against the public policy of this state and is to that extent void and unenforceable. (California Labor Code §2870.)

Prior Inventions or Works of Authorship. Except as listed below, Employee will not assert any rights to any inventions or works of authorship as having been created, made, or acquired by Employee prior to having been employed by Company.

Employee identifies these rights as follows:

6. <u>Restrictions on Competitive Employment after Termination</u> (where allowed)

For a period of [insert reasonable number of months or years] after he or she leaves the Company, and within a [insert reasonable geographic area] radius of the Company's place of business at _____, Employee will not directly or indirectly work for a competitor of the Company or solicit any customer of the Company for whom Employee performed services while employed by the Company.

7. <u>Enforcement/Injunctive Relief</u> (California)

Employee's work for the Company requires the rendering of a special, unique, unusual, extraordinary, or intellectual nature to the Company and involves extraordinary ingenuity and effort, loss of which cannot be reasonably or adequately compensated in damages in an action at law. Employee's compensation will be at a rate of not less than $6,000 per annum.

Employee understands that any breach of this Agreement by Employee is material and will irreparably and immediately harm the Company and that the Company cannot reasonably or adequately be compensated in damages by that breach. Employee understands that the Company will be entitled to injunctive relief, which may include restraining Employee from performing any services or doing any other act that would breach this Agreement.

However, no remedy conferred by this Agreement is intended to be exclusive of any other remedy existing at law, equity, or by statute, or otherwise, and each and every remedy shall be cumulative and in addition to remedies detailed herein.

8. Heirs and Assigns

The terms of this Agreement will be binding on the Employee's heirs, assigns, and legal representatives.

9. Severability-Enforceability

The provisions of this Agreement are severable. In case any one of them is held to be invalid or unenforceable, the remaining provisions of this Agreement will continue to be binding.

10. Waiver

The Company's failure to enforce any provision of this Agreement shall not in any way be construed as a waiver of any such provision or prevent the Company from enforcing that provision or each and every other provision.

11. <u>Modification of Agreement</u>

Modifications to this Agreement must be in writing and, to be effective, signed by the party to be charged. Only a duly authorized officer of the Company may sign a modification on behalf of the company.

Date:

Company

By_____

_____

(Title)

Date:

By_____

Employee

EXHIBIT B:　Employee's Agreement of Confidentiality and of Assignment

IN CONSIDERATION OF MY EMPLOYMENT by Acme Corporation or its divisions or subsidiaries in a capacity which makes available to me confidential information concerning the technology and trade secrets on which the Corporation's business depends or is involved, I agree:

To keep confidential and not disclose or use, either during or subsequent to my employment, any secret or confidential technology, information or trade secrets of the Corporation, except as required in my employment with the Corporation or as authorized in writing by the Corporate legal counsel; and

To assign to ACME CORPORATION all inventions made by me, alone or jointly with others, in the course of such employment, relating to the business of the Corporation or resulting from tasks specifically assigned to me by the Corporation.

This Employee's Agreement of Confidentiality and of Assignment shall continue in effect for the duration of my employment with ACME CORPORATION, whether at the location at which it was signed or to an affiliated company of the corporation either in the continental United States or overseas.

THIS AGREEMENT does not, of course, bind either party to any specific period of employment.

_____

Date　　　　Signature of Employee

_____

Location and Division　　Full Name of Employee-Typewritten
  or Department

　　ACME CORPORATION　　　　　　　　　　　　　　　　BY:

_____

Date　　　　Signature of Division or
　　　　　　　　　Corporation Officer

_____

Division or DepartmentName of Division or Corporation Officer

_____

Exempt　　　　　　Nonexempt　　　Employee's Social Security No.

EXHIBIT C: Termination Agreement

As you are now leaving the employ of the Acme Corporation, the firm wishes to reaffirm to you your obligation to the Acme Corporation to retain in strictest confidence certain confidential and proprietary company information. As you will recall, prior to this time you have signed a "Confidentiality and Assignment Agreement" under which you agreed to respect the confidentiality of the proprietary information and the trade secrets of this corporation.

Listed below are the areas to which you have been exposed during your employment with this corporation and which are considered by this corporation to involve proprietary information. It is in these specific areas alone that you are bound by your obligations of nondisclosure.

(List or itemize the areas)

_____   _____

(Company Counsel's Signature)   (Employee's signature)

                                     _____

                                     (Date)

NOTES

1. Stevenson and Roberts, _Intellectual Property_, Harvard Business School, Pub. #9-384-188 (as revised) (1984): 1.
2. Miles, "Information Thieves Are Now Corporate Enemy No. 1," _Business Week_ (May 5, 1986): 120.
3. Adams, "Trade Secret Program," _Protecting and Profiting from Trade Secrets 1977_ 73 (Practicing Law Institute, Handbook Number 83), as cited in O'Brien, "Establishing a Company Policy and Program for Intellectual Property Rights," 50 _Albany Law Review_ (1986): 539.
4. Epstein and Levi, "Protecting Trade Secret Information: A Plan For Proactive Strategy," _The Business Lawyer_ 43 (May 1988): 889.
5. Eels and Nehemkis, _Corporate Intelligence and Espionage_ (1984), as cited in Epstein and Levi, "Protecting Trade Secret Information: A Plan For Proactive Strategy," _The Business Lawyer_ 43 (May 1988): 889.
6. Greenwald, "Corporate Cloak and Dagger," _Time_ (August 30, 1982): 62-63.
7. Klitzke, "Trade Secrets: Important Quasi-Property Rights," _The Business Lawyer_ 41 (February 1986): 555.
8. Epstein and Levi, op. cit., 887-888.
9. O'Brien, "Establishing a Company Policy and Program for Intellectual Property Rights," _Albany Law Review_ 50 (1986): 541.
10. Chisum, _Patents: A Treatise on the Law of Patentability, Validity, and Infringement_, vol. 4, Section 16.02(1), 16-4 (1978).
11. Stevenson and Roberts, op. cit., 3; and, see Burge, _Patent and Trademark Tactics and Practice_ (New York: John Wiley, 1980).
12. O'Brien, op. cit., 545.
13. For example, _Underwater Devices, Inc. v. Morrison-Knudsen Co., Inc._, 717 F. 2d, 1390 (Fed. Cir. 1983).
14. Stevenson and Roberts, op. cit., 3-4.
15. Ibid., 5.
16. 17 _U.S.C._ Section 102(a)(1982).
17. Bender, "Protection of Computer Programs: The Copyright/Trade Secret Interface," _University of Pittsburgh Law Review_ 47 (1986): 914.
18. 17 _U.S.C._ Section 102(b)(1982).
19. Black, _Black's Law Dictionary_ (Revised 4th ed.) (St. Paul, MN: West Publishing, 1968), 1665; see also 15 _U.S.C._ Section 1127 (1982 and Supp. III 1985).
20. Stevenson and Roberts, op. cit., 7.
21. Ibid.; see also Illinois Institute for Continuing Legal Education, _Intellectual Property Law for the General Business Counselor_, Illinois Bar Center, 1973.
22. _Restatement of Torts_, Sections 757(b)(1939).
23. Uniform Trade Secret Act, 14 _U.L.A._ 537, 542 (1980).
24. _Restatement of Torts_, Section 757 and 758 (1939) and _Central Plastics Co. v. Goodson_, 537 P. 2d 330 (Okla. 1975).
25. Klitzke, op. cit., 558-559.
26. _Carpenter v. United States_, 108 S. Ct. 316, 320 (1987).
27. Klitzke, op. cit., 560.
28. _Greenburg v. Croydon Plastics Co._, 378 F. Supp. 806, 812 (E.D. Pa. 1974). Phillips, "The Concept of Reasonableness in the Protection of Trade Secrets," _The Business Lawyer_ 42 (August 1987): 1046.
29. _E.I. duPont de Nemours & Co. v. Christopher_, 431 F. 2d 1012, 1017 (5th Cir. 1970), cert. denied, 400 U.S. 1024, rehearing denied, 401 U.S. 967 (1971), as cited in Phillips, "The Concept of Reasonableness in the Protection of Trade Secrets," _The Business Lawyer_ 42 (August 1987): 1046.
30. Ibid, _E.I.duPont_, 1017.
31. Richey and Bosik, "Trade Secrets and Restrictive Covenants," _The Labor Lawyer_ 4 (1988): 24.
32. _Hollingsworth Solderless Terminal Co. v. Turley_, 622 F. 2d 1324 (9th Cir. 1980).
33. Uniform Trade Secrets Act, Section 1 (2) (1979).
34. Ibid., 1(4).
35. Borgman, "The Adoption of the Uniform Trade Secrets Act: How Uniform is Uniform?", 27 _IDEA_ 78 (1986).
36. Uniform Trade Secrets Act, Section1 (2)(i) and (ii)(1979).
37. Ibid., Section 1(1)(1979).

38. <u>SI Handling Sys., Inc. v. Heisley</u>, 753 F. 2d 1244 (3d Cir. 1985), as cited in Richey and Bosik, "Trade Secrets and Restrictive Covenants," <u>The Labor Lawyer</u> 4 (1988): 25.
39. <u>Valco Cincinnati, Inc. v. N&D Machining Serv., Inc.</u>, 492 N.E. 2d, 819 (Ohio 1986), as cited in Richey and Bosik, "Trade Secrets and Restrictive Covenants," <u>The Labor Lawyer</u> 4 (1988): 26.
40. Richey and Bosik, op. cit., 26-27.
41. Schwab and Jordan, "Protecting Technology through Litigation," <u>Pittsburgh Legal Journal</u> 135 (April 1987): 6.
42. Uniform Trade Secrets Act, Sections 2 and 3 (1979).
43. Uniform Trade Secrets Act, Section 2 (1979), and Borgman, "The Adoption of the Uniform Trade Secret Act: How Uniform is Uniform?", <u>IDEA</u> 27 (1986): 81-82.
44. Uniform Trade Secrets Act, Section 3 (1979).
45. Ibid., Section 4.
46. Brown & Swanson, "Maintaining the Competitive Edge—Lawful Protection of Trade Secrets," <u>Employee Relations Law Journal</u> 10, no. 3, (Winter 1984-85): 387.
47. Ibid., 388.
48. Ibid., 389.
49. Ibid., 388.
50. Ibid., 390.
51. Ibid., 390-391.
52. Ibid., 391.
53. Hyde, "Legal Protection of Computer Software," <u>Connecticut Bar Journal</u> 59 (August 1985): 298.
54. Bender, op. cit., 909 (1970).
55. 416 U.S. 481 (1974).
56. 524 F. Supp. 171 (N.D. Cal. 1981).
57. 17 <u>U.S.C.</u> Sections 101-810 (1982).
58. 17 <u>U.S.C.</u> Sections 101, 117 (1982).
59. Bender, op. cit., 921-922.
60. Ibid., 922-924.
61. Ibid., 915-918.
62. Ibid., 918-921.
63. Solomon, "The Copyrightability of Computer Software Containing Trade Secrets," <u>Washington U. Law Quarterly</u> 63 (Spring 1985): 162.
64. Ibid., 132.
65. Milgrim, "Trade Secrets," <u>Business Organizations</u> 12 Section 502, 5-2-5-52, (Mathew Bender and Co., 1983).
66. <u>SI Handling Sys., Inc. v. Heisley</u>, 753 F. 2d 1244 (3d Cir. 1985).
67. Richey & Bosik, op. cit., 27.
68. Ibid., 28.
69. Ibid., 28-32.
70. Annot., "Employee's Duty, In Absence of Express Contract, Not to Disclose or Use In New Employment Special Skills Or Techniques Acquired In Earlier Employment," 30 <u>A.L.R. 3d</u>, 637 (1970), as cited in Coolley, "Is It Time To Change Your Client's Employment Agreements?", <u>The Practical Lawyer</u> 31, 8 (December 1985): 26.
71. 30 <u>A.L.R. 3d</u> 644 (1970), as cited in Coolley, op. cit., 27.
72. Coolley, op. cit., 28.
73. Many of the guidelines are adapted or derived from Coolley, op. cit.
74. 127 U.S. 342 (1890).
75. Coolley, op. cit.
76. Ibid., 15.
77. <u>United States v. Dubilier Condenser Corp.</u>, 289 U.S. 178, (1933), 187-189.
78. Ibid., 187-188.
79. Ibid.
80. Coolley, op. cit.
81. <u>Small v. Heywood-Wakefield Co.</u>, 13 F. Supp. 825 (D. Mass. 1936), aff'd. 87 F. 2d 716 (1st Cir.), cert. denied, 301 U.S. 698 (1937); see also Coolley, op. cit., 16.
82. Coolley, op. cit., 16.
83. Neumeyer and Stedman, <u>The Employed Inventor in the United States</u> (Cambridge: MIT Press, 1971),43; see also Coolley, op. cit., 17.
84. Coolley, op. cit., 17.
85. Ibid.
86. Ibid., 17-18.

87. Ibid., 18.
88. MBL(USA) Corp. v. Dickman, 112 Ill. App. 3d 229, 67 Ill. Dec. 938, 445 N.E. 2d 418 (1983).
89. Electro-Craft Corp. v. Controlled Motion, Inc., 332 N.W. 2d, 902 (Minn., 1983).
90. Phillips, "The Concept of Reasonableness in the Protection of Trade Secrets," The Business Lawyer 42 (August 1987): 1049.
91. Epstein and Levi, op. cit., 959.
92. The exhibit is a slight adaptation of one which appears in Brown and Swanson, op. cit., 374.
93. Phillips, op. cit., 1049.
94. This exhibit is an adaptation of the Union Carbide contract which appears in O'Brien, op. cit.
95. Phillips, op. cit., 92.
96. Klitzke, "Trade Secrets: Important Quasi-Property Rights," The Business Lawyer 41 (February 1986): 563, citing High v. Trade Union Courier Publishing Corp., 31 Msc. 2d, 8, 69 N.Y. S. 2d 529 (1946).
97. Epstein and Levi, op. cit., 905.
98. Schneider and Halstrom, "A Program for Protecting Proprietary Information," The Practical Lawyer 18, 6 (October 1972): 71, 79-80.
99. This exhibit is an adaptation of one which appears in Schneider and Halstrom, op. cit., 71.
100. Brown & Swanson, op. cit., 385-386.
101. Epstein and Levi, op. cit., 887-890.
102. Brown & Swanson, op. cit., 386.

8
Marketing and Advertising Issues for the 1990s

INTRODUCTION

Although a number of America's best-known firms suffered significant financial reverses in the 1980s, many others substantially expanded sales and profits. The successful companies, such as Hewlett-Packard, Delta, and 3M, shared a common devotion—excellence in design and application of their marketing concepts. In these companies, marketing is concerned not merely with selling, but with satisfying customers' needs.[1]

"Marketing," according to noted commentator Philip Kotler, "is a social and managerial process by which individuals and groups obtain what they need and want through creating and exchanging products and value with others."[2] Companies are placing an increasing emphasis on marketing: developing, improving, and implementing successful marketing strategies will continue to be one of the highest priorities of American firms in the 1990s as studies indicate it has in the 1980s.[3] The importance of marketing has grown as society has become more affluent. The fact that marketing visibility contributes enormously to customer patronage also presents a risk. When marketers and firms engage in deceptive or questionable practices, they risk jeopardizing company image and goodwill. Critics suggest that marketing contrives consumer demand, that production creates rather than satisfies the urgency of wants. Moreover, as another prod to marketers' proper conduct, government is an omnipresent force, ready to be directed by political forces to further regulate the marketing system.

Advertising, the use of media to present products and services, is an essential and visible element in marketing. In 1989 firms spent over $128 billion, up from $102 billion in 1986, on advertising in the United States.[4] Whereas the "challenge now is to break through the clutter as well as public indifference," as suggested by a leading marketer, images apparently take precedence over words.[5] Today, advertisements rely more on the visual image than yesterday's classics such as David Ogilvy's Rolls-Royce advertisement: "At 60 miles an hour, the loudest noise in this new Rolls-Royce comes from the electric clock."[6] In the 1990s advertisers face new challenges to craft better methods of communicating with consumers. For instance, despite 1988 expend-

itures of $25.8 billion in the medium (22% of the $118.3
billion spent on U.S. advertising in 1988), television
advertising, concludes a recent study, has a minimal effect on
consumers' choices.[7]

Because of the public's concern for an economic system
that efficiently communicates accurate and complete information about products and services, government regularly
intervenes in the marketing and advertising process.   The
Federal Trade Commission (FTC) continues to prevent and deter
unfair trade practices and unfair and deceptive advertising,
and the Food and Drug Administration (FDA) prohibits the
distribution of misbranded, unsafe or adulterated food and
drugs.[8] For example, in January of 1989 the FTC charged the
Campbell Soup Company with deceptive advertising as a result
of the firm's assertion that its soups could reduce heart
disease risks, although the advertisement failed to disclose
an alleged high sodium content in the soups.[9] Moreover, firms
are sensitive to shareholder and consumer pressures. After
three years of complaints of racial stereotyping from shareholders, religious groups, and consumers, Colgate-Palmolive
announced in 1989 that it would rename "Darkie," a toothpaste
it sells in Asia, as well as redesign its logotype, a minstrel
in blackface.

In addition, complaints from children, of whom the
average viewer typically watches over 30,000 television
commercials per year, about misleading advertising induce
sponsors to cancel four or five commercials a year.[10]   For
instance, in 1988 an eleven-year-old girl wrote Penny Power,
with 130,000 subscribers the childrens' version of Consumer
Reports, to complain that Hasbro's television commercials for
its "Army Ants" created the illusion that the artificial
insects, dressed in military gear, could move and shout.
Hasbro subsequently discontinued the commercial "for marketing
and other business reasons."[11]

RESPONSES TO MARKETING'S IMPACT ON SOCIETY, COMPETITION, AND CONSUMERS

Marketing is the "most visible of all functional departments
in an organization . . . [and] [t]hrough salesperson-customer
interactions, advertising and sales promotion programs,
publicity, channel members, and products . . . marketing
manifestations are omnipresent."[12] Three major factors create
significant pressure on firms' marketers to engage in
questionable, counterproductive (for society's and consumers'
welfare), or even unethical or illegal activities. Limits of
consensus of acceptable behavior (for instance, Federal Trade
Commission or antitrust regulations) vary greatly depending on
the public's mood or the economy's stability.   Moreover,
marketers' ethnocentrism, an emotional attitude that a
person's functions or mode of operation is superior to others,
may "predispose them toward an expanded view of limits of
consensus governing" proper marketing activities when the
questionable, but successful, behaviors exist beyond the
acceptable range.[13] The emphasis on utilitarian cost-benefit
analysis often omits any subjective appraisal of societal
costs and benefits in the calculus.[14]

One commentator notes that criticisms of marketing comprise three basic categories: marketing's impact on society, its influence on business competition, and its effect on consumer welfare.[15] Among marketing's purportedly negative impacts on society are creation of excessive materialism, manipulation of demand, overstimulation of demand for private goods at the expense of public goods, cultural pollution that debases values and inhibits privacy, and excessive political power that protects particular industries' interests at the expense of a predominant public interest. Manipulation of demand, the most damaging criticism of marketing, according to Professor Galbraith, "embraces a huge network . . . engaged in selling goods . . . [and] it . . . [also means] the management of those who buy goods."[16] Another critic, Vance Packard, observes the result of such marketing efforts to channel the thinking and purchasing habits of the consumers "is that many . . . are being influenced and manipulated, far more than we realize, in the patterns of our everyday lives."[17]

Responses to these criticisms include, first, the fact that consumers' needs and values are molded by many factors (family and education, for instance), not merely mass media and consumers' repeat purchases, an essential element of successful marketing, only when product values satisfy expectations. Second, company, industry, and government regulations discourage many product and packaging techniques that are pollutants, and the trend over the last two decades is that firms should bear the entire costs of their operations, including private and social costs. Third, public opinion surveys indicate that only a small percentage of people consider marketing (advertising) as irritating or that it needs change.[18] Moreover, whereas business does exert powerful political influence through marketing, countervailing forces also act to check or deflect business' political power achieved through marketing.

Marketing, in addition to influencing society, also affects business competition and various fair competition statutes, as discussed in Chapter 13, directly regulate marketing activities. Criticisms of marketing's effect on business competition include three alleged abuses: business expansion by acquisition rather than by internal development of novel and important products; the use of large marketing and promotional expenditures by industry firms to create entry barriers for other firms and, thereby, to increase substantially above normal profits; and predatory competition, which includes offering unusually low prices, threatening to terminate supplier relationships, and disparaging competing firms' products.[19] Responses to these abuses caused by overzealous competitors are that antitrust and fair competition laws, as applied by the courts, adequately prevent anticompetitive mergers, often strip barriers to entry not based on real economies of large scale, and sanction predatory competition.[20]

Although Americans have realized one of the highest standards of living in the world due, in some degree, to the existing marketing system, critics have identified deficiencies in that system that adversely impact consumer welfare. Critics assert that consumers actually pay more for products and services because middlemen add markups in excess of the value their services, expensive promotion costs in the distribution process force higher consumer prices, and markups on many products and services are grossly disproportionate to their true costs of production or provision.[21] Many of these arguments have their public genesis in the 1926 publication The Tragedy of Waste, in which the author noted and decried that selling and distribution costs rose as a percentage of product costs from 19.8% in 1850 to 50.4% in 1920.[22] Others answer these charges by pointing out that a rising spread between production costs and retail prices, rather than indicating profiteering, normally results from inefficiency of the retailer, inflation, more extensive promotion, or better or more desirable products or services.[23]

Other consumer complaints relate to high-pressure and insidious marketing and selling techniques by which consumers exercise purchasing decisions they later regret, to unsafe or poor quality products, and to planned material functional and style obsolescence. Such criticisms notwithstanding, statutory protection affords much consumer liberty to rescind the purchase of certain products within a specified time frame, and producers and retailers have an increasingly greater legal burden to provide products free of defects and that actually deliver marketed benefits. Increasingly better educated consumers who intelligently compare product values are the most effective antidotes to actual planned obsolescence.

ADVERTISING FUNCTIONS AND DYSFUNCTIONS

Advertising is a major activity by which firms persuade target buyers to purchase their goods or services. It comprises "nonpersonal forms of communication conducted through paid media under clear sponsorship."[24] Advertising has two primary and correlative functions: informing and persuading.[25] In this regard, the distinguishing characteristic of modern advertising is that it attempts to modify consumer desires and needs beyond life's basic necessities. John Kenneth Galbraith posits in "The Dependence Effect" that advertising's primary function is to manufacture demand. Other commentators, such as Robert Arrinton in his article "Advertising and Behavior Control," cite the importance of advertising's informational value and assert that, instead of creating desires, advertising merely redirects them.

Galbraith does recognize that the consumer understands that an "advertisement is an ad, not a factual news story":[26] ". . . [B]ecause modern man is exposed to a large volume of information of varying degrees of unreliability . . . he establishes a system of discounts that he applies to various sources almost without thought."[27] Nonetheless, as Martin Mayer skeptically notes in his book Madison Avenue, U.S.A., whereas the purposes of advertising are clear, "Only the very brave or the very ignorant . . . can say exactly what advertising does in the marketplace."[28] In 1984 advertising expenditures in the United States comprised over $89 billion, with Procter & Gamble accounting for $872 million, which represents 6.2% of its 1984 sales.[29] Advertising accounts for approximately one-fifth of the aggregate selling costs of American industry.

One point on which all agree is that false or deceptive advertising is morally wrong. As fully discussed in Chapter 13, in 1937 the Wheeler-Lea Amendments empowered the Federal Trade Commission (FTC) to forbid unfair or deceptive practices, in addition to its previously granted powers to prohibit unfair methods of competition. Deceptive advertisements are harmful to consumers because such ads cause them to have false beliefs. Moreover, deception lowers the normal level of trust and truthfulness that is essential to the proper operations of society and its economic system. If everyone in the economic system acted deceptively, the system would cease its effective or efficient service to society. Further, acts such as deception and lying are inherently wrong whether their consequences are destructive or not.[30]

Three types of deceptive advertisements[31] are distinguishable: deceptive pricing, deceptive promotion, and deceptive packaging. Deceptive pricing includes such activities as advertising "wholesale" prices falsely or advertising a substantial price cut from a regular price where the regular or "list" price is speciously high. Moreover, deceptive promotion comprises practices such as exaggerating the product's attributes, conducting rigged contests, or falsely presenting the product's or services's accomplishments. Deceptive packaging includes advertising on the box a price reduction when the sale's price is, in reality, the normal price, or packages that are deceptively large or less than fully filled.

In its Advertising Code of American Business, the American Advertising Federation (AAF) declares that "advertising shall tell the truth, and shall reveal significant facts, the concealment of which would mislead the public."[32] There are a number of definitions of "deceptive advertising," including one that "causes a significant percentage of potential customers (i.e., those at whom it is directed or whose consumption behavior is likely to be influenced by it) to have false beliefs about the product."[33]

The Federal Trade Commission (FTC) and the United States Postal Service are the agencies with primary responsibility for regulating false and misleading advertising. In cases of explicit representation, the factual controversy consists of whether adequate evidence exists to support the advertisement's claim, as whether its product is more effective than a competing product or whether "more doctors recommend" its product.[34] In instances of implicit misrepresentation, however, where the alleged implication, if present, would be false, the issue becomes whether the offending implication can in fact be culled from the advertisement.[35] Three questions underlie the rendering of such a factual determination in cases of implicit misrepresentation: (1) the composition of the group that must be considered to determine whether the offensive implication should be derived from the advertisement, (2) after determining the scope of the audience, the number threshold of persons who interpreted the advertisement as containing the implication to conclude that the implication in fact is present, and (3) whether the foregoing (1 and 2) determinations are accomplished by reliance on consumer sampling or solely on the interpretation of the advertisement by the fact finder.[36]

The FTC and U.S. Postal Service have responded variously to these subjective guidelines regarding implicit misrepresentation.   For instance, courts have diversely determined that the audience to be considered includes almost everyone, "the most ignorant and unsuspecting purchaser," "the ignorant, the unthinking and the credulous," and "consumers acting reasonably under the circumstances."[37]   Yet, the most recent FTC positions provide less protection to the gullible consumer, as, for example, in Cliffdale Associates, Inc., in which the commission noted that ". . . an advertisement . . . [is] not considered deceptive merely because it could be unreasonably misunderstood by an insignificant and unrepresentative segment of the class of persons to whom the representation is addressed."[38]

In regard to the second question, supra, the most protective decisions require only that there be one deceived person, even if he or she is a gullible individual of below normal intelligence.[39]   Nonetheless, recent FTC decisions have established the threshold as a "significant" or "substantial" number of deceived consumers.[40]   The last issue, represented in the aforementioned question 3, relates to the method by which a determination is made that the requisite audience would believe the scrutinized advertisement yields the offensive implication.[41]   As the complainant does not have any burden of establishing that any consumer, in fact, interpreted the implication in the advertisement, the fact finder may find that the representation is implied by merely reviewing the advertisement.   In some cases, consumer surveys and expert testimony are occasionally introduced as evidence for consideration by the fact finder.

Naturally, such imprecision in measuring deception in advertising troubles marketers.   Critics of the present, uncertain process regarding the standard of proof of deception have proposed three different modes of proof in cases of alleged implied deception.   The issue in such cases is what consumers perceive, which the advertiser is not specially situated to determine.[42]   First, reformers assert, the FTC might utilize marketing studies used by the advertiser to determine whether the advertiser knew or should have known that consumers would, in fact, perceive the inaccurate or deceptive implication in the advertisement.   Second, the FTC might demonstrate consumer deception by consumer surveys buttressed by expert evidence.   In order to establish a sufficient consumer deception in this manner, the FTC could establish fixed percentages that sufficiently demonstrate that deception in fact occurred.   Last, critics of the present process of proving deception assert that the FTC could promulgate trade rules that define what "misleading implications can be assumed to flow from specified product claims or descriptions."[43]

IMAGE ADVERTISING AND THE FIRM'S FREE SPEECH

Corporate image advertising "describes the corporation itself, its activities, or its views, but does not explicitly describe any products or services sold by the corporation."[44]   Image advertisements comprise a various range of subjects, from "direct image advertising," which attempts to differentiate the firm from its competitors, to "direct issue advertising," which sets forth the firm's viewpoint on public issues.[45] Firms initiated image and issue advertising to address declining public confidence in American business in the 1960s.[46] For instance, Mobil Oil in the late summer of 1970 began image advertising by purchasing one-quarter of a page in the opinion-editorial section of the New York Times. In so doing, Mobil "crossed the line from low profile to going public," and fifteen months later placed such ads on a weekly basis to discuss "our [Mobil's] thoughts, our concerns, our beliefs, our practices."[47] Later, the company inaugurated a fortnightly column, "Observations," published in 185 newspapers. Advocacy advertising, as practiced by Mobil, produced results: a 1976 Louis Harris opinion poll indicated the public's perception of the company as more concerned about consumers, the energy crisis, good government, and honesty to consumers than its six major competitors.[48]

Presently, the phenomenal upsurge in U.S. corporate image advertising, which swelled from $292 million in 1976 to $714 million in 1985, is characterized by Dow Chemical activities. In the mid-1980s Dow began a national advertising campaign, budgeted at over $50 million dollars,[49] to change the firm's image of a napalm producer and toxic waste dumper to one of a concerned corporate citizen. Earlier image campaigns such as "Dow lets you do great things", sparked a response from commentators and the FTC staff, which proposed various standards for regulating image advertising.[50] The commission, however, refused to adopt the staff recommendations, but did recognize its option to exercise "such enforcement actions in the future as it deems appropriate and consistent with its understanding of its constitutional and statutory obligations."[51]

There are many objectives of image advertising, which firms believe offset the deleterious effects of negative public opinion in such areas as sales, potential investment in companies' shares, personnel recruitment, and government regulation.[52] Specifically, image advertising publicizes the firm's desirable activities, rebuts specific criticism and corrects misconceptions resulting from negative publicity from allegedly biased media and critics. It addresses political issues by demonstrating the potentially negative impacts of government restrictions and sponsors public service communication to mitigate public hostility to company activities as well as enhance public awareness of the company activities such as research and development.[53]

Under current law, the category of speech determines the degree of its constitutional protection. In noncommercial speech, the courts' various interpretations of First Amendment rights prohibit the government from arbitrating truth or falsity of an expression or from sanctioning citizens and corporations from communicating false, noncommercial information.[54] Nonetheless, the Supreme Court has ruled that commercial, as opposed to noncommercial, speech is not entirely protected by the First Amendment. Consequently, the Court has underlined the government's power to regulate false or misleading assertions, such as deceptive advertising, in the marketplace.[55] Therefore, the critical distinction is whether the company's image advertisement lies within the commercial or noncommercial category.

Although company-sponsored editorial advertisements that respond to the value of spending legislation clearly escape government determination of falsity, those informational ads that combine product information with firms' comments on issues of public importance are vulnerable to governmental regulation. Unfortunately, under current legal standards, it is at times difficult to classify corporate image advertising as either commercial or noncommercial speech. For instance, in response to an FTC complaint, an administrative law judge (ALJ) analyzed an R. J. Reynolds Tobacco Company's 1985 advertisement that the nexus between smoking and health was unresolved based on a study that tested the effect of various risk factors on the occurrence of coronary disease. The ALR determined that the ad was noncommercial speech and, as such, beyond FTC regulation, even though the ad logically appeared as persuading smokers not to end their tobacco use.

Yet, a federal appellate court in National Commission on Egg Nutrition v. FTC,[56] another case involving an apparent mixture of commercial and noncommercial speech, affirmed the FTC's finding that a trade association's generic advertisements of eggs without mentioning a specific brand were commercial speech and, hence, subject to FTC jurisdiction.[57] The court found that the advertisements' claim that no scientific evidence tied egg consumption to an increased risk of heart disease (contrary to existing evidence) was an attempt to persuade the public to buy the product, not statements of opinion.[58]

1989 SUPREME COURT CUTBACK IN FIRST AMENDMENT PROTECTION OF BUSINESS ADVERTISING

Since 1976 commercial advertisements and other messages, although not to the same extent as other forms of speech, have been entitled to First Amendment protection. Yet, in the 1989 decision in Board of Trustees, State University of New York v. Fox, the Supreme Court continued its more recent tendency to reduce First Amendment protection for commercial speech. One constitutional lawyer deemed the ruling "a serious blow to the protection of commercial speech." In the Court's opinion, written by Justice Antonin Scalia, government restrictions on commercial speech can be broader than that absolutely necessary to regulate a particular type of communication. The restriction can be a "reasonable attempt to regulate, not "a perfect fit," decreed the Court. The State University of New York adopted a regulation to restrict commercial access to college dormitories. As a result of a housewares representative's arrest in a dormitory for violating the regulation, a group of students challenged the regulation as violating their First Amendment rights to host sales parties. The Supreme Court ruled, in ordering the lower federal courts to examine the reasonableness of the regulation, that government officials need not adopt the "least restrictive" means of regulating commercial speech, such as advertising, as reported June 30, 1989, by the Wall Street Journal.

ENLIGHTENED MARKETING

Although there are numerous benefits in the present system of marketing, the process is also vulnerable to abuses that effectively inhibit marketing from realizing its full promise.[59] Enlightened marketing, in which the marketer or businessperson realizes that his or hers and the firm's long-term interests require forthright marketing within the established system, may not absolutely maximize the firm's revenues at all times. Nonetheless, enlightened marketing, characterized by five principles identified by marketing scholar Philip Kotler, will enhance the firm's long-term financial performance, as well as reinvigorate the nation's economic system. Kotler's five principles of enlightened marketing include: consumer-oriented marketing, innovative marketing, value marketing, sense-of-mission marketing, and societal marketing.[60]

Consumer-oriented marketing simply means that the firm should view its marketing activities from the perspective of the consumer rather than the seller's. In this regard, Peter Drucker views consumerism as a product of the "shame of the total marketing concept . . . [as] essentially a mark of the failure of the concept . . . [in which our present marketing and advertising] are meaningless to the consumer."[61] Kotler asserts that marketers must also exercise innovative marketing, in which marketers are creative in a fundamental manner—by continually searching for better ways to enhance consumers' welfare. Moreover, whereas hard-sell tactics may yield short-term gains, the marketer should press instead for value marketing. Value marketing requires the marketer to push for better values in the product offering by pressuring the development of a better product.

In addition, the firm should define its business position "in broad social terms, not narrow product terms."[62] In this manner, the firm and its marketers develop a sense of purpose and direction that energizes and ennobles the firm's activities. The enlightened marketer can best serve the business and economic system by balancing three elements in marketing decisions: consumer desires, business financial performance, and society's welfare.

In a Harvard Business Review article,[63] substantial majorities of subscriber respondents indicated that firms should eliminate untruthful or misleading ads (91%), establish and enforce a code of ethics (65%), upgrade the intellectual level of ads (62%), and increase the information content of ads (59%). A vehicle for realizing these goals of enlightened marketing, notes Kotler, is the firm's formulation and communication of lucid policies to its employees regarding proper marketing activities.[64] Such ethical or proper conduct policies can include matters relating to advertising standards, customer service, pricing, distributor relations, and product development.[65] Furthermore, although supporting the need for firms to employ certain types of marketing "fluff," which others call "puffery," Theodore Levitt suggests the critical need to understand the difference between duplicity and embellishment. He asserts that the consumer wants "truth" as well as the "alleviating imagery and tantalizing promises" of the marketer and designer.[66] Nonetheless, Levitt decries any failure of the firm ". . . to mount vigorous, meaningful programs to protect the consumer, to standardize product grades, labels, and packages, to improve the consumer's information-getting process, and to mitigate the vulgarity and oppressiveness" in much of the nation's marketing.[67] Toward these ends, Levitt proposes that American business: (1) exert pressure to prevent any industry from obtaining exemptions from reasonable and popular legislative restrictions, (2) work with government to assure a healthy commercial environment, (3) support legislation to provide consumers with information that facilitates comparisons between products, prices, and packages, and (4) support improved legislation relating to quality stabilization.[68]

CONCLUSIONS

In today's globally competitive business world, the marketing function is a critically important success factor. The marketplace determines which products and firms will succeed or fail. Consequently, any successful firm must provide product quality and innovation that serve the customer's needs. In this regard, the efficient marketplace requires, notes the Supreme Court, ". . . dissemination of information as to who is producing and selling what product . . . the free flow of commercial information is indispensable."[69]

Whereas marketing and advertising may, at times, control behavior or create wants that are artificial, not naturally the consumer's, they serve a useful function in our society. The law proscribes most of the negative consequences of marketing and advertising. Firms have an obligation to abide strictly by statutory and regulatory prohibitions concerning competitive relations, and product, promotion and pricing decisions. The FTC and the FDA have responsibilities to enforce such legal standards, but the business firms themselves, admittedly often in response to consumer pressure, should enforce proper business conduct standards. Firms should take a proactive role, further, in applying enlightened marketing that is, at once, consumer- and society-oriented.

NOTES

1. See Peters and Waterman, Jr., In Search of Excellence: Lessons From America's Best-Run Companies (New York: Harper & Row, 1982); Peters and Austin, A Passion for Excellence: The Leadership Difference (New York: Random House, 1985).
2. Kotler, Marketing Management, 6th ed., (Englewood Cliffs, NJ: Prentice-Hall, 1988), 3.
3. Ibid., 2.
4. Collins, "Image and Advertising," Harvard Business Review (January-February, 1989): 93.
5. Ibid., 93-94.
6. Ibid., 94.
7. Lipman, "Television Ads Ring Up No Sale in Study," Wall Street Journal (February 15, 1989): B-6.
8. Corley and Read, The Legal Environment of Business (New York: McGraw Hill, 1987), 434.
9. Rothenberg, "Advertising," New York Times (January 27, 1989): 29.

10. Hinds, "Young Consumers: Perils and Power," New York Times (February 11, 1989): 16.
11. Ibid.
12. Hensel and Dubinsky, "Ethical Dilemmas in Marketing: A Rationale," Journal of Business Ethics 5 (1986): 63.
13. Ibid., 65.
14. Ibid.
15. Kotler, Marketing Management, 2nd ed. (Englewood Cliffs, NJ: Prentice-Hall, 1972), 804.
16. Galbraith, The Affluent Society (Boston: Houghton Mifflin, 1958), 158; Kotler, op. cit., 2nd ed., 806.
17. Packard, The Hidden Persuaders (New York: Pocket Books, 1957), 1; Kotler, loc. cit., 2nd ed., 806.
18. Ibid., Kotler, 2nd ed., 809.
19. Kotler, op. cit., 2nd ed., 810–812.
20. Ibid.
21. Ibid., 812–816.
22. Ibid., 813.
23. Ibid., 816.
24. Kotler, op. cit., 2nd ed., 663.
25. Santilli, "The Informative and Persuasive Functions of Advertising: A Moral Appraisal," Journal of Business Ethics 2 (1983): 27.
26. Levitt, "The Morality (?) of Advertising," Harvard Business Review, Advertising: Better Planning, Better Results, (Harvard Business School, 1980): 182.
27. Ibid., 182–183.
28. Kotler, op. cit., 6th ed., 664.
29. Kotler, op. cit., 6th ed., 617.
30. Carson, Wokutch, and Cox, "An Ethical Analysis of Deception in Advertising," Journal of Business Ethics 4 (1985): 99–102.
31. Kotler, op. cit., 2nd ed., 816–817.
32. Carson, op. cit., 94.
33. Ibid., 96.
34. Schmidt, Jr., and Burns, "Proof or Consequences: False Advertising And The Doctrine of Commercial Speech," University of Cincinnati Law Review 56 (1988): 1275.
35. Ibid., 1276.
36. Ibid., 1277.
37. Ibid., 1278–1279.
38. Trade Reg. Rep. (CCH) Section 22,137 (FTC 1984); Schmidt, op. cit., 1278.
39. Gelb v. FTC, 144 F. 2d 582 (2nd Cir. 1944); Schmidt, op. cit., 1278–1279.
40. Schmidt, op. cit., 1279.
41. Ibid.
42. Ibid., 1289.
43. Ibid., 1290.
44. Lin, "Corporate Image Advertising and the First Amendment," Southern California Law Review 61 (1988): 461.
45. Ibid.
46. Ibid., 462.
47. Ross, "Public Relations Isn't Kid-Glove Stuff at Mobil," Fortune (September, 1976), as cited in Esterquest, Mobil Oil and Advisory Advertising, pub. no. 380-149 (Revised, 1984), Harvard Business School, 1.
48. Ibid., 3.
49. Rice, "Dow Chemical: From Napalm to Nice Guys," Fortune (May 12, 1986): 75.
50. Lin, op. cit., 460.
51. Ibid.
52. Ibid., 462.
53. Ibid., 462–467.
54. New York Times v. Sullivan, 376 U.S. 254 (1964), and First National Bank of Boston v. Bellotti, 435 U.S. 765 (1978); Lin, op. cit., 468.
55. Lin, op. cit., 469.
56. 570 F. 2nd 157 (7th Cir. 1977), cert. denied 439 U.S. 821 (1978).
57. Lin, op. cit., 476.
58. Ibid.
59. Kotler, op.cit., 2nd ed., 835.

60. Ibid., 836-837.
61. Ibid., 836.
62. Ibid., 837.
63. Greyser and Reece, "Businessmen Look Hard at Advertising," <u>Harvard Business Review, Advertising: Better Planning, Better Results</u> (Harvard Business School, 1980): 141.
64. Kotler, op.cit., 2nd ed., 838.
65. Ibid., 839.
66. Levitt, op. cit., 184.
67. Ibid.
68. Ibid.
69. <u>Virginia State Board of Pharmacy v. Virgina Citizens Consumer Council, Inc.</u>, 425 U.S. 765 (1976).

9

Financial Accounting and Reporting: Duties of Accountants and Firms

INTRODUCTION

Before the creation of the Securities and Exchange Commission (SEC) in 1934, financial reporting shenanigans were commonplace and generally unsanctioned because the Federal Trade Commission, which regulated firms before the birth of the SEC, had no formal disclosure requirements.[1] For instance, Associated Dry Goods, ALCOA, and United Fruit, among other firms, issued annual reports setting forth net income figures without divulging revenues.[2] Di Giorgio Fruit Corporation deducted expenses from the firm's equity account instead of from revenues, thereby artificially reconstructing an annual loss into an annual profit.

Other firms manipulated earnings and stock prices by gross adjustments of depreciation charges; American Can (now Primerica) charged $500,000 in depreciation in 1912 and raised that figure fivefold in 1913 to hold profits constant before cutting depreciation to $1 million in 1914 to double profits, thereby stampeding the stock price from $11 to $50. "There are still a lot of warts on financial statements today . . . but— . . . investors today are in a much better position to make an informed decision than they were back then," notes Clarence Sampson, chief accountant at the SEC.[3]

In the present, accountants are much more independent and conscious of their duties to accurately and fairly report financial affairs to the public. Prior to the SEC's creation in 1934 and its 1938 decision to approve for general use those accounting principles having substantial authoritative support, "the individual morality of the [independent] auditor could no longer be relied upon to deter the growing power of the managerial class."[4] Deceptive accounting prices prior to SEC regulation promoted a "two-tiered" market structure in which information asymmetries provided ample opportunities and potent incentives for stock market manipulation, enriching the company and market insiders at the expense of the investing public. The institution of disclosure regulations since has vitiated most, but not all, avenues of abuse.[5]

For instance, ESM Government Securities illegally pledged the same assets as security for various loans until its financial failure. Moreover, Saxon Industries, which in 1981 rose to a _Fortune_ ranking as the 381st-largest industrial company, actually manufactured inventories over a fourteen-year period by false bookkeeping entries, in the process costing shareholders and creditors over $200 million after the firm's eventual bankruptcy.   Furthermore, when firms delay "writing down" assets caused by bad investment until opportune times, such a writedown taken after the event "makes you think you can't believe any of the numbers over the last few years [after the acquisition, but before the writedown]," notes David Hawkins, Harvard Business School finance professor.[6] Standard Oil Co. (SOHIO) waited until its fourth quarter 1985 financial report to writedown $1.15 billion of its $1.8 billion purchase of Kennecott, even though the purchase had been overpriced and ill-timed from the time of acquisition four years earlier.[7]

Inventory valuation can have a substantial effect on bottom-line profits as well.   Whereas operating profits for U.S. firms rose only 4% to 7% in 1988, some companies reported huge gains of 25% to 100% due primarily to rising prices of inventories, which gains are not spendable income.[8]   Although not deliberately deceptive, this accounting practice and those that are fraudulent have created the perception that accountants and firms manipulate financial reports at the expense of clarity, fairness, and honesty.   Growing public expectations that public accountants should aggressively serve the public interest have led to a substantial increase in lawsuits against them.   For instance, in 1989 British partners in Arthur Young agreed to pay $42.5 million to settle claims of negligence in that firm's audits of the former Johnson Matthey Bankers Ltd. in 1982 and 1983.

STATE OF PUBLIC ACCOUNTING IN THE UNITED STATES

Modern accounting, which has its roots in fourteenth-century England where store owners recorded ledger balances and inventory, expanded with the growth of rationalism and directed the activity of capitalism.   In America, as new methods of financing development required more advanced accounting methods for management and control, the advent of railroads and large corporations was a catalyst for the use of financial reports as public summaries of firms' economic performances and expectations.   The important role of accountants concomitantly grew with the heightened appreciation that dependable financial information is critical for the existence of a free society and, specifically, for necessary disclosure through accounting statements.

The organized accounting profession began in the United States with the establishment of the American Institute of Certified Public Accountants (AICPA) in 1887.   Throughout its history, the AICPA has implemented numerous rules that govern its membership, and it has refined the process for promulgating accounting standards.[9]   Today, the Institute's 264,000 members are regulated through AICPA rules and the state boards of accountancy.   Moreover, the AICPA supports the Financial Accounting Standards Board (FASB), established in 1972, which is the private sector body that promulgates accounting principles, rules, and interpretations.[10]

Through the Securities Act of 1933[11] and the Securities Exchange Act of 1934,[12] the Securities and Exchange Commission

(SEC) indirectly controls independent accountants by establishing the type and extent of financial information that public companies must disclose to the public.[13] Consequently, by having the statutory power to prescribe the content of a company's financial information and to define accounting and technical terms, the SEC has authority to establish accounting principles.[14] For instance, to improve the basic professional standards of independent accountants who report financial statements that are filed with it, the SEC has adopted "Regulation S-X," and the agency periodically publishes its decisions concerning accounting problems. Nonetheless, the SEC has delegated responsibility for the promulgation of accounting principles and proper accounting methods to the FASB. Except when specialized or regulated industry accounting standards constitute alternative rules, only the FASB has the authority to establish a "generally accepted accounting principle" (GAAP).[15] In addition, the AICPA also issues statements on auditing standards through the Institute's Auditing Standards Board (ASB), which forms "generally accepted auditing standards" (GAAS) to which both the AICPA and the SEC require auditors to adhere.[16]

Although the two basic categories of GAAP are principles that measure and those that disclose, other areas of accounting principles, such as cost accounting, managerial accounting, nonprofit, and governmental accounting are not under the jurisdiction of the AICPA or the FASB.[17] For example, the recently established Governmental Accounting Standard Board (GASB) regulates governmental accounting standards. Moreover, the National Association of Accountants (NAA), whose membership consists primarily of accountants employed in commercial and industrial firms, as opposed to public accountants who serve the public, has authorized its Management Accounting Practices Committee (MAPC) to develop guidelines for management accounting policies, concepts, and practices.[18]

ACCOUNTANTS' COMMON LAW LEGAL LIABILITY IN CONTRACT AND TORT

The profession of accounting has assumed an increasingly central role in commerce and finance and, as a result, has become a vulnerable target for lawsuits involving auditing and nonauditing functions brought by clients and third parties.[19]

The majority of states follow the rule that a professional is not liable, _ex contractu_, for any breach of warranties of performance or of contract even to his or her clients. The law recognizes that professional services involve inexact sciences and skilled judgment in dealing with random factors that cannot be precisely measured. Hence, the law requires not perfect results, but rather "the exercise of that skill and judgment which can be reasonably expected from similarly situated professionals."[20] Nonetheless, if a professional offers a client an express warranty regarding a particular result, a breach of contract may well lie.

Moreover, an accountant must comply not only with the express and implied provisions of his or her contract, but also must exercise a standard of care required by the undertaking.[21] This standard is consistent with the general negligence principle that requires the court or jury to determine whether a defendant, who allegedly breached a duty of care, has been negligent because his or her conduct is short of that care that a reasonable person would have exercised under similar circumstances.[22]   Reasonable care requires that an accountant employ the common ability and skill of those members of the accountancy profession in providing services to the client.[23] The accountant's duty of care, ordinarily a matter for expert testimony in alleged breaches involving professionals, dictates adherence to "generally accepted accounting principles" (GAAP) and "generally accepted auditing standards" (GAAS), and to the Code of Professional Conduct (CPC).[24] The code, for example, imposes affirmative duties to maintain independence from the client, carefully supervise associates, and offer reasonable taxation advice and strategies.[25]

If the accountant represents to the client that he or she has special skill or superior knowledge, then the accountant must satisfy a higher standard of care consistent with his or her representations. Normally, however, if the professional in good faith conforms to the professional standards, he or she will have satisfied the duty of care the circumstances require.[26]   Consequently, although the accountant is not relieved of criminal liability under federal securities law if intentionally causing a false statement or omission of a material fact in a financial statement filed with the SEC, the public accountant will be relieved of any negligence liability when he or she complies in good faith with GAAP and GAAS.[27] Nevertheless, accountants are not immune from liability when pro forma compliance with GAAP or GAAS ignores practicalities.[28]

Moreover, in negligence suits in which accountants are defendants, the plaintiff must prove that he or she suffered because of relying upon the accountant's work product.   For instance, in Bunge Corp. v. Eide,[29] the court ruled that a creditor, who allegedly relied on an accountant's inflated valuation of inventory when lending money to the borrower, was not entitled to recover damages. The court posited that the creditor failed to follow prudent lending practices as it extended credit to avoid a loan loss.[30] Further, the damages recoverable in tort are those that are the proximate, as well as natural, result of the accountant's misconduct.[31]

Because accountants professionally represent certain facts to clients, other particularly important tort theories are those of negligent and fraudulent misrepresentation.   The elements of negligent misrepresentation include the accountant's (1) furnishing false information during the course of his or her business, (2) which is supplied for the guidance of others in their business affairs, (3) during which the accountant failed to exercise reasonable care or competence in either gaining or communicating the information with the result that (4) the plaintiff justifiably relied on the information that (5) directly resulted in the plaintiff's damage, of which there was actual monetary loss.[32] Although a negligent misrepresentation occurs when the misrepresenter asserts a fact of his or her own knowledge without knowing whether it is true or false, a nonnegligent mistake will not establish negligent misrepresentation.[33] The chief difference between negligent and fraudulent misrepresentation is that the latter claim requires the plaintiff to demonstrate that the misrepresentation was made with "fraudulent intent," that is, with "dishonesty or bad faith."[34]   Generally, fraudulent misrepresentation must be based on material representations of past or existing facts.

When providing professional services for a client, a public accountant must act in good faith with reasonable care without fraud.[35]   At common law, liability claims for the accountant's ordinary negligence were restricted to those parties with whom the accountant was in contractual privity. In the 1980s the liability of public accountants to third parties, such as creditors and equity investors, with whom the account has no privity been further expanded.

In Ultramares Corporation v. Touche,[36] Judge (later Justice) Benjamin Cardozo, in dismissing the action for negligence, restricted recovery for an auditor's negligence to the auditor's client and those other specific persons the auditor actually knew would receive and rely on the audit information.   In Ultramares, Stern & Company employed the accounting firm of Touche, Niven, and Company to prepare and certify a balance sheet, which, upon completion of the audit, reported assets in excess of $2.5 million and a net worth of over $1 million.   In reality, the assets were fictitious and the firm was insolvent.   Relying upon a certified balance sheet, Ultramares Corporation made unsecured loans to Stern & Company, which subsequently defaulted and filed bankruptcy. Ultramares brought suit against Touche alleging negligence in the audit preparation.   This "limited privity rule" was adopted by other jurisdictions and remained the majority standard until the Restatement principle three decades later.

The Restatement rule[37] extends public accountants' liability for negligence beyond those parties with whom the accountant is in limited privity.   Although sharing the Ultramares court's concern that relaxing the privity standard would subject the accountant to a potentially unlimited liability to an indeterminate class of people, the Restatement (Second) of Torts drafters established a two-pronged standard of duty: (1) an accountant's duty extends to a person or limited class of persons the accountant intends or knows will utilize the misleading information, and (2) the duty extends only to the type of transaction that the accountant intended to influence.[38]   Thus the Ultramares limited privity rule and the Restatement rule differ only with regard to who is considered a third party beneficiary to a contract between an accountant and the client.   The limited privity rule requires the accountant's knowledge of the specific identity of beneficiaries; the Restatement rule does not.

Whereas a majority of jurisdictions obey the Restatement's modified privity standard, a minority, including New Jersey,[39] Wisconsin,[40] and North Carolina,[41] allow negligence actions by all foreseeable third parties against accountants grounded in the theory of simple negligence.   In addition, the most extreme example of the definitional expansion of a "foreseeable third party" occurs in International Mortgage Co. v. Butler.[42]   International Mortgage Co. (IMC) reviewed Butler's audit and accompanying unqualified opinion letter regarding the financial statements of Westside, Butler's client.   Butler had no knowledge of IMC at the time of the audit, that the financial statements were to be transmitted to IMC, or that IMC was relying on them. The California Court of Appeals, nonetheless, held that the accountant could be liable to IMC for damages from Westside's failure to deliver the promised deeds. It is clear that the defendant-accountant would not have been liable under the limited privity rule or the Restatement standard.

RESPONSIBILITIES OF THE INDEPENDENT AUDITOR

CPAs provide tax and management advisory service, but their primary function is auditing.[43] For instance, the accounting profession derives 60% of its annual revenue from auditing.[44] This auditing function is critically important for many reasons. "The investor making a decision to buy or sell securities, the banker deciding whether to approve a loan, the government in obtaining revenue from income tax returns . . . [rely] upon [financial] information provided by others."[45] Directly or indirectly, nearly everyone has a financial interest in corporate enterprise, and, hence, dependable financial information.[46]

Through the auditing process, the public accounting profession attests or provides assurance as to the fairness and dependability of financial statements. Two stages of the attest function are: first, the examination or audit of the underlying accounting records and supporting evidence, and second, the issuance of the auditor's report. Typical auditing procedures include the examination of tangible assets, confirmation of account balances, vouching transactions, observation of certain activities, questioning management, and checking computations.[47]

Originally, the independent auditor's primary function was the discovery of theft, bookkeeping discrepancies, and other indicators of proper or improper management for the client's benefit. Today, however, the audit's most important purpose is the unbiased report of the firm's financial condition for the benefit of third parties.[48] Toward this end, the independent public accountant or auditor completes the audit process's five stages: (1) planning the audit by understanding the firm's physical operations and accounting system, (2) preliminarily evaluating the firm's internal control system to form a basis for reliance thereon, (3) performing compliance tests that indicate whether the internal control system is properly operating, (4) evaluating and modifying the independent auditor's planned audit program to conform to the results of the compliance tests, and (5) evaluating the obtained information to determine whether the firm's financial statements accurately manifest the true economic conditions of the firm.[49] Following this evaluation, the independent auditor issues a written report of the audit, the "opinion." In the opinion, the independent auditor expresses "an opinion on the fairness with which they [financial statements] present financial position, results of operations, and changes in financial position . . ."[50] In this regard, there are four categories of audit reports promulgated by independent public accountants: unqualified opinions, qualified or adverse opinions, and disclaimer opinions. In the unqualified opinion, the independent public accountant, although not warranting that the numerical figures in the financial statements are precise or that fraud is absent, does report without any exceptions, reservations, or qualifications that the firm's financial statements fairly reflect its financial positions, operations' results, and changes in financial position.[51]

The independent auditor issues a qualified or adverse opinion, depending on the materiality of the deficiency, if the firm's financial statements are not in compliance with GAAP.[52] Elements that are grounds for a qualified opinion include: "a lack of competent evidential matter, restrictions on the scope of the auditor's examination, departures from GAAP in the financial statements, changes in accounting principles being applied, or significant uncertainties which affect the financial statements."[53] If any of the foregoing grounds materially and pervasively affect the financial statements' fairness of presentation, the independent auditor must issue an adverse opinion.[54] The disclaimer opinion indicates that the independent accountant who audited the financial statements expresses no opinion because it is objectively impossible to determine if the financial statements presented are consistent with GAAP.[55]

An area related to auditing financial statements is that of issuing "solvency" letters. Firms or lenders that seek to reduce or diffuse their own exposure to legal and financial risks often seek written assurances from independent auditors that a firm planning to substantially increase its debt in a leveraged buyout is solvent and will remain so in the near future. Although such instruments do not possess the weight of an audit opinion, borrowing firms, lenders, and investment banking institutions have requested them with increasing frequency in the merger and acquisition mania of the late 1980s. Solvency letters raise many of the same issues as audits, including legal liability of the independent auditors and opinion shopping by the firms seeking such letters. "If a leveraged buyout runs into trouble, there is no question that accounting firms that provide these letters may wind up as a 'deep pocket' in a later lawsuit."[56]

In fulfilling the audit function, the independent accountant (auditor) has a number of affirmative responsibilities. First, he or she must be accurate in methods to discover and report the firm's true financial position. Second, as a surrogate for the public, the independent accountant must remain independent of the firm's management. The independent accountant owes the duty of independence to the board of directors, the firm's shareholders, and the public.[57] Third, the independent accountant must fully disclose all material aspects of the firm's financial condition. His or her duty of disclosure requires him or her to "report embezzlement, refuse an improper engagement, and place a warning on statements . . . about the company's liquidity and ability to continue as a going concern."[58]

In his or her affirmative duty to detect material errors and irregularities, including fraud, the independent auditor fulfills a function that the public considers the independent auditor's most important role.[59] "Fraud does not appear on the face of a company's records, but often indications of it will appear in the form of irregularities," and, hence, the auditor can only reveal fraud by closely examining irregularities.[60] Whereas the Statements of Auditing Standards (SAS), specifically Number 16, affirms the independent auditor's clear responsibility to detect management fraud, that same SAS does not require the auditor to guarantee the accuracy of the firm's financial statements.[61]

The Court, in United States v. Arthur Young & Co.[62] has typecast the accountant as a "public watchdog," whose "ultimate allegiance [is] to the . . . [firm's] creditors and stockholders, as well as to the investing public . . . [and such] function demands that the accountant maintain total independence from the client at all times and requires complete fidelity to the public trust."[63] The Supreme Court reasoned that the public accountant's responsibility to detect, not merely search for, errors and irregularities, is based upon, first, the accountant's being in a better position and more skilled to detect errors and irregularities than anyone else, and, second, upon society's significant reliance on the accuracy of information provided by the accountant.[64]

To aid the public accountant's detection of fraud, the AICPA has developed a list of business environment symptoms of financial statement fraud. The list enumerates the following symptoms: (1) a dominating senior management in conjunction with compensation wed to reported performance or an ineffective board of directors, (2) deterioration of sales volume or quality, (3) excessive interest of top-level management regarding the effect of accounting alternatives on earnings per share of stock, and (4) unusual pressures extant, such as inadequate working capital, substantial investment in a volatile sector, and debt restrictions that hamper management actions.[65]

Many of these symptoms were present, for instance, in the Boston Company, the 114-year-old upper-crust banking firm, which admitted in 1989 it had cooked its own books, overstating pretax profits by $44 million for the first three-quarters of 1988. The deceptive accounting began shortly after the October 1987 stock market crash, when the firm was short of its performance goals established by its flamboyant and subsequently terminated president, James von Germeten, an advocate of rapid growth who "came down hard on subordinates who didn't deliver."[66] Missing the performance goals would translate into sharply reduced management bonuses, which approached $1 million for certain top executives.[67]

THE PROFESSION'S RESPONSE TO PUBLIC EXPECTATIONS AND PROBLEMS PLAGUING ACCOUNTING

A recent study of allegedly fraudulent activities of public firms reveals that 87% of the frauds are accomplished through the use of misleading financial information, that high-level management is involved in 66% of the alleged frauds, and 45% of the cases entail breakdowns in internal controls systems.[68] An audit failure occurs when a firm experiences "serious financial difficulties soon after receiving an unqualified opinion by the independent auditor that the company's financial statements are accurate."[69]   Fraudulent reporting is one cause of audit failures.

Although many cases of unlitigated fraud may escape public discovery, the number of litigated cases alleging fraud and the aggregate of reported allegations of financial fraud suggest that over 99% of all audits are free of financial fraud.[70]   Nonetheless, when financial fraud occurs, it usually results in huge losses to creditors and investors and affects confidence in the financial reporting process in general. Moreover, lessened public confidence in the reliability of financial information can adversely affect all firms that issue financial statements, because creditors and investors will demand higher return rates due to increased uncertainty about financial reports' accuracy.[71]   Between 1980 and 1985, the Big Eight accounting firms, which employ about 12% of practicing CPAs, paid over $175 million in judgments and settlements in cases involving disputed audits.[72]

To respond to the public's expectations concerning the role of the public accountant, the accountancy profession has taken certain self-regulatory steps, including the AICPA's creation of the National Commission on Fraudulent Financial Reporting (NCFFR) in 1986, and the Auditing Standards Board's drafting of ten proposed changes in auditing standards adopted by the accounting profession in February 1988.

Earlier, in 1985, the AICPA, through its committee on professional conduct, established the Anderson Committee to evaluate the institute's professional code of conduct.[73]   The AICPA sought such review because of public skepticism of the accounting profession, following charges of diminished auditor independence, casual attitude toward management fraud, and growing commercialism of the profession.[74]   The Anderson Commission Report, issued in September of 1986, suggested a massive overhaul of CPA professional standards, as well as the manner in which the profession enforces its code provisions.[75.]

The NCFFR, commonly referred to as the Treadway Commission, was constituted to recommend ways to improve the integrity of the public firms' financial reporting.   Unlike the Cohen Commission, established in 1974, which evaluated the internal accounting controls reporting system, the NCFFR, according to commission chairman James Treadway, examined "the entire financial reporting process—everything that may have an impact, or potential impact, on the system."[76]   The NCFFR's forty-nine recommendations directed to the SEC, public companies, independent public accountants, and the educational institutions have as their purpose the promotion of accurate, reliable financial reporting.

Among the NCFFR's recommendations are: (1) every public firm should establish an audit committee comprised of independent directors, (2) senior management should openly and firmly acknowledge in a report that the firm, not the independent auditor, has primary responsibility for the accuracy and honesty of the financial reporting process, including financial statements, (3) the independent accountant, although not expected to guarantee the accuracy of the firm's financial statements, should take affirmative steps to assess the potential for fraud and is responsible for detecting and determining fraudulent financial reporting, and (4) the accounting profession should revise auditing standards to enhance the quality and accuracy of the audit and to improve public communication concerning the accountant's role in auditing financial statements.[77]

The internal audit function, as distinguished from the independent audit committee, the NCFFR admonishes, should maintain a proper degree of independence from the firm's organization. One method of assuring this independence is to require the chief internal auditor to report directly to the firm's chief executive officer or to a senior financial officer whose responsibility does not include preparation of the firm's financial statements.[78] In addition, the chief internal auditor should have unfettered access to the audit committee. The NCFFR characterizes the internal auditors, who often monitor internal control and prepare financial statements, as providing "the first line of defense against fraudulent financial reporting."[79] Other commission-prescribed crucial management responsibilities include implementing an effective system of internal controls.

The NCFFR analysis offers the foregoing recommendations as well in response to problems plaguing accountants that the commission identified in its investigation of financial reporting. Specifically, the commission identified, first, the lack of adequate communication between the independent auditor and the client firm, and, second, the nonaccountant's confusion with accounting standards. One important factor that inhibits meaningful information transfer from the independent auditor to the client firm is that the standard audit report, often little more than "boiler plate" presented to the client at the conclusion of the audit process, is often devoid of meaningful information. The audit report does not inform the client of the specific difficulties found with the firm's accounting system.

In addition, investors referring to the audit report usually are not sufficiently skilled to decipher the financial reports.[80] The average investor needs objective and comparable data, not stilted language, "technicalese," and expressions understood only by accountants.[81] Moreover, accounting statements contained in financial reports are often misleading to the nonaccountant because he or she does not understand the language of accountancy. Further, there is even dispute among accountants as to what is "misleading" in terms of financial statements. Accordingly, facts that appear to represent fairly the financial condition of a firm may not do so because accounting "facts" represent probability, not absolutes.[82] Unfortunately, alternative accounting choices generate different "facts" for the same event (e.g., LIFO versus FIFO), accounting principles and, therefore, "facts" change, and accounting "facts" may appear as arbitrary because accounting standards, such as GAAP, are little more than guidelines.[83] Reflecting the confusion, the courts have determined that adherence to the accountant's GAAP or GAAS standards does not conclusively protect the accountant from being answerable to clients, investors, and creditors.[84]

Likewise, there often exists a lack of clear standards regarding various accounting issues. For example, specific accounting problems have many equally acceptable solutions because GAAP's inherent inflexibility tolerates equally acceptable alternatives. The mere existence of the variety of alternatives for solving a given problem allows each accountant considerable discretion for designing creative, often inconsistent, accounting solutions.[85]

Perhaps the accounting profession's most significant response to the public expectation of fair, honest, and reliable financial reporting is its adoption in 1988 of ten Statements on Auditing Standards (SAS) proposed by the Auditing Standards Board (ASB). Under the new standards that supersede SAS Number 16, the independent auditor has an increased responsibility to detect and report fraud. The auditor now has an affirmative duty to design the audit to discover material errors and irregularities. Another standard, which displaces SAS Number 17, recognizes that the independent auditor may have a duty to report illegal activities to authorities beyond the firm. Further, the new standard that supplants SAS Number 34 requires the independent auditor to evaluate the economic viability of the firm and craft certain statements in the audit report if there is doubt as to the firm's continued existence.[86]

These foregoing SAS changes respond directly to criticism, including that of Congressman Ron Wyden, who introduced a bill in 1986 that would require auditors to search for "any illegal act," that "[a]ccountants have . . . [placed] too much trust in management, . . . [acquiesced] too readily to management's interpretations of accounting principles, . . . [overlooked] obvious abuses of financial reporting, and . . . [been] too sympathetic to their client's interests."[87] Consequently, no longer can independent auditors either assume that management has not misrepresented material facts or ignore the ultimate effect of those misrepresentations on the firm's viability.

STANDARDS FOR MANAGEMENT ACCOUNTANTS

On June 1, 1983, through its Management Accounting Practices Committee (MAPC), the National Association of Accountants (NAA) established standards of appropriate conduct for management accountants, those accountants who work within an industrial concern or firm, as opposed to public accountants who offer their services to the public at large.[88] The MAPC developed and published these management accounting standards in a series of Statements of Management Accounting. Statement 1(B) contains the provision that establishes the overall objectives of management accounting: (1) the management accountant will provide information, and (2) the management accountant should participate in the management process.[89]

Management accountants select and provide to various management levels financial information needed for planning, assessing, and directing operations, for protecting the firm's assets, and communicating with interested parties outside the firm. Furthermore, management accountants directly manage the firm.[90]

Several standards have been developed to regulate the activities of management accountants. Statement 1(C) of the NAA's code includes two major sections. One section establishes four primary criteria for proper conduct in the areas of competence, confidentiality, integrity, and objectivity.

The other important 1(C) section provides guidelines for resolving ethical conflicts faced by management accountants.[91] The duty of competence requires that the management accountant maintain an appropriate level of professional knowledge, obey all laws, regulations and technical standards, and prepare complete, lucid reports after a thorough analysis of reliable and relevant data.

To fulfill the confidentiality criterion, the management accountant must refrain from revealing confidential information in the course of work; inform all subordinates and superiors of the confidential nature of all information; review, monitor, and restrict access to the confidential information; and prohibit the illegal or unethical use of the confidential information for personal profit or advantage. Moreover, to maintain integrity, the management accountant must avoid conflicts of interest, recognize and communicate limitations that preclude effective performance, communicate all professional opinions whether favorable or not, and not discredit the profession. To realize the objectivity criterion, the management accountant communicates information fairly, in an unbiased manner, and fully discloses all relevant information.[92]

The second principal area of the MAPC-created standards for management accountants relates to the resolution of ethical conflict. The management accountant should discuss ethical problems with his or her immediate supervisor, and successively higher levels of management, until a final resolution is achieved. Additionally, he or she should conduct confidential discussions with an impartial third party advisor to discover all possible courses of action. Finally, as a last resort the management accountant must resign if he or she has exhausted all internal sources in striving for a solution.[93]

OPINION SHOPPING

Business firms have demonstrated a pronounced willingness to change accountants for a variety of reasons, including the desire to obtain more favorable accounting treatment regarding a particular issue or transaction.[94] When a company substitutes auditors in an effort to improve the reported financial position of the firm, or surveys several accounting firms to gain their views to select a desired opinion, the firm has probably engaged in opinion shopping.[95] As employed by the SEC, opinion shopping involves an attempt by a public company to: (1) "find an accountant who will approve its proposed accounting treatment, (2) make its decision about which auditor to engage contingent upon receiving the desired answer from a consulted accountant, and (3) use an accounting method in a way that frustrates the true reporting objectives of financial statements."[96]

Several specific factors have led to increased opinion shopping. Fierce competition among accounting firms has added to auditor switching and created an environment for opinion shopping.[97] Moreover, the accounting profession's desire to maintain previous growth rates has placed competitive pressure on independent auditors to acquire small firms and reduce fees in order to maintain clients.[98]   Several firms have, in an attempt to enhance their financial performances, resorted to "creative bookkeeping," and the concomitant, aggressive interpretation of GAAP.[99]

For instance, In re Stephen O. Wade,[100] two savings and loan associations suffered significant financial losses through trading in treasury bond futures, losses that the firms desired to defer. When the firms' current independent auditors informed them that the losses should be recognized in the instant period of loss, the firms replaced the auditors with an accounting firm that would issue an unqualified opinion allowing the desired loss deferral. The SEC sanctioned participating partners in the second firm for improper conduct, after ruling the loss deferral to be incorrect.

Likewise, In re Broadview Financial Corp.,[101] a savings and loan holding company received a $4 million payment from a developer as a direct result of a $20 million loan to that same developer. The company wished to recognize the entire payment immediately as current revenue and "shopped" the transaction to a number of "Big Eight" accounting firms, when the company's existing independent auditors opined that the revenue must properly be deferred. When one of the "Big Eight" firms agreed to treat the income as current, the company dismissed its existing auditors. The SEC disagreed with the desired treatment, consequently, and the company restated its affected financial statement.

Auditor independence is an essential element in the financial reporting process. Opinion shopping creates several unique problems, including raising questions about the independence of auditors, for ". . . independent auditors should not only be independent, in fact, they should avoid situations that may lead outsiders to doubt their independence."[102] Because the nature of the independent auditor is to objectively assess the financial statements of a paying client, the auditor could have pronounced difficulty in rendering an objective opinion that adversely affects the client, especially in a time of increasing competition among firms for clients.[103]

Three specific problems often attend a firm's change of auditors. First, the firm may ask the auditor to provide an opinion on a subject with which the auditor does not have complete information. Although the auditor may modify the exploratory opinion he or she rendered during the opinion shopping process, that auditor usually is quite hesitant to change his or her opinion after being hired by the firm.[104] Second, an auditor who permits him- or herself to be "shopped" places his or her ability to negotiate in future transactions with the hiring firm at risk.[105]   Third, the public may question the integrity of the auditor if the company that selected him or her cannot provide a sound reason for changing auditors.[106] The mere threat of losing a client's account may also cause independent auditors to change opinions out of accommodation.[107]

CONCLUSIONS

Well-advised management decisions regarding cash flow, asset deployment, market entry, product pricing, taxation, and other tactical decisions depend on accurate accounting methods and information.[108] If management acts on inadequate disclosure or erroneous information, the usually resulting bad management decisions can imperil the firm's existence, the equity of investors, and the loans or advances of creditors. Both independent accountants and management accountants can enhance the provision of accurate and fair financial information by acting with integrity. Toward this end, in 1988 the AICPA, the leading membership body of U.S. accountants, approved a program of mandatory self-regulation and peer review whereby all institute members are required to undergo a quality review every three years.[109]   Edmund Coulson, then the recently appointed SEC chief accountant, commended the program, referring to it as "a positive initiative for quality prac-tice" but indicated that the SEC would strive for non-AICPA accountants to be subject to peer review as well.[110]

Nonetheless, just as great, if not more substantial, a responsibility for fair and accurate financial reporting lies in the nation's business firms, specifically management.   In virtually every firm, upper management establishes that organization's tone—where the honest and ethical actions of managers either are or are not subjugated to corporate drives for growth and greater profit.   The notorious Equity Funding scandal of the early 1970s, like that of the Boston Company in 1988, illustrates how a chief executive's admonition to subordinates to achieve high growth objectives can lead to false accounting entries and the defrauding of the investing public.[111]

To instill and maintain a culture of honesty, firms of all sizes, whether publicly traded or not, should promulgate and enforce internal controls to assure that deceptive financial accounting and reporting will be detected and prevented.   Just as important is another Treadway Commission recommendation that firms create written codes of conduct that establish procedures to monitor and enforce compliance as well as protect employees from reprisal for revealing fraud and errors in financial reporting.[112]

NOTES

1. Jereski, "You've Come a Long Way, Shareholder," Forbes (July 13, 1987): 282.
2. Ibid., 282–283.
3. Ibid., 283.
4. Stewart, "Ethics and Financial Reporting in the United States," Journal of Business Ethics 5 (1986): 402.
5. Ibid., 403.
6. Weberman, "Rumpelstilzchen Accounting," Forbes (February 24, 1986): 30.
7. Ibid.
8. Winter, "Manufacturers' Profits Picture Clouds Up," Wall Street Journal (January 12, 1989): 2.
9. Chaffee, "The Role and Responsibility of Accountants in Today's Society," The Journal of Corporation Law (Winter 1988): 863, 866.

10. Ibid.
11. 15 U.S.C., Sections 77a and 77aa (1982).
12. 15 U.S.C., Sections 78a and 78kk (1982).
13. Smolevitz, "The Opinion Shopping Phenomenon: Corporate America's Search for the Perfect Auditor," Brooklyn Law Review 57 (1987): 1084.
14. Ibid.
15. Adler, "Accounting Principles," Trial (August 1988): 37.
16. Smolevitz, op. cit., 1093.
17. Adler, op. cit., 37.
18. Woelfel, "Standards of Ethical Conduct for Management Accountants," Journal of Business Ethics 5 (1986): 365.
19. Shroyer, William Mitchell Law Review 14 (1988): 77.
20. Ibid., 79.
21. 16 American Jurisprudence 2d, "Accountant's Liability to Client for Negligent Performance of Duties," Section 2 (1978).
22. B&B Insulation, Inc. v. Occupational Safety and Health Review Commission, 583 F. 2d 1364, 1370 (5th Circ., 1978), 57 American Jurisprudence 2d, "Negligence Section" 75, (1971), as cited in Hagen, "Certified Public Accountants' Liability for Malpractice: Effect of Compliance with GAAP and GAAS," Journal of Contemporary Law 13 (1987): 76.
23. Restatement (Second) of Torts, Section 299A, Comment e (1965).
24. Shroyer, William Mitchell Law Review 14 (1988): 82-83.
25. Ibid., 83.
26. Corpus Juris Secundum 65, "Negligence," Section 1(4)(1966), and Hagen, "Certified Public Accountants' Liability for Malpractice: Effect of Compliance with GAAP and GAAS," Journal of Contemporary Law 13 (1987): 78.
27. See SEC v. Arthur Young & Co., 590 F 2d 785 (9th Circuit 1979), Goss v. Crossley (In re Hawaii Corp.) 567 F. Supp. 609 (D. Hawaii 1983), and Hagen, "Certified Public Accountants' Liability for Malpractice: Effect of Compliance with GAAP and GAAS," Journal of Contemporary Law 13 (1987): 78.
28. Hochfelder v. Ernst & Ernst, 503 F. 2d 1100 (7th Cir. 1974), reversed on other grounds, 425 U.S. 185 (1976); see Shroyer, op. cit., 83.
29. 372 F. Supp 1058 (D.N.D. 1974).
30. Ibid., 1064; see Shroyer, op. cit, 83.
31. Shroyer, op. cit., 86.
32. Restatement (Second) of Torts, "Information Negligently Supplied for the Guidance of Others," Section 552 (1977).
33. Shroyer, op. cit., 88.
34. Ibid., 91.
35. See Weiner, "Common Law Liability of the Certified Public Accountant for Negligent Misrepresentation," San Diego Law Review 20 (1983): 233.
36. 255 N.Y. 170, 174 N.E. (1931), 441.
37. Restatement (Second) of Torts, op. cit.
38. Ibid.
39. H. Rosenblum, Inc. v. Adler, 93 N.J. 324, 461 A. 2d 138 (1983).
40. Citizens State Bank v. Timm Schmidt & Co., 113 Wis. 2nd 376, 335 N.W. 2d 361 (1983).
41. Raritan River Steel Co. v. Cherry, Bekaert & Holland, 79 N.C. App. 81, 339 S.E. 2d 62 (1986).
42. 177 Cal. App. 3d 806, 223 Cal. Rptr. 218 (Cal. Ct. App. 1986).
43. Hagen, "Certified Public Accountants' Liability for Malpractice: Effect of Compliance with GAAP and GAAS," Journal of Contemporary Law 13 (1987): 65-66.
44. Farris "Accountant Malpractice," Washington State Bar News 41 (June 1987): 29.
45. Meigs et al. Principles of Auditing, 8th ed. (1985): 2.
46. Ibid., 5.
47. Hagen, op. cit., 67.
48. Garrison, Washington and Lee Law Review 44 (1987): 187.
49. Hagen, op. cit., 68.
50. American Institute of Certified Public Accountants, AICPA Professional Standards, "Auditing," Section 110.01 61 (CCH, 1985).
51. Hagen, op. cit., 69.
52. Ibid., 70.
53. Ibid., 70.

54. Handbook of Accounting and Auditing (Burton, Palmes, and Kay, eds., 1981), 16-5 through 16-6, as cited in Hagen, op. cit., 71.
55. Hagen, op. cit., 71-72.
56. Berton, "Legal Time Bomb: Big Accounting Firms Risk Costly Lawsuits By Reassuring Lenders," Wall Street Journal (January 14, 1988): 1.
57. Farris, op. cit., 27.
58. Ibid.
59. Cook, "The AICPA at 100: Public Trust and Professional Pride," J. Acct 163 (May 1987): 376.
60. Pacific Acceptance Corp. v. Forsyth, 92 N.S.W.W.N. 29, (1970), and Chaffee, "The Role and Responsibility of Accountants in Today's Society," The Journal of Corporation Law (Winter 1988): 844-885.
61. Chaffee, op. cit., 881.
62. 465 U.S. 805 (1984).
63. Ibid., 817-818.
64. Chaffee, op. cit., 882.
65. Raab, "Detecting and Preventing Financial Statement Fraud: The Roles of the Reporting Company and the Independent Auditor," Yale Law & Policy Review 5 (1987): 527.
66. Chipello and Anders, "Boston Co.'s Chief Departs the Firm with Usual Drama," Wall Street Journal (January 30, 1989): 1.
67. Ibid., 4.
68. Raab, op. cit., 520.
69. Ibid., 514, 520; see also Berton, "Self-Regulation by Accountants Divides Industry," Wall Street Journal (June 20, 1986): 21.
70. Raab, op. cit., 514-515.
71. Ibid., 514.
72. McComas, "How Accountable The Accountants?" Fortune (August 18, 1986): 56.
73. Anderson and Ellyson, "Restructuring Professional Standards: The Anderson Report," Journal of Accountancy (September 1986): 92.
74. Ibid.
75. Ibid.
76. Liebtag, "Profile: James C. Treadway, Jr.," Journal of Accountancy (September 1986): 78, 80.
77. Szabo, "Above-Board Bottom Lines," Nation's Business (October, 1988): 56; Berman, "Checking Financial Fraud," Commentary (February, 1988): 8; Liebtag, "Profile—James C. Treadway, Jr.," Journal of Accountancy (September 1986): 78, and Chaffee, "The Role and Responsibility of Accountants in Today's Society," The Journal of Corporation Law (Winter 1988): 883.
78. Raab, op. cit., 521.
79. Ibid., 521.
80. Chaffee, op. cit., 887-888.
81. Reynolds, "What Investors Want from the Annual Report," Wall Street Journal (January 18, 1989): 1.
82. Chaffee, op. cit., 887-888.
83. Ibid.
84. Ibid., 888.
85. Ibid., 889.
86. Ibid., 884-885.
87. Boland, "Myth and Technology in the American Acccounting Profession," Journal of Management Studies 19 (1982): 113.
88. Woelfel, op. cit., 365.
89. Ibid.
90. Ibid.
91. Ibid., 366.
92. Ibid., 367-368.
93. Ibid., 368.
94. Smolevitz, op. cit., 1103.
95. Ibid.
96. Ibid., 1104.
97. Ibid., 1105.
98. Ibid.
99. Ibid., 1107.
100. Securities Exchange Act Release, Number 21095 (June 25, 1984Fed. Sec. L. Rep. (CCH) Section 73, 432, at 63, 130, as cited in Goelzer, "The SEC and Opinion Shopping: A Case Study on the Changing Regulation of the Accounting Profession," Brooklyn Law Review 52 (1987): 1062.

101. Accounting and Auditing Enforcement Release Number 54, <u>6 Fed. Sec. L.</u>
     <u>Rep.</u> (CCH), Section 73,454 at 63,196 (April 17, 1985), as cited in
     Goelzer, "The SEC and Opinion Shopping: A Case Study on the Changing
     Regulation of the Accounting Profession," <u>Brooklyn Law Review</u> 52
     (1987): 1063.
102. <u>American Institute of Certified Public Accountants, Statement of</u>
     <u>Auditing Standards</u>, Number 1, Section 220.03 (Supp. 1984).
103. Smolevitz, op. cit., 1109.
104. Ibid.
105. Ibid.
106. Ibid.
107. Ibid., 1110.
108. Farris, op. cit., 29.
109. Berton, "Accountants Vote Required Program of Self-Regulation," <u>Wall</u>
     <u>Street Journal</u> (January 14, 1988): 12.
110. Ibid.
111. Longenecker, "Management Priorities and Management Ethics" 4 (1985):
     68.
112. Szabo, op. cit., 56.

10
Computer-Based Information Systems

INTRODUCTION

During 1987 and 1988, a teen-age high-school dropout bypassed AT&T's computer security systems and copied $1.2 million worth of computer programs and destroyed computer files valued at $174,000.[1] In late 1988 a widely publicized computer system near-disaster was the virus spread through government computer networks by a computer science graduate student. The virus multiplied so quickly that it overloaded a series of computer networks within hours. Fortunately it destroyed no data, but it could have had it been designed to do so.[2] There has been considerable attention to these and other similar "outside invasions" of publicly and privately owned Computer-Based Information Systems (CBISs), perhaps due to our fascination with movies such as Wargames.

Although the problems for computer security from hackers and viruses are real enough, the true menace to CBIS security is from the "inside" of organizations. Experts agree that the greatest threat, which accounts for at least 80% of the breaches to CBIS security, is internal.[3] Two days after he was fired for disruptive behavior and disregard for company policy, a computer programmer from a Fort Worth securities firm planted a "virus program" in the company's computer systems that destroyed 68,000 sales commissions records in just several days.[4] A computer consultant employed by Security Pacific Bank of California obtained a security code that allowed him to electronically transfer $7 million from the company to a Swiss bank account.[5] And currency traders, either within Volkswagen AG or with a financial firm that handled Volkswagen's corporate funds, covered up $259 million of trading losses through the alteration of computer programs and erasure of data tapes.[6]

These examples of breaches of computer security vividly illustrate that CBIS security is one of the more challenging business conduct issues facing business firms today. Computers have permeated the business world such that information-related activities now dominate the workplace. Furthermore, our computer networks for handling information are now so extensive that almost $1 trillion is transmitted among financial institutions every workday, an amount equal to 25% of the GNP.[7] It is very clear that the opportunities to breach CBIS security systems in modern-day business firms, and in all other types of today's "computerized" organizations as well, are virtually limitless.

In reality, security is only one part of a broader issue of information "access," which also involves the related issues of "privacy" and "power." Other important social, legal, ethical, and business conduct issues that firms face today in managing information and operating CBISs include: responsibility for information "accuracy," "automation" of the workplace, and the "ownership" of information and software. These various social, legal, and ethical issues have emerged mainly as the result of both the unique nature and the rapid outpouring of computer and communication technologies that comprise the backbone of corporate CBISs. Prior to consideration of these various issues, the main focus of this chapter, the current CBIS milieu is reviewed briefly to highlight the technological-organizational-managerial context in which these issues persist.

THE CBIS MILIEU

A CBIS is an information system with one or more computers forming the core. Actually, such a system is comprised of five elements: hardware, software, data, procedures, and people. Technological advancements in computer hardware and, increasingly, in computer software have pushed CBISs to the forefront of business operations and management today. These new and emerging technologies pose real challenges to effective organization of the data, procedures and people within business firms. Not surprisingly, management of the overall CBIS is evolving to meet these technological advancements and organizational challenges. The more recent technological advancements in computer hardware and software have included, among others, parallel processors, laser disks, and hypertext.[8] Also, new superconductors appear to be forthcoming within the 1990s. These and other future advancements in information processing and storage technology likely will continue to pose new challenges and create difficult issues for management. However, advancements in information transmission technology leading to greater sharing of information, combined with increasing commitment of firms to develop and utilize more widely integrated, broader based CBISs, appear to have the greatest potential impact upon the social, legal, and ethical business conduct issues for management in the future.

The rapid scientific advancements in computer and communication technologies have enabled small and large firms alike to benefit from more accurate, more timely, more analytical, and just _more_ information with which to conduct business. In fact, today's large business firms have come to depend upon CBISs in virtually every aspect of their operations. And even the smallest companies can employ PCs, LANs, FAXs, and electronic mail to facilitate information processing in their business operations. By 1997 it is estimated that more than 5 million personal computers will be used in small businesses throughout the United States, with another 10 million being used in large businesses. In addition, satellite-based communication services are expected soon to provide worldwide interpersonal and intracorporate communication among even the smaller computer systems.[9]

We are now in an "information age," in which CBISs have proliferated to the extent that more people in organizations are involved in information-related work than in any other single activity. This proliferation has occurred because of the many business functions that CBISs can perform or aid in performing. To date, CBISs have proven useful in improving operational efficiency, increasing decision-making effectiveness, enhancing competitive position, identifying new opportunities, adding customers, providing better service, and improving products, among others. And whereas this is an impressive list, CBISs surely will contribute to organizational success in added ways in the future. The use of CBISs, in particular the use of computers to process information, has had and is continuing to have significant impacts upon how these various business functions are carried out, such that fundamental changes in business operations and interrelationships are both necessary and desirable to stay competitive. Inevitably, changes in the manner of conducting business tend to exacerbate long-standing social, legal, and ethical issues for management, or they create new issues of even greater proportion for business firms and for society generally. Such is the case with CBISs, as discussed later.

The extent of CBIS proliferation is a direct result of the available technology and the resources committed to CBIS development and implementation. The evolution of computer and communication technology has been occurring at such a rapid rate that the growth of corporate CBISs has not been inhibited in a meaningful sense by any lack of sophisticated hardware and software. In fact, the infusion of information processing technology has in general led, not lagged, many firms' ability to use it to its fullest extent. This is due to a number of factors, including the shortage of trained personnel, overemphasis upon automation of information processing tasks to the exclusion of enriching and extending the scope of these tasks, and a failure to recognize the resulting, sometimes intangible, benefits to be gained from CBISs. Many experts agree that technological developments in computer and communications systems will continue to be forthcoming at a rate that will challenge firms' capacity to employ them to the fullest extent with the resources available to most firms.

In large businesses, CBISs have become a significant portion of the corporate budget. According to a Datamation survey of the top ten companies in each of twelve selected industry sectors, budgeted spending for CBIS was $32 billion in 1988, up from an actual $29 billion in 1987.[10] The industrial and automotive sector led the list with CBIS expenditures of nearly $8 billion, closely followed by electronics with almost $6 billion and banking with $4.5 billion in 1987. Overall, of all 120 firms, budgeted spending for CBIS in 1988 averaged 2.1% of total revenues.[11]

The top ten electronics firms are their own best customers for CBIS, spending 4.0% of their total revenues for in-house information systems in 1987.[12] This percentage would be even higher, except that the computer manufacturers of this group give themselves discounts on the computer hardware. The rapidly changing nature of the computer manufacturing industry demands that these firms employ their own CBIS products in every facet of their businesses. The top ten utilities firms also are big users of CBIS. In 1987 they spent $2.5 billion on CBIS, excluding large sums spent on computer-based switching systems and transmission facilities that are not counted in CBIS budgets.[13]

From a more recent Datamation survey, the average corporate CBIS budget in 1988 was $1.82 million, expected to have grown in 1989 to approximately $1.90 million.[14] Although this is a modest increase and smaller than expected due primarily to the decentralizing of CBIS organizational structures and accompanying staffing changes, it is nonetheless a substantial resource commitment that likely will continue to increase in the future.

Another CBIS development that is impacting the conduct of business and business interrelationships among firms is Electronic Data Interchange (EDI). EDI is a form of electronic communication involving the direct computer-to-computer exchange of standards business documents, thus far primarily those to do with daily purchasing transactions and the flow of materials from supplier to customer. The number of potential applications of EDI may be virtually unlimited, however. One consulting firm predicts a $1.3 billion domestic market for EDI networks and systems by 1991.[15] Some firms have already required their suppliers to go to this means of doing business. Many experts believe that electronic data interchange will virtually eliminate paper purchasing transactions among large firms in the 1990s.

As CBIS use has grown, concomitant with the rapid increase in mergers and acquisitions and the increasing need to integrate more business functions, communications among CBISs in firms' various divisions and subsidiaries also have proliferated. This high demand for network connectivity among CBISs is challenging the dissimilarities among proprietary systems and calling for an "open-system" approach to CBIS operations.[16] Due to the proprietary nature of different computer hardware, one manufacturer's hardware has not been compatible with all others with whom the firm does business. Among CBIS-user firms, there is a growing clamor for connectivity among CBISs through operating-system software standardization. This will allow for easier combination and extension of CBISs and corresponding greater integration of business functions and activities throughout firms and industries generally. The administrative arm of the European Economic Commission promulgated in 1980 the first open-system policy for CBISs that has pioneered the current movement.[17] By 1987 open systems were 34% of the total U.S. market of $43 billion, and they are estimated to grow to 48% of $54 billion by 1991.[18] Interestingly, some experts believe that this movement to an open system or standard interconnectivity among CBISs could promote still more merger activity and lead to "megacorporations" forming at a rapid rate.[19]

The organizational structures of CBIS units are changing in response to the newer computer technologies, especially microcomputer technology, which has led to a burgeoning of "end-user" computing and "distributed" CBISs in many firms. According to a recent Datamation survey, General Electric tops the list of U.S. corporations, excluding the computer manufacturers, with 45,000 personal computer systems installed. The top three firms each have at least 40,000 systems and average six employees per installed system.   IBM leads the personal computer manufacturers with 200,000 installed systems and approximately one employee per installed system.[20]

In reaction to the growing demand for CBIS applications development, coupled with an increasing number of personal computer systems and computer-savvy CBIS end-users in all parts of organizations, operational units in many firms have taken the initiative for developing their own CBISs. This has influenced the CBIS organizational units to decentralize more and to reorganize themselves somewhat to support both large-system CBIS development and operation, together with a broad range of smaller scale CBIS applications and end-users. One popular organizational approach to serving end-user, micro-computer-based information systems is the "information center," which has demanded a new breed of computer profes-sional, one with a broad range of microcomputer-system knowledge combined with an understanding of the business applications to which they can be applied.   Whereas the Information Center (IC) is still a relative new approach, a few firms have already abandoned it in favor of other more de-centralized forms of distributing the responsibility for CBIS. Some firms are putting CBIS staff in independent business units, which focus on a very specific aspect of the firm's business.   This is still another organizational approach to getting CBIS technology and know-how closer to the workforce it supports.[21]   Clearly, our organizational know-how for utilizing CBIS technology most effectively is still evolving.

The CBIS has not had the impact upon the overall structure of organizations predicted by some scholars earlier. Organi-zations in the 1980s were predicted to have flatter management hierarchies, smaller managerial spans of control, more centralization, and higher degrees of routinization in lower and middle level jobs.[22] However, structural changes have not occurred consistently in these respects, and some organiza-tions have experienced an increase in the size of management and even taller hierarchies. For example, aggressive CBIS development at Travelers Insurance Company has enabled a doubling in business volume concomitant with a decrease in the clerical workforce and an increase in managerial personnel.[23] In this and other similar situations, the greater volume and the increased complexity of business brought about by informa-tion technology has required more and better trained profes-sionals and managers, especially at the middle levels, to direct the work and make the nonroutine decisions that more complex operations require.

The effect of CBIS technology upon organizations in the future is unclear. According to Professor Shoshana Zuboff of Harvard University, it will depend in great part upon the extent to which organizations use CBIS technology to "inform-ate" as well as to "automate" their operations.[24]   If the emphasis is conventionally upon automating clerical work, then relatively tall hierarchies will continue in order to legit-imize managerial authority and ensure tight control over organizational operations. But if informating all organiza-tional jobs also becomes a priority, then the collective knowledge base of the organization will grow, task-related learning will be encouraged, and the organizational hierarchy likely will diminish in both size and formality.[25] The effect of CBISs upon management and managers has been mixed to date. In the information systems (IS) area itself, along with the growth in CBIS management overall has come the emergence of the chief information officer (CIO) as an important member of top management.   In firms where information processing technologies are seen as playing a key role in their future, the CIO is typically at the vice president level.   In firms that are more predominantly transaction processing oriented, the CIO is often a director, typically at the middle managerial level. According to a 1988 Coopers & Lybrand survey of 400 top IS executives across the United States, 59% considered themselves to be CIOs, but only 27% reported directly to the top of the firm.[26] CIOs are seen by some as a new breed of "information elite" who will rise to the top of the firm, as senior accountants rose to become chief financial officers in the 1960s, by means of their control over information, the key corporate resource of the "information age." Others see the CIO as the chief architect of the firm's CBIS strategic plans, but do not see the CIO on a direct path to the top.[27] In any event, the CIO has become an important position in technologically progressive firms employing CBISs widely, because managing information as a resource has become essential to corporate success.

The growing corporate CBIS budgets and the trend toward large-scale open systems surely represent a greater commitment by American business firms to utilize computer-based information systems to support more and more facets of their operations. It is also reasonable to expect an increase in CBIS usage at the executive level.   However, in a recent 1988 survey of America's top 500 CEOs conducted by _Personal Computing_ magazine, approximately four of five (78.6%) CEOs reported that they do not use computers themselves.[28]   This percentage of nonusers has remained constant since 1986.   In contrast, 27% of all white collar workers used computers themselves in 1988, up from 19% in 1986.[29] About two-thirds of the user CEOs said that they liked to use computers because they provided better access to information and increased their personal productivity.[30]   Approximately two-thirds of the nonuser CEOs said that computers were "difficult to learn," which made them reluctant to try or that their subordinates used computers for them instead. Among all CEOs, however, there is a growing sentiment that "those top executives who do not now use computers, and those who never will, are slowly losing ground to a lot of other people who do—like their employees."[31]   One widely accepted view of the central role of the CEO is the exercise of leadership through the skillful use of language.[32] Increasingly, the corporate language is the language of computers, with which everyone will eventually have to converse.

CBIS technology is having an impact upon middle and lower level managers throughout organizations as well.   These managers now have easier access to information, enabling them to be better informed about their respective areas of responsibility.   And CBISs also are providing enhanced decision support, especially for the nonroutine, ill-structured decisions managers face with increasing frequency in today's complex business environments.   In addition, more managerial effort is required to understand and direct the work of subordinates whose tasks are becoming increasing automated and informated.[33]   Information overload also has increased the rigors of day-to-day management.   Some middle and lower level user managers attempt to protect themselves from useless data by utilizing specially designed software, which ranks incoming data and messages by order of importance.[34]   These and other CBIS effects are imposing more stringent demands upon managers to become more computer-savvy, more analytical, and less resistant to changes in business operations brought about by CBISs.

Summary

The corporate world is increasingly characterized by reorganization, decentralization, cost reductions, mergers, and multinational expansion.   The CBIS milieu in today's reorganized, decentralized, cost-conscious, recently merged, multinational corporations consists of:

- More than half of the workforce engaged in information processing activities.

- Rapid changes in computer technology affecting virtually all information processing, storing, and retrieving and most other dependent activities.

- More investment in and growth of CBIS functions, accompanied by increasing distribution of CBISs toward more end-user responsibility for and control over information processing activities.

- Emergence of communication networks that facilitate electronic data interchange within and among firms, their suppliers, and customers.

- Movement toward open systems that reduce the incompatibilities among CBISs, thereby broadening and expanding the opportunities for integration of business operations, mutual business ventures, and mergers.

- Some elimination of routine jobs due to automation, accompanied by increases in the size of management due to the increased demands of understanding and directing more complex, higher tech jobs.

- Emergence of the chief information officer to handle strategic planning and top-level management of the information resource.

- Still a substantial number of CEOs who are not personally involved with CBIS technology nor expect to become so in the near term.

In this rapidly changing, increasingly complex business environment, the basic functions of management and the skills of managers are, by necessity, changing dramatically. However, certain critical social, legal, and ethical issues have been ignited or rekindled by CBISs, and these issues will have a significant impact upon the evolution of corporate management in the 1990s.

SOCIAL, LEGAL, AND ETHICAL BUSINESS CONDUCT ISSUES

In addition to changes already noted in the nature and structure of organizations and their management, which computer and communication technology in great part have rendered, business firms are confronted with certain critical social, legal, and ethical issues surrounding CBISs. From the viewpoint of the firm overall, these are issues that require a formal, prescribed course of action if the firm is to maintain integrity in its operations, project a positive image to its customers and to society, and remain competitive in the long run. But from the viewpoint of the individual manager in the firm, they are in reality dilemmas in day-to-day informal situations and are not always easily dealt with in that they often involve conforming to social norms, interpreting legal opinions, and making difficult choices between what is right and wrong.[35] The issues or dilemmas that we focus here on here are: access to information, which encompasses the separate issues of privacy, security, and power; responsibility for information accuracy; ownership of information and software; and automation and information of work. Understanding these issues or dilemmas has, in general, been quite perplexing because they are so varied in nature. For example, even though ownership is primarily a legal matter and privacy a social and legal phenomenon, they both have ethical ramifications as well. Such is the case for most, if not all, of these issues or dilemmas. Moreover, "information" itself is not a simple concept, referring, on the one hand, to a process as in "information of work" and, on the other, to the output of that process as in "ownership of information." Each of these information-related issues or dilemmas is examined here in respect to its impact on the conduct of business and its management in the 1990s. Then some guidelines are offered relative to formulating and promulgating the corporate code of conduct as a means of addressing certain aspects of these issues.

Access to Information

Society, and especially U.S. corporate society, advances as a result of the creation, availability, and intelligent use of knowledge. Information is knowledge that has been derived from data.[36] Raw data abound in our society, and are being produced at a Herculean rate. In most situations, there is no shortage of existing data, but the needed data may not be immediately available or, if so, it is not used wisely. Today, computers can generate vast quantities of data, and they can be stored in large computerized databases at relatively low cost. So, aside from the motivational aspects, the real challenges to knowing and advancing knowledge lie in

the availability of data and our use of the information
derived from it.

In addition to the data being available, there must be
access to data before they can be used as information to
impart knowledge. Professor Richard Mason has suggested that
"our main avenue to information is through literacy."[37] He has
identified three requirements for literacy: possession of the
intellectual skills, including reading and reasoning, to
utilize information; access to the computer and communication
technologies for processing and transmitting data; and access
to the data itself.[38] In spite of the increasing availability
of computers in our educational systems at all levels, it is
not clear that students are becoming more literate, albeit
they are learning to use computers. In fact, scholastic
aptitude test scores of students have not been increasing as
one might expect, and they have declined in some areas. This
suggests that although computer technology has become less
costly, especially in respect to computing power, and therefore is increasingly affordable, it has not yet had the mass
effect upon improving learning and reasoning performance that
some have predicted. Moreover, it is still relatively more
expensive than some other forms of information that are
available in libraries free. And whereas large corporations
have the resources to provide computers for every five-to-ten
employees, smaller firms are usually less able financially to
do so to improve the computer literacy and general literacy of
their employees.

Access to large computer databases is much greater today
as a result of advances in communications technology and
relational database software. However, it is still relatively
expensive for many individuals and firms alike. To access
information providers such as CompuServe and The Source, one
must pay both a connection fee and usage charge, which can be
much more costly than a nominal telephone bill. Information
utilities such as Dialcom, Telemain, GE Quik-Comm, Notice,
Connect, and OnTyme provide electronic mail and other information services to corporate clients for a combination of,
typically, a basic fee, on-line time charges, file-size
charges, and charges for discretionary storage.[39] These
charges are sufficiently high to preclude most individuals and
small firms from subscribing.

Privacy. One thorny issue concerning information access
is the matter of privacy. The risks of invasion of privacy in
business situations stem from a number of different factors,
including the wide range of users, uncontrolled data communications, links to corporate databases, access to highly
processed information as in office automation systems, and
even unprotected physical environments.[40] Professor F. Warren
McFarlan of Harvard suggests that it is useful to separate the
issue of privacy into concerns external to the firm and
concerns internal to the firm's operations.[41] Relative to
external transfer of information among firms, the nature of
the information and the organizational units and people
involved must be considered. What types of information may be
exchanged? And with whose permission? As firms increasingly
link their CBISs to those of their suppliers and customers,
will intrusion into each other's files and databases be

controllable?   According to a report by an American Bar Association task force, the risks in Electronic Data Interchange (EDI) include, among others, unauthorized disclosure to third parties, interception during transmission, and transmission to the wrong parties.[42]   Lawyers informed about EDI believe that participating firms will eventually wind up in court over various privacy-related matters because the status of EDI is not yet well defined in the law.   Another concern is whether any individual or group of employees of the firm have the right to stop the information transfer process.   One might observe that the information is improper or irrelevant and it could impair the firms' ability to make good decisions or take appropriate actions.   The increasing value of information for decision-making can necessitate close surveillance by all responsible parties over the firm's data and information resources if the firm is to retain a competitive edge.

Concerns about the use of information inside the firm are perhaps even more troublesome.   Is all information within the firm's databases available to all units and individuals throughout the firm?   What information should an employee be required to divulge about him- or herself to others in the firm, and under what circumstances?   To what extent should an employee's work be scrutinized, and by what means?   According to the U.S. Office of Technology Assessment (OTA), new computer-based employee monitoring and surveillance technologies are becoming increasingly intrusive and can possibly contribute to work-related stress.[43]   OTA data reveals that in 1987 about 6 million workers were monitored by computers, 90 percent of them were women, and most were clerical workers.[44] In other OTA findings, the National Institute of Occupational Safety and Health found that heavily monitored clerical workers showed more stress than a control group that was not monitored; and Harvard professor Shoshana Zuboff reported that turnover increased by almost 100 percent after a large retail chain introduced computer monitoring of its collections staff.[45]

Perhaps the most serious internal privacy concern from the loss of control of information is the resulting loss of autonomy by organizational groups and individuals, according to Professor Deborah Johnson of Rensselaer Polytechnic Institute.[46]   Loss of autonomy means loss of status as a responsible group or person, leading to loss of self-respect in extreme cases.   If business firms diminish individual autonomy to increase profits, there is no real net gain to society as a whole, according to Johnson.[47]

Security. Computer security is perhaps the most difficult issue affecting business conduct in the information age because the lack of it can bring about huge financial losses rather quickly.   The total losses to business from computer security breaches today are estimated to be at least $3 billion to $5 billion annually according to Ernst & Whinney.[48] The cost of computer security is also enormous, growing from an estimated $588 million in 1988 to nearly $1 billion by 1992, according to Frost & Sullivan, Inc., a New York-based market research firm.[49]   Total shipments of all types of software and hardware security mechanisms have been estimated to be considerably higher.

The matter of computer security is not really a moral issue, because crimes committed via computer-based information systems are clearly dishonest and offenders must be punished as for other crimes. However, ensuring that one's computer system is secure is not an easy matter today, especially with the increasing emphasis upon more open, more widely integrated CBISs to improve the efficiency of a firm's operations and to improve the effectiveness of decision-making to enhance its competitiveness.

As noted earlier, the primary threat to computer security is from employees and those associated with the firm in some way who actually know something about the firm's operations. The typical computer crime felon has the following character-istics: young, median age 25 years, ranging from 18 to 46 years; very skilled, high performing computer professional, sometimes a manager; in a position of trust, performing his or her own job responsibilities; works with a close friend or associate also skilled in computers; to impress others, ignores commonly accepted practices that eventually escalates into a serious crime; is able to rationalize harming the organization, which is viewed an impersonal entity; and enjoys using computers to challenge his or her intellect, wherein the crime is viewed as a game.[50]

Computer viruses are one danger to the security of CBISs, and they can emerge in any firm. In December 1987 the world's largest computer firm, IBM, had to shut down its entire worldwide computer network for two hours. Thousands of large computers were infected by 500,000 instances of a "virus" program, which injected a self-replicating holiday greeting throughout the system, and for eight weeks afterward indivi-dual computers had to be shut down because of recurrences of the virus.[51]

The six most common computer viruses are called Pakistani Brain, Scores, Israeli Virus, nVir, Alameda Virus, and Lehigh, and researchers have identified more than thirty different and widely diverse strains of these viruses.[52] The Computer Virus Industry Association has documented virus attacks on nearly 90,000 personal computers during 1988, according to assoc-iation president John McAfee.[53]

Some software products on the market provide limited protection against computer viruses, including IBM's RACF and two other products, Top Secret and ACF2, all for mainframe computers.[54] A new generation of "integrity shells" software products will offer fuller protection for corporate CBISs. The key to total protection, which may not really be possible in fact, seems to lie in continual vigilance by CBIS staffs and by everyone in the firm involved with information process-ing, which will eventually be nearly everyone.

The two major pieces of legislation dealing with computer security passed by Congress and enacted into law to date are the 1986 Computer Fraud and Abuse Act,[55] and the 1987 Computer Security Act.[56] The latter is a major step forward in improving the security of information in federal computer systems. The primary thrust of the former act is to make illegal the unauthorized entry into computers of government agencies, committing computer fraud or theft across state lines either physically or electronically, or the posting of passwords on electronic bulletin boards that would allow

unauthorized access to government computers.[57]   The teen-age
computer hacker mentioned earlier who invaded AT&Ts computer
system was convicted and fined $10,000 in January 1989 under
this statute.[58]

Almost all states have also passed laws prohibiting
specific computer-related activities.[59]   However, the nature
of those activities and the severity of the punishments vary
considerably.   For example, in some states unauthorized
computer access is considered a felony; in others it is
considered a misdemeanor, and is not even mentioned in the
criminal code in still others.[60]

Many problems with computer security result from such
things as utilities failures, electromagnetic discharges, and
the like.[61] Also, Edward Yourdon, a notable computer analyst,
believes that the Achilles' heel of information security is
software maintenance.[62] He estimates that firms spend roughly
$22 billion annually fixing software problems, much of which
involves working on programs someone else wrote.   This can
seriously undermine the integrity of the firm's information
systems.   Although these are not directly social, legal, or
ethical issues as such, they also help to point out the
enormity of the challenge to CBIS and information security
faced by business firms.   The need for computer security of
corporate CBISs is enormous.   According to Patrick J.
McGovern, chairman, International Data Group, currently, some
50 million people have direct access to corporate computers;
by 1992 this number will grow to about 350 million; and by the
year 2000, the computing population is estimated to reach over
2 billion.[63]   McGovern believes that new ground rules are
needed for guardianship of domestic CBISs involving all
employees sharing the responsibility for information protection. On the international level, there are serious jurisdic-
tional and compliance questions to be answered.   For example,
if information is stolen or damaged in transit through another
country, who is responsible for investigation and prosecution?
Lincoln D. Faurer, president and CEO, Corporation for Open
Systems International, believes that global open systems
interconnection will mandate that both corporate and governmental users will have to balance the virtues of greater
accessibility and information sharing with their respective
needs to maintain adequate security.[64]

Power.   Information is power, and CBISs that process
information give power to those who control them.   Power
derived from information processing systems can take various
forms, including possession power, expertise power, monitoring
power, and competitive power.   The CBIS department can be
powerful by virtue of the fact that it has the responsibility
for information processing and storage, to the extent that
these activities are centralized and information is viewed as
one of the firm's critical assets by top management, which is
increasingly the case. Information systems professionals also
can hold power from their expertise, especially if they use it
to gain political clout within the organization wherever
possible. This can pose social and political problems in some
organizations when the value systems of information system
designers embedded into the firm's CBISs differ from those who
use or manage the systems.[65]   The key here would seem to be

education of computer professionals in the social effects of computers upon organizations and their operation. Power over other individuals is also derived from computer systems used to monitor and control them, which is also a privacy-related matter as discussed earlier.

One of the principal functions that a CBIS can provide for a firm is to increase its competitive position in the market-place through locking in clients and locking out competitors.[66] In other words, CBISs offer the potential for new kinds of monopolies in today's information age. A number of different firms are linked electronically to their customers or sup-pliers to encourage them to be business partners and to reduce transaction costs. This is desirable because it can lead to lower total costs and lower prices to consumers, which is surely the aim in using any technology. However, some firms have been criticized for using their information channels in ways that seem as anticompetitive- and even anticon-sumer-oriented. Perhaps the most classic example is in the computer-based airline reservation industry, which has been studied by Douglas G. Copeland and Professor James L. McKenney of Harvard University.[67] Copeland and McKenney conclude that this situation illustrates the role of scale economies, the congruence between task and technology, and the importance of intelligence persistence by the dominant firms in a highly competitive market where success is highly dependent upon exploiting opportunities by adapting evolving technology, which is essential to free enterprise.[68] Of course, this is a complex issue that sometimes must be settled in the courts, as is the case in this instance.

Information Accuracy. Concerns about data and information accuracy are far-reaching and complicated, and they center around two primary questions. How do firms ensure that their data is accurate? Who will bear the liability for dissem-ination of inaccurate information? Common practice in centralized CBIS departments is to employ validation and verification procedures to ensure that when data are created and entered electronically into corporate databases, they are accurate. Stored data are also verified periodically and when updated. However, as firms move increasingly into distributed information systems where the responsibility for CBIS develop-ment and operation is decentralized more to users, it becomes increasingly difficult and costly to ensure the accuracy of data. Moreover, it has become so easy to process data with both mainframes and microcomputers that the total amount of processed data, especially in large organizations, is enor-mous.

The central position of responsibility for data integrity in CBIS organizations is the data administrator. Database management systems software that incorporates data diction-aries are used to manage the data and provide data integrity. As databases are increasingly shared among partner firms in open system business relationships, more sophisticated database management software will be needed to ensure the accuracy of the data used in the ensuing transactions. Also, the responsibility of data administration will broaden to encompass CBIS managers, user managers, and others involved in data and information exchange.

The responsibility or liability for inaccurate information is a troublesome and challenging issue. In transactions between firms, and especially where third parties are involved such as in purchasing-type electronic data interchange (EDI) situations, computer and communications technology apparently have advanced faster than the law or courts can keep up.[69] Because EDI transactions are paperless, some firms have entered into "trading partner agreements" to preauthorize EDI transactions and specify terms and conditions. The agreement ordinarily also places liability when there are problems with a transaction. However, apportioning liability among the trading partners and among the communication networks and software vendors involved is complicated, according to how many parties are involved. "Under the provisions of negligence law, errors in business transactions must be fixed quickly after they are discovered or the liability goes up dramatically", according to J.T. Westermeier, a partner at the Washington, D.C. law firm of Abrams, Westermeier, and Goldberg.[70]

Another related concern is whether the type of data affects liability for dissemination of erroneous information, and if so, how is it affected. Professor F. Warren McFarlan of Harvard University implies that "medical data, credit data, and customer buying behavior data" may present different requirements for data accuracy and different liabilities for each type.[71] In any event, the matter of responsibility for data integrity is highly complex, and the base of responsibility will surely broaden with the broadening of CBIS networks within and among business firms.

Ownership of Information and Software. Concerns about information accuracy raise the issue of ownership of information and accompanying software, discussed to some extent in Chapter 7. Information as intellectual property has become a more complex issue as the result of computer and communication technologies. Computer-generated information is easy to produce and to share with others, so it is difficult to safeguard. Patents, copyrights, and oaths of confidentiality, among other means, are commonly used to protect computer-generated information as intellectual property, albeit often with limited success.

Professor Richard O. Mason of Southern Methodist University has focused on the field of artificial intelligence and expert systems to illustrate what firms are up against in dealing with the problems of ownership of information.[72] "Practitioners of artificial intelligence proceed by extracting knowledge from experts, workers, and the knowledgeable, and then implanting it into computer software where it becomes capital in the economic sense."[73] This process, in effect, transfers control of the knowledge (i.e., information) to those who own the ensuing computer software and the hardware in which it is processed. The question here is—is this type of exchange of information warranted, and if so, under what circumstances? And how are the knowledge contributors to be recognized and compensated? Mason believes that these are crucial questions to be answered as more intelligent CBISs are developed, for "nowhere is the potential threat to human dignity so severe as it is (here)."[74]

The ownership of computer software and the liability for malfunctions of computer programs also are concerns for business firms. Because the software of a CBIS controls the operation of the hardware, it is a different form of property that did not exist prior to the computer era, and therefore it has posed new legal problems. At present, there are three main forms of legal protection to software creators: copyright protection, patents, and trade secrecy laws.[75] Each of these has some real limitations here, however. And whereas patents would probably give software creators the protection they most need, there is some question as to whether or not patents can and should be applied more broadly to computer software. Perhaps what is needed is some new legal mechanism to protect the ownership of computer software.[76]

Professor Barbara Johnson sees the moral issue of owner-ship of computer software "inextricably tied to the metaphys-ical question: What are (computer) programs?" Regrettably, this question has not been answered precisely enough to resolve all the legal questions.

In general, the courts have attempted to distinguish between the general use and specific application of computer software in respect to the use of patent law. However, suggests Johnson, "the Court's struggle with patent protection of programs suggests that the patent system cannot be used to achieve protection for all programs."[77] It seems that business firms, professional organizations, and individuals alike can help to minimize the problems associated with recognition and protection of ownership of computer software by "taking the law seriously, the spirit of it, not just the letter."[78]

Automation and Information of Work

Computers and CBISs have done much to automate work, especially clerical work, and consequently to increase the efficiency of business operations. But this accomplishment does not adequately distinguish the potential of information processing technology from earlier generations of machine technology, such as typewriters and calculators. CBIS technology is used to automate various productive and admin-istrative operations, but it also is capable of generating vast amounts of information about the underlying productive and administrative processes through which organizational work is done. This characteristic of CBIS technology has been termed "information" by Professor Shoshana Zuboff of Harvard University to parallel the term "automation."

Although the automation of work has some very positive consequences for business firms by increasing efficiency, reducing costs, and thereby lowering prices and raising profits, it also has some serious social consequences. In situations where computers have replaced people in certain structured, routine tasks, job displacement has surfaced as an ugly consequence. It can be argued that jobs for people are not really lost here, because new jobs will be created to develop and maintain the computers and associated technology employed in these applications. The relative magnitude of jobs lost and jobs gained is under debate in business and academic circles, but at the very least, people are displaced and must be retrained, which is a real cost to business and ultimately to society generally.

Zuboff, in her book <u>In the Age of the Smart Machine</u>, vividly illustrates "how the need to defend and reproduce the legitimacy of managerial authority can channel potential innovation toward a conventional emphasis on automation."[79] Under these circumstances, Zuboff believes that "managers emphasize machine intelligence and managerial control over the knowledge base <u>at the expense of developing knowledge in the operating work force</u>" (emphasis added by authors).[80]   An enlightened management could employ both the automating and informating capabilities of their CBISs to retain jobs and give them more meaning and significance to the jobholders and to the firm as a whole. This would be an enviable accomplishment for any firm, that of using information technology more fully while also using people more fully and thereby creating a better climate for the growth of business and free enterprise.

Guidelines for Meeting the Challenges of CBIS

A number of guidelines are offered to help resolve the issues and meet the challenges brought about by CBISs.

1. A code of professional conduct should be adopted by firms for their CBIS professionals. The code of the Association of Computing Machinery (ACM) or the code of the Data Processing Management Association (DPMA) can serve as a starting point for developing one's own code for its computer professionals.[81] Although CBISs will continue to be increasingly distributed among nonprofessionals, the firm's computer professionals will remain the backbone and center of expertise for the entire organization. It is vital that they conduct themselves in a socially, legally, and ethically responsible manner.

2. All employees involved in the handling of data and information must be educated in the importance of building and maintaining the firm's information resources. As John deButts, retired chairman of American Telephone and Telegraph, has so aptly stated, "The more interdependent (corporate) society becomes, the more crucial is the performance of the <u>individuals</u> who make it up."[82] Business firms are becoming more interdependent through open systems networks and business partnerships stemming from advancements in computer and communications technologies. Each and every employee must accept more responsibility for the firm's information, because the possibilities for information problems are growing accordingly.

3. Relative to security and reliability of information, three principles adopted by AT&T seem appropriate for most organizations: (1) "Information must be timely, accurate, and available to people when and where they need it," (2) "In an emergency or disaster situation,

computer resources must be immediately recoverable,"
and (3) "Maximum security of proprietary information is
imperative".[83]   In today's CBIS environment, security
of information is a shared responsibility among users,
providers, and facilitators of information.   This
requires everyone's cooperation.

4. Firms should strive to balance their needs for information about other firms, customers, suppliers, competitors, other special groups, and individuals against the
needs and interests of these groups and individuals in
retaining their privacy and autonomy.   The view that
private business, in seeking profits, does so by
providing what people want and exists for the purpose
of fulfilling human needs and enhancing human life
seems relevant here.[84]   To use CBISs to diminish the
privacy and autonomy of others seems to be contra-
dictory to the fundamentals of capitalist ideology.
Firms must protect their own security and privacy while
recognizing the need for others to do the same.   This
often requires a delicate balance between providing
freedom of action while maintaining adequate control,
which will surely be a continuing challenge in the
information age of the 1990s.

5. Firms must recognize the importance of strategic
planning for CBIS. The chief information officer (CIO)
must assume the primary role in this endeavor.
Apparently CIOs in many firms are not yet members of
top management, which limits their organizationwide
perspective and often hampers their ability to influence the adoption of sound CBIS strategic imperatives
for the firm.   An effective CIO functioning at the top-
management level can provide the kind of imaginative
leadership that will be needed in the 1990s to maximize
the competitive potential offered by CBIS technology.

6. Firms need to focus on evaluating their CBISs more
critically than in the past.   In addition to determining the more tangible efficiencies realized from
traditional cost-saving CBIS applications, firms must
learn to recognize and assess the more intangible
benefits derived from improved effectiveness in
decision-making.   This is a most difficult task, and it
includes consideration of the social, legal, and even
ethical aspects of CBIS use for which there are more
questions than answers, as discussed in this chapter.
Nonetheless, the benefits to be derived from implementation of emerging CBIS technology appear to be
enormous, especially in the areas of decision support
and expert systems, so firms must be able to evaluate
them carefully along with other capital investments.

7. The computer literacy of all employees must be increased in order to take fuller advantage of CBIS
technology and to enhance "organizational literacy,"
i.e., learning and reasoning generally.   This effort
should initially focus on the managerial ranks, because

managers will increasingly be responsible for managing more complex task and operations brought about by continually evolving CBIS technology. CEOs need to be computer literate, for this will enable them to better understand the new technologies and provide leadership in marshalling the information resources of the firm toward realization of the maximum possible benefits from their employment. More computer-literate workers should perform better in an automated _and_ informated organization and likely be more fulfilled as well.

8. Firms need to promulgate a formal code of conduct for computer-based information systems that addresses the various social, legal, and ethical issues described herein and illustrated at the end of the chapter. The segments of actual codes presented here are rather limited in scope, perhaps because of the complex, unresolved nature of many of these issues. Nevertheless, firms must formulate and articulate their stances on these issues, because these issues will increasingly affect the firms' activities and general business climate in the information age of the 1990s and beyond. Harry B. DeMaio, of Deloitte, Haskins, & Sells, has offered some specific guidelines for an information ethics code that can serve as a beginning: (1) Make it Workable, (2) Make It Consistent, (3) Tailor It to Your Organization, (4) Guide. Don't Trap, and (5) Enlist Support.[85] The last point deserves reinforcement. Unless one's own management colleagues actively adopt and support a code of conduct, it will not be regarded as credible nor will it be accepted by employees generally. An organizational climate and code that encourages acceptance is decidedly preferable to that based more on enforcement.

CONCLUSIONS

Computer-based information systems have taken business from an age of automation to an age of information, where the central focus must now be on managing information as a vital resource. The prevailing CBIS milieu is very complex and becoming increasingly so, to such an extent that there are no real individual CBIS experts. The complex nature of computer and communication technologies is such that no one person can be highly knowledgeable about all aspects of these technologies. This will call for more team-building and more sharing of expertise and group responsibility for CBIS. Furthermore, growth in CBIS linkages and networks coupled with the increased sharing of information and the formation of electronically based business partnerships has brought about the need to reexamine our views and approaches to business conduct. Clearly, managers of the 1990s and beyond will need to be more adept and knowledgeable about CBIS technology and its application.

Various social, legal, and ethical issues stemming, in part, if not in full measure, from CBIS technology weigh heavily upon our views and approaches to business conduct in the 1990s.   Access to information, involving questions of privacy, security, and power, is both easier and riskier now because of the power of computers and their increasing availability. Responsibility for the accuracy of information is becoming a growing problem because of the volume of information generated and the distribution of responsibility for CBIS implementation and management. Ownership of information and information-generating software has brought about some difficult legal questions that have not yet been fully answered. Finally, the matter of automating and informating the workplace has confounded certain social aspects of operating businesses. To further complicate matters, these various issues tend to be somewhat interrelated. More than ever, managers must be resolved to seek to understand these issues and their impact upon their firm and upon the conduct of business generally. A firm must set forth its framework for responsible business conduct and action, and its managers must be prepared to make tough choices between what is right and wrong within this framework.[86]

NOTES

1. Alexander, M., "Prison Term for First U.S. Hacker-Law Convict," _Computerworld_ (February 20, 1989): 1-2.
2. Honan, "Avoiding Virus Hysteria", _Personal Computing_ (May 1989): 16.
3. Thackery, "Computer Security: The Menace Is from Inside," _The Office_ (October 1988): 45-48.
4. Ibid., 64.
5. Keefe, "It Can't Happen Here", _Computerworld_ (April 6, 1988): 15.
6. Wilder, "Altered Systems, Data, Blindside Volkswagen in Record-Breaking $259 Million Computer Fraud," _Computerworld_ (March 16, 1984): 4.
7. "Is Your Computer Secure?", _Business Week_ (August 1, 1988): 65.
8. "Innovation in the '90s: The Critical Questions", _PC Computing_ (September 1989): 72-87.
9. Ahituv and Neumann, _Principles of Information Systems for Management_, 2nd ed. (Dubuque, IA: Wm. C. Brown, 1986): 497.
10. "Industry by Industry IS Survey," _Datamation_ (November 21, 1988): 4-7.
11. Ibid.
12. Ibid.
13. Ibid.
14. Hodges, "IS Budget Growth Slides," _Datamation_ (April 1, 1989): 18-22.
15. Schatz, "EDI: Putting the Muscle in Commerce & Industry," _Datamation_ (March 15, 1988): 56-64.
16. Carlyle, "Open Systems: What Price Freedom?" _Datamation_ (June 1, 1988): 54-60.
17. Runyon, and Tate, "Europe's Economic Approach," _Datamation_ (May 15, 1989): 36-40.
18. Ibid.
19. Ibid.
20. Reed, "The Top 100 Companies with PCs," _Datamation_ (September 1989): 71-90.
21. Kerr, "The New IS Force," _Datamation_ (August 1, 1989): 18-23.
22. Leavitt, and Whistler, "Managing in the 1980s," _Harvard Business Review_, 36, 6: 41-48; and Whistler, _The Impact of Computers on Organizations_ (New York: Praeger, 1980).
23. Penzias, "Managing in a High-Tech World," _PC Computing_ (August 1989): 109-115.
24. Zuboff, _In the Age of the Smart Machine_ (New York: Basic Books, 1988), 9-11.
25. Ibid., 387-392.

26. Carlyle, "CIO: Misfit or Misnomer?" Datamation: (August 1, 1988): 50-56.
27. Ibid.
28. Nelson, "CEOs: Computing in High Places," Personal Computing (April 1989), 70-84.
29. Ibid.
30. Ibid.
31. Ibid., 71.
32. Jonas et al., "The Person of the CEO: Understanding the Executive Experience," Academy of Management Executive, III, 3 (August 1989): 205-215.
33. Penzias, op. cit., 113.
34. Carlyle, "Managing IS at Multinationals," Datamation (March 1, 1988): 54-66.
35. Toffler, Tough Choices: Managers Talk Ethics (New York: John Wiley, 1986), 20.
36. Kroenke, Management Information Systems (Santa Cruz, CA: Mitchell Publishing, 1989), 14.
37. Mason, "Four Ethical Issues of the Information Age," MIS Quarterly (March 1986): 10.
38. Ibid.
39. Simone, "E-Mail, The Global Handshake," PC Magazine (August 1989): 175-202.
40. Fuori and Aufiero, Computers and Information Processing, 2nd ed. (Englewood Cliffs, NJ: Prentice-Hall, 1989), 627-628.
41. McFarlan, "Editor's Comment," MIS Quarterly (March 1988): iii-vi.
42. Betts, "Lawyers Fret Over Risks of EDI Growth," Computerworld (January 19, 1989): 16-17.
43. "Worker Monitoring and Privacy," The Futurist (March-April 1988): 51.
44. Kleiman, "Computer Monitoring Puts Workers on the Defensive," The Orlando Sentinel (Sunday, April 23, 1989): E-15.
45. Ibid.
46. Johnson, Computer Ethics (Englewood Cliffs, NJ: Prentice-Hall, 1986), 66.
47. Ibid., 67.
48. "Is Your Computer Secure?" Business Week (April 1, 1988), cover story.
49. Keefe, op. cit., 13-17.
50. Wolk and Luddy, Legal Aspects of Computer Use (Englewood Cliffs, NJ: Prentice-Hall, 1986), 121-122.
51. Cohen, "Computer Viruses: A Contemporary Affliction," Datamation (September 15, 1988), in "Computer Security: Issues and Trends," special section.
52. McAfee, "The Virus Cure," Datamation (February 15, 1988): 29-40.
53. Honan, "Avoiding Virus Hysteria," Personal Computing (May 1989): 85-92.
54. Keefe, op. cit., 16.
55. Athey and Zmud, Introduction to Computers and Information Systems, 2nd ed. (Glenview, IL: Scott, Foresman, 1988), 500.
56. Glickman, "The Computer Security Act of 1987: Resolve is Not Enough," Datamation (September 15, 1988), in "Computer Security: Issues and Trends," special section.
57. Zmud, loc. cit.
58. Alexander, op. cit., 12-13.
59. Athey and Zmud, op. cit., 639.
60. Ibid.
61. Farhoomand, and Murphy, "Managing Computer Security," Datamation (January 1, 1989): 67-68.
62. Yourdan, "The Achilles Heel of Information Security," Datamation (September 15, 1988), "Computer Security: Issues and Trends," special section.
63. McGovern, "Planning for Information Security: Grassroots and Global Concerns," Datamation (September 15, 1988), "Computer Security: Issues and Trends," special section.
64. Faurer, "Building Secure Worldwide Communications Networks," Datamation (September 15, 1988), "Computer Security: Issues and Trends," special section.
65. Johnson, op. cit., 79-80.

66. Parker, C.S., _Management Information Systems: Strategy and Action_ (New York: McGraw-Hill 1989), 19-20.
67. Copeland and McKenney, "Airline Reservations Systems: Lessons From History," _MIS Quarterly_ (September 1988): 353-370.
68. Ibid.
69. Betts, op. cit., 17.
70. Ibid.
71. McFarlan, op. cit., v.
72. Mason, op. cit., 9-10.
73. Ibid., 9.
74. Ibid., 9-10.
75. Johnson, op. cit., 87-103.
76. Ibid., 95.
77. Ibid., 102.
78. Ibid., 103.
79. Ibid., 390.
80. Ibid.
81. Couger,   "Preparing IS Students to Deal With Ethical Issues," _MIS Quarterly_ (June 1989): 217-218.
82. deButts, "Securing Our Future Through Technology," _Datamation_ (September 15, 1987), "Computer Security: Issues and Trends," special section.
83. Kavner, "Reliability and Security in Information Management," _Datamation_ (September 15, 1988), "Computer Security: Trends and Issues," special section.
84. Johnson, op. cit., 67.
85. DeMaio, "The Information Ethics Issue: It's Time for Management Action," _Datamation_ (September 15, 1988), "Computer Security: Issues and Trends," special section.
86. Toffler, op. cit., 24-38.

11
Business Dealings and Relationships: Truthfulness, Integrity, and Deception

INTRODUCTION

At least one-fifth and as many as one-half of the American public view unfavorably the honesty standards of business executives, according to Gallup Survey data from 1976 until the present and the April 29 - May 1, 1986, New York Times survey. These attitudes reflect that the business sector and executives in their business dealings and relationships are facing a crisis of confidence. Gerald Mitchell, chairman and CEO of Dana Corporation, recognizes the long-term negative consequences when business executives and transactions are perceived as dishonest or deceptive. Mitchell emphasizes, "Integrity and trust is the most important part of management. Otherwise, everything collapses—your communication, credibility, customer image, respect; your identity with the company. None of this is possible without integrity and trust. If I can't trust you, we have nothing."

Aside from the consideration that wealth without honest labor is one of Gandhi's seven sins, the individual cannot relinquish his or her critical role in affecting responsible business behavior. By merely asserting that untrustworthiness or deception that falls short of illegality is acceptable and that it is government's responsibility to regulate unethical or immoral business conduct, a business executive or employee overlooks the inherent risk to our economic system and is "advocating a police state."

Rather, "it is difficult to believe that effective [regulation] can be brought about only by a Gestapo" for "[i]ndividual integrity is the mortar cementing the foundations of our [economic] system."[1] Moreover, to one great nineteenth-century philosopher, "A liar is a coward; he is a man who has recourse to lying because he is unable to help himself and gain his ends by any other means."

No doubt, there is a significant pressure on executives and employees to practice deception, for their firms' or their own benefit, toward customers, suppliers, labor unions, government officials, superiors, or their peers. Consequently, as one executive has commented, "[i]f the law as written gives a man a wide-open chance to make a killing, he'd be a fool not to take advantage of it. If he doesn't, somebody else will."[2] For instance, firms that trumpet the false threat of bankruptcy to sever burdensome contractual obligations owed to employees represent those who will take advantage of an opportunity for self-gain, regardless of the lack of good ethics in such conduct.

This line of seizing the business opportunity without eschewing deception reflects the modus operandi accorded prominence through the British statesman Henry Taylor, who asserted that "falsehood ceases to be falsehood when it is understood on all sides that the truth is not expected to be spoken."[3] Normative ethical rules of integrity and forthrightness, according to the last two statements, simply are inoperative in most business situations.

Yet, a number of major firms' executives have witnessed the long-term economic harm to their firms when their executives and labor unions, distrustful of each other, negotiate according to the old rules of confrontation and bluff or deception—of gaining and holding a myopic advantage regardless of the long-term damage to their enterprises or the free enterprise system itself. The resulting lack of trust breeds work environments in which job restrictions and classifications choke productivity, and, with the exception of progressive firms such as IBM, companies have rejected forms of job security such as an annual wage and retraining and helping redundant workers find jobs outside the firm. Further, lack of trust, as the 1989 Eastern Airlines strike has tragically demonstrated, often leads to a zero-sum confrontation that results in an abrogation of important labor or management prerogatives, or, worse, the destruction of the firm as a viable concern.

Consider the situation where corporate bondholders are sacrificed when the firm's management piles on debt to make the firm an uninviting target for a corporate takeover. The solemn and binding covenants in corporate bonds are vitiated by the downgrading of the bonds as a result of the additional debt. Other firms, such as Washington Public Power, with the acronym WHOOPS, have defaulted on billions of dollars of bonds and, before the dust has settled, have issued more equity or debt. In yet other cases, like those of Triangle Industries and E-II Holdings, management's and investment bankers' maneuverings essentially have prevented bondholders from realizing the full economic value of their bonds. Bonds are not what they used to be—and certainly not necessarily a safe investment for widows and orphans with such machinations by financiers.[4]

The person described above who is committed to success at any cost and who, detached from sentiment or conscience, exploits others ruthlessly is the prototype of the "gamesman"— the successful 1970s and 1980s executive as described by author Michael Maccoby. According to Maccoby, in a recent work, The Leader, the successful manager in the 1990s and beyond must rid himself of the gamesman's hollow style. Instead, integrity along with competence is the essential characteristic of effective leadership.

Vernon Loucks, president and chief executive officer of Baxter Travenol, a firm with over $5 billion in sales and 66,000 employees, reflects this new leadership. Loucks decries deception: "Ethics is simply and ultimately a matter of trust." Whereas "[p]eople act in their economic self-interest," any "system based on that fact must also be grounded on mutual trust, among individuals and among organizations."[5]

ATTITUDES FOR THE 1990S

In his essay entitled "Ethical Duties Towards Others: 'Truthfulness,'" Immanuel Kant underscored that "exchange of our sentiments is the principal factor in social intercourse, and truth must be the guiding principle therein" because "[w]ithout truth social intercourse and conversation become valueless."

According to Kant, a person does a man no injustice by lying to him when that man has lied to the former; however, that second prevarication does contravene, instead, the right of society. Nonetheless, in this vein, not every untruth is a lie; it is a lie only when the actor has represented to the other person that the former will share his thought. In Kant's view, whether a lie is told with good or bad intent, "a lie is always evil," in spite of the fact that since some men are malicious, to be "punctiliously truthful is often dangerous."

The fact that all people are not well intentioned gives rise to the lie pressed on a person by necessity—the "white lie." Nevertheless, in Kant's opinion, the only case in which a person can justifiably utter a white lie is when the statement is coerced and will serve an improper use. Nonetheless, few would endorse Kant's view that it is wrong to lie even to protect the physical health of innocent people. Yet, in another essay, Kant asserts that it would be wrong to lie to a potential murderer about the location of the intended victim.[7]

In 1747 Dr. Isaac Watts admonished businessmen concerning prudent conduct. In his estimation, a businessman should "judge things as they are, to speak to them, when properly called thereto . . . neither adding or diminishing, neither depreciating a commodity, nor putting false color upon it."[8] Nearly two and one-half centuries later, a number of important studies have documented the values of American managers. In some regards, those values fall considerably short of Watts' advice.

For example, a 1980 _Fortune_ article, "How Lawless are Big Companies," by Irwin Ross concludes that 11% of the more than 1,000 firms studied had committed serious infractions of the law.[9] Moreover, according to the 1977 _Harvard Business Review_ article, "Is the Ethics of Business Changing,"[10] American business executives were more critical of their peers' ethical conduct than they had been fifteen years earlier. These studies are especially important since "managers view ethical decisions through the prism of their own personal values,"[11] according to the authors of a 1984 study, "Values and the American Manager: An Update," and because "[t]he behavior of one's superiors is the primary guidepost for unethical behavior."[12] Further, managers' personal values directly and indirectly influence the organization's strategy and behavior.[13]

Conclusions from the foregoing 1984 study of managerial values[14] include the following:

- Most often managers cite establishing or sustaining an effective organization as their paramount objective.

- Maintaining a positive image contributes to the firm's effectiveness.

- Managers consider society a more important shareholder than stockholders themselves.

- Of all personal qualities, managers most highly regard "integrity," and this selection applies whether the manager is rating the most desirable quality in subordinates, peers, or superiors.

- The majority of managers believe that the organizational environment is the most important determinant of proper behavior.

It is obvious that being truthful is of paramount importance to managers who wish to lead as well as enhance a healthy, productive working climate. Certainly, then, the "essence of 'charismatic' leadership is managers with integrity" and employees, subordinate managers, and peers will "follow more readily one whose values are clear, consistent, principled, and fair."

The 1990s comprise an era when sophisticated communication and employee interaction demand increased levels of cooperation at the value-added areas of a firm's activities, at the same time that hierarchical managerial power continues to diminish. The resulting interdependence of all the firm's employees, together with its suppliers and customers, demands a degree of trust and honest business interaction unprecedented in this century.

Aside from establishing a healthy working environment that increases production, truthfulness and trust can revitalize a flagging firm. During the 1980s, General Motors, with 750,000 employees the world's largest corporate bureaucracy and auto manufacturer, faced starkly plunging sales and profits, low employee morale, and a shrinking market share. With a notoriously rigid bureaucratic structure and top-down management style bordering on autocracy, GM invested billions in a "high-tech spending binge" that failed to stem the downward spiral and "often came across as antipeople." In contrast, Ford crafted a sense of community and teamwork, implementing participatory management in a genuinely cooperative effort to increase production, and reduce defects. By 1986 Ford earnings surpassed GM's.

As a consequence of its difficulties, GM in 1987 launched its Quality Network program, which accorded union workers unprecedented authority in setting policy and negotiating terms of employment. GM rapidly realized startling improvements in a number of areas, including the union's attitude toward management.   Newly instituted information sharing sessions have permitted frank interrank discussions.   The apparent willingness of senior management and employees to negotiate forthrightly in a collaborative, rather than antagonistic and bluffing, manner may help the company reverse course.[15] In this way, GM's management and its employees, rather than hurling hand grenades, are instilling trust as an integral part of the culture. Paradoxically, GM has emulated its historic rival, Ford, which radically transformed its culture to one of truthfulness and trust. Although the GM and Ford examples are instructive and emphasize what truthful conduct and good will can accomplish, difficulty arises in establishing standards of truthfulness and deception.

Business Deception, Bluffing, and Puffery

One author has defined business deception or bluffing as "an act which attempts to misrepresent one's intentions or overstate the strength of one's position in the bargaining process."[16] Moreover, according to the widely noted commentator, Albert Carr, business deception or bluffing occurs when business people employ "conscious misstatements, concealment of pertinent facts, or exaggeration . . . to persuade others to agree with them."[17] Carr's article has sparked much comment and offers a basis for discussion.

In the Carr scheme of economic jousts, if the business individual refuses to deceive, "if he feels obligated to tell the truth, the whole truth, and nothing but the truth," he not only ignores opportunities but is significantly disadvantaged in his business dealings.[18] Whereas these individuals may abide by strict codes of ethics and proper conduct in their private lives, in business affairs they become law abiding but unsentimental game players who apply the rules of poker. The Carr gamesman knows the rules, possesses insight into how other key players think, and responds effectively to opportunities; the gamesman trusts that others will protect themselves accordingly. Obviously, this stratagem of deception is inconsistent with Vernon Loucks's assertion that "in the long run, the ethical course of action is the profitable course . . . I also don't think we've ever really improved on the Golden Rule."[19] Rather, in Carr's analysis, the cardinal measures of every gamesman's business activity are whether that activity is, first, legal, and, then, profitable. Further, in a twist on the Golden Rule, as Bruce Henderson commented in "Brinksmanship in Business" in the March-April 1967 Harvard Business Review, many businessmen attempt to do unto others what they hope will not be done unto them.

Business deception can be active or passive. Active deception entails the making of a statement that the maker knows is false. Examples of active deception include: a job applicant's misrepresenting his or her age, experience, religion, or education on the employment application; a firm's statement that it will close a plant if the union refuses to renegotiate a wage and salary contract, even though the firm has no intention of actually shutting down operations; or when union leaders misreport the union's intention to strike in sympathy with another of the firm's unions.

On the other hand, passive deception "is not affirmatively false, but ignores the truth passively by concealment."[20] Examples of passive business deception are: when a firm has decided on a course of bankruptcy and delays communicating it to employees, shareholders, or the financial markets; or when an employee answers on a disclosure form that he or she does not own stock in a supplier firm which he or she has selected for the firm's business, even though that employee's father-in-law has controlling interest in the supplier firm.

There is, however, a distinction between affirmation of fact and puffery, which is an opinion concerning value, or the nature of the property or services involved in a negotiation. No legal sanctions attach to a statement that is merely an expression of opinion as opposed to an affirmation of fact.[21] For instance, when a party to a transaction to his detriment relies on the other party's affirmation of fact, which is both material and wrong, the aggrieved party often has a remedy in contract or tort law—by virtue of the legal theories of fraud, misrepresentation, or breach of warranty. In successful suits under these legal theories, the aggrieved party must have the right to rely on the statement made by the other party. Consequently, according to one author on the subject, "If one knows that the truth is not being spoken or is in a position where reliance is unreasonable, it is difficult to find that he has been the victim of a lie." Moreover, the same writer asserts that mere puffery is not unethical either because the injured party was aware that such statements were false. According to this line of reasoning, individual industries and professions should determine whether puffery should be regulated, if at all, and proceed appropriately.[22]

Workable Standards of Truthfulness in Business Interactions

Indisputably, Kant's extreme principles of truthfulness aside, many free market advocates aver that business lies and deceptions are wrong—and there is a moral presumption against such activities. Most 1990 circa businesspeople, judging from studies indicating that integrity and forthrightness are key success characteristics of the modern manager, endorse the application of normative ethical rules of forthrightness and honesty to internal and external business relationships and dealings. Certainly, to many, that application is preferable to the dated business environment described by Carr: "Cunning deception and concealment of one's strengths and intentions, not kindness and openness, are vital . . . no one should think any the worse of the game of business because its standards of right and wrong differ from the prevailing traditions of morality in our society."[23]

Still, what is preferable is not necessarily what exists: in business negotiations people routinely deceive each other. Further, all reasonable parties do not perceive exaggerated positions, akin to poker, in the bargaining process to be mere statements of opinion. In addition, trust is an essential element in negotiation and relationships, within and outside the firm, if the economic system is effectively to operate. In fact, as one executive has noted, "[I]t is not at all the case that businessmen do not expect the truth to be spoken. On the contrary, almost all day-to-day business is conducted verbally or on the basis of nonlegal documents. The economic system would collapse without mutual trust on a practically universal scale among business executives."[24]   Bribery, questionable payments, lies, and material deception are unnecessary burdens on that system.

Although there may be a moral presumption against lying or deception in business affairs, many have identified special justifications for such deception to be permissible.[25] In the short term, too, deception, not illegal, can be profitable. For example, in negotiations, concealing one's minimally acceptable position or discovering the other party's actual position enables a person to cement the deal at the other party's minimally acceptable position.[26] Unfortunately, too, the penalty for such action is often remote, because lies frequently are difficult to prove, often parties are only involved in a single transaction, and word of deceitful practice does not necessarily spread sufficiently to punish the liar or material deceiver in his or her subsequent attempts at business dealing.[27]

Whereas a businessman cannot justify lying or business deception merely because such act serves his self-interest, or provides a profit to the firm, commentators have recognized exceptions to the rule prohibiting lying or deception. First, when a firm has been bulldozed to near or actual bankruptcy by the deception of others, especially competitors, a firm may resort to deception due to economic necessity. The presumption against lying or deception cannot prevail when a person or firm acts in self-defense. Whereas deception cannot be condoned simply because its practice is ubiquitous, certainly in a business negotiation when a firm is the victim of deception it is permissible to direct deception against the deceiving or lying party.[28] Consequently, according to this line of reasoning, "one may presume one is justified in bluffing (by means of lying and deception about one's negotiating position) in ordinary circumstances, unless either: (1) one has special reasons to suppose that the other party will not do the same (e.g., one might know that the individual with whom one is dealing is unusually scrupulous or naive), or (2) one has special reasons for thinking that one will not be harmed by the bluffing of the other party . . ."[29]

Restoring American Productivity: Commitment to Integrity, Truthfulness, and Trust

It is not only proper for firms and employees to adhere to high standards of integrity, truthfulness, and trust, it is also vital for the continued economic existence of those firms.   For instance, Peter Drucker levels much of the responsibility for the decline in American manufacturing productivity on management's compulsive preoccupation with profits, particularly short term, and this commercial myopia's resulting impact on labor relations.[30] In labor negotiations, often by its own choice and by management's dogmatic attachment to redundant, dated attitudes, employees have not realized job security benefits such as annual wages and retraining policies. Instead, to preserve short-term profits, management has conceded to workers the costlier work rules and job restrictions that strangle productivity.   For instance, Japanese-owned auto plants in America—such as Honda in Tennessee and Toyota in California—produce 30% to 50% more autos per worker per day than the major American firms, with only three to five job classifications compared to the sixty or more in the plants of the three major American automakers.

In Drucker's learned economic diagnosis, management and labor are equally culpable. The lack of trust, based in part on the historically adversarial and deceptive management-labor relationships, often impedes the vitally necessary changes in the rules of the workplace. Yet, fortuitously, the 1990s are an appropriate period to establish integrity, truthfulness and trust in the firm because the modern employee, in contrast to his or her forebears, is better educated and more concerned with noneconomic factors such as integrity of managers in the workplace, respect from supervisors and other managers, and the firm's public image. A firm's respect for the individual, above all, means being truthful to and trusting with employees—treating them as autonomous, respected, and valuable members of the firm. The direct results of this integrity and treatment are institutional solidarity, "strong culture," and "corporate integrity"—"from which alone long-term profitability flows."[31] To realize this healthy and productive environment, a manager should consider the organization as an "ongoing human society" and "take very seriously [his] role as manager of human lives."[32]

CONCLUSIONS

At least one chief executive of a _Fortune_ 500 firm has pointedly emphasized that ethical issues involving honesty and truthfulness are not only recent concerns. As that CEO noted, "It was about 560 B.C. . . . . when the Greek thinker Chilon registered the opinion that a merchant does better to take a loss than to make a dishonest profit. His reasoning was that a loss may be painful for a while, but dishonesty hurts forever . . ."[33] The merchant, according to this venerable tenet, should not bribe, lie, or deceive to realize profit.

In a 1987 hypothesis, one experienced commentator posited that the vast majority of managers are neither moral nor immoral but amoral—they simply believe that different rules apply in business than in other spheres of a person's life.[34] The amoral manager envisions ethical decisions as independent and isolated, not integrated, with managerial decision-making and competence.[35] The upright firm should carefully hone its definition of and approach to truthfulness and deception; moreover, it should simultaneously nurture emphasis on conscience, respect for the individual worth of every employee, discussion of ethical and business conduct problems at all levels, and greater awareness of the "importance of moral considerations in the formation of management policy."[36] Until senior management embraces the concepts of ethical management, the transformation of the organization to one of integrity and truthfulness, and higher productivity will not occur.[37]

Certainly, businesspeople are engaged in a number of activities and situations with differing common rules. Whereas the gamesman of the 1970s may be ethically neutral, the successful manager in the 1990s must continuously and consciously integrate his or her approaches to truthfulness and deception in his or her managerial perspective. The basis of

private morality is a regard for the truth; the more forthright an individual, the more he or she gains respect and
power to lead effectively. In such integration, the manager
may not eliminate ethical disagreement and ambiguity; however,
he or she will help ensure profitability within the confines
of obedience to the laws and standards of ethics. In so
doing, the manager preserves and validates the integrity of
the firm and the economic system. Toward this end, the firm
should establish and publicize its standards in areas in its
code of conduct to ensure consistent and ethical practices and
to cultivate discussion and standardization of such guidelines
in the business sector. This process creates the strong
culture of integrity which is essential to long-term profitability.

NOTES

1. Kintner, <u>An Antitrust Primer: A Guide to Antitrust and Trade
   Regulation Laws for Businessmen</u>, 2nd ed. (New York: MacMillan, 1973),
   226.
2. Carr "Is Business Bluffing Ethical," <u>Harvard Business Review</u>
   (January-February 1968): 143.
3. Ibid.
4. Sloan, "The Rape of the Bondholder," <u>Forbes</u> (January 23, 1989): 67-69.
5. Loucks, "A CEO Looks at Ethics," <u>Business Horizons</u> (March-April
   1987): 4.
6. See <u>Lectures on Ethics</u> (Methuen, 1930); rpt. (New York: Harper & Row,
   1963), 224-235.
7. Kant, "On the Supposed Right to Tell Lies from Benevolent Motives,"
   <u>Moral Rules and Particular Circumstances</u>, edited by Brody (Englewood
   Cliffs, NJ: Prentice-Hall, 1970), 32-33, and Wokutch and Carson, "The
   Ethics and Profitability of Bluffing in Business," <u>Westminster
   Institute Review</u> 1, no. 2 (May 1986).
8. Beach, "Bluffing: Its Demise As a Subject Unto Itself," <u>Journal of
   Business Ethics</u> 4 (1985): 191.
9. Ross, "How Lawless Are Big Companies?", <u>Fortune</u> (December 1980):
   57-63, as cited in Posner and Schmidt, "Values and the American
   Manager: An Update," <u>California Management Review</u> 26, no. 3, (Spring
   1984): 203.
10. Brenner and Mollander, "Is the Ethics of Business Changing?" <u>Harvard
    Business Review</u> (January-February 1977).
11. Posner and Schmidt, op. cit., 210.
12. See Loucks, op. cit., 2.
13. See England, "Personal Value Systems of American Managers," <u>Academy
    of Management Journal</u> (March 1967): 53; McMurry, "Conflicts in Human
    Values," <u>Harvard Business Review</u> (May-June 1963): 130; Guth and
    Tagiuri "Personal Value and Corporate Strategies," <u>Harvard Business
    Review</u> (September-October 1965): 123.
14. Posner and Schmidt, op. cit., 214-215.
15. Ibid.
16. Schlesinger and Ingrassia, "GM Woos Employees By Listening to Them,
    Talking of Its 'Team,'" <u>Wall Street Journal</u> (January 12, 1989): 1, 6.
17. Carr, op. cit., 143-144.
18. Ibid.
19. Loucks, op. cit., 6.
20. Beach, op. cit., 192.
21. <u>Sessa v. Riegle</u>, 427 F. Supp. 760, aff. 568 F. 2d 770 (1978).
22. Beach, op. cit., 195.
23. Carr, op. cit., 145.
24. Blodgett, "Showdown on 'Business Bluffing,'" <u>Harvard Business Review</u>
    (May-June 1968): 164.
25. Wokutch and Carson, op. cit., 77.
26. Idem, 79.
27. Idem, 78.

28. Idem, 81
29. Idem, 82.
30. Drucker, "Workers' Hands Bound by Tradition," <u>Wall Street Journal</u> (August 2, 1988): 20.
31. Newton, "The Internal Morality of the Corporation," <u>Journal of Business Ethics</u> 5 (1986): 250.
32. Buchholz, <u>Fundamental Concepts and Problems in Business Ethics</u> (Englewood Cliffs, NJ: Prentice-Hall, 1989), 24.
33. Loucks, op. cit., 1.
34. Carroll, "In Search of the Moral Manager," <u>Business Horizons</u> (March-April 1987): 11-12.
35. Idem, 14.
36. Randall, "The Executive's Conscience," <u>Harvard Business Review</u> (January-February 1968): 150.
37. Carroll, op. cit., 15.

12
Insider Trading and
Securities Laws

INTRODUCTION

The decision in early 1989 by Drexel Burnham Lambert to plead guilty to six felony charges of fraud and disgorge $650 million in penalties has further riveted the public's attention to the widespread corruption on Wall Street. Drexel had been bludgeoned into a plea bargain by fear of prosecution under the Racketeer Influenced and Corrupt Organization statute (RICO), which allows the judge to exert some control over the defendant's assets before trial. "They put a gun to Drexel's head," said one observer. "This was purely an issue of survival." Later, in July of 1989, a federal jury found Marcus Schloss & Co. guilty of two felony counts of securities fraud and conspiring to trade on inside information regarding the firm's purchase of American Brands stock. Few shed any tears. No other form of business conduct, with the exception of price fixing, has raised the public's moral disapproval and brought such opprobrium to the offenders as improper use of nonpublic information. "We are dealing with a very systemic type of problem—a systemic corruption that undermines the financial world and that is not, unfortunately, an exaggeration," observes John Carroll, a Drexel prosecutor.

In fact, not since the mid-1930s when the Securities and Exchange Commission (SEC) exposed ubiquitous fraud and theft on Wall Street leading to the great market crash of 1929 has the federal government exposed such venality in the financial markets. The scope of the apparent wrongdoing is substantial, not only in America but in the markets of its close trading partners.

Arbitrageur Ivan Boesky and Kidder Peabody investment banker Martin Siegel have recently been convicted of securities fraud. At least forty other Wall Streeters, including Drexel merger specialist Dennis Levine, have been convicted of illegal insider trading. Kidder, Peabody & Co. paid the federal government more than $20 million as settlement of charges of illegal insider trading in the stocks of takeover targets. Boyd Jefferies, former chairman of The Jefferies & Co., a major brokerage firm in the trading of takeover stocks, resigned to plead guilty to criminal securities fraud. From 1981 to early 1987, the SEC initiated 125 insider trading cases, compared to only seventy-seven during the forty-seven years prior to that time.[1]

The Commodity Futures Trading Commission and the U.S. Attorney's office in Chicago on January 23, 1989, following a two-year undercover investigation, cracked down on allegedly widespread fraud at the Chicago Mercantile Exchange and Board of Trade. Accusations include systematic fraud and theft by as many as 100 brokers and traders, most of whom have been subpoenaed to testify in the investigation. The alleged abuses parallel insider trading techniques: a commodities broker who receives a large order for soybeans from a customer might then buy some soybeans futures himself. He could then sell at a higher price to fill the customer's order or sell to others when the price rises as a result of the large purchase order. In February of 1989, however, the Chicago Board of Trade postponed any move to restrict its trading practices.

In France, Roger-Patrice Pelat and other close friends of French President François Mitterand allegedly purchased huge blocks of Triangle Industries' stock immediately before Pechiney S.A. of France announced plans to acquire Triangle. French investigators have revealed the financiers used confidential government information to garner trading profits of over $10 million.

In Japan, Hiromasa Ezoe, the former Recruit Company chairman, sold unlisted shares in Recruit Cosmos, a company subsidiary, to influential politicians and bureaucrats. The buyers realized enormous profits when Ezoe arranged for Recruit Cosmos to become a publicly held company in 1986. Ten Japanese government cabinet members, including Finance Minister Kiichi Miyazawa, are implicated, and by February 1989, three had resigned. The scandal eventually forced the resignation of the prime minister, as well. The scandal was a major reason that the ruling Liberal Democratic party suffered a stunning defeat on July 23, 1989, in elections to the upper house, thereby threatening the LDP's single-party rule. The runup of stock prices for selected insiders, although unethical, may not be illegal. Nonetheless, revelation of this impropriety closely followed intense foreign pressure on the Japanese government and securities industry to ban the rampant insider trading in the country's stock exchanges.

Despite vigorous enforcement of antifraud laws brawny with sanctions that include huge financial penalties and prison terms for offenders, those who abuse the insider trading,[2] short-swing profits[3] laws have not been deterred. A depressing study released in late 1987 by the New York Stock Exchange indicates that the huge increases in volumes and prices that accompany hostile takeovers ceased for only two months immediately following Boesky's December 1987 conviction. A study of prebid trading in the stock of acquisition targets conducted by Data Resources indicates that in the year following July 1, 1986, 70% of the 130 takeover targets' stock rose at a higher rate than the New York Stock Exchange Composite Index.[4] As a further indicator of the globalization of the crime, more than one-third of all cases of suspected insider trading in 1986 and 1987 involved foreign brokerage firms.[5]

"It is hard to debate there isn't some larger malady this is a symptom of," asserts Bob Gordon, president of Twenty-First Securities Corporation. Apparently, the public agrees.

In a <u>Wall Street Journal</u>/NBC News Poll taken after the Boesky revelation, 83% of the respondents believed insider trading was commonplace. Greed has again replaced fear of detection; as a result there is a substantial erosion of the public's confidence in the financial markets' fairness.

HISTORY OF REGULATIONS

Rule 10b-5 proscribes the use in interstate commerce of "any device, scheme, or artifice to defraud . . . or . . . any act, practice, or course of business which operates as a fraud or deceit upon any person, in connection with the purchase or sale of any security."[6] This rule was promulgated in 1942 pursuant to the Securities and Exchange Act of 1934, which declares illegal the use "in connection with the purchase or sale of any security . . . any manipulative or deceptive device or contrivance . . ."[7]

A related rule, Section 16(b)[8] of the 1934 act, explicitly allows corporations to recover profits from short-swing purchases and sales or sales and purchases within six months of their equity securities (stock and convertible debentures) by statutorily defined insiders.   Under this rule, the officer's or director's intent or the presence of inside information is irrelevant.   The exercise of a stock option constitutes a purchase. The restriction may apply even though the purchase and the sale involve different types of equity securities.   Under rules of beneficial ownership, an officer or director is deemed to be the owner of shares issued in the name of a spouse or children.

Under the short-swing rule, an officer or director may complete as many purchases as he or she wishes without regard to any time constraints provided he or she does not sell the equity-security.   Recovery by the firm is automatic if a profit can be projected by matching the lowest acquisition price and the highest selling price during the period.

Prior to the promulgation of rule 10b-5, the common law rule held that an insider (for instance, a firm's director) was not obligated to seek out the party on the other side of the transaction and reveal his or her "specialized" knowledge. Nonetheless, in 1934 the report of the Senate Banking and Currency Committee, buttressing the Securities Exchange Act of 1934, assailed this common law rule: "Among the most vicious practices unearthed . . . was the flagrant betrayal of their fiduciary duties by directors and officers of corporations who use their positions of trust and the confidential information which came to them in such positions to aid them in their market activities."

INSIDER TRADING

Insider trading refers to the buying or selling of securities by a person who has obtained nonpublic information, which is likely to be important to a reasonable investor and who employs that nonpublic information in breach of an obligation of confidence or trust.

Types of persons who periodically obtain information of this sort include a firm's executives, directors, and large shareholders. This confidential business information belongs to the corporation, to its shareholders. Securities laws dictate the time and method that certain important information can be released to the public. The disclosure of information, however, lies within the discretion of a firm's executive management. Nonetheless, the firm's executives must exercise that discretion in conformity with the obligations prescribed by reason of their fiduciary relationship with the firm and its shareholders.

A classic example of insider trading involved Paul Thayer, then chairman and chief executive officer of LTV Corporation. As a director of Anheuser-Busch and Allied Corporation, Thayer learned that LTV would make a tender offer for Grumman Corporation stock, and, further, that Allied would tender takeover bids for Supron Energy Corporation and for Bendix. Thayer shared this confidential information with his stock-broker and with a woman who maintained a "private personal relationship" with him.

The firm's employees are also prohibited from selling or giving away inside information to someone who is likely to use it. Moreover, if the person to whom the employee sold or gave the information knew, or should have known, that the firm's employee was breaching a fiduciary duty in disclosing the nonpublic information, that person, the "tippee," is also liable for illegal insider trading.[9] Only if the tipper is without sin, is the tippee as well.

Like classic corporate insiders, professionals such as Dennis Levine, who provide services in confidential business transactions, have a duty to refrain from trading or tipping based on the nonpublic information garnered in the course of performing services. These professionals include attorneys, accountants, and investment bankers. While employed at Drexel, Levine learned nonpublic information that Coastal Corporation intended to make a tender offer for American Natural Resources Company and apparently realized a profit of over $1.3 million trading on the basis of that inside information and in fifty-four transactions overall from which he received $12.6 million in illegal profits.

Unlike Thayer and Levine, Thomas Reed did not secure nonpublic information through his employment. Rather, Reed allegedly procured nonpublic information from his father, a member of the AMAX board of directors and chairman of an AMAX subsidiary. AMAX had been engaged in nonpublic merger negotiations with the Standard Oil Company of California (SOCAL). Unwittingly, expecting his disclosure to be maintained as confidential, Reed's father discussed the merger strategy with his son.

As a consequence, Thomas Reed bought call options, which provided him the right to buy 100,000 shares of AMAX at prices of $45 or $50 a share. On March 5, 1981, AMAX announced that it had received a SOCAL offer for $78.50 per share, and the price of AMAX rose appreciably. Reed received about $430,000 upon the exercise of the options he had purchased. Reed surrendered his profits to the government in settlement of the civil action. Although Reed was acquitted in the criminal action, the civil action's court opinion establishes that securities trading that violates a confidence obtained through a confidential relationship is prohibited.[10] Moreover, the SEC has cast an increasingly wide net for persons, including financial columnists,[11] trading based on nonpublic information; and people convicted of illegal insider trading are now subject to penalties equal to triple the amount of losses avoided or profits made, in accord with the Insider Trading Act of 1984, as well as incarceration.

Materiality of NonPublic Information

Insider trading involves the use of nonpublic information likely to be important to a reasonable investor. The term used to describe the "importance to a reasonable investor" is "materiality." Examples of information regarded as material[12] are:

- The pendency of an acquisition or divestiture of the firm's substantial business or division.

- A major change in the firm's dividend policy.

- A sharp decline or increase in the firm's projected earnings.

- Significant unexpected losses by the firm.

- Significant new products or services offered by the firm.

- Extraordinary management developments.

- Major contracts.

- Stock splits.

- New major scientific discoveries or inventions by the firm.

- Significant curtailment or expansion of operations.

- Initiation of significant litigation and later developments in which the firm is a party.

- The gain or loss of a major contract.

- A merger with another firm.

- An acquisition of another firm.

The profitable use or disclosure of nonpublic information in the foregoing material areas will violate the federal securities laws and result in civil and criminal penalties for the user or discloser as well as the firm.

Principles Underlying the Prohibition Against Insider Trading

Regulation of insider trading has received strong support among those who consider noneconomic values as the basis on which government should establish the ideal content of laws in our society. It has, on the contrary, had much weaker support among those who wish to base securities regulations on a purely economic basis.[13]

Professor Henry Manne has little concern for the betrayal of trust inherent in illegal insider trading. In fact, Manne and his law-and-economics adherents contend that unregulated insider trading benefits the market and the firm.[14] Specifically, the Manne school claims that: (1) insider trading improves market efficiency, (2) insider trading is an appropriate means of compensating the firm's executives and providing a greater incentive to promote the firm's business, and (3) insider trading is a victimless act.

There are several aspects of the market efficiency argument. First, the Manne school contends that insider trading would enhance a more accurate and rapid pricing of the firm's securities. The market price does not presently reflect inside information; hence, the market price is often inaccurate. If insiders were allowed to trade, the inside information would reach the market sooner. Second, insider trading would reduce the considerable price fluctuations in the securities markets because insider trading would permit the market to assimilate the information more gradually. Third, insiders, because of their free and fluent access to the firm's material, confidential information, are the most efficient disseminators of that information. Last, insider trading would lessen the misallocation of resources occasioned by those investors unaware of all information important in the pricing of a firm's stock.

This market efficiency argument, however, assumes that the primary goal of the federal securities laws is to promote short-term market efficiency. Overlooked is the fact that securities laws were promulgated to protect the public—to assure them that the market is not rigged. If the market is unfair, professional and public investors will find investment alternatives, including those in other countries. Moreover, information is property and the theft of that property erodes the incentives to invest and form capital.

Insider trading costs firms and their shareholders vast sums of money as insiders usually cause a runup in the price of stock of the target company. The result is a higher price that the acquiring firm must pay. Litton Industries, which acquired Itek, advanced an identical allegation in its lawsuit against Dennis Levine and Lehman, his employer at the time of his criminal act. Further, there is no guarantee that insiders will allow the unimpeded flow of the material, nonpublic information to the public. For instance, thirteen employees of Texas Gulf Sulphur Company[15] issued a press release that denied the actual discovery in 1963 of an abundant vein of silver, zinc, and copper near Timmins, Ontario. Four days later, as thirteen key employees purchased company stock and options, Texas Gulf issued a second release admitting the size of the discovery.

A second argument that the Manne school posits in support of insider trading is that it provides incentives for corporate executives to make the firm more profitable through new business developments. This argument requires a belief that other forms of incentives, including promotions, lateral employment opportunities, bonuses, and stock options are inadequate substitutes for the booty from insider trading. Further, an insider can also benefit from advance warning of negative news about the firm by selling short or purchasing put options in advance of the publication of the harmful information.

The Manne school also contends that insider trading has no victim because a person who places an order to buy or sell a particular stock has already determined that transaction price as fair. On the contrary, there are numerous victims: the acquiring companies whose costs of mergers and takeovers are substantially increased; the market specialists and market makers whose primary responsibilities include stabilizing the trading in the firm's stock but who cannot make rational pricing decisions when an insider trades in larger blocks of shares; and, most consequentially, the financial markets as a whole because of investor cynicism and mistrust.

The Racketeer Influenced and Corrupt Organization Law (RICO)

Under RICO, "racketeering" entails engaging in a pattern of certain serious crimes through the vehicle of a business or organization. Anyone convicted under RICO must forfeit the gains from crime together with the convicted person's interest in the "racketeering enterprise." Further, the prosecution may seek a pretrial restraint by which the judge exerts some control (e.g., freezes assets, assigns a monitor) over the defendant's assets. The Securities and Exchange Commission, prior to trial, can seek a court order freezing the assets of a person or firm accused of violating securities laws, like the prohibition of using material inside information for gain. Such pretrial orders can effectively close down a business, as happened to Princeton/Newport LP, which was liquidated four months after its officers were indicted in August 1988, under RICO. Whereas white-collar criminals are the chief target of RICO, securities cases still account for less than 1% of the total cases brought under RICO. Nonetheless, RICO has become a powerful and controversial prosecutorial bludgeon in the government's attack on securities fraud.

Related Activities: Going Private, Tender Offers, and the Merger and Acquisition Disclosure Law

One area of the law that is similar to insider trading regulation is that of "going private" in which insiders buy out public shareholders. These insiders may have delayed their purchase until they obtained material nonpublic information that positive events were imminent.[16] Of course, this transaction may be entirely efficient. The insiders, after taking the firm "private," will own the firm's equity and may perform better. Moreover, insider trading in connection with tender offers is prohibited as well.[17]

A third related area is in the realm of merger disclosure. The federal securities law is, as has been noted, designed to protect investors against stock manipulations. Pursuant to this dictate, a public firm is prohibited from making misleading, incomplete, or untrue statements about facts that are material to its fortunes. The public firm also has a positive duty to reveal "material" information. Recently, for example, Basic Incorporated falsely denied in public statements that it was conducting merger discussions with Combustion Engineering, which ultimately acquired Basic. The Supreme Court in the Basic case held that firms may have to disclose merger discussions even before fruition appears likely.

Materiality, in this instance, depends on the facts of each case while considering the significance of the possible merger and the likelihood of its completion.[18] Some corporate attorneys advise their clients not to comment at all on mergers. Others interpret the ruling to mean that the right to silence directly diminishes as the merger or acquisition talks proceed. When an accord between the firms appears imminent, disclosure must be made.

Requirements of disclosure regarding material, nonpublic information are being extended by the courts and by the Securities and Exchange Commission. Unfortunately, the requirements are complex and often as vague as the insider trading laws. There is no question, however, that at all times material, nonpublic information must be disclosed.

Guidelines to Avoid Violations of Insider Information (Rule 10b-5) and Short-Swing Profits Prohibitions (Rule 16-b)

In the case of insider information regulations, the firm is well advised to carefully monitor employee compliance with the following guidelines:

1. Material nonpublic information about the firm should be shared only with those fellow employees in the firm whose proper tasks require their use of the information.

2. Never disclose sensitive or nonpublic information to anyone outside the firm.

3. Do not buy or sell the firm's stock, options, other securities, or another firm's securities or direct someone else to buy or sell them for you, when you have knowledge of material nonpublic information concerning the firm until that information has been disclosed to the public and assimilated through the medium of widest circulation, the Dow-Jones broad tape, and no new major developments remain undisclosed.

4. Do not trade in another firm's stock, options, or other securities if you believe its value will be influenced by the firm's activities or plans.

5. Do not buy or sell the stock, options, or other securities of a customer firm based on any nonpublic
information you possess about that customer firm.

In the case of short-swing profits regulations, the firm
should ascertain that officers and directors and other
statutorily defined "insiders" comply with the following
guidelines:[19]

1. The officer or director should consider a periodic
   investment program through which that person makes
   regular purchases of securities under an established
   program where the timing of the purchases is beyond
   that person's control.

2. Officers and directors should consider buying or
   selling the firm's securities during a forty-five-day
   period beginning seven days after the firm's annual
   report has been disseminated to shareholders and
   otherwise broadly circulated, provided no new material
   undisclosed developments occur within that forty-five-
   day period.

3. Officers and directors should contact the chief executive officer of the firm, prior to the purchase or sale
   of the firm's securities, to ascertain that there is no
   pending important development that should be publicized
   before an insider could properly participate in a
   market transaction at the following times:
   (a) Following release and wide dissemination of quar-
       terly results.
   (b) When there is a relative stability in the market
       for the firm's securities and in the firm's opera-
       tions.
   (c) Following the wide dissemination of information on
       the current results and status of the firm.

4. Officers and directors should avoid transactions when
   a development of major importance is approaching or has
   approached ripeness for disclosure.

5. Officers and directors should wait until after the
   release of earnings, dividends, or other important
   matters regarding the firm have appeared in the press
   before purchasing or selling the firm's securities.
   Further, officers and directors should avoid any transactions just prior to releases of important information.

CONCLUSIONS

The ethics of insider trading and related areas of disclosure
have been the subject of debate for many centuries. The issue
was discussed by Cicero, who posed two hypothetical situations
concerning insider trading. The first involved an honest
merchant carrying grain to famine-stricken Rhodes, who knows

other ships carrying grain are also on their way there. Should he report that fact to the Rhodians even though it will depress the price they will pay for his grain?   The second example involves a vendor who sells a building with a hidden defect.   Cicero resolved that full disclosure in both instances was ethical and expedient.[20]

Government regulation has unnecessarily intruded in many business activities.   Deregulation in other industries has brought benefits to the consumer, whereas deregulation in the securities industry would threaten the public with less information and with improper behavior by insiders.   Some securities regulations, like the Rule 10B-5 application to illegal insider trading, are excessively vague.   That ambiguity allows federal prosecutors great latitude in convicting wrongdoers who sully the market.   Certainly, a more precise definition of insider trading would be welcomed by business.

The securities laws are essential in the present environment of perceived widespread wrongdoing to maintain the public's confidence in the integrity of the financial markets and the public's ability to secure a fair return on investment.   The prices of the vast majority of securities reflect available public information about companies and the economy. By promulgating and enforcing the standards and guidelines proffered in this chapter, firms can assure the public that fairness and efficiency go hand in hand.

NOTES

1. <u>Wall Street Journal</u> (February 6, 1987): 20.
2. 17 <u>C.F.R.</u> Section 249.10b-5, Securities and Exchange Act of 1934.
3. Ibid.
4. Weiss, Power, and Crock, "Insider Trading: Business as Usual," <u>Business Week</u> (August 24,1987): 21.
5. Ricks, "Foreign Brokerages Appear Frequently in Insider-Trading Reports, Study Says," <u>Wall Street Journal</u> (June 6, 1988): 3.
6. 17 <u>C.F.R.</u> Section 106-5(a),(c).
7. <u>U.S.C.</u> 78j(b).
8. 15 <u>U.S.C.</u> Section 78p(b)(1982).
9. Sturc, Associate Director of the Division of Enforcement of the Securities and Exchange Commission, in a speech delivered October 17, 1986, <u>Vital Speeches of the Day</u> 53 (April 15, 1987): 405.
10. Ibid., 406.
11. <u>Carpenter v. United States</u>, 108 S. Ct. 316 (1987).
12. A number of these examples of material information appear in the very thorough codes of conduct of SmithKline Beckman, Chicago Pacific, Fireman's Fund, and First Union.
13. Levmore, "In Defense of the Regulation of Insider Trading," <u>Harvard Journal of Law and Public Policy</u> 11 (Winter 1988): 101.
14. For a detailed examination of the points in the Manne argument which one of the authors has summarized, see Manne, <u>Insider Trading and the Stock Market</u> (1966).
15. <u>S.E.C. v. Texas Gulf Sulphur Co.</u>, 401 F. 2d 833 (2d Circuit 1968) certiorari denied, 394 U.S. 976 (1969).
16. Clark, <u>Corporation Law</u> 507 (1986).
17. 17 <u>C.F.R.</u> Section 240.143-3 (1987).
18. Green, "Confusion Over Merger-Disclosure Law," <u>Wall Street Journal</u> (June 24, 1988): 21.
19. Some of these guidelines are adaptations of New York Stock Exchange recommendations.

20. Lawson, "The Ethics of Insider Training," <u>Harvard Journal of Law and Public Policy</u> 11 (Summer 1988): 737-740; see also Cicero, <u>De Officiis</u>, Book III (Alhambra, CA: Miller Translation 1968).

13
Fundamental Honesty, Law Compliance, Fair Competition, and the Antitrust Laws

INTRODUCTION

The rule of man, as opposed to the rule of law, was firmly established in England many centuries ago when "the dungeons of the barons' castles were full of both men and women put in prison for their gold and silver and tortured with pains unspeakable.'"[1] Clearly, the rule of law is preferable, although still onerous for society. Now not in constant fear of the whims of its rulers, society has the far different burden of following the law, because the rule of law has efficacy only if it enjoys the respect and active support of those it protects from tyranny.

Present-day law requires no ordeal by water, walking over red-hot ploughshares, or placing one's hand in a glove of red-hot iron or in a large pot of boiling water to prove one's innocence. Although trial by ordeal was formally abolished in England in 1219, the equally ancient trial by combat survived into the fourteenth century. There was scant mercy for the accused or for the guilty, as when a woman convicted of the capital offense of perjury was unable to pay the fine imposed on her. The court, "by way of dispensation let her eyes be torn out."[2] Those who could not evade the excesses of this nonjurisprudential system sought protection of sanctuary, a right that survived until the eighteenth century in England.

Our society is one in which the rule of law, not that of man or woman, is supreme. In fact, the rule of law is the foundation of our society—one in which individuals and businesses find harmony in conducting their activities in accordance with the laws of cities, states, and nations where they operate. Respect for the law means respect for society, and it is a catalyst for conducting oneself in accord with standards that go beyond legal requirements—such as avoiding conflict of interest and enhancing good corporate citizenship. In this way a law-abiding person or firm is naturally a highly ethical one as well. Respect for the law implies a respect for others' rights. It is an easy process to transfer that respect to an ethical concern for society.

As society has become more complex, government rule making, in the form of statutes, regulations, and ordinances, has become more pervasive. Laws that apply to all members of society, like prohibitions against defamation, slander, murder, and larceny, also apply to employees of businesses.

Other laws, like antitrust statutes, apply to individuals and firms in the context of employment and their economic activities, respectively.   It is essential that everyone knows enough about the law to determine when it is appropriate to seek advice from more knowledgeable individuals.   Further, from a legal procedure viewpoint, "ignorance of the Law excuses no man" because it is "an excuse every man will plead, and no man tell how to refute him."   Each person, in private or business life, has responsibility for acquiring sufficient knowledge of the law so as to fulfill his or her responsibility to society and to his or her firm.

OVERVIEW OF COMPETITIVE PRACTICES AND ANTITRUST LAWS

The objectives of the antitrust laws are to foster free enterprise, the hallmark of the American economic system, by protecting and nurturing business competition. The ability to compete is the sine qua non of a system in which market forces dictate company policy.   The antitrust laws help ensure that the results of market forces are not adulterated by unfair and predatory business practices. By protecting vigorous competition in purchasing and selling, the laws have allowed the business sector to flourish.   Nonetheless, even though such laws enhance the firm's chance for success, almost every leading corporation has violated the law, often because of ignorance or poor judgment by managers and employees.

To many businesspeople, antitrust laws apply to a huge firm's activities, certainly not to their firms.   Yet, there are very few areas of economic activity beyond the potential reach of antitrust laws.   From local undertakers' operations to foreign firms' acting at the behest of their own foreign governments, antitrust regulation has become a prominent feature of every manager's environment.[3]

In few areas is the adversarial relationship between business and government more evident than antitrust and trade regulatory laws.   These laws, whether of the United States or Japan, are the result of social policy decisions to organize the economic system through competitive markets.   Antitrust laws, whether federal or state, are varied and complex. Business firms depend for compliance on leadership from organizations' top levels and on the individual cooperation and effort of all the firms' employees.   Violation of the antitrust laws may result in severe criminal and civil sanctions, and in the sapping of the firm's vitality, or worse.

There are four major antitrust and trade regulation laws: the Sherman Act, Clayton Act, Federal Trade Commission Act, and Robinson-Patman Act.   Most states have enacted their own antitrust and trade regulation statutes that mirror the federal acts.   Further, state laws prohibit behavior in intrastate (wholly within one state) commerce, whereas federal laws proscribe behavior in interstate (activities involving two or more states) commerce.   Consequently, the state laws are generally satisfied by compliance with the federal laws. Moreover, foreign antitrust laws in Europe and Japan are similar to the U.S. federal statutes.

Adam Smith laid the foundation for antitrust statutes a century before their enactment by pointing out in <u>Wealth of Nations</u> that in a system of business competition, effective competition was not a natural adjunct: "People of the same trade seldom meet together, even for merriment and diversion but the conversation ends in a conspiracy against the public, or in some contrivance to raise prices."[4] The modern antitrust laws are a result of the American public's historic and similar distrust of bigness.

Following the Civil War (1861-65), the American economy entered a period of unparalleled growth due to several dynamic factors: the transportation and demographic developments that created a national market, the invention of new technologies able to manufacture goods in larger quantities, the exploitation of pronounced economies of scale, and the generation of huge amounts of capital to finance this rapid growth. In fact, the annual rate of growth of output per capita between 1870 and 1890 was 2%, compared to 1.5% prior to 1860.[5]

Successful late nineteenth-century firms followed one or both of two fundamental growth strategies: vertical integration forward into marketing or backward into producing raw materials, and horizontal combination when independent competitors consolidated to avoid declining prices and unprofitability, and often, failure. By the 1880s firms entered agreements to reduce price competition and instituted self-imposed restraints of output. The early vehicle was the pool by which managers established the participating firms' market shares and uniform margins of profit; however, entry into new uncovenanted markets and entrance of nonparticipating firms destroyed the efficacy of the pool.

Later, because pools were no better than "ropes of sand," according to John Rockefeller, many industrialists employed the trust to centralize market control with restrictions that would bind all participating firms. In this economic medium, leading firms in an industry would form a trust by exchanging trust certificates for common stock—thereby giving legal control of the firms to the trust. Although the trust would on occasion intervene in the actual operations of the trust's firms, as when it vertically integrated or closed an inefficient plant, the trust more often resembled a cartel as the trust executed pricing and output decisions.[6]

Citizens, especially farmers for years afflicted by the abuses of the railroad trusts, and small businessmen, so vigorously condemned the business trusts that both the Republican and Democratic parties included antitrust platform planks in their 1888 presidential campaigns.[7] This counteraction to trust-rigged outputs and increased prices led to the enactment of the Sherman Act in 1890.[8]

The Sherman Act (1890). This act, the first modern antitrust law, remains the primary instrument for bringing government and private antitrust lawsuits against unfair competition. Although courts in America had struck contracts held to be a restraint of trade prior to the enactment of the Sherman Act, these common law actions required initiation by private individuals, not the government. In this way, the Sherman Act embodied a new public policy of government action to prohibit restraint of trade and monopoly in foreign and interstate commerce.

Because the Sherman Act's statutory language was vague and the courts generally unsympathetic, early judicial interpretations were extremely narrow.   In addition, enforcement was timid: the government litigated only twenty-two cases in the statute's first fifteen years and attacked only one of the trusts at which the Sherman Act purportedly aimed.   That attack on the Sugar Trust failed because the court, in a narrow-gauged reading of "interstate commerce," forestalled, for a time, the statute's applicability to manufacturing.[9]

The most important elements of the Sherman Act are Sections One and Two.   Section One provides that "Every contract, combination in the form of trust or otherwise, or conspiracy, in restraint of trade or commerce among the several States, or with foreign nations . . . and offending corporations, persons, and associations . . . shall be deemed guilty."

Section One's enactment raised the question of what constitutes a *restraint of trade*.   The Supreme Court in the Standard Oil case[10] determined that the scrutinized act must be an unreasonable restraint of trade to be illegal, because every contract restrains trade to some degree.   Consequently, the fact finder (usually the jury, at times the judge) must consider all the circumstances in each case to determine whether a restrictive practice is unreasonable.   In applying this "rule of reason standard," then, every case must be judged individually and the courts would have wide discretion to restrict or expand the activities considered to be unfairly competitive—as opposed to the later approach that automatically attaches illegality to certain activities.

A number of relevant factors provide insight as to whether or not a restraint is reasonable, including the following: the nature of the restraint and its effect, whether or not it visibly has coerced or attacked rival competitors, the legitimate business purpose of the restraint, whether a more narrow restraint would adequately achieve that purpose, any competitive advantages for the market as a whole, and the nature and history of the restraint.[11]   Under this standard, practically every formal agreement among firms—especially sellers—with the purpose of inhibiting independent action in the market is illegal.[12]   Consequently, most vertical restraints, like resale and franchise location restrictions, must pass the "rule-of-reason" test.[13]   Nonetheless, if the restraint, including price fixing,[14] enhances a fair market and promotes an end to injurious competition, it may very well not be an "unreasonable restraint."

Moreover, certain agreements or practices have such a decidedly "pernicious effect on competition" and are, hence, per se violative of Section One of the Sherman Act, regardless of the surrounding circumstances.   Per se violations include concerted activities such as production output restraints, price fixing,[15] boycotts of particular buyers or sellers, and division of customers or territories.   Almost every vertical price fixing, as resale price maintenance, is deemed a per se violation unless protected by state fair trade legislation.[16] The legally sufficient establishment, alone, of the agreement or practice automatically tars it as illegal under the per se rule, regardless of the reasonableness of the restraint or its economic justification.   In addition, Section Three of the Clayton Act proscribes vertical restrictions as exclusive dealing or tying arrangements.

Section Two of the Sherman Act provides that any corporation, person, or association "who shall monopolize, or attempt to monopolize, or combine or conspire with any other person or persons, to monopolize any part of the trade or commerce among the several states, or with foreign nations, shall be deemed guilty . . . "

Section Two prohibits market structures characterized as *monopolies* because the seller concentration is so pronounced. There are two critical questions in every Section Two lawsuit: whether the defendant possesses or has made an attempt to possess monopoly power, which question requires a definition of the relevant market; and, assuming the defendant in fact possesses monopoly power, whether such power was fairly acquired as a result of superior performance, as through strategic foresight or development of patents.[17] Because power to monopolize includes the power to unreasonably restrict competition or control prices, almost every agreement or conspiracy to monopolize also violates Section One of the Sherman Act.   Moreover, unlike Section One, which requires two separate entities for a conspiracy, Section Two conspiracy violations can be successfully prosecuted based on the conduct of a single actor.[18]

Nonetheless, it is difficult to prove the existence of a monopoly under the case law—a fact that certainly explains the infrequency of Section Two lawsuits attacking monopolies.   For instance, in the landmark <u>Alcoa</u> case,[19] the court reversed long-held doctrine that a firm's size alone or a firm's unexerted power could not be the basis for a violation of the Sherman Act.   In <u>Alcoa</u>, the court determined that the firm's maintaining a high level of seller's market concentration constituted a violation.   Yet, although declaring Alcoa's 90% share of the relevant market as a monopoly, the court also suggested that market shares that ranged from 64% to 72% under alternative definitions of the relevant market would not have established a monopoly.[20]

For much of the life of the Sherman Act, a political consensus, supported since the 1940s by economists, has asserted that pronounced concentration in markets and sectors produces poor performance.   When a few sellers dominate a market, the argument continues, consumers typically are exploited through higher prices and fewer choices.   Yet, the Federal Trade Commission (FTC) failed in its atttempt[21] to break up the principal firms in the concentrated breakfast cereal industry, and that failure apparently ended government efforts to deconcentrate markets where the target firms had grown by internal expansion.[22]

The Clayton Act (1914). The Clayton Act,[23] enacted twenty-four years after the Sherman Act, was passed to correct the earlier statute's vagueness as to what indeed constituted a restraint of trade.   Further, through its Section Seven, the Clayton Act also sought to decelerate the merger movement from which had emerged a number of larger corporations in the decade before 1914.   The Clayton Act strengthened the Sherman

Act by defining practices as unlawful "where the effect . . . may be to substantially lessen competition or tend to create a monopoly." No longer did the government have to prove actual monopoly or conspiracy to convict a firm of antitrust violations.

Section Two of the Clayton Act deems it illegal for any corporation, association, or person engaged in commerce to "discriminate in price between different purchasers or commodities of like grade and quality . . . where the effect of such discrimination may be substantially to lessen competition or tend to create a monopoly." Consequently, a seller cannot legally grant lower prices to favored buyers. Price differentials are permissible though, when based on actual difference in the "cost of manufacture, sale, or delivery resulting from the differing methods or quantities in which such commodities are sold," or when made "in good faith to meet an equally low price of a competitor." Section Two protects, for instance, retail merchants from "predatory" competition practices by "chain stores."

Section Three of the Clayton Act prohibits two specific actions by a seller or lessor that promote a monopoly condition: first, exclusive dealing whereby sale or lease is made on condition that the purchaser or lessee refrains from dealing in some regard with the seller's or lessor's competitor; and second, a tying arrangement where a seller or lessor allows the buyer or lessee access to one product line provided the buyer or lessor purchases or leases other of the seller's products as well. Under exclusive dealing and tying agreements, larger firms would be able to unfairly force their goods on small retail merchants.

Section Four provides that the successful private plaintiff "injured . . . by reason of anything forbidden in the antitrust laws . . . shall recover threefold the damages . . . sustained, and the cost of the suit including a reasonable attorney's fee." Moreover, Section Eight, invoked infrequently, prohibits interlocking directorates. The trend over the last two decades indicates private antitrust lawsuits are much more frequently brought than government actions.

Section Seven, as amended by the 1950 Celler-Kefauver amendments[24] to the Clayton Act, prohibits corporate mergers when there is an acquisition of "the whole or part of the stock or . . . assets of another corporation engaged also in commerce in any section of the country, the effect of such acquisition may be substantially to lessen competition, or tend, to create a monopoly." As in Section Two of the Sherman Act, Section Seven lawsuits under the Clayton Act require the definition of the relevant product market, based on the availability of sufficient substitute products or alternative sources of supply, and of the relevant geographic market, based on a measure of the effective competitive range for the product and firms in question.[25] Unlike Section Two, however, there has been a plethora of suits pursuant to Section Seven attacking mergers, because the Department of Justice "Merger Guidelines" direct a challenge against almost any significant merger.[26] Under Section Seven, the government has attacked horizontal,[27] vertical,[28] and conglomerate[29] mergers.

The Federal Trade Commission Act (1914).   President Woodrow Wilson vigorously and successfully urged Congress to pass this act, as he did the Clayton Act, to correct weaknesses in the Sherman Act, specifically the Supreme Court's Standard Oil case's[30] "rule of reason" doctrine which was insufficiently strong to combat trusts.   The Federal Trade Commission Act,[31] as amended by the Wheeler-Lea Act of 1938,[32] declares illegal "[u]nfair methods of competition in commerce, and unfair or deceptive acts and practices in commerce," and it established a commission (the Federal Trade Commission) to research economic and technical issues in antitrust enforcement to provide guidance to the courts and to implement the act itself.   As a result, the Federal Trade Commission (FTC) regulates a variety of business practices that tend to harm businesses or consumers.   Further, in the S&H case, the Supreme Court held that the FTC would be justified in designating a practice as unfair if it "considers public values beyond simply those enshrined in the letter or encompassed in the spirit of the antitrust laws."[33]   In addition, no private right of suit lies under Section Five of the FTC Act.[34]

Apparently, Congress intentionally employed vague language in the FTC Act, "unfair methods of competition," because it is impossible to specifically designate or define all practices that impair competition.   "The standard of 'unfairness' under the FTC Act is, by necessity, an elusive one, encompassing not only practices that violate the Sherman Act and the other antitrust laws, . . . but also practices that the Commission determines are against public policy for other reasons."[35] Nonetheless, critics assert that the FTC Act's vague language and the commission's unspecific guidelines allow the FTC "to roam freely in search of business practices that are inconsistent with personal and social values of individual commissioners."[36]

Under the "deceptive acts and practices" criterion, the FTC has ordered "misleading advertisers" to disseminate corrective advertisements to cure the "deceptions," and has issued "cease and desist" orders, as for example, to Mary Carter Paints to prohibit the deceptive advertisement, "Buy one gallon, get one free."[37]   In addition, the FTC is empowered to issue orders directed to an entire industry, without first bringing proceedings against an individual firm.[38]

Robinson-Patman Act (1936).   Congress enacted the complex and vague Robinson-Patman Act[39] primarily to save the nation's small businesses through the government's regulating price discrimination.   The growth and economic strength of chains during the Depression created a severe disparity in the profit margins of chain organizations and smaller firms, with the latter usually unable to obtain the same special prices or brokerage concessions from suppliers as the former.

The Robinson-Patman Act amended Section Two of the Clayton Act, and it prohibits price discrimination "where the effect . . . may be substantially to lessen competition or tend to create a monopoly . . . or to injure, destroy, or prevent competition with any person who either grants or knowingly receives the benefit of such discrimination or with customers of either of them." (Emphasis added.) With the addition of the phrase "to injure, destroy, or prevent competition," a

firm's action no longer had to substantially lessen competition to be illegal.   Rather, the firm's activity could be
unlawful if it merely injured competition.

Under the act, price discrimination is defined as the
selling of commodities of like grade and quality at dissimilar
prices to different customers.   This discrimination is not
prohibited per se: if the price differential reflects
differences in costs in dealing with buyers or if the price
differential is necessary to respond to a competitor's lower
price, then the price discrimination is legal.   Other defenses
a firm can raise against the charge of unlawful price discrimination   are   that   the   price   changes   are   "in response   to
changing conditions affecting the market or the marketability
of the goods concerned, such as, but not limited, to actual or
imminent deterioration of perishable goods, obsolescence of
seasonal goods, distress sales under court process, or sales
in good faith in discontinuance of business in the goods
concerned."

Moreover, the Robinson-Patman Act prohibits discrimination
through brokerage fees, special promotion allowances (as for
advertising), or special services or facilities unless that
benefit is "available on proportionally equal terms to all
other customers competing in the distribution of such products
or commodities."   Also, under all prohibitions of the statute,
sanctions can be levied against the purchaser who solicits the
favored treatment as well as the offending seller.

Given the vagueness of the statute, the resulting uncertainty and caution among businesspeople in the use of prices,
allowances,   and   services   are   pronounced.   As   a   result,
businesspeople have become more concerned about maintaining
cost data, dwell more on cost pricing than demand pricing, and
shy away from price competition, instead, by differentiating
on the basis of promotion and service.   Under the act, the FTC
can establish limits on quantity discounts and forbid brokerage allowances except to independent brokers.[40]   In its impact,
the Robinson-Patman Act clearly protects individual, often
inefficient, firms, usually at the expense of the competitive
process.

Violation of Antitrust Laws

Antitrust violations can result in serious consequences.
Criminal violations of the Sherman Act are felonies, punish-
able, in the case of a corporation, by fines up to $1 million
for each offense, and in the case of an individual, by fines
up to $100,000, and by a prison term as long as three years
for each offense.   The felony conviction of an individual may
result in the denial of certain basic citizenship rights, such
as voting and holding political office.

Moreover, all firms, customers, competitors, or other
persons who suffer injury by a Sherman Act violation, or by
certain Clayton Act violations, may recover treble damages,
essentially three times the amount of any actual damage.
Obviously, treble damages will greatly exceed the amount of
any conceivable financial benefit gained by the firm or the
person through the illegal acts.   In addition, any state,

through its attorney general, may sue on behalf of that state's injured residents to recover treble damages as well.

Third, violations of the laws or FTC regulations usually result in sanctions, including injunctions, which are enforced by monetary penalties and contempt of court proceedings, and divestment. The scope of the injunctions, usually broad, can impair a firm's ability to remain competitive in a market or industry. Court-ordered divestment of portions of a firm's business units often causes an upheaval so profound as to inhibit the firm's economic development.

In addition, any person or business injured by an antitrust violation may bring a lawsuit to recover three times the actual damages together with litigation expense. The firm's cost of defending an antitrust suit is substantial: from hundreds of thousands of dollars for simple defenses to millions of dollars for more complex cases, together with many thousands of hours of key employees' time defending the case. All of these factors, the expense of litigation and the severity of the sanctions, frequently compel firms to settle the case before trial. The consent decree occasioned by settlement can prohibit a firm's activity that is not itself illegal. Under the best of circumstances, a consent degree significantly impairs the firm's operations and subjects its managers to the threat of court sanctions, including penalties against the firm of up to $10,000 per day.

Conduct and Practices Involving Competitors, Suppliers, or Customers that Violate or May Violate Antitrust Laws

Certain types of conduct are so indefensible that the courts deem them per se violations of the antitrust laws, regardless of their effect on competition or the motives of the firms involved. Per se violations are a magnet for criminal as well as treble damages, penalties against the firm, and the employees involved in the proscribed activities. Additionally, the courts can find a forbidden conspiracy or agreement without a written contract or express words of assent. The following examples of generally per se violations concern agreements with:

1. A competitor firm to limit competition in product quality.

2. A competitor firm to restrict production of goods in order to raise prices through limited supply.

3. A competitor, supplier, or customer to indirectly or directly stabilize or affect prices (whether maximum or minimum), pricing procedures, credit terms, discounts, transportation costs or arrangements, or other terms and conditions of sale.

4. A competitor firm to divide markets through allocation of sales territories, classes of customers or suppliers, or product lines.

5. A competitor firm, a customer, or a supplier to refuse to sell to or purchase from a third party.

6. A firm's purchase of goods from a supplier or customer on that other party's buying goods from the firm.

7. A competitor firm, supplier, or customer to boycott selling to or purchasing from a third party.

8. A supplier or customer to fix or influence the supplier's or customer's resale pricing, or to fix or influence terms and conditions of the resale.

9. A supplier or customer to refrain from dealing in a competitor's products.

10. A supplier or customer that conditions the sale of one product on the purchase by the other party of another product as well.

Yet another class of business practices and transactions may violate the antitrust laws if they "unreasonably restrain" trade or damage a competitor. Following are examples of possibly illegal actions.

1. Any business practice or transaction that may result in a firm's acquiring a substantial portion of sales in any trade channel or geographic area.

2. Any practice or transaction involving selling below cost or below marginal cost designed to damage or fatally wound a competitor firm.

3. Any purchase of the assets or shares of another firm, especially if that firm is in a business even tangentially related to the purchaser's business.

4. Any practice or transaction that appears to involve an unfair method of competition or that may be deceptive to a customer or supplier.

5. An agreement with a customer that the latter will purchase all of his or her product requirements from the firm, to the exclusion of purchasing competitive products from a third party.

6. An agreement with a customer that essentially restricts that customer's right to resell to a particular type of customer or in a specific geographical area.

A third class of potential antitrust offenses comprises those discriminatory practices that are harmful to competitors, suppliers, or customers. As long as harm to competition or a competitor is present, the reasonableness of the price or terms of sale discrimination are not material. Specific examples of this category of potential violation appear under the earlier discussion of the Robinson-Patman Act.

CURRENT DEVELOPMENTS IN ANTITRUST LAW

For three decades before the mid-1970s, antitrust law increasingly enlarged the rights of those perceived as victims of other firms' economic power. However, the trend of rights expansion was reversed by the landmark opinion in <u>Sylvania</u>,[41] in which the Supreme Court proclaimed a "rule-of-reason" approach for almost all nonprice restraints involving a firm's arrangements with customers, dealers, agents, or suppliers. Only when collaboration among competitors is so pernicious that it "touches the nerve of the free market system" does the Court apply the per se or a hybrid per se rule.[42] Moreover, the Court has given great weight to the claim that some restraints—exclusive contracts among them—actually are enhancers of competition, and that "much single-firm behavior, such as low but profitable pricing, is normally the essence of healthy competition." [43]

Further, a firm's large size is no longer a lightning rod for hostile government agency lawsuits. In 1980 the FTC dismissed charges against DuPont for its domination of the titanium oxide market, after stating that a firm's activities that create a monopoly are not unlawful when they are the result of aggressive competition based on scientific technological advantages. The Department of Justice espoused a doctrine that antitrust enforcement should seek to accomplish efficiency, which the department deemed to be maximum production at the lowest price.[44] In 1981 the Department of Justice dismissed the case against IBM, under attack for thirteen years because of its dominant position and activities in the computer industry, and settled its case with AT&T on the same day by severing AT&T's local telephone monopoly from that firm.[45]   As a consequence of concern about international competition, business alliances, such as Abbott's and 3M's new venture "Corporate Alliance" to cut hospital costs, are growing at an annual rate of 20%. Alliance is a response to cost pressures directly resulting from low inflation and increasingly intense private competition, as government has focused its antitrust action on price fixing.

Over the next few years, the FTC ended its investigation of the four largest U.S. auto manufacturers, and the Department of Justice replaced the outdated 1969 Merger Guidelines with new guidelines in 1982 and in 1984; and it later issued Restraint of Trade Guidelines in 1985.   The 1982 Merger Guidelines create the presumption that mergers, no matter what size, are beneficial and efficient. The 1984 guidelines encourage mergers that eliminate duplication, enhance economies of scale, or would serve as a lifeboat to a firm whose weak market position would likely deteriorate further without the merger.[46] Moreover, the new guidelines on restraints manifest the view of the Reagan administration that many types of restraint agreements between a firm and its customers, dealers, agents, or suppliers are beneficial for consumers.

In 1986 the Supreme Court virtually discarded predatory pricing as an antitrust cause of action in <u>Matsushita Electric Industrial Co. v. Zenith Radio Corp</u>.[47] In that case the Court found predatory pricing schemes inherently implausible and even less likely when the scheme requires the participation of more than one firm.[48]

The result of the Justice Department's accommodating merger guidelines, "large size is beneficial" philosophy, and the Supreme Court's greater use of the rule-of-reason doctrine and its permissive attitude toward certain restraints of trade has been an explosion in business merger activity. This frenetic activity has significantly restructured the nation's economy. For instance, following the 1985 mergers between RCA and General Electric, and between General Foods and Philip Morris, the number of mergers in 1986 increased at a fissionable rate to over 4,000 worth $190 billion. In contrast during the first six months of 1980, only 856 mergers were promulgated.[49]

GUIDELINES FOR COMPLIANCE WITH ANTITRUST LAWS

Any employee of a firm who fails to comply with the law jeopardizes the reputation and viability of the firm. Sanctions imposed for violation of antitrust laws have included judgments in excess of $100 million. Hence, it is important for a firm and its employees to strictly adhere to the following guidelines:

1. The firm should clearly establish that any employee who fails to abide by the guidelines herein shall be severely disciplined and, perhaps, discharged.

2. No employee shall enter any agreement or understanding, whether formal or informal, with a competitor firm's employee regarding the following elements of the business policy of either party or of the business relationship of either party to any third party: costs; past, present, or future prices, profits, or product offerings; service; production or sales volume; manufacturing facilities or capacity; share of the market, terms or conditions of sale; sales territories; marketing or distribution methods; customer characteristics or selection; supplier classification or selection; or any other subject that might directly or indirectly affect prices.

3. An employee may obtain information concerning a competitor's pricing, including schedules, only from sources other than competitors. Any employee obtaining such information should record next to the information the date received and the source of the information. Such procedure provides a basis for demonstrating that the information was obtained lawfully.

4. When a firm markets the same product in the same geographic markets directly to users or retailers as well as through distributors, the firm should consider the distributors as competitors within the meaning of the antitrust statutes. Consequently, no employee should enter any discussion with distributors anyone could infer was actually an agreement not to compete with the other for specific customers, or types of customers, in product types, or in geographic areas.

5. A boycott can occur even when the agreement is between two firms not in competition. Consequently, employees should refrain from discussing with a customer, supplier, competitor, or anyone else a refusal to buy from a supplier or to sell to a customer.

6. The antitrust laws do not prohibit every contact with a competitor—only those that result in understandings, conspiracies, or agreements to limit or restrict competition. Every employee, though, should discuss any potential contact with a competitor with the firm's legal counsel.

7. An employee should not attend a meeting of a trade association to which the firm does not belong without obtaining permission from the firm's legal counsel and should never attend a surreptitious meeting of competitors.

8. An employee should not join any trade association without approval of the firm's secretary and legal counsel.

9. An employee should participate in civic, technical, professional, industry associations, or government committees. However, no matter how formal or informal the meeting, the employee should disengage from any discussion the propriety of which that employee is uncertain. Further, the employee should depart from any such meeting and record in the minutes that departure. These proscriptions apply to contacts before and after the meetings.

10. An employee should seek the legal counsel's opinion concerning (a) the content and promulgation of any marketing plan or activity that might weaken a competitor, and (b) the permissibility under law of any proposed acquisition, merger, or joint venture.

11. In international business transactions and practices that affect the trade and commerce of the United States, an employee should abide by all of the guidelines contained in this section.

12. An employee should refrain from entering any agreement or understanding with or exerting pressure on a purchaser or lessee of the firm's product that restricts the purchaser's or lessee's right to establish the price to resell or lease that product. Further, the employee should not enter any like agreement when the firm is the purchaser or lessee of a product, or participate in any activity between two or more distributors or dealers to establish, rig, stabilize, or influence the resale price.

13. An employee should never (a) dictate or suggest to customers where or to whom they should sell, (b) use the firm's purchasing power to promulgate sales, or (c) use

delivery of a product in demand or short supply as a carrot. Package sales are permissible only if the seller lacks sufficient economic power in regard to any specific product to force the buyer to purchase the entire product package.

14. It is proper for a firm's employee to insist that a firm's distributors and dealers adequately promote the firm's products as a primary line and to use ethical salesmanship to demonstrate to distributors and dealers the advantages of carrying the firm's product line exclusively. Nonetheless, an employee should (a) not insist that a distributor or dealer abandon a competitor's product line or market the firm's products exclusively, (b) gain approval of the firm's legal counsel for all long-term arrangements to provide a customer's requirements, and (c) refrain from discussing the cancellation of a distributorship or dealership without consulting the firm's legal counsel.

15. The firm's legal counsel should review the firm's price schedule before dissemination. An employee should not deviate from the terms and prices of the schedule without permission. An employee should offer every customer the same terms and prices as well as the same advertising and services.

16. An employee may sell to one customer at a lower price than to another customer if the primary reason is to match a competitor's offer, provided the competitor's product competes directly with the firm's product. Further, the firm may not offer a better price, except when the contract is awarded on the basis of bids. The employee must record and confirm, as accurately as possible, the salient elements of the competitor's offer, such as the source of the competitor's price, the price, the competitor's identity, the date of the competitor's offer, the product involved, and all documentation such as invoices, proposals, or correspondence the customer voluntarily provides. In such cases, the firm's offer should be ripe for acceptance only for the same duration as the competitor.

CONCLUSIONS

Whereas the kernel of antitrust legislation dates to the law of seventeenth-century England, basic antitrust principles are now integral elements of the economic and political philosophy of the United States. Admittedly, the fair competition and trade laws are vague, and their enforcement and interpretation vary with society's attitudinal changes toward business and with the "iliction returns," in Mr. Dooley's vernacular. For instance, the rule-of-reason test has given way to the per se approach, particularly in regard to issues concerning a firm's size. Recent attitude shifts favor corporate growth and mergers as being beneficial to the consumer.

Conservative critics, the University of Chicago economists and adherents, attack wide-ranging antitrust regulation. They hold a number of beliefs including: that efficiency should be the exclusive goal of all commercial law; that the law should reprehend, not protect, what is inefficient; that the market punishes inefficiency better and more quickly than the law; and that law is economics and efficiency is justice. The Chicago School's beliefs are compatible only with the most minimal law—that which "proscribes only clear cartel agreements and mergers that would create a monopoly in a market that included all perceptible potential competition."[50]

Liberal critics such as Lester Thurow and John Kenneth Galbraith comprise the "statists." Statists believe that American political, economic, and social institutions have "outgrown antitrust." Concern about the firm's market penetration and massive size is misplaced: a closer integration of business and government is the solution to assuring social welfare and, therefore, policy direction should be based on planning. Models to emulate include Japan's Ministry of International Trade and Industry (MITI).[51]

On the other hand, those traditionalists favoring antitrust laws perceive a direct causal relationship among structure, conduct, and performance. Traditionalists view healthy and free competition as the nucleus of the free enterprise system; in turn, many of the political and social freedoms enjoyed by U.S. citizens depend on the free enterprise system. The objectives of the antitrust laws nurture that desired competition and enhance the rise of the gross national product without a concomitant diminution in the quality of life. As federal antitrust action in some areas waned during the Reagan administration, state attorneys general recently have enforced more stringent state guidelines to force a $4 million settlement from Minolta for manipulating retail camera prices, and $16 million from Chrysler for odometer fraud. Moreover, the U.S. Supreme Court, in an important 1989 decision, <u>California v. ARC America Corp.</u>, ruled that states may indeed allow consumers who suffer indirect financial loss as a result of anticompetitive business activities to sue the violators, even though federal antitrust law does not permit such indirect purchaser lawsuits.

Almost every firm, especially those that market products and services in any manner, face potential exposure under antitrust laws and must develop antitrust compliance programs.[52] In spite of its critics, antitrust will continue to develop incrementally and offer constructive resolution of business conduct problems—a resolution vital for the health of our economic system.

NOTES

1. Hibbert, <u>The English: A Social History 1066-1945</u>, (New York: W.W. Norton, 1978), 138.
2. Idem., 141-143.
3. Kasper, <u>Note on U.S. Antitrust Laws</u>, Harvard Business School Pub. 378-127 (1977), 1-2.

4. Adam Smith, <u>The Wealth of Nations</u> (New York: Pelican Books, 1974), as cited Ibid., 3.
5. Fox and Sullivan, "Antitrust—Retrospective and Prospective: Where Are We Coming From? Where Are We Going?" <u>N.Y.U. Law Review</u> 62 (November 1987): 937.
6. Ibid., 938-940.
7. Ibid., 940.
8. Ch. 647, 26 Stat. 209 (1890), as amended at 15 <u>U.S.C.</u> Sections 1-7 (1982).
9. Kasper, op. cit., 4.
10. <u>Standard Oil Company of New Jersey v. United States</u>, 221 U.S. 1 (1911).
11. Kasper, op. cit., 9.
12. Buchholz, <u>Business Environment and Public Policy</u>, 3rd ed. (Englewood Cliffs, NJ: Prentice-Hall, 1989), 216.
13. Kasper, op. cit., 9.
14. See <u>Appalachian Coals, Inc. v. United States</u>, 288 U.S. 344 (1933), as cited in Buchholz, op. cit., 216.
15. <u>United States v. Trenton Potteries Co</u>, 273 U.S. 392 (1927).
17. Kasper, op. cit., 7.
18. Buchholz, op. cit., 224.
19. <u>United States v. Aluminum Co. of America</u>, 148 F. 2d 416 (1945), reviewing 44 F. Supp. 97, (1945).
20. Kasper, op. cit., 7.
21. See <u>Kellogg Co.</u>, 99 F.T.C. 8, 267 (1982).
22. Fox and Sullivan, op. cit., 943-944.
23. Ch. 323, 38 Stat. 739 (1914) codified as amended at 15 <u>U.S.C.</u> Sections 12-27 (1982 and Supp. II, 1984).
24. 15 <u>U.S.C.</u> Section 18 (1982 and Supp. II, 1984).
25. Kasper, op. cit., 11.
26. 15 <u>U.S.C.</u> Section 18 (1982 and Supp. II, 1984).
27. <u>U.S. v. Von's Grocery Co.</u>, 384 U.S. 270 (1966), and <u>U.S. v. Brown Shoe Co., Inc.</u>, 370 U.S. 294 (1962).
28. <u>U.S. v. duPont de Nemours & Co.</u>, 353 U.S. 586 (1957).
29. <u>F.T.C. v. Procter and Gamble Co.</u>, 386 U.S. 568 (1967).
30. <u>U.S. v. Standard Oil Company of New Jersey,</u> 221 U.S. 1 (1911).
31. 15 <u>U.S.C.</u> Sections 41-58 (1976).
32. Ibid.
33. <u>FTC v. The Sperry and Hutchinson Company</u> 405 U.S. 233 (1972), 244.
34. <u>Carlson v. Coca-Cola Co.</u>, 483 F. 2d 279 (9th Cir. 1973).
35. <u>FTC v. Indiana Federation of Dentists</u>, 106 S. Ct. 2009 (1986), 2016.
36. Gellhorn, "Trading Stamps, S&H, and the FTC's Unfairness Doctrine," <u>Duke Law Journal</u> 903 (1983): 940.
37. <u>FTC v. Mary Carter Paint Co.</u>, 382 U.S. 46 (1965), as cited in Kasper, op. cit., 9.
38. Kasper, op. cit., 12.
39. 15 <u>U.S.C.</u> Section 21(a) (St. Paul, MN: West, 1973 & Supp., 1986).
40. See Kotler, <u>Marketing Management</u>, 6th ed., (Englewood Cliffs, NJ: Prentice-Hall, 1988), 158.
41. <u>Continental T.V., Inc., v. GTE Sylvania, Inc.</u>, 433 U.S. 36 (1977).
42. Fox and Sullivan, op. cit., 954-955.
43. Ibid., 955.
44. Buchholz, op. cit., 226-227.
45. Ibid.
46. Fox and Sullivan, op. cit., 952-953.
47. 475 U.S. 574 (1986); see also <u>Cargill, Inc. v. Monfort of Colorado, Inc.</u>, 107 S. Ct. 484 (1986).
48. Idem, 588-593.
49. Buchholz, op. cit., 229.
50. Fox and Sullivan, op. cit., 957-958.
51. Ibid., 960-961.
52. Jaglom, "How To Develop a Corporate Antitrust Compliance Program," <u>The Practical Lawyer</u> 31, no. 5 (1985): 75-86.

14

International Business Relationships and Practices

INTRODUCTION

"Perhaps for the first time since the United States became a modern industrial economy, the most important influence shaping the trend of business conditions in the years ahead will be our external trade . . . a shift of historic proportions," notes economist Paul McCracken.[1] Yet, from a 1980 deficit of $31 billion, the 1988 trade deficit soared to $171 billion, roughly 10% of America's gross national product. The result of the internationalization of business and industry is the loss of over three million American jobs in manufacturing, a 2% reduction in the gross national product, and a sinking median family income measured in constant dollars. In a span of a few years, the United States, formerly the largest creditor nation, has become the leading debtor nation, and, if present trends continue, U.S. individuals, institutions, and government may owe foreign investors $700 billion more than they owe us by the end of 1990.

Furthermore, the World Competitiveness Report, a business survey of thirty-two nations issued in July 1989 by the World Economic Forum, ranks the United States third in international economic competitiveness, behind Japan and Switzerland. The authors define competitiveness as "the ability to take advantage of opportunities in the international marketplace." The Japanese business environment has been enhanced by the government's policy of promoting international business involvement, according to the article appearing in the <u>Wall Street Journal</u> (p. A-4) on July 5, 1989. In addition, the report ranks the United States sixth behind Finland and Sweden in "innovative forward orientation."

One observer, Harvard professor Quinn Mills, places part of the blame for the nation's trade problem on American foreign policy, which, in a global contest with the Soviet Union, has supported political stability in Third World nations at almost any cost. These less-developed countries have become client states—they expect the United States to "bail them out of tough economic times by buying their products" no matter the quality, price, or need. As Mills reasons, "[T]hese policies sacrifice our long-term economic strength for short-term political influence."[2]

American business, by enhancing its international participation, not only helps the nation but also itself.

International markets provide new demand for a firm's products—thereby allowing larger production runs and, often,
marginal product costs that are lower than the product's
average costs.   Moreover, foreign markets offer greater
returns on capital because of lesser competition and a larger
growth rate of consumption.   Finally, firms must export
products to foreign markets or risk extinction when American
markets are sated.[3]

Yet, for a variety of reasons, primarily lack of knowledge
and formidable bureaucratic obstacles, relatively few American
firms export.   A mere 250 U.S. firms account for 85% of the
nation's exports.   The General Accounting Office estimates
that another 11,000 domestic firms could export; if they did,
they would generate at least $4 billion in sales and create
125,000 jobs.   Moreover, by the end of 1992 the European
community will become the world's largest trading bloc—320
million people annually producing $2.4 trillion worth of goods
and services—by eliminating all barriers to free trade among
its members.   The United States, with 247 million people and
a $3.9 trillion annual economic output, must expand its inter-
national trade to transform the European challenge into an
opportunity.

The United States presently accounts for about 10% of
world trade in manufacturing, a substantial drop from 15% in
1970 and 13% in 1980.   Since manufacturing still accounts for
80% of U.S. and of all world trade, this nation needs to boost
manufacturing.   A recent Massachusetts Institute of Technology
(MIT) study indicates that U.S. manufacturing output must increase to 26% of GNP from its current level of 22% to balance
the nation's international trade imbalance.   In addition,
notes Ford Motor president Harold Poling, "Global competition,
international capital flows, and the integration of the
worldwide economy have added new dimensions to the conduct of
business." Growing market economics have transformed yesterday's developing countries, like Korea and Taiwan, into
present-day fierce competitors. "Whoever controls the Pacific
controls the world," according to Senator Albert Beveridge in
1900, and in the last three decades the dynamic of American
economic history has focused on the North Pacific.   For
example, in 1980 for the first time, trade between the United
States and the Pacific zone ($117 billion) exceeded the
nation's trade with Western Europe ($115.9 billion)—a fact
that underscores the new technological and economic axis of
the United States and Japan.

The concept of markets has changed just as rapidly, notes
Walter Wriston, retired chief executive of Citicorp: "The
global marketplace is reality.   Money and ideas can and do
move to any place on this planet in seconds, and there is no
longer any place to hide from the judgement of others."   For
example, foreign competitors have hastened an industrial
sunset for USX and LTV, two firms that did not export and
Japan's Bridgestone bought Firestone.

Since new products are increasingly more expensive to
develop, and shorter life cycles require earlier global
marketing, "competitiveness is already beyond the reach of the
purely national company," asserts Harvard Business School
professor Christopher Bartlett.   Increased economic interdependence among the world's nations is reflected in the

phenomenal growth in global trade: 7% per annum from 1948 to 1973, a rate that has far outpaced growth of worldwide GNP. As a result, exports and imports are now much more important to a nation's economic health.   Further, direct foreign investment flows, another trapping of global interdependence, grew annually at 13% from 1960 to 1975.   National economies are continuing to expand and to become more interdependent.[4] Success in business more often requires success in international trade: in the 1990s it is "trade or perish."

CREATING AND ENHANCING THE FIRM'S OPPORTUNITIES

Succeeding in the international sector requires the firm's determined commitment to developing a strategy based on the interrelationship of three factors: the market, the product, and the business person.   Whereas mastery of the first two elements assists in determining a starting point of export operations, the last is more important in actually maintaining export activities.[5]   The firm can determine which foreign markets to serve by discussing the matter with foreign contacts and by examining market information, in journals, general business papers, almanacs, and world trade publications,[6] which provide names, addresses, and information about potential foreign customers.

After assessing and selecting the relevant markets to exploit, the firm should consider the attributes of the product it wishes to sell to the chosen markets.   International markets have unique technical, climatic, and perceptual variances that might require product modifications.   For instance, a heavy duty detergent sold in Germany may include enzymes that act as catalysts for cleaning—which additions are of no value in England, where laundry is boiled at high temperatures, which destroy the enzymes.[7]   Further, it is particularly important to accentuate the value of the product to the foreign consumers by demonstrating that the product accomplishes the task the customer has in mind.   Finally, successfully pursuing foreign business requires patience and perseverance in large quantities.   Firms should select customers within the chosen markets for patient cultivation. Often these time commitments appear severe by American standards.[8]

Another method of increasing foreign sales is through countertrade, a market some observers believe is a market equal to at least 30% of the over $2 trillion in international sales.   Countertrade is "an umbrella term encompassing a wide range of barterlike activities in international trade."   In international barter transactions, a buyer may require payment in goods rather than cash.[9]   Counterpurchase is a prevalent form of countertrade in which the contract is specifically stated in a selected currency.   The seller delivers the desired products to the purchaser, and the seller agrees to purchase products from the original buyer equal to more than a portion or all of the original sale price.[10]

For instance, General Electric won the contract to construct a large electric generator project in Romania by contracting to market that country's products in a sum equivalent in value to the construction contract.   Moreover,

Chrysler sealed a deal to sell trucks to Jamaica in return for Chrysler intermediaries' exporting Jamaican alumina. Likewise, FMC, Northrop, McDonnell Douglas, and Occidental Petroleum have expanded their international sales through countertrade.[11]

Countertrade, the annual value of which exceeds $100 billion, is a particularly attractive marketing mechanism for firms that are not undisputed industry leaders. In 1990 with the mounting foreign debt crisis many countries are experiencing, countertrade is a particularly useful tool for firms to sell their goods to countries and firms that are without sufficient foreign exchange. In addition, a great number of smaller U.S. firms can use countertrade to find low-cost sources of procurement, enter the international market, and develop good customer relations.[12]

The firm considering countertrade should observe the following guidelines[13] offered by one noted observer of international trade:

1. Firms with good trading expertise, extensive networks, and excellent control of the internal divisions or subsidiaries can usually handle the countertrade transaction internally. Other firms may wish to hire a trading company, at 1% to 2% above the incremental costs of the firm's own trading arm.

2. The firm should incorporate the trading cost in prices for its products.

3. The firm should develop a knowledge base concerning the target countries' government, regulations, and politics.

4. The firm should accept only countertrade products about which it has an expertise.

5. The firm should understand the process thoroughly and be prepared to negotiate every aspect of countertrade. For instance, the American firm could establish penalties if the foreign firm or government provided products that did not satisfy the American firm's quality and delivery specifications.

Moreover, one of the nation's most brilliant marketers, Harvard professor Ted Levitt, asserts that "the globalization of markets is at hand."[14] This globalization translates into a "commonality" where firms sell standardized products everywhere. Levitt offers constructive advice to firms that wish to create or increase their international presence. By standardizing its products, a firm can realize enormous economies of scale that allow a subsequent lowering of prices to the substantial regret of competitors. Second, firms should develop products that are functional, advanced, reliable, and optimally low-priced. Third, according to Levitt, firms should concentrate their product strategies on what people want rather than attempting to sell a different line of products specifically tailored to each country based on what people may like.

Not surprisingly, Levitt pointed out that Henry Ford's Model T and the modern Japanese firms have vindicated this strategy of depressing product cost and price while improving product reliability and quality. In addition, Outboard Marine Corporation improved its product installation and credit service to customers and reduced its product costs by collapsing the traditional three-tiered distribution channels in Europe into a more manageable two-level structure. When SmithKline Beckman successfully introduced the decongestant Contac 600 in Japan, the firm employed only thirty-five wholesalers instead of the customary 1,000 or more. The Outboard Marine and SmithKline successes demonstrate a fourth element of Levitt's advice: firms should challenge prevailing international practices with sustained and vigorous support systems, product quality and reliability, low prices, and implacability and audacity.[15]

In addition, successful international advertising, one of the most important elements of trading, conducted in one country can be a critical sales success factor in others as well. The advertising campaign that establishes and maintains a firm's branded image expands the firm's product line even when the firm's support resources are not locally at hand in those foreign markets. "The lasting image of quality and value given by a strong advertising proposition helps us overcome local pricing turbulences and other factors which always occur and about which we can do almost nothing," according to one successful chief executive. Moreover, the centralized control implied by internationalized advertising provides an effective control over widely dispersed activities, and it usually reduces the cost of developing advertising in each foreign market.[16]

The key to success in international advertising, according to one chief executive, is the firm's effective strategic planning.[17] On formulating such a strategy the firm should clarify the marketing policy by determining whether global sales represent an opportunity for selling new or, on the other hand, existing products, and whether centrally produced advertising is feasible and cost saving. Next, the firm can organize to reflect advertising needs by resolving what degree of management control (central line or more local autonomy) is necessary, the benefits of standardizing service like consumer research, and whether a smaller staff operation is capable of producing and executing advertising concepts. Deere, for instance, produces several hundred works of advertising a year in a dozen foreign languages.

The firm's next step is assuring, after examining the firm's product advertising in a major market, that the "buying proposal," the content of the advertisement, actually transfers to the international market's consumers. For instance, the heavy duty cleaning and the cosmetic benefits of Procter & Gamble's Tide and AMC's Jeep, respectively, represent "buying proposals," or content. On the other hand, the second element of advertising, the "creative presentation," or the form of the advertisement, usually is not an effective international traveler, as Esso's unfortunate use of its tiger in Malaysia, where tigers have actually eaten members of the local human population. Consequently, whereas the firm almost always can transfer the content of a successful advertisement to the international market, it must modify the form in which the content is presented in most instances.[18]

International marketing techniques, like the ones noted above, can substantially increase consumer demand in large markets for products with similar characteristics.[19] The firm can achieve greater economies of scale through the products' common design—in this way the firm's position in one major market translates into a strengthened presence in others. As a result of this standardization, the firm can lower its costs and increase its profits because of realized economies of scale. For instance, Caterpillar exploited its international sales volume for equipment parts to preempt any competitor's spending the substantial investment to compete—by standardizing its products and thereby decreasing its cost per unit, Caterpillar created a formidable barrier to competition. The successful exporting firm does not have to market a "world product," but rather one in which its product variations all share essential design similarities. In this way, the firm can accommodate some local differences in consumer taste, as IBM has, without ceding lower production costs, according to Michael Porter, a leading authority in the field of competitive strategy.[20]

Adroit international human resource practices of American firms can contribute greatly to success. American firms have begun to or have enlarged their international presence greatly in the last few years and derive a substantial part of their aggregate sales and operating profits from foreign markets.[21] Yet, one observer who has compared U.S. and Japanese firms' activities has remarked that "American companies have shown little evidence of realizing how much Japan owes its phenomenal success to high performing international managers . . . Japanese companies go about equipping their expatriate personnel for the exacting task of working and living in an alien culture."[22]

The American firm that assigns a manager overseas must pay especially close attention to four variables that particularly contribute to expatriate managerial success: the manager's personality traits, technical competence, family situation, and the environment. The cost per expatriate failure to the employing firm is $55,000 to $80,000.[23] Consequently, to avoid the failure or premature return of international managers, firms should carefully select, train, and sensitize their managers to "reduce the often painful and agonizing experience of transferring into another culture and avoid the great damage that culture shock and cultural misunderstanding can do to a firm's operating relationships."[24]

Certainly, semiacculturation training includes the identification of potential culture collisions including threats and bribery, currency speculation, language, and customs.[25] A culturally sensitive firm should refrain from threatening to "move operations to another country" in the "face of unwanted regulation, environmental constraints, and labor relations." Further, whether or not bribery is wrong in a moral sense, it is foolish, since "there are no secrets in the American republic, only varying lengths of time until all is revealed." Further, many of the payments classified as bribes a decade ago were really payments extorted from American firms by foreign concerns, governments, or persons as the price of doing business, a subject discussed in the next section.

Another collision zone lies in a firm's manipulations in international finance, such as currency speculation. The firm should avoid moving large funds in anticipation of the appreciation or depreciation of a national currency. Not only does such action contribute to that rise or fall in value, it also fuels the animus of local decision-makers.

Moreover, whereas an executive's knowledge of the host country's language is helpful, English still remains the lingua franca of business. Nonetheless, unwary managers' ignorance of the host country language can lead to their becoming "showroom managers, sitting in well-decorated offices with a staff of secretaries but having little control over operations . . . decisions are made without them."[26]

To avoid this unfortunate scenario, the international manager should be aware of some helpful pointers when conversing in English with foreigners: (1) use standard English, avoid slang, (2) use short, simple concrete phrases, (3) be specific and illustrate with examples, (4) avoid long discourse, encourage a dialogue, (5) occasionally interject questions to determine the foreigner's comprehension of the conversation's salient elements, (6) summarize essential items, (7) express regret at not speaking the foreigner's language, be patient when he gropes for a word, and compliment the foreign counterpart's English, (8) if possible, provide the other party in advance of the conversation a digest of any ideas that may be difficult for that party to comprehend, (9) take notes and provide the foreign counterpart a detailed report of the meeting, (10) avoid using humor because foreigners, who at best experience difficulty in understanding it, may be offended because they do not customarily commingle humor and business affairs.[27]

Additionally, American managers abroad face cultural dilemmas of other sorts. When Americans nod their heads, they are nonverbally communicating yes. Italians and Japanese use similar body language to impart no. Scandinavian firms establish loosely defined hierarchies, whereas French businesses are rigidly hierarchical. Consequently, a Scandinavian employee may bypass a middle manager, whereas a French manager may only reluctantly speak to an employee. Moreover, there are subtle differences in greetings and language. "At your earliest convenience" is a polite phrase for expedited action to Americans; however, Europeans often interpret it as a request that does not demand immediate attention. Finally, whereas Americans thank others in advance of the latters' providing services, Italians and Germans think it absurd to thank someone for doing what is expected.[28] According to Robert Shuter, director of the Center for Intercultural Communications, "Corporate culture is a minisociety where all backgrounds tend to meet," and "Americans, Europeans and Asians all think of themselves as the center of the universe."

GIFTS, BRIBES, AND THE FOREIGN CORRUPT PRACTICES ACT

The Foreign Corrupt Practices Act of 1977 (FCPA),[29] which originated in the post-Watergate scandal morality, is one of

the most controversial U.S. federal laws.   Discovery of
payments in the 1970s by large American firms to the prime
minister of Japan and the Italian president subsequently
caused their resignations.   Many American corporations had
provided payments to foreign politicians for favors or to
foreign agents fronting for government officials to secure
business.   Because there was doubt about their legality, these
payments were termed "questionable."   Some payments were
undoubtedly bribes;   others were political contributions,
consulting fees, or expediting gifts.   The revelation of
questionable payments tarnished American business to   the
extent that corporate leaders had not been "held in such low
regard since perhaps the days of the Great Depression," and
business was "close to the bottom rung in measures of public
trust and confidence."[30]

The ensuing furor catalytically led the Securities and
Exchange Commission (SEC) to investigate many American firms
and in 1974 to establish a disclosure program to determine the
extent of the questionable payment practice by firms.   Whereas
the SEC had no legal authority to sanction the firm's illegal
or questionable payments, or its firm's false bookkeeping, the
agency could act against firms that failed to actually
disclose their illegal transactions.   The response from
business firms regarding questionable or illegal payments to
foreign officials was unsettling.   Over 500 firms disclosed
such payments, aggregating many hundreds of millions of
dollars.   Four companies alone, including General Tire &
Rubber, paid over $200 million in questionable payments.

Business leaders responded that the questionable payments
were a necessary cost of doing business, that they were more
often products of extortion than bribes, that competitors in
other countries use such payments, that such payments reflected a local practice that Americans should not arrogantly
contravene, and that such payments were in the best interest
of the firms' shareholders.

Critics of such practices asserted, however, that, aside
from the payments that were illegal under the laws of the host
countries, the remaining questionable payments corrupted the
free enterprise system.   According to one treasury official,
"when the major criterion in a buyer's choice of a product is
the size of a bribe rather than its price and quality and
reputation of its producers, the fundamental principles on
which a market economy is based are put in jeopardy."[31]
Moreover, the criticism continued, such questionable payments
were counter to the values of the American public, destructive
to foreign relations, bred corruption in allied governments,
and tarnished the American reputation for honesty and integrity.

Congress moved with dispatch based on the finding of
firms' widespread use of bribes and as a result of the
consensus that bribery was unethical and unnecessary.
Congress constructed and enacted a bill that includes two
methods to prevent U.S. firms from bribing foreign officials:
first, accurate disclosure and record-keeping of all payments,
whether to foreign officials or not, made by firms; and,
second, the criminalization of firms' foreign bribery.   The
entire legislative process had required less than one year
when President Carter signed the bill into law on December 19,

1977, and it was codified as an amendment to the 1934 Securities Exchange Act.

For the first four decades of their existence, the federal securities laws neither required nor prohibited "specific managerial practices in the operation of a business, other than a business in one of a handful of closely regulated industries." However, the FCPA of 1977 empowers the SEC to "tighten the noose of responsibilities and liabilities on corporate directors, officers, and managers."[32] Whereas the civil injunction against and the criminal prohibition of a corporation's or a person's foreign payment appear in the FCPA's antibribery provisions, the disclosure requirements appear in the form of accounting provisions. The act's prohibitory sections concerning bribery apply to all "domestic concerns," whereas the record-keeping and internal controls provisions extend only to those U.S. companies registered under the 1934 Securities and Exchange Act.

The FCPA deems it unlawful for any U.S. business firm or "any individual who is a citizen, national, or resident of the United States"[33] to use an instrument of interstate commerce (such as the telephone or the mail) in furtherance of a payment or offer to pay money or "anything of value," directly or indirectly to any foreign official with discretionary authority, any candidate for foreign political office, or any foreign political party, if the purpose of the payment or offer is made "corruptly" to induce the recipient's act or refraining from an act in such a manner as to assist the firm in obtaining or retaining business for or with or directing business to any person.[34] The sanctioned "corrupt" action, by FCPA standards, does not have to violate the law of the host country.

The FCPA does not include in any of the aforementioned three classes of recipients any foreign governmental employee "whose duties are essentially ministerial or clerical."[35] The act, hence, clearly does not proscribe "facilitating" or "grease" payments to induce those employees to perform customary services that, were it not for the payment, they might refuse to effect. Moreover, the FCPA forbids payments or offers of anything of value to any person, foreign or domestic, when the payor knows or has reason to know "that all or a portion of such money or thing of value will be offered, given, or promised, directly or indirectly,"[36] to any of the statutorily defined classes of recipients. This section concerning suspect payments poses a significant dilemma for a firm because in most cases it will be unclear that the firm actually knew the payment would be passed on or offered to another, and, therefore, the prosecution will rest on whether the firm had reason to know that fact. In this regard, according to former SEC chairman Hills, "You do not have the right to close your eyes when you drop off a large payment."[37] Further, if a U.S. parent company deliberately employs its foreign or domestic-controlled subsidiary as a conduit for payment of a bribe, the parent firm has violated the act.

The SEC has civil enforcement authority concerning violations by SEC registrants or persons commercially related to those registrants, such as the executives of a registrant firm. In addition, the Department of Justice (DOJ) possesses civil and criminal enforcement authority over domestic concerns—any person who is a citizen, national, or resident of the United States, or any U.S. business concern, including a sole proprietorship, not a registrant under the 1934 Securities Exchange Act.

The FCPA imposes severe criminal penalties on violators of the antibribery provisions of the act. A registrant company and a nonindividual domestic concern are subject to a fine up to and including $1 million for every prohibited payment. Any individual who is a domestic concern, and any officer, shareholder, or director acting in the stead of a registrant or domestic concern, who willfully violates the law, are subject to fines up to and including $10,000, or imprisonment for five years, or both. Any registrant company's or domestic concern's employee or agent who is a U.S. citizen, national or resident, or is otherwise subject to the jurisdiction of the United States, can be fined up to and including $10,000 and imprisoned for five years, but only if such registrant company or domestic concern is itself adjudicated guilty of violating the antibribery provisions of the FCPA.

The firm's executives most vulnerable in an antibribery prosecution include the chief executive officer, chief operations officer, financial vice president, controller, tax director, treasurer, internal auditor, members of the board of directors (especially those serving on the audit committees), and executives in foreign sales and operations.[38]

Although there is no FCPA criminal liability attached to failure to maintain accurate books and records and an effective system of internal accounting controls, severe penalties exist for willful violations through the general sanctions under the 1934 Security Exchange Act. Registrant firms and those persons who control the direction, policies, or management of a firm are subject to a fine up to and including $10,000 and imprisonment of up to and including five years, or both, for their willful violations of the accounting provisions. The most vulnerable executives, in the case of a record-keeping or internal controls deficiency, are the chief executive officer, the chief operations officer, the financial vice president, controller, tax director, treasurer, internal auditor, and members of the board of directors (especially those serving on the audit committees).

Even if an executive who violates the act escapes a fine or imprisonment, a federal court will likely issue an injunction that restrains further prohibited acts. Noncompliance with the injunction is sanctioned as contempt of court or a sentence to jail without any right to jury trial. In addition, third party lawsuits are available to aggrieved persons who contend the firm concealed a material fact.

ACCOUNTING PROVISIONS: REQUIREMENTS OF RECORD-KEEPING AND INTERNAL CONTROLS

The basic requirements of the accounting provisions apply to all registrants under the 1934 Securities Exchange Act.[39] The FCPA's accounting provisions probably have served a more effective deterrent to illicit payments by public corporations than any other part of the act. Terse and straightforward like the antifraud sections of the federal securities laws, the cardinal provision requires every company registered under the 1934 act to "make and keep books, records, and accounts, which, in reasonable detail, accurately and fairly reflect the transactions and dispositions of the assets" of that company.[40]

The second requirement of the FCPA's accounting provisions, like the first a substantial governmental intrusion into managerial practices, directs every company registered under the 1934 act to "devise and maintain a system of internal accounting controls sufficient to provide reasonable assurances"[41] that: (1) transactions are executed in accordance with management's general or specific authorization, (2) transactions are recorded as necessary to permit preparation of financial statements in conformity with generally accepted accounting principles or any other criteria applicable to such statements, and to maintain accountability for assets, (3) access to assets is permitted only in accordance with management's general or specific authorization, and (4) the recorded accountability for assets is compared with the existing assets at reasonable intervals, and appropriate action is taken with respect to any differences.[42]

The accounts of an SEC reporting firm's foreign subsidiaries are consolidated with the parent firm's accounts. Consequently, a U.S. firm must institute and maintain the FCPA's required controls for its foreign subsidiaries in order to comply with the section mandating "preparation of financial statements in conformity with generally accepted accounting principles."   Therefore, certain practices, such as over-billing, which are not prohibited by a foreign country's laws, or by the antibribery section of the FCPA, may violate the accounting provisions of the act.

In the drafting stage of the bill that became the FCPA, accountants sought to delete "accurately" from the wording because that word "connotes a concept of exactitude that is simply not attainable."   Congress in the end accepted the standard of "in reasonable detail" in defining specifically the firm's obligation to maintain books and records.   Lawyers deprecated the FCPA's lack of a materiality standard—"materiality" means whether the disclosure would be important to a prospective buyer or seller of securities or to stockholders in exercising their rights to vote.   The SEC believed that materiality was too narrow a standard—that, for example, a smaller firm's $300 payment might be material, whereas a huge conglomerate's $20,000 might be immaterial.   Consequently, Congress determined the appropriate test to be one of "reasonableness," because such a standard provides flexibility in addressing each case's facts and circumstances.

The SEC was particularly concerned with attacking the three basic record-keeping shortcomings uncovered in its investigations: records that completely failed to reflect improper transactions; records that were falsified to disguise aspects of improper transactions that were accurately and correctly recorded otherwise; and records that accurately recorded the payments' sums but neglected to record the qualitative portions that would have revealed the illegality of the transaction.[43]

CRITICISMS OF THE FCPA

Criticisms have been leveled against the FCPA.[44]   The act, unenthusiastically received by American business and foreign nations, comprises a unilateral assault on bribery.   The antibribery provisions are vague, and they fail to define key terms such as "corruptly," "in furtherance of," "knowing or having reason to know," and "obtaining or retaining business." In addition, the act holds American firms liable for the acts of their agents in foreign countries without providing any guidance as to the degree that the firms should investigate those agents.   These and other ambiguities place an unfair burden on American business.

In spite of increases in exports, American firms are distinctly disadvantaged by the FCPA because in many foreign nations, entities expect and consider payments as a common business practice.   It is not surprising that other countries have not enacted legislation similar to the FCPA, even though most have legislation deeming as illegal any bribes to their own public officials.   Further, empirical evidence indicates that U.S. firms have suffered significant harm.   The FCPA's deleterious effects include lost deals because of refused payments, and overcautious American firms that refuse legitimate business because of uncertainty that a proposed transaction may violate the FCPA.[45]

Reflecting the haste with which Congress drafted and ratified the act, the accounting provisions of the FCPA contain ambiguous language as well.   For example, the act did not adequately define "accurately and fairly," "in reasonable detail," "internal accounting controls," and "reasonable assurances," even though these concepts comprise the linchpins of the act.   Moreover, neither the record-keeping nor the internal controls provision is limited to material transactions or to those in excess of a specific dollar amount.[46] Although the act is vague in these and other regards, every business transaction is fraught with "potential criminal liability."   Further, whereas the act's disclosure requirements are extremely burdensome and not cost-effective, they apply to every stock issuer subject to the 1934 act, even those firms without any international business.[47]

1988 AMENDMENTS

In 1988 Congress enacted an omnibus trade bill.   Part I is titled "Foreign Corrupt Practices Act Amendments."   The 1988 amendments modify the FCPA in several important aspects.

1.   Foreign Trade Practices.

   a. The FCPA, before the 1988 amendments, prohibited payments to foreign officials and certain other foreign persons in order to obtain, retain, or direct business.   The 1988 amendments tighten this prohibition by clarifying that the FCPA extends to payments made to influence a "foreign government or instrumentality thereof to affect or influence any act or decision of such government or instrumentality, to benefit the firm's business."

b. The 1988 amendments exclude from prohibited payments those made to facilitate or expedite a "routine governmental action." The FCPA originally excluded from its prohibitions any payments made to an employee of a foreign government or instrumentality whose duties are essentially "ministerial or clerical." Consequently, the amendments moved the focus of this exception to the payment's purpose from that of the position of the official receiving the payment. The act, as amended provides examples of "routine govern- mental action": obtaining licenses, processing government paper and work orders, obtaining phone service, protecting perishable products from deterio- ration, and actions of a similar nature.

c. The 1988 amendments provide for an affirmative de- fense, the applicability of which the firm must demonstrate, for payments that are "lawful under the written laws and regulations" in the official's country, or for the payment that "was a reasonable and bona fide expenditure, such as travel or lodging expenses "incurred by an official provided it was directly related to the promotion of the product or service or the execution or performance of a contract.

d. The 1988 FCPA amendments also attempt to clarify the original FCPA's lack of definition concerning "reason to know"—as the FCPA proscribes payments to a third party if the payor has "reason to know" that the third party will utilize the payment in contravention to the FCPA. The amendments define a person's "knowing" as being "aware" of or having a "firm belief" that such result is "substantially certain."

2. **Attorney General: Guidelines and Opinions Regarding Foreign Trade Practices**.

The 1988 amendments establish a procedure under which the attorney general may issue general guidelines regarding foreign payments, describing actions that would or would not violate the Department of Justice's present enforce- ment policy. Further, the attorney general is empowered to respond to specific inquiries by firms concerning conformance of their conduct and such an opinion letter serves as a "rebuttable presumption" of conformity with present DOJ guidelines, with final adjudication in the discretion of the courts.

3. **Penalties and Injunctive Relief Regarding Foreign Trade Practices**.

The 1988 amendments substantially increase the maximum criminal fine to $2,000,000 for a company and $100,000 for individuals. Moreover, the FCPA amendments create a civil penalty of up to $10,000 for business firms and individ- uals, and, further, empower the attorney general to seek injunctive relief against firms or individuals violating or about to violate the FCPA.

4. Accounting and Control Standards.

    a. The FCPA requires certain companies to maintain records in "reasonable detail" to accurately report transactions involving their assets. The act requires these companies to establish internal accounting controls that provide "reasonable assurance" as to the accounting systems' integrity. The 1988 amendments, attempting to alleviate the unnecessarily detailed and costly records, defines the terms "reasonable assurances" and "reasonable detail" as "such level of detail and degree of assurance as would satisfy prudent officials in the conduct of their own affairs."

    b. The 1988 amendments provide that a failure to comply with accounting requirements will not produce criminal liability except in the case of "knowing" violations. Criminal penalties apply to those who "knowingly fail to implement a system of internal accounting controls of knowingly falsify any book, [or] record, or account . . ." kept pursuant to the FCPA.

    c. The FCPA, prior to the 1988 amendments, did not delineate the degree to which a parent company can be held responsible for a subsidiary firm's lack of compliance with the mandated accounting provisions. Consequently, the 1988 amendments indicate that a company is "conclusively presumed" to have discharged its responsibility in this regard when it proceeds "in good faith to use its influence, to the extent reasonable under the . . . circumstances, to cause such domestic or foreign [subsidiary] firm to devise and maintain a system of internal accounting controls consistent with FCPA requirements.

GUIDELINES FOR COMPLIANCE

Given the ambiguities of the FCPA, even with the 1988 amendments in place, every firm that comes within the purview of the act should adhere to the following guidelines,[48] in addition to the various suggestions made in earlier sections of this chapter.

    1. A firm should incorporate clear and complete recapitulations of the FCPA, and, in addition, conflict-of-interest policies in its code of conduct that require the disclosure of the conflicts of interest as well as transgressions of prohibited activities. For instance, adherence to this guideline would reveal a firm's executive's ownership or interest in a customer's or supplier's business; a record of a transaction between the firm and that customer or supplier that failed to reflect the ownership would not accurately and fairly reflect the transaction or the disposition of the firm's assets required under the FCPA.

    2. In its self-regulation, a firm should especially focus on specific types of transactions in which the SEC has

maintained an historic interest: legal and illegal political contributions; payments to government officials; illegal or questionable rebates to customers; commercial bribes or kickbacks; violations of customs or currency control laws; violations of laws regulating tobacco, drugs, narcotics, alcohol, or firearms; income tax evasion; self-interest dealings by insiders or their agents; and transactions that manipulate sales, earnings, or other financial data or reports.

3. The firm should discourage any facilitating or expediting payment, except as a measure of last resort, to end damaging delays and refusals by foreign governmental officials to carry out their duty. The firm should consider each such facilitating payment and must dismiss out of hand any request by the firm's foreign manager or agent unless the circumstances that call for facilitating payments satisfy the following criteria:

a. The action the firm seeks is a "routine governmental action," is legal or is reasonable and a bona fide expense incurred in the promotion of a product or the execution of a contract.

b. The firm has made all reasonable efforts to obtain action without payment, regarding a "routine governmental action."

c. The payment is not substantial in regard to "routine governmental action."

d. The payment is not made to obtain an action or decision by a foreign official to award new business or continue business with the firm in regard to "routine governmental action."

e. The transaction is accurately described in the firm's books and records in accord with the firm's internal guidelines and policies.

f. The manager in charge of the foreign transaction furnishes a complete report of the payment and any subsequent transactions to the firm's designated internal auditor for report periodically to the audit committee of the board of directors.

4. Under any circumstances, the firm's appropriate activity head must approve any payment over $100 or a smaller amount if considered substantial under the particular circumstances. That activity head should approve such payment only when it is appropriate in consideration of the damage the firm will suffer if foreign official action is refused or delayed extensively, and after consultation with the firm's legal counsel.

5. The firm should direct all employees or agents to report to the legal counsel any approach or request to participate in any illegal or unrecorded disbursement, whether domestic or foreign.

6. Before the firm retains a foreign representative, it should consider the totality of circumstances,

including: the manner the representative proposes to secure business, the commission requested, and other factors, including the representative's background, character, and reputation. These circumstances must satisfy the firm that there was no reason to know, nor was there a basis for reasonably suspecting, that the representative's conduct would be inconsistent with the requirements of the FCPA.

7. The firm should direct all employees to respect the firm's record-keeping and reporting systems. Specifically, the firm should require all employees to comply with generally accepted accounting rules and controls, to avoid any false or misleading entries or failure to make required entries in the firm's books and records, and to assure that documentation evidencing each transaction shall adequately represent the purpose of such payment.

8. The firm's documentation should record not only financial data but also other information that would call the reviewer's attention to a possible impropriety or illegality.

9. The firm should prohibit any employee or agent from selling, transferring, or disposing of any assets of the firm; or from ordering, authorizing, or paying for materials, supplies, or any other item or service without a written authorization in accordance with the firm's written policy.

10. The firm should prohibit any employee or agent from issuing checks, cash, or drafts without approval documentation supporting the reason for disbursement.

11. Moreover, the firm should direct any employee or agent who has properly disbursed a check, cash, or draft to record such action in the appropriate system accounting for the disbursement.

12. The firm should require all salaried employees and its subsidiaries to complete and sign on an annual basis a certificate of compliance with the FCPA. Any employee not in compliance or uncertain of his or her compliance, should discuss the matter with a superior and record the facts of the transaction in the compliance certificate.

INTERNATIONAL TRADE PRACTICES

Even though the benefits of international trade are substantial, nations often institute economic sanctions that restrict the unimpeded flow of international trade. Often, the major trading nations settle their policy differences through trade agreements. The world's two major trading organizations, the General Agreement on Tariffs and Trade (GATT), formed in 1947, and the United Nations Conference on Trade and Development

(UNCTAD), formed in 1964, provide frameworks for multilateral trade negotiations and agreements.

GATT, with nearly ninety-five members representing the sources of the substantial majority of international trade, promotes nondiscrimination—that is, a country grants to all GATT members every concession it grants to one or more. Although GATT has strengthened the free flow of goods and services across international borders, it has not eliminated protectionism.[49] Unfortunately, GATT does not cover trade in services or international financial investment and cannot effectively counter foreign industrial policies.   It is apparent in 1990 that agreements that govern the international trading system are drastically in need of revision.

The United States enacted its first international trade law in 1789, as a result of the Constitution, which vests in Congress the authority to regulate foreign commerce and "to lay and collect taxes, duties, imports and excises."   That Tariff Act of 1789 sought to stimulate domestic manufacturing through protective duties.   Thereafter, Congress increased tariffs in times of war or domestic economic crisis and reduced tariffs during peace and economic expansion.   In 1916 Congress created the precursor of the U.S. International Trade Commission (ITC), whose mission was to promulgate Congress's technical tasks concerning tariff legislation.   Four years after establishing the highest tariffs in history in the Smoot-Hawley Tariff Act of 1930, the catalyst for massive trade-barrier retaliation by the nation's trading partners, Congress enacted the Reciprocal Trade Agreements Act (RTAA). Smoot-Hawley, which increased tariff schedules for over 20,000 products, caused U.S. exports to plummet from $5.2 billion in 1929 to $1.6 billion in 1933 and helped trigger the worldwide depression.

Through the RTAA, the Congress delegated tariff-modifying authority to the president, who could, thence, reduce duties up to 50% through trade agreements.   After voicing his opinion that "unhampered trade dovetails with peace," Secretary of State Cordell Hull concluded thirty-two bilateral trade agreements with twenty-seven countries.   Since 1934 U.S. trade policy has generally reflected the principle of liberal trading; however, many U.S. political values have been codified and appear in the requirement of reciprocal trade concessions and in protection against injurious imports.

According to I.M. Destler, in _American Trade Politics: System Under Stress_, (20th Century Fund, 1987), trade barriers, including tariffs on imports, do not eliminate trade imbalances.   Although many decry the significant U.S. merchandise trade deficit with Japan, there is a rising antiprotectionist sentiment in the nation.   For instance, according to the authors of "Anti-Protection: Changing Forces in United States Trade Politics" (Institute for International Economics, 1987), "the growing antiprotection phenomenon does seem to have made a significant difference" in the successful opposition to product-specific trade protection from 1975 to 1985.

In general, sanctions relate to the refusal to export to or import from the target nation goods, services, or capital. Sanctions include boycotts, divestiture (for instance, divesting of shares in banks that provide loans to South Africa), and divestment (for instance, firms withdrawing from business activities within South Africa). One of the economic sanctions a nation can impose to coerce the target nation to comply with a desired behavior pattern—social, political, or economic pattern—is that of the *boycott*. A number of foreign nations have laws that impose boycotts on trade with other nations. The United States has itself imposed commercial boycotts that prohibit the importation and exportation of technical information and products. In the case of the Soviet Union, a number of totalitarian countries in East Europe, and the People's Republic of China, U.S. boycotts restrict the export of goods or technical information that could be used to America's detriment. In the case of North Korea, Cuba, Vietnam, and Cambodia, U.S. laws restrict almost all exports of U.S. goods or technical information.

On the other hand, the United States has prohibited domestic firms, their foreign subsidiaries, and controlled affiliates from aiding any boycott directed against a country friendly to the United States. Under the Export Administration Act (EAA) of 1979, an act addressing the import of U.S. technology by an adversary nation, and its 1985 amendment, the president can limit the export of products through licensing controls imposed for reasons of national security, foreign policy, or limited domestic supply.[50] Firms that cooperate in the furtherance of a prohibited international boycott can suffer severe sanctions: loss of the right to export, and fines of up to $50,000 or five times the value of the exports involved, whichever is greater. Individuals who violate the EAA can suffer the same fines and imprisonment for up to and including five years. Moreover, the Ribicoff Amendment to the Tax Reform Act of 1976 subjects violators to adverse tax consequences. Moreover, if a firm or person knowingly violates the act by exporting items restricted for national security or foreign policy purposes, sanctions include a fine five times the value of the exports involved or $100,000, whichever is greater, or incarceration for up to and including ten years, or both.

Among the boycott-related activities prohibited by U.S. law are: refusing to conduct business with boycotted countries or blacklisted persons; furnishing information about business relationships with boycotted countries or blacklisted persons; furnishing information about any person's race, sex, religion, or national origin, or membership or support of charitable organizations supporting a boycotted country; or discriminating against individuals or firms on the basis of race, sex, religion, or national origin. The firm must report any boycott request to the U.S. government.

Although foreign policy restrictions, like the one applied against the Soviet natural gas pipeline in 1982, generate more publicity, the most extensive use of the Export Administration Act of 1979 relates to protection of national security.[51] The act's provisions authorize the Commerce Department to compile a list of those products and technical data that could be militarily useful to the nation's adversaries. The list of thousands of items includes microprocessors and semiconductors.

CONCLUSIONS

According to Richard Voell, president of the Rockefeller Group, in a speech in Hawaii in April of 1987, "Once . . . in America, we were the most . . . powerful nation in the history of mankind . . . so dominant . . . that in 1941 Henry Luce, publisher of _Time_ magazine, predicted that the twentieth century would be 'the American Century.'" Nearly five decades later, "we're getting our tail kicked by nations one-tenth our size."

In that same year, 1987, in a September speech to the American Mining Congress, George Keller, Chevron's then chairman and CEO asserted, "Because of the fast pace of technology, we now have . . . a 'transitional economy.' To compete effectively today in almost any field you have to adapt to a worldwide market which has no room for the inefficient." If America is to unbind the economic Gulliver it once was, firms will have to view, as Walter Wriston, "the planet as a single marketplace" and act upon the comprehension as Harvard's Robert Reich that as "our economy becomes so entwined with the world's . . . the nation's borders lose their commercial significance."

Determined competition from firms in Japan, South Korea, and West Germany have emphasized the vulnerability of American firms at home and abroad. Twenty years ago, imports comprised only 8% of America's ultimate consumers' demand; now they account for 15%. Yet, American firms can recapture markets and enhance their position in others. American firms must invest more in new production and technology, increase capacity, cut production costs, produce standardized products of good quality, and secure market share in the context of the world as a single market. Firms that increase their presence in international trade, in the long run, assure their own vitality.

Nonetheless, there is no easy formula for success in international business. In order to create and keep customers, firms must be innovative and entrepreneurial and, most of all, develop a global strategy. Without addressing the world as one market, managers will be unable to "recognize the nature of competition, justify the required investments, or sustain the change in everyday behavior needed."[52]

NOTES

1. Poling, "Can We Make U.S. Industry Competitive Again?" U S.A. Today (November 1987): 22.
2. Mills, "Destructive Trade-Offs in U.S. Trade Policy," Harvard Business Review (November-December 1986): 119.
3. Buchholz, Business Environment and Public Policy, 3rd ed. (Englewood Cliffs, NJ: Prentice-Hall, 1989), 557-558.
4. Encarnation, Note on Comparative Poltical Economy, Publication #3854-161, Harvard Business School (1984).
5. Pezeshkpur, "Systematic Approach to Finding Export Opportunities," Selling in Foreign Markets edition, Harvard Business Review (1981): 47.

6. The following agencies provide helpful information to the firm which wishes to invade or enlarge its share in an international market: Bureau of Export Development, U.S. Department of Commerce; Export-Import Bank of the U.S.; Export Trade Services Division, U.S. Department of Agriculture; U.S. Customs Service, Department of the Treasury; Office of Commercial Affairs, Bureau of Economic and Business Affairs; and the Federal Trade Commission, all in Washington, DC.
7. Pezeshkpur, op. cit., 49-51.
8. Ibid., 51.
9. Yoffie, "Profiting from Countertrade," Harvard Business Review, Pub. #84316 (May-June 1984): 7, and see 3-5.
10. Ibid.
11. Ibid., 6-7.
12. Ibid.
13. Ibid.
14. Levitt, "The Globalization of Markets," Harvard Business Review, Pub. #83308 (May-June 1983): 92, and 93-102.
15. Ibid., 94-101.
16. Killough, "Improved Payoffs from Transnational Advertising," Selling in Foreign Markets edition, Harvard Business Review (1981): 36-37.
17. Ibid., 38-39.
18. Ibid., 41.
19. Hout, Porter, and Rudden, "How Global Companies Win Out," Harvard Business Review (September-October 1982): 20.
20. Ibid., 26.
21. "International 150 U.S. Companies Ranked by Foreign Sales," Business Week (April 18, 1986): 290-292, as cited in Dowling, "Human Resource Issues in International Business," Syracuse Journal of Int'l Law and Com. 13 (1986): 255.
22. Murray and Murray, "Global Managers for Global Business," Sloan Management Review (Winter 1986): 75.
23. Mendenhall and Oddou, "The Dimensions of Expatriate Acculturation: A Review," Acad. Mgmt. Rev. 10 (1985): 39, cited in Dowling, op. cit., 257.
24. Robock and Simmonds, International Business and Multinational Enterprises, 3rd ed. (Homewood, IL: Irwin, 1983) 562, as cited in Dowling, op.cit., 263.
25. Galbraith, "The Defense of the Multinational Company," Harvard Business Review (March-April 1978): 83, 91.
26. Mauser, "Losing Something in the Translation," Selling in Foreign Markets edition, Harvard Business Review (1981): 100.
27. Ibid., 101-102.
28. Rose, "Cultural Collisions to Watch Out For," Working Woman (January, 1987): 21-22.
29. 15 U.S.C. Section 78a, 78m, 78dd-1, 78dd-2 (1982); see also Longobardi, "Reviewing the Situation: What Is to Be Done with the Foreign Corrupt Practices Act," Vanderbilt Journal of Transnational Law 20 (1987): 431.
30. Wolfson, U.S. Senate, Committee on Banking, Housing and Urban Affairs, Foreign Corrupt Practices and Domestic and Foreign Investment Disclosure: Hearing on S. 305, 95th Congress, 1st Session, March 16, 1977, 215, as cited in Buchholz, Business Environment and Public Policy, 3rd ed. (Englewood Cliffs, NJ: Prentice-Hall, 1989), 565.
31. Buchholz, op. cit., 566-567.
32. Baruch, "The Foreign Corrupt Practices Act," Harvard Business Review, Pub. #79101, 1, (January-February 1979).
33. 15 U.S.C. Section 78dd-2(d)(1)(A) (1982).
34. Baruch, op. cit., 5.
35. 15 U.S.C. Section 78dd-2(d)(2) (1982).
36. 15 U.S.C. Section 78dd-2(a)(3) (1982).
37. Baruch, op. cit., 6.
38. Ibid., 7.
39. 15 U.S.C. Sections 78m, 78dd-1 (1982), and see Longobardi, "Reviewing the Situation: What Is to Be Done with the Foreign Corrupt Practices Act," Vanderbilt Journal of Transnational Law 20 (1987): 441.
40. 15 U.S.C. Section 78m(b)(2)(A)(1982).
41. 15 U.S.C. Section 78m(b)(2)(B)(1982).

42. Baruch, op. cit., 4; see also 15 <u>U.S.C.</u> Section 78m(b)(2)(B)(i)-(iv)-(1982).
43. Baruch, op. cit., 2-3.
44. Longobardi, op. cit., 442-493, which forms an important basis for the discussion of criticisms of the FCPA.
45. Ibid., 447.
46. Baruch, op. cit., 4.
47. Longobardi, op. cit., 448.
48. A number of the guidelines are based on derivations from Baruch, "The Foreign Corrupt Practices Act," <u>Harvard Business Review,</u> Pub. #79101 (January-February 1979).
49. Buchholz, op. cit., 557-558.
50. Madison, "Congress, Administration Split on How to Plug Technology Leaks to Soviets," <u>National Journal</u> (February 19, 1983): 380-381, as cited in Buchholz, op. cit., 557.
51. Buchholz, op. cit., 557-558.
52. Hout, Porter, and Rudden, "How Global Companies Win Out," <u>Harvard Business Review</u> (September-October 1982): 30.

Bibliography

Ackerman and Bauer. <u>Corporate Social Responsiveness</u>.
    Reston, 1976.
Ahituv and Neumann. <u>Principles of Information Systems for</u>
    <u>Management</u>, 2d ed. Dubuque, IA: Brown, 1986.
Athey and Zmud. <u>Introduction to Computers and Information</u>
    <u>Systems</u>, 2d ed. Glenview, IL: Scott, Foresman, 1988.
Barland. <u>Ethical Issues in Business</u>. Englewood Cliffs, NJ:
    Prentice-Hall, 1988.
Bowen. <u>Social Responsibilities of the Businessman</u>. New
    York: Harper & Row, 1953.
Buchholz. <u>Business Environment and Public Policy</u>, 3rd ed.
    Englewood Cliffs, NJ: Prentice-Hall, 1989.
— — —. <u>Fundamental Concepts and Problems in Business</u>
<u>Ethics</u>. Englewood Cliffs, NJ: Prentice-Hall, 1989.
DeGeorge. <u>Business Ethics</u>, 2d ed. New York: Macmillan,
    1986.
Eells and Walton. <u>Conceptual Foundations of Business</u>.
    Homewood, IL: Irwin, 1961.
Epstein and Nickles. <u>Consumer Law</u>, 2d ed. St. Paul, MN:
    West Publishing, 1981.
<u>Federal Regulatory Directory</u>, 5th ed. Congressional
    Quarterly, 1986.
Fuori and Aufiero. <u>Computers and Information Processing</u>,
    2d ed. Englewood Cliffs, NJ: Prentice-Hall, 1989.
Galbraith. <u>The Affluent Society</u>. Boston: Houghton
    Mifflin, 1958.
Gribbin. <u>The Hole in the Sky</u>. New York: Bantam, 1988.
Hare. <u>Moral Thinking</u>. Atlanta: Clarendon Press, 1981.
Hemphill. <u>The Consumer Protection Handbook</u>. Englewood
    Cliffs, NJ: Prentice-Hall, 1981.
Hibbert. <u>The English: A Social History 1066-1945</u>. New
    York: Norton, 1978.
Johnson. <u>Computer Ethics</u>. Englewood Cliffs, NJ: Prentice-
    Hall, 1986.
Jones, et al. <u>Approaches to Ethics</u>. New York: McGraw-
    Hill, 1962.
Kolb and Ross. <u>Product Safety and Liability</u>. New York:
    McGraw-Hill, 1980.
Kotler. <u>Marketing Management</u>, 2d ed. Englewood Cliffs, NJ:
    Prentice-Hall, 1972.

— — —. Marketing Management, 6th ed. Englewood Cliffs, NJ:
    Prentice-Hall, 1988.
Kroenke. Management Information Systems. Santa Cruz:
    Mitchell, 1989.
McGuire. Business and Society. New York: McGraw-Hill,
    1963.
Madden. Products Liability, 2d ed. St. Paul, MN: West,
    1988.
Maritain. Moral Philosophy. New York: Scribner, 1964.
Norman. The Moral Philosophers. Atlanta: Clarendon Press,
    1983.
Nozick. Anarchy, State, and Utopia. New York: Basic
    Books, 1974.
Packard. The Hidden Persuaders. New York: Pocket Books,
    1957.
Parker. Management Information Systems: Strategy and
    Action. New York: McGraw-Hill, 1989.
Peters and Austin. A Passion for Excellence: The
    Leadership Difference. New York: Random House, 1985.
Peters and Waterman Jr. In Search of Excellence: Lessons
    from America's Best-Run. New York: Harper & Row,
    1982.
Schneck. Acid Rain. Los Angeles: Tasa, 1981.
Sidgwick. The Methods of Ethics, 7th ed. New York: Dover,
    1966.
Smith. The Wealth of Nations. Gretna, LA: Pelican, 1974.
Toffler. Tough Choices: Managers Talk Ethics. New York:
    Wiley, 1986.
Velasquez. Business Ethics: Concepts and Cases. Englewood
    Cliffs, NJ: Prentice-Hall, 1982.
Wolk and Luddy. Legal Aspects of Computer Use. Englewood
    Cliffs, NJ: Prentice-Hall, 1986.
Zuboff. In the Age of the Smart Machine. New York: Basic
    Books, 1988.

Index

About the Authors

WALTER W. MANLEY II is Professor of Business Administration at Florida State University and President of the Exeter Leadership Training Institute.

WILLIAM A. SHRODE is Chairman of the Department of Information and Management Sciences at Florida State University. His research has been published in journals such as *Decision Sciences, Academy of Management Journal, AIIE Transactions,* and *Public Administration Review.*